Barry Commoner and the Science of Survival

Urban and Industrial Environments
Series editor: Robert Gottlieb, Henry R. Luce Professor of Urban and Environmental Policy, Occidental College

For a complete list of books published in this series, please see the back of the book.

Barry Commoner and the Science of Survival

The Remaking of American Environmentalism

Michael Egan

The MIT Press
Cambridge, Massachusetts
London, England

MIT Press books may be purchased at special quantity discounts for business or sales promotional use. For information, please e-mail special_sales@mitpress.mit.edu or write to Special Sales Department, The MIT Press, 55 Hayward Street, Cambridge, MA 02142.

This book was set in Sabon by Graphic Composition, Inc. Printed and bound in the United States of America.

Printed on recycled paper.

Library of Congress Cataloging-in-Publication Data

Egan, Michael, 1974–
Barry Commoner and the science of survival : the remaking of American environmentalism / by Michael Egan.
p. cm. — (Urban and industrial environments)
Includes bibliographical references and index.
ISBN-13: 978-0-262-05086-9 (hardcover : alk. paper)
1. Environmentalism—United States—History. 2. Commoner, Barry, 1917– — Influence. I. Title.
GE197.E33 2007
363.70973—dc22

2006030288

10 9 8 7 6 5 4 3 2 1

for kieran and joshua
axe and handle

Contents

Preface

This book seeks to take a first step in filling a hole in the current literature on the history of American environmentalism since World War II. The biologist Barry Commoner is frequently invoked in works of environmental history, but little of substance has firmly situated his larger role in that history. During the 1970s, Commoner became famous for his Four Laws of Ecology, and many will recall his presidential campaign of 1980, but rarely is the context of Commoner's place in the history of American environmentalism properly appreciated. His influence on postwar science, environmentalism, and politics runs much deeper and is far more complicated than the literature suggests. This book means to engage with Commoner's social and environmental activism. In addition to being one of the most important environmental leaders of the postwar period, Commoner was a very able biologist who did groundbreaking work on the tobacco mosaic virus, free radicals, and genetic theory. While *Barry Commoner and the Science of Survival* concentrates on Commoner's use of science as a political tool, it does less justice to his scientific career outside the public arena; that important story remains to be written.

History, though, is an exercise in collaboration. We organize our thoughts and research in tandem with the intellectual generosity of others. In this way, I am indebted to more people than I could ever hope to acknowledge here. I must begin, however, with the protagonist of this story. In my first meeting with Professor Commoner, I asked a series of general and awkward questions that he very patiently answered. At the end of that meeting, he gave me a tour of the Center for the Biology of Natural Systems, then stopped me and said: "You're Michael; I'm Barry." I took it as a sign of acceptance. He also duly informed me—without a shred of self-consciousness—that I was tackling an excellent and important topic. He was right. I hope that the following pages do justice to his career in the public spotlight, the trust he placed in me, and the amount of time he made available for me.

Barry Commoner and the Science of Survival began as a doctoral dissertation at Washington State University, where I found myself deeply interested in the relationships between science, environmentalism, and social justice. In a seminar, LeRoy Ashby encouraged me to pursue these questions in a research paper that turned out to be the substance of chapter 4. My instinct is that I have broken—at some point—every one of his "rules" for writing in this book—but, I hope, not the spirit with which they were delivered. The dissertation benefited from the careful and thoughtful comments provided by Ron Doel and Paul Hirt. I especially want to acknowledge Ron's kindness and encouragement; while tirelessly offering comment and answering questions, he never wavered in his enthusiasm for the questions I was asking. He and Paul are my friends. Paul's supervision of my graduate work and dissertation struck an excellent balance between teacher and one who strongly believed in my intellectual freedom and that I should chart my own path. He has seen more drafts of these chapters than he or I would likely care to count, and if his good direction is reflected in the pages that follow, then this book is a much better piece of work than I ever deserved to write.

This study has also benefited from the attention and care that Bob Brulle, Ben Cohen, Jeff Crane, Amy Crumpton, Andrew Duffin, John Hausdoerffer, Maril Hazlett, Linda Lear, Neil Maher, Kevin Marsh, and Laurie Mercier offered in insightful readings of various sections and chapters. In addition, for suggestions, conversations, and directions, I am grateful to Kevin Armitage, Sue Armitage, Mary Braun, Laurie Carlson, Arthur Daemmrich, Matthew Eisler, Hilary Elmendorf, Sara Ewert, Michael Fellman, Dale Goble, Hugh Gorman, Denis Hayes, Sam Hays, Katie Johnson, Steve Kale, Peter Kuznick, Christophe Lécuyer, Jack Little, Alan Loeb, Tim Luke, Gregg Mitman, Cyrus Mody, Tammy Nemeth, Sheldon Novick, Bill Robbins, Philip Scranton, Thomas Seiler, Steve Shay, Adam Sowards, Jeffrey Stine, Heather Streets, Noël Sturgeon, Paul Sutter, Jay Taylor, Patricia Thorsten, Jessica Wang, Sylvia Washington, Charlie Weiner, Laurie Whitcomb, and Tony Zaragoza. What light this work does offer is amplified by the generosity of these colleagues and friends. I, of course, remain solely responsible for its enduring shortcomings.

At Washington State University, I was the recipient of the College of Liberal Arts' Boeing Graduate Fellowship in Environmental Studies and the Department of History's Claudius O. and Mary W. Johnson Fellowship. Both the college and the department were especially energetic in encouraging my studies and research. Similarly, my new colleagues at McMaster University have been most supportive and an Arts Research Board grant helped to defer some of the costs of the photographs. I am also grateful to archivists across the country for their help in locating documents: Kenn Thomas at the Western Historical Manuscript Collection at the University of Missouri-St. Louis; Patricia E. White at the Special Collections and University Archives at Stanford University; Lucia Munch at the AAAS Archives; and especially the genial staff of the Manuscript Reading Room at the Library of Congress. I should also make special reference here to Sharon Peyser of the Center for the Biology of Natural Systems, who assisted in coordinating my interviews with Professor Commoner and helped me to get access to a number of papers in their files. At MIT Press, Clay Morgan and Bob Gottlieb have been instrumental (and patient) in shepherding this work to its completion. I am especially grateful to three anonymous readers, whose comments were intellectually invigorating.

Finally, I have enjoyed the unfailing love of family, near and extended. My parents have been a constant source of support—moral and intellectual; my grandmother, a source of inspiration; and my brother and sister, companions. My children, Joshua and Jordan, served as wonderful distractions from work as well as poignant reminders of its larger significance. This work begins and ends with Janice: friend, partner, beloved.

In our progress-minded society, anyone who presumes to explain a serious problem is expected to offer to solve it as well. But none of us—singly or sitting in committee—can possibly blueprint a specific "plan" for resolving the environmental crisis. To pretend otherwise is only to evade the real meaning of the environmental crisis: that the world is being carried to the brink of ecological disaster not by a singular fault, which some clever scheme can correct, but by the phalanx of powerful economic, political, and social forces that constitute the march of history. Anyone who proposes to cure the environmental crisis undertakes thereby to change the course of history.

But this is a competence reserved to history itself, for sweeping social change can be designed only in the workshop of rational, informed, collective social action. That we must act now is clear. The question which we face is how.

—Barry Commoner, *The Closing Circle,* 300

Introduction

The New Apparatus

You have to describe the country in terms of what you passionately hope it will become, as well as in terms of what you know it to be now. You have to be loyal to a dream country rather than to the one to which you wake up every morning. Unless such loyalty exists, the ideal has no chance of becoming actual.

—Richard Rorty

On 2 February 1970 *TIME* magazine incorporated a new "Environment" section. The editorial staff chose for that issue's cover a haunting acrylic painting by Mati Klarwein of Barry Commoner, its appointed leader of "the emerging science of survival." Commoner was set in front of a landscape half of which appeared idyllic and the other half apocalyptic, presumably suggesting the environmental choices facing humankind. The urgency of those choices was implicit. The decision to put the biologist from Washington University in St. Louis on the cover stemmed less from Commoner's celebrity than from his relative ubiquity. As *TIME* editors hunted for their first cover story relating to the environment, they discovered that Commoner had lectured widely on a variety of environmental topics and had gained notoriety in sounding the alarm on environmental problems ranging from nuclear fallout and air pollution to water contamination and toxic chemicals in the city, on the farm, and in the home. In choosing Commoner, *TIME* acknowledged both the extent and the complexity of that crisis as well as affirming Commoner's role as a key voice of dissent in the larger environmental discourse.

After World War II, the American popular imagination recognized the existence of an environmental crisis in the United States. Amid a period of high Cold War tension, Americans welcomed the "Age of Ecology," the rapid expansion of legislation relating to environmental protection, and the proliferation of popular publications lamenting the condition of the Earth's ecosystems, all of which pointed toward a specific and growing ecological fear. *TIME*'s devoting a cover story and a new section to the environment a couple of months before the first Earth Day (22 April 1970) tapped into a collective anxiety over the state of the environment that suggested, in Commoner's words, "a sign that the finely sculptured fit between life and its surroundings [had] begun to corrode."[1] For many, the popular genesis of the new ecology movement was the publication in 1962 of Rachel Carson's *Silent Spring,* which described—rather ominously—the potential of a "silent spring," one without birds singing. *Silent Spring* concentrated on the fact that chemicals designed to kill bugs—notably DDT—produced unforeseen environmental hazards and were often toxic to birds, fish, children, and small animals. But it also paved the way for a decade of effective criticism of American industrialism and helped shape the context of postwar American environmentalism.[2]

Indeed, World War II might be seen as a pivotal point in American environmental history, wherein Americans effectively sought to replace nature with human technologies.[3] This endeavor was fraught with unanticipated consequences, many of which were deleterious to the physical environment and human health. As a result of this transition, the scope and scale of environmental decline grew markedly. Commoner wrote in *The Closing Circle:* "The period of World War II is . . . a great divide between the scientific revolution that preceded it and the technological revolution that followed it."[4] That technological revolution led to an outpouring of polluting technologies, which contributed to what might be regarded as a tragic tableau of the Progressive Era fallacy that humans could infinitely shape and dominate the environment.

In addition to pesticides such as DDT, many other miracle chemicals became prominent and dangerous parts of the American landscape. Synthetic detergents quickly replaced natural soap until it was discovered that their suds did not break down, and thus polluted surface waters. The manufacture of plastics emitted dangerous chemicals into the environment. The disposal of these new synthetic products also resulted in problems because they were not biodegradable, and their incineration released dioxin and other poisons into the air and water before working their way into the food chain. Nuclear technology was perceived as a clean and viable energy alternative to coal, but its hazardous waste defied safe disposal. Increased demands on agriculture led to greater dependence on synthetic fertilizers and pesticides, the runoff of which contaminated local waters. The dispersal of ammonium perchlorate, an additive used in rocket fuel and munitions since the 1950s, threatened the widespread contamination of groundwater. Flame retardants, known as polybrominated diphenyl ethers, were detected in alarming quantities in the milk of nursing mothers in the United States and Canada. The growing demand for high-performance automobiles led to greater fuel consumption—the fuel contained lead—and higher levels of carbon dioxide, and contributed to urban smog. Further, new methods of food production, continued urban expansion and suburban sprawl, and the nonchalant disposal of harmful waste materials all contributed to a variety of health and environmental problems locally, nationally, and globally. As Commoner warned in *Science and Survival:* "The age of innocent faith in science and technology may be over."[5]

The historian Samuel P. Hays has argued that the impetus for popular environmental concern after World War II was the product of a desire on the part of a newly affluent middle class to enjoy a higher standard of living. His interpretation of the rise of environmentalism suggests that this newfound energy for protecting the environment was part of a history of consumption: environmental quality had become a desirable product. But Hays's analysis overlooks the history of production during and after World War II (Commoner's technological revolution), which provoked stern reaction from a much broader social base. Ironically, the technical decisions that went into producing the amenities that characterized the postwar era also precipitated the most significant threat to the physical environment in human history. The environmentalism that responded to that threat—as this study proposes to show—was never so homogeneously middle class or interested solely in a clean environment as a quality-of-life issue. Indeed, in many instances American environmentalism was reactionary and addressed much more pressing issues of survival. In Commoner's environmental activism, a clean environment was rarely just a desirable commodity; it was a social necessity. So while a good deal of energy behind postwar environmentalism came from a growing interest in "the good life," it is important that we also trace the response to the production decisions that introduced a host of new environmental hazards throughout the American landscape.[6]

Individually, and sometimes cumulatively, these new hazards galvanized the American public into action, frequently in agreement with Commoner's assertion. By 2000, a Gallup poll found that 83 percent of Americans were sympathetic to the goals of the environmental movement.[7] But the year after Rachel Carson's *Silent Spring* was published, the historian Arthur Ekirch, Jr., mused on the "paradoxical ability" of Americans "to devastate the natural world and at the same time to mourn its passing."[8] While Americans seemed to agree with the broadest goals of environmental protection, the Gallup poll also noted that only 16 percent were "active participants," whereas more than half of those polled were sympathetic but uninvolved. It was a recurring phenomenon. Within a couple of decades of the energy crisis that rapt the American consciousness during the mid-1970s, for example, American drivers had pushed gas and oil consumption to per capita levels higher than those prior to the oil crisis of the 1970s.[9] Hal Rothman has suggested that Americans are "halfhearted" environmentalists, reluctant to make the difficult choices that might alter their current lifestyles.[10] Americans are buying and consuming more plastics, emitting more toxins into the air, and encouraging wasteful industries that promote cost-efficiency over environmental responsibility. And the consequences of these decisions have hardly been benign. The nation's wild places are under siege by developers; sprawl has turned many American cities into wastelands; cancer rates have steadily increased, especially among children; more children are developing asthma and other respiratory diseases; carbon dioxide levels continue to increase; and Americans are still consuming a disproportionate and—many would argue—unsustainable share of the Earth's resources.[11] The environmental crisis, then, is two-pronged: the first is the objective hazards wrought upon nature and human health, and the second is the relative apathy of the American public to address it.

To make matters worse, in 2004, two young environmental writers, Michael Shellenberger and Ted Norhaus, proclaimed the "death of environmentalism." Reflecting on the environmental movement's failing efforts to confront global warming, they argued that modern environmentalism was incapable of responding to this new ecological crisis. According to Shellenberger and Norhaus, the American environmental movement's "foundational concepts, its methods for framing legislative proposals, and its very institutions are outmoded," and "what the environmental movement needs more than anything else right now is to take a collective step back and rethink everything."[12] While the leaders of national environmental organizations were energetic in their denials of Shellenberger and

Norhaus's claims, it was clear that the essay had landed a serious blow. The criticism that modern environmentalism was outmoded was not new, however. Seventeen years earlier, Commoner had argued that the environmental movement had lost its way and was failing to realize its promise. In a long piece in *The New Yorker,* Commoner reflected upon the progress of the American environmental movement: "The environmental movement is old enough now . . . to be held accountable for its successes and failures. Having made a serious claim on public attention and on the nation's resources, the movement's supporters cannot now evade the troublesome, potentially embarrassing question: What has been accomplished?" Commoner's response: Not enough. In spite of the groundswell of environmental concern that preceded and followed Earth Day, the state of the environment seventeen years later was not markedly improved. "The original thrust of the environmental movement," Commoner reminded his readers, "envisioned not an environment that was a little less polluted than it was in 1970, or holding its own against an expanding economy, but an environment free of mindless assaults on ecological processes."[13] So where did the movement stand in 1987? "The question is whether the movement's goal can be reached by the present spotty, gradual, and now diminishing course of environmental improvement or whether some different course must be followed."[14] Commoner had long been navigating such a different course.

This study charts the course of American values toward the environment since World War II, using Barry Commoner as a lens. Insofar as a coherent thesis directs, justifies, and coordinates the chapters that follow, it is that the growing recognition of an environmental crisis emerging during the postwar era fostered a restructuring of environmental activism defined by a novel apparatus. That apparatus consisted of the importance of dissent; the dissemination of accessible technical information; and the need for a more public discussion of environmental risk. The adoption of this apparatus and its effective use were the mechanisms of Commoner's science of survival—method and practice—and constituted the remaking of American environmentalism. The following narrative traces Commoner's efforts to develop an effective apparatus, its early successes in the 1960s, its ultimate defeat in mainstream environmentalism in the 1970s, and its more recent renewal or revival with the advent of the environmental justice movement.

One of Commoner's biggest obstacles involved captivating the American public and alerting them to the dangers inherent in environmental hazards. Indeed, he quickly discovered that initiating a public dialogue on social problems and risk analysis was particularly difficult in the state of Cold War conformity that emerged after World War II. Conformity stimulates and bolsters a tyranny of an unwitting majority, and allows little room for dissenting thought. In many respects, then, Commoner's challenge to the Cold War social conformity and his role as a public intellectual constitute his most significant contributions to American social activism. Commoner outlined the central tenets of his political activism in a commencement address titled "The Scholar's Obligation to Dissent," in which he discussed his social duty as a scholar:

> The scholar's duty is toward the development of socially significant truth, which requires freedom to test the meaning of all relevant observations and views in open discussion, and openly to express a concern with the goals of our society. The scholar has an obligation—which he owes to the society that supports him—toward such open discourse. And when, under some constraint, scholars are called upon to support a single view, then the obligation to discourse necessarily becomes an obligation to dissent. In a situation of conformity, dissent is the scholar's duty to society.[15]

Because the postwar era was marked by a prevailing consensus and conformity—in no small measure a reaction to a decade of economic depression during the 1930s and then cultural uncertainty during World War II—the need for dissenting opinions had rarely been greater. Historically, however, dissent has rarely been easy. Because the very act of dissent upsets the delicate conformity upon which social stability is founded, conformists are frequently considered the defenders of social interests and dissenters are regarded as selfish individualists. But in *Why Societies Need Dissent,* Cass R. Sunstein argues that the opposite is perhaps more accurate. "Much of the time," he claims, "dissenters benefit others, while conformists benefit themselves."[16] Commoner's dissent, this first branch of the new apparatus, sought to create a forum in which questions and concerns might be raised.

Information and its dissemination were equally important. For a democracy to function properly, dissent and open discourse are vital, but these freedoms are not terribly useful if the public lacks the tools necessary to make informed decisions. Acknowledging this, Sunstein also notes that "conformity is often a sensible course of action. . . . One reason we conform is that we often lack much information of our own."[17] Providing information, however, was the scholar's primary mission. As Commoner asserted in his commencement address, "The scholar's duty is . . . not to truth for its own sake, but to truth for society's sake."[18] To that end, Commoner saw the public intellectual's role as vital to the moral glue that countenanced social progress. In effect, through this devotion to dissent, public intellectuals embodied "a self-appointed moral conscience of their society."[19] Their role, in Commoner's reading, was to translate and distribute widely to a lay audience the technical information that would assist in broader public participation in decision-making. During the 1950s and 1960s, Commoner was instrumental in building a science information movement, a movement of activist scientists who sought to provide accessible scientific information to an increasingly concerned public.

The final pillar in Commoner's apparatus was risk. As a biologist, Commoner applied his understanding of his social responsibility to questions of environmental risk. In the years following World War II, specialists had managed to reduce risk assessment to a series of statistics that measured hazards in parts per million (or parts per billion) and actuarial equations of what constituted acceptable social risk. These equations were designed to objectively determine the statistical threats to human health from newly introduced hazards. Environmental pollutants were noticeably harmful to human health at varying levels of exposure. Statistically, then, risk assessment calculated acceptable levels of risk based on a predetermined number of people (in a predetermined subset) experiencing specific health problems that could be related to their exposure to a specific pollutant. The problem, however, was that these kinds of evaluations typically do not account for the geography of race or class. Even within "acceptable" parameters of risk, some people, communities, or regions experienced disproportionate exposures to environmental hazards. Further, just as risk varies in space, it also varies over time; evaluations of acceptable risk were subject to change as new scientific knowledge became available and to changing public opinion. In *Uncertain Hazards: Environmental Activists and Scientific Proof,* Sylvia Noble Tesh shows that lay citizens interpret risk differently than experts and that statistical objectivity is rarely a criterion.[20] But here was the impetus for Commoner's dissent and his distribution of scientific information: even if it was not as scientifically quantifiable, the public deserved to participate in a credible forum on what constituted acceptable risk.

The history of the quantification and qualification of risk assessment, therefore, plays a critical role in this study. I submit that the modern environmental movement is engaged in a struggle to alter the manner in which risk is identified and assessed; in light of Shellenberger and Norhaus's recent diagnosis, it is a struggle the environmental movement is currently losing. In his seminal study of risk analysis, the sociologist Ulrich Beck argued that the production of wealth was inevitably connected to the production of societal risks. Because the postwar technological revolution had introduced a variety of hazards that defied easy solution, Beck argued that society had turned its attention from the production of goods to the management of those hazards and the social controversies that ensued. But by shifting society's focus away from production, a perpetual vicious circle emerged as new hazards continually presented themselves, thereby founding what Beck termed "risk society."[21] With respect to environmental concerns, these risks were manifested in threats to human health, the mismanagement or overexploitation of resources—or what economists might call natural capital—and the unforeseen social and environmental costs of technological progress. As Frederick Buell summarized the situation: "No longer does society need to deal only with social conflict resulting from the unequal distribution of environmental goods; it now has to cope also with the tensions and conflicts that come from the inequitable distribution of environmental bads."[22] To Commoner, questions of what constituted acceptable risk, who made that determination, and what groups of people were most susceptible to risk required fundamental revision. He insisted that these questions demanded public participation; scientific experts or policy makers had no moral authority to make these kinds of decisions unilaterally. What Commoner was advocating through environmental protest was a radical overhaul of how democracy and the governance of production in the United States worked.

Commoner's new apparatus challenged one of the central tenets of American technological progress: that expert management and technical expertise were apolitical. Following this powerful tenet, the history of the American twentieth century might profitably be read as a story of the rise of the modern technological nation. According to Thomas P. Hughes, Americans would see in that story "that not only their remarkable achievements but many of their deep and persistent problems arise, in the name of order, system, and control, from the mechanization and systematization of life and from the sacrifice of the organic and the spontaneous."[23] The rise of the modern technological nation is characterized by the growing stock placed in expertise and the development of an "iron triangle" of government, industry, and science, which effectively limited the potential for open, democratic politics and public input.[24] "Leaving it to the experts" clearly constituted a shift toward unquestioning conformity and a related suppression of information. Commoner found this unacceptable. Such an "objective" approach ignored or downplayed public concerns and pressing social questions of what criteria and ethical standards should be used to regulate pollution and protect human health. Throughout his career, Commoner's writings and activism pointed to the tension between expertise and the public interest; the two were not universally compatible.

Indeed, it is important to note that the science under debate throughout this study was—at the outset of the various struggles—rarely conclusive. As Commoner grappled with government and industrial scientists over the relative safety of fallout from aboveground nuclear testing or the potential hazards of mercury, existing knowledge and scientific data could not conclusively support either argument. To the extent that Commoner constituted a voice of caution in a world addicted to technological optimism and progress, he also presented a powerful critique of post-World War II expertise. That new technologies were introduced to the public and integrated into the marketplace before their safety had been fully established was, to Commoner, a palpably dangerous feature of the postwar technological revolution. Industrial scientists were exposing society to unanticipated risks and dangers.

However, pivotal to Commoner's new apparatus was—paradoxically—the authority of science as a form of knowledge and as a rhetorical tool. Commoner never disputed science's usefulness, but rather how it was used. And this is one of the more compelling features of postwar American environmentalism: Donald Worster has commented that "what is especially surprising . . . is that the campaign against technological growth has been led not by poets or artists, as in the past, but by individuals within the scientific community. So accustomed are we to assume that scientists are generically partisans of the entire ideology of progress . . . that the ecology movement has created a vast shock wave of reassessment of the scientist's place in society."[25] For more than fifty years, Barry Commoner was at the vanguard of that scientists' movement. Scientists were intellectual leaders, but they were also prominent actors in the debate over environmental policy. As much as the atomic bomb raised palpable concerns over the potential for social and environmental destruction, it also gave rise to a fierce moral debate within the broad scientific community that had spawned it. In the wake of the bomb, science had become politically interesting, and scientists had immersed themselves—often fractiously—in politics. A bitter disagreement broke out among scientists over how they should use their newfound social and political prestige. Connections between the social responsibility of postwar scientists and modern environmentalism exist within the framework of what values are inherently important to American society and how those values changed after World War II.

To properly understand Commoner's role and radicalism and his emergence as a leading spokesperson in American environmentalism, we must start by recognizing the extent to which the technological leviathan against which he railed was firmly entrenched within the American popular imagination. Chapter 1 introduces the culture and context of consumer and technological enthusiasm after World War II, and examines the early postwar debates among scientists over their social responsibility, particularly in relation to the public discourse of risk. The detonation of the atomic bomb made it abundantly clear that scientists had uncovered forces that required considerable caution, and decision-making now demanded political and moral assessment just as much as it did scientific. Within the scientific community, Commoner and a small group of scientists sought to emphasize scientists' responsibilities to the public. The historian Donald Fleming has called these younger activists "politico-scientists."[26] The undercurrent throughout Chapter 1 examines the changing shape of American science in response to American technological optimism and the popular acceptance of the importance and centrality of technology to the modern condition.[27]

According to Fleming, one of the pivotal roles of the new politico-scientists was to serve as a kind of fifth estate. In addition to mediating between experts and laypeople, politico-scientists were dedicated to providing accessible scientific information to the public as a kind of highly specialized fourth estate. This responsibility came directly from Commoner's apparatus, and was central to the politico-scientists' belief that a functioning democracy required an informed citizenry. The single most important case involving the science information movement—of which Commoner was the primary founder—was raising public concern over the hazards from atmospheric nuclear weapons testing. Chapter 2 relates Commoner's participation in the debate over nuclear fallout and explores the importance of information as a necessary tool for democracy and for environmentalism, as it helps to discern and define acceptable risk through social as well as scientific means.

Shedding light on the connection between science and activism is critical to our environmental understanding because it helps us to appreciate how scientists came to be among the intellectual leadership of the new environmentalism. Commoner would call the 1963 Nuclear Test Ban Treaty one of the first major victories for the modern environmental movement. For Commoner, the transition from opposition to nuclear fallout to environmental concerns such as fertilizers and air pollution was perfectly natural. Advocating a more holistic approach to science and health problems, he became one of the leading popular ecologists of the 1960s, marking the rise of modern ecology as a popular field of inquiry critical to identifying the social and environmental health of the American landscape. Chapter 3 recounts Commoner's adoption of popular ecology after the Test Ban Treaty and his focus on the dangers presented by the petrochemical industry. Moreover, whereas chapter 2 examined the importance of information, chapter 3 explores how the politico-scientists presented that information. Environmentalists borrowed one of their most effective rhetorical methods from the Puritan evangelists of the First Great Awakening (eighteenth century). As nature's prophets, ecologists would use their scientific status to insist that the world was on the brink of ecological destruction from a variety of human-induced causes. In so doing, Commoner and others capitalized on their authority as scientists, but also appropriated a field in which they had little formal training. By 1970, on the eve of Earth Day, *TIME* magazine would refer to the ecological messages as the new jeremiad, conflating ecology with environmental politics. The rhetoric of the jeremiad was particularly effective in making headlines and generating an audience for the necessity of greater environmental responsibility, but it also strongly associated the environmental movement (and ecology) with alarmist diatribes in order to drive people to environmental action.

The "Age of Ecology" and the jeremiads spawned by it that swept the United States in the 1960s—made popular by the Test Ban Treaty and Rachel Carson's *Silent Spring*—helped raise the general ecological literacy of citizens and laid a path for subsequent environmental action that would lead to the first Earth Day in 1970. After deliberating on the significance of Earth Day, chapter 4 follows a particularly well-publicized debate in which Commoner contributed to a major rift in the environmental movement by engaging in a vociferous debate with Paul Ehrlich, another popular and charismatic ecologist, over the origins of the environmental crisis. The rift itself is historically significant for understanding the divisions within American environmental interests, the politics of environmental concern, and the breadth of environmentalism. Perhaps the jeremiad's great failing was that it gave rise to a cacophony of voices and interests that diluted concern for the environment and deflected interest from pressing social issues relating to environmental degradation. The jeremiad's tenor lent itself to singular explanations for environmental decline, and limited Commoner's success in asserting that environmental problems could be addressed only in conjunction with poverty, civil rights, and peace.

During the euphoria of Earth Day, Commoner began to change his message from one of social activism to an increasingly blunt attack on the economic systems that gave rise to the environmental crisis. Indeed, the 1970s might be read as a decade of crisis. The decade began with the environmental crisis, which was followed in swift succession by the energy crisis—spurred by the OPEC oil embargo—and the economic crisis, which followed on the heels of the energy crisis. As analysts scrambled to make sense of these crises, Commoner pointed to the fact that they all derived from the same root cause. Chapter 5 examines the shock waves of the 1970s oil crisis and expands on the relationship between risk and economics. As Commoner boldly outlined in *The Closing Circle* (1971) and *The Poverty of Power* (1976), there was a clear enemy, and it was free market capitalism, which governed the means of production in socially irresponsible ways. It was not a new argument; to Commoner, the American economic system was complicit in diminishing the integrity of science after World War II.

The 1980s were a decade of mixed gains for environmentalism. The Reagan administration was overtly hostile to environmental interests, but in reaction to that, membership in environmental groups swelled and activists found new ways to enforce important pieces of environmental legislation. For Commoner, the 1980s constituted a decade of returning to age-old foes: waste disposal, dioxin, and other toxic threats. What had become abundantly clear to him through his career was that Americans did not experience these threats equally. Chapter 6 discusses the relationship between poverty and environmental risk. As Commoner and numerous other observers noted, there was a direct association between one's socioeconomic standing and the extent to which one was exposed to environmental pollutants in the United States. Poor and disempowered communities were much more likely to suffer exposure to dangerous toxins. Commoner was one of many environmentalists to point to this disturbing link between poverty and environmental health. Environmental justice—the combination of social and environmental activism—has recently provoked divisions within American environmentalism which stem from a question of priorities. Rather than representing a direct threat to existing strands of the movement, however, Commoner saw environmental justice as a welcome expression of environmentalism's pluralism at the end of the twentieth century.

Commoner's active role in all of these issues helps us to understand the relationships between these disparate elements of environmental decline and the movement that sought to arrest that decline. Cumulatively, these chapters explain the relationship between Commoner's social and environmental dissent and his efforts to alert the American public. But his activism involved a complication of standard environmental concerns. To Commoner, environmentalism was intimately and inextricably linked to other social movements that collectively expressed a sense of disillusionment and disenchantment in postwar America. The consistent thread throughout these disparate movements was a struggle for social empowerment, particularly as it related to the postwar technological revolution. "Social guidance of technological decisions is vital not only for environmental quality but for nearly everything else that determines how people live: employment; working conditions; the cost of transportation, energy, food, and other necessities of life; and economic growth," Commoner wrote in 1987. "And so there is an unbreakable link between the environmental issue and all the other troublesome political issues. . . . Environmentalism reaches a common ground with all the other movements [civil rights, women's rights, gay and lesbian rights, antiwar, against nuclear power and for solar energy, world peace, . . . the much older labor movement], for each of them also bears a fundamental relation to the choice of production technologies."[28]

In gauging his successes and setbacks, *Barry Commoner and the Science of Survival* explores the significance of Commoner's social and scientific activism. As a discipline built around the significance of empirical and reproducible data, science was supposed to be a self-correcting enterprise. Its self-correction was designed to enhance scientists' grasp of scientific knowledge, but also to guard the larger public citizenry from the dangers of faulty science and its application. But if the environmental crisis was any indication, the watchdog had, in effect, inadvertently surrendered its bark. And to Commoner and his colleagues there was a clear correlation between recent technological mistakes and the erosion of the central tenets of open scientific endeavor. As he rightly noted in *Science and Survival,* one of science's major duties to society is "prediction and control of human intervention into nature."[29] The story that follows suggests that after World War II, American science failed to keep human well-being as its primary objective, but also that American science was the tool most relied upon to evaluate and resolve the environmental crisis. Commoner's work to galvanize the public into action against numerous environmental problems tells an engaging story about dissent in America and the significance of a more public conversation about environmental health and risk.

1
In the Thunderclap's Wake

When the late war ended in a thunderclap, it left two noteworthy developments in its wake. Science had become politically interesting, and scientists had become interested in politics.

—Joseph H. Rush

It would be rather difficult to overstate the cultural significance of the Great Depression and World War II on the postwar American psyche. After almost two decades of depression and war, the American public was desperate for a rest—a return to normalcy (whatever that was)—and the promise of a restored individual and national affluence. This meant affordable homes; affordable cars; machines to help remove the burdens of household work; chemicals that ensured greener lawns, more abundant produce, and cleaner clothes. And cheaper, too. World War II restimulated a long-flagging economy and created an outlet for production. After the war, "big ticket" items were in demand and more affordable than they had ever been. Americans with money to spend were lured by new technologies that proliferated in the market. The unprecedented growth of new technologies—and, more important, the popular acceptance of them—suggested the realization of a brave new world. This new wave of chemicals, machines, and conveniences helped usher in a novel kind of consumer culture that Lizabeth Cohen has called a "landscape of mass consumption."[1] Combined with the beginning of the Cold War, mass consumption bred a kind of mass consensus or conformity, against which dissent was not a welcome feature of sociopolitical discourse.

Behind this culture of consumerism was a deep-seated technological optimism, firmly rooted in American history. In the 1930s, the historian Charles A. Beard, an acute observer of the American condition, hailed technology as "the supreme instrument of modern progress" and "the fundamental basis of modern civilization."[2] During World War II, innovation and production levels exceeded even the wildest dreams of American policy makers. The proximity fuse, solid fuel rockets, and radar enhanced American military objectives; DDT and other pesticides helped ensure that hostile fire claimed more casualties than did disease for the first time in modern warfare; and the atomic bomb provided ominous closure. After the War, American technologies came home, and human ingenuity promised to re-create the landscape in ways heretofore unimagined and to put nature and its resources to even more effective use. The prosperity of postwar America and the convenience that these new technologies offered seemed almost idyllic.

In a sense, the postwar consumer culture was a reaffirmation of the long-dormant notion that the American character was a product of unlimited economic abundance.[3] Referring to the popular belief that energy and resources were limitless, the historian Robert Righter observed: "Americans who, during the war had conserved, afterwards consumed."[4] Critics castigated this internalized mass consumption as neglecting social needs, but after so much social upheaval in previous decades, Americans seemed unwilling to upset or question the economic growth they enjoyed.[5] The result was a public that was uninformed, uncoordinated, complacent, and generally unwilling to confront imminent environmental threats. According to Elmo Richardson, Americans "had nothing more to draw upon to cope with that threat than the economic materialism, the bureaucratic inertia, and the political gamesmanship practiced by the men of the Truman–Eisenhower era."[6] Reservations about the growing technological output typically came from voices outside the mainstream and, as a result, were easily dismissed as irrelevant and even un-American.

While mass consumption is an indisputably significant cultural feature of the postwar period, it is important to recognize the mechanism that made consumption after World War II so environmentally problematic. If consumption was the expression of American environmental decline, production was its architect. The explosion of technological production that coincided with World War II brought with it new kinds of environmental hazards—which assaulted human bodies as well as natural landscapes—and dramatically shifted the perception of environmental protection from a luxury pastime to a social necessity. Human civilizations have always consumed goods and resources, but how those products were fabricated after World War II changed markedly. Over the decade following the conclusion of World War II, human-made materials—many of which did not break down in nature, but wrought havoc on natural ecosystems (in both their production and disposal)—replaced organic materials. Synthetic fibers replaced cotton and wool; detergents replaced soaps; and a variety of chlorine-based chemicals replaced more benign, natural products.

The acceptance of these new products is relatively easy to understand. In *Guns, Germs, and Steel: The Fates of Human Societies,* the Pulitzer Prize-winning physiologist Jared Diamond outlined why some inventions succeed and others do not. "The first and most obvious factor," Diamond contended, "is relative economic advantage compared with existing technology."[7] These newer goods were invariably cheaper to produce in mass quantities than their organic predecessors, resulting in higher profits for producers and cheaper market prices for consumers. The outcome was that American culture and society in the postwar era became infatuated with what they saw as technological progress. Commoner's critique of post-World War II technology focused on his concern for what he called widespread "technological displacements," this practice of introducing new technologies with severe environmental impacts to replace older technologies with less destructive effects. "The chief reason for the environmental crisis," Commoner argued, "is the sweeping transformation of productive technology since World War II. . . . Productive technologies with intense impacts on the environment have displaced less destructive ones. The environmental crisis is the inevitable result of this counterecological trend."[8] As more environmental problems found their way into media headlines and the public's psyche and concern, Commoner's critique of science appeared more prescient and foreboding. "If we are to survive the new age of science," he wrote in 1964, "scientists and citizens alike need to learn why this massive contamination has come about."[9]

This first chapter traces the rise of two important developments: the technological leviathan that would culminate in the post-World War II technological revolution, and the body of scientists who came to recognize a change in how science was conducted and presented a stern voice of caution against unregulated technological progress. While research and development produced considerable technological growth and significant advances in the scientific understanding of the natural world, the new realms of knowledge also—unwittingly and somewhat paradoxically—increased the gulf between what was known and what it was desirable to know, thereby providing a context for heightened risk.[10] When public interest in science grew markedly after the atomic bomb demonstrated the awesome destructive powers unleashed by nuclear science, politically concerned scientists such as Commoner took that opportunity to force themselves into the public arena in order to cater to the public's desire for more information. And in the years directly after World War II—in the thunderclap's wake—independent and socially conscious scientists such as Commoner increasingly found themselves asking epistemological questions—What is science for? and how should it be used?—which mirrored similar questions in the public arena as new technologies fundamentally changed the lives of average Americans across the country.[11] The rise of the politico-scientists and their role in ultimately helping to develop both the intellectual and political wings of the American environmental movement begins with scientists' debates over their own social responsibility in the postwar world. These debates were instrumental in Commoner's creation of the new apparatus and his science of survival.[12]

Because of the major scientific advances during and after World War II, the potential dangers of which required far greater caution and understanding, this new breed of politico-scientist sought to enter the political arena and influence policy decisions. Scientists figured on all sides of the policy-making spectrum, but what is especially intriguing here is the increase in questions among scientists about their responsibility to the larger society. If the debate between scientists focused on how science ought to be used, politico-scientists turned their attention to questions of what the new guidelines governing science—secrecy and national security, closed labs, and more specialized science—meant in the broader social and scientific context. One of the most fundamental flaws in the postwar science, they contended, was the absence of conduits through which risk might be publicly assessed and disclosed, and they frequently sought to make this appeal to public citizens. Commoner was one of the first and, retrospectively, the most durable of a new generation of politico-scientists who emerged after World War II. His professional career, briefly delayed by service in the U.S. Navy during the war, effectively began in this new climate of postwar science and political activism.

The central question of this chapter, then, asks: How did American scientists perceive themselves and their social responsibility after World War II? After the thunderclap, during a period of high political tension, Commoner was an important participant in an effort to democratize scientific information in reaction to a conservative push by the federal government, accepted by many physical scientists, in which many branches of science reached new levels of privacy and secrecy. This phenomenon was most vehemently played out in the opposition to aboveground nuclear weapons testing in the late 1950s and early 1960s (the subject of the next chapter) and in subsequent protests against the industrial production of synthetic chemicals. And while politically active scientists were not a novel feature of the postwar landscape—scientists have always been political—the new scale of hazards necessitated a greater urgency in the struggle to ensure that science become primarily an instrument of peace, dedicated to human welfare. Science had become more immediately relevant outside the laboratory, and certain scientists—Commoner included—sought to demonstrate science's political importance not only to a still largely uninformed public traditionally comfortable in leaving science and science policy to the experts, but also to the experts themselves, who tended not to adequately consider the social ramifications of their work.

"Scientists," Richard Lewontin has correctly observed, "do not begin life as scientists . . . but as social beings immersed in a family, a state, a productive structure, and they view nature through a lens that has been molded by their social experience."[13] Barry Commoner grew up in Brooklyn, New York. Born 28 May 1917, the son of Russian immigrants, he experienced the Great Depression, during which his parents lost their savings. Despite his urban environment, Commoner was fascinated by nature and became an avid biology student in high school. In 1933 he enrolled at Columbia University with enough money for only one semester, and worked his way through college. During the 1930s, Columbia was a hub of social activism. "I'm a child of the Depression," Commoner later noted, referring to his being influenced by the numerous rallies to support the Spanish Loyalists, to support Socialist and Communist meetings that promoted and defended labor union movements, and to protest lynchings in the South.[14] He was a careful reader of Friedrich Engels, and later saw

J. D. Bernal's *The Social Function of Science* as a prime example of how scientists might function as socially responsible (and engaged) experts.[15]

Of that period, Commoner remembered, "I began my career as a scientist and at the same time . . . learned that I was intimately concerned with politics." That perspective helped him to develop a social conscience, which he applied to all his activities, and before he had completed his undergraduate studies at Columbia University, he was deeply committed to participating in "activities that properly integrated science into public life."[16] By the time he entered Harvard in 1937, Commoner was convinced of his public and political duty as a scientist to disseminate his scientific findings as broadly and as publicly as possible. At Harvard, Commoner studied under the biologist Kenneth V. Thimann, who, since arriving in the United States from England in 1930, had worked to organize scientists concerned about their social role. Thimann was in regular contact with K. A. C. Elliott, a chemist at the Franklin Institute in Philadelphia, who founded the radically oriented American Association of Scientific Workers, a progressive group of scientists who, according to Elizabeth Hodes, "pioneered awareness and involvement of scientists in social concerns and political activity."[17] Commoner found himself at home in this radical "science and society" milieu, which Peter Kuznick has called "a small though vocal and influential portion of the scientific community [that] became radicalized, believing that the full realization of science's potential demanded a socialist transformation."[18] By 1939, Commoner had become a member of the executive committee of the Boston-Cambridge branch of the American Association of Scientific Workers, and a firm advocate of its guiding principles: "Scientists must advise the public, make scientific advances accessible, and undertake research with social needs in mind."[19] Here, in the 1930s, then, Commoner was acquiring the tools that would serve him throughout his career.

Commoner's Jewish background also played a role in shaping his worldview; "it was a big, big hurdle to overcome." Commoner noted that he had been "very lucky," but that his rather un-Jewish name "helped" him avoid the harsher effects of American anti-Semitism. When he was born, Commoner's last name was spelled "Comenar," but very conscious of the stigma against Jews in America, Commoner's uncle, Avrahm Yarmolinsky, chief of the Slavonic Department at the New York Public Library—whom Commoner would frequently refer to as his "intellectual uncle"—recommended changing the spelling of his last name to the more anglicized "Commoner." Yarmolinsky also recognized and encouraged Commoner's potential as a biologist early on, and bought him his first microscope. When he was a teenager, Commoner's teachers at Madison High School earmarked him for the academic world and for a career as a biologist. Commoner recalled being taken aside by a couple of his teachers, "and they said since you're a Jew it'll be very hard for you . . . so you'll have to work twice as hard as everyone else, but they had confidence in me and they said they were going to apply to City College for me." At this point, Commoner's uncle intervened, insisting that even with a degree from King's College—a two-year college to which promising Italians and Jews were shunted—Commoner would "just be a New York Jew." Yarmolinsky pushed to send Commoner to Columbia University. Yarmolinsky's wife, the poet Babette Deutsch, was a lecturer at Columbia, and together they were able to get Commoner accepted. At Columbia, Commoner excelled. He planned to do graduate work there until one of his mentors, the visual physiologist Selig Hecht, told him that as a Jew, even eight years at Columbia would do him no good, and that he had applied to Harvard on Commoner's behalf. World War II ultimately helped to diminish the anti-Semitic feelings in America, but that initial experience, combined with growing up in a poorer section of Brooklyn, contributed to Commoner's more radical perspective.[20]

During World War II, Commoner served in the U.S. Navy. He was sent to the air cadet training center at Corpus Christi, Texas, to operate the low-pressure chamber. There, he invented a successful breathing technique for high-altitude pilots without oxygen, for which he received a letter of commendation. It was also during his wartime service that he discovered firsthand that scientific innovations often possessed unanticipated and undesirable side effects. In 1942, Commoner headed a team working to devise an apparatus that would allow torpedo bombers to spray DDT on beachheads to reduce the incidence of insect-borne diseases among soldiers. The new device was tested in Panama and at an experimental rocket station off the New Jersey coast that was infested with flies. The apparatus was a success, and the DDT was tremendously effective in killing the flies. Within days, however, new swarms of flies were congregating at the New Jersey rocket station, attracted by the tons of decaying fish—accidental victims of the DDT spraying—that had washed up on the beach. As the flies fed on the dead fish, Commoner witnessed an eerie foreshadowing of how new technologies brought with them environmental problems that their inventors had not anticipated.[21]

But unwavering faith in science and technology's role in the American marketplace was not a new phenomenon—rather, it was a product of the Enlightenment and the engine of modernity. Advances in science and technology promoted a deeply rooted sense of progress in American culture, which manifested itself in a unique brand of millennialism.[22] According to Robert V. Bruce, "Science and technology [were] the prime instruments of irreversible change in the thought and life of mankind."[23] Central to that faith was the integrity of the scientific method, the critical and empirical approach to the collection of knowledge. "The Scientific Spirit," the columnist Walter Lippmann asserted in *Drift and Mastery* in 1914, was "the discipline of democracy."[24] The best environment for scientific endeavor, he intimated, was a society that valued individualism, free initiative, and mass education. As it had evolved during the latter stages of the nineteenth century, science embraced those democratic ideals both in theory and in practice. As the American philosopher Charles Peirce posited in 1878, the scientific method was profoundly social and democratic. It demanded that scientists arrive at the truth through mutual engagement and public discourse. Disagreement in science—embodied in peer review—was an example of dissent that ultimately strengthened the overall body of work. Collaboration, criticism, and communication were the cornerstones of the scientific method.[25]

Indeed, the intellectual impact of an earlier war strongly influenced the scientific spirit in the United States. Coming out of the Civil War, American science and philosophy sought to make sense of the new United States, brutally scarred from violent differences over secession, slavery, reconstruction, and, in the decades to follow, immigration. Amid these social tremors, Charles Darwin's *On the Origin of Species* (1859) and *The Descent of Man* (1871) threatened to overturn the existing and ardent theological order that had structured so much of the societal framework. War and evolutionary theory had shaken America to its core, and the nation's collective intellectual culture was in need of nearly as much reconstruction as its political structure. After years of political instability revolving around sectionalism and political corruption, a veritable whirlwind of scientific and technological innovation followed. Rather than contributing to the malaise of the period, however, science and technology served as the bulwark for the nation's metaphysical revitalization and the dawn of a new age that Charles and Mary Beard would call "the Second American Revolution."[26]

In the quarter-century following the conflict, Alexander Graham Bell's telephone (1876), Thomas Edison's incandescent lightbulb (1879), the first hydroelectric power plant in Appleton, Wisconsin (1882), and electric light and power to which Nikola Tesla, William Stanley, and Elihu Thomson contributed during the 1880s all promised to reshape the material foundation of American society. Overseas, the Russian chemist Dmitri Mendeleev introduced the periodic table of elements (1869), Karl Benz and Gottlieb Daimler invented the internal combustion engine (1885), and Guglielmo Marconi patented wireless telegraphy (1896). In addition, the continuing rapid expansion of railroads, communication, and machine manufacturing heralded a mode of living that we might begin to recognize as "modern."

If Commoner referred to the period following World War II as a technological revolution, surely the period following the Civil War constituted a similar kind of paradigm shift in American culture and its relationship to science and technology. The rise of the machine changed the way Americans worked. More factory and industrial jobs created remarkable demographic changes in America as urbanization represented one of the most significant migrations in American history. The 1920 census indicated that for the first time more Americans lived in cities than in rural areas.[27] In just over a century, Jefferson's agrarian republic had been transformed into an urban-industrial juggernaut. The organic city of the eighteenth century gave way to the urban metropolis, complete with what the urban planner Lewis Mumford called the "underground city"—the vast complex of subway and service tunnels, water and gas mains, and sewers—and the "invisible city"—the electric and communications grids. American science and technology were bearing fruit.[28]

The boom in technological progress and economic growth meant that industrial production, too, climbed dramatically as the nation organized itself into gargantuan production and communication systems.[29] The historian Ruth Schwartz Cowan noted that in 1869, agricultural products made up 53 percent of what was produced in the United States, while only 33 percent of the Gross Domestic Product came from manufacturing. Just thirty years later, however, those figures were reversed, and half the nation's output was in manufactured goods, even though farm acreage had increased markedly as a result of westward migration and settlement.[30] Industrial productivity encouraged further technological innovation, and the Gilded Age welcomed in a new era that Thomas P. Hughes has called an era of popular "technological enthusiasm" in the United States.[31] Technological optimism was so great in America that the intellectual historian Perry Miller described Americans "[flinging] themselves into the technological torrent," conscious "that here was their destiny."[32] Confidence in American technology had increased to such an extent that many Americans were convinced they had won the war against nature. The natural world, they believed, was dominated by and subject to human ingenuity and endeavor.[33]

By World War I, leading American corporations—General Electric, Du Pont, General Motors, and Bell Telephone—were establishing and funding their own research laboratories. Industrial scientists dismissed the broadly inquisitive methods of the independent inventors in favor of more direct, applied research, much more in tune with the mantra of efficiency and utilitarianism that typified the age. Efficiency and utilitarianism, themes introduced and praised during the Progressive era, lingered after World War I, and continued to demonstrate their centrality to Americanism in the auto industry and in the continuing success of efficiency experts such as Henry Ford, Frederick Taylor, and Charles Bedaux. Economic growth and technological optimism also welcomed back individualism and entrepreneurialism in formidable style. Whereas the economic depression at the end of the Gilded Age had bloodied the middle-class American entrepreneur, the Progressive era offered the entrepreneurial spirit another chance. As John Opie observed, "No one who looked at the American character in the nineteenth century and the first half of the twentieth century said that Americans were cautious."[34]

Scientists also embraced that American entrepreneurial spirit, and as the growth of industrial laboratories suggested, they cultivated relationships with their financial supporters to strengthen their research abilities by establishing science and technology as the cornerstone of progress during the first half of the twentieth century. The Great Depression of the 1930s injured the popular sentiment that science and technology were the harbingers of unmitigated progress. Populist voices—continually present since the Gilded Age, but generally muted by the more optimistic spirit toward technology's promise—pointed to the loss of jobs as a product of greater reliance on scientific expertise and its machines. While this sentiment galvanized radical scientists to think about their social role during the 1930s, wartime distractions put these concerns on the back burner. Just as war salvaged the American economy, it also reified the American technological spirit. The continued cooperation between science and industry contributed to maintaining the American enthusiasm for technological growth, which resulted in the realization of the technological revolution that occurred once post-World War II affluence allowed more consumers to enjoy the fruits of scientists' labors.[35]

And there's the rub. Whereas Lippmann and Peirce lauded American science's democratic principles, the economist Thorstein Veblen—a former student of Peirce—warned in 1918 that knowledge reflected the material circumstances of its conception.[36] During and after World War II, those circumstances were increasingly shaped by an omnipresent military influence that dominated scientific research agendas across the country.[37] In 1939, the federal government had allotted $50 million per year to science research, 18 percent of all private and public spending on research and development.[38] By the end of the war, the federal investment was $500 million, and constituted 83 percent of private and public spending on scientific research.[39] In 1955, the annual research and development budget was $3.1 billion. By the early 1960s, that budget had climbed above $10 billion, and to $17 billion by 1969. Moreover, since 1940 the federal budget had multiplied by a factor of 11. The budget for research and development had increased some 200 times.[40] Where that money went also changed; in 1939 the bulk of government-funded research was done in agency laboratories, but by 1969 more than three-quarters of it was performed by private industry, universities, and nonprofit institutions.[41] While the money was a significant boon to scientific research, it also suggested that the American research agenda was integrally connected to political interests. After World War II, that meant military development and, eventually, the space race. Of the $17 billion in funds made available in 1969, $8.2 billion came from the Department of Defense and $4.5 billion from NASA.

Upon departing the White House in 1961, President Dwight D. Eisenhower warned against the growing predominance of the military-industrial complex. From his vantage point in 1962, Supreme Court Justice William

O. Douglas echoed Veblen's concerns. "The new centers of power are in the hands of those who control science; and one who traces the controls back to origins often finds the Pentagon in the central position," he wrote in a pamphlet titled *Freedom of the Mind.* "Those who finance the scientific revolution," he continued, "usually control those who work for them. The impact of this control on our universities is so great that their autonomy is threatened."[42] Moreover, that powerful influence impressed upon the scientific community the importance of secrecy as a means of ensuring national security, but it also meant doing science in a relative vacuum, in direct contradiction of the collaborative spirit and the democratic principles of scientific discourse. As a result, new discoveries risked not receiving the full scrutiny that the scientific method required. According to Stuart W. Leslie, "the Cold War redefined American science."[43] American science was beholden on a grand scale to the immediacy of the political pressures of the period at the same time that it was married to a public enthusiasm for technological progress.

As Americans embraced risk, science and technology continued to raise the stakes throughout the twentieth century. In the mid-1960s, Commoner reflected on this entrepreneurialism and technological optimism, conceding that "there is considerable disagreement about the medical hazards of the new pollutants: about the effects of DDT now found in human bodies, about the diseases due to smog, or about the long-range effects of fallout." But that there was disagreement was a fundamental element in risk assessment. "The crucial point," he continued, "is that the disagreements exist, *for they reveal that we have risked these hazards before we knew what harm they might do.*"[44] In addition, Commoner noted that the powers of modern science meant that "the permissible margin for error has become very much reduced. In the development of steam engines a certain number of boiler explosions were tolerated as the art improved. If a single comparable disaster were to occur in a nuclear power plant or in a reactor-driven ship near a large city, thousands of people might die and a whole region be rendered uninhabitable."[45] To Commoner, the persistence of technological optimism after World War II threatened to embrace such risks uncritically.

If there was a singular event that alerted American scientists to the reduction of their autonomy, it was the atomic bomb. The bomb and its use also definitively resolved a major ethical dilemma among scientists that had raged for half a century. American scientists' complicity with war and politics destroyed any notions that they—especially physicists—were engaged in a pure and autonomous undertaking. In addition, the aftermath of World War II signaled the beginning of a renewed epistemological examination among scientists of their role in the world order. Concerned scientists concentrated not only on how science was funded, but also on questions pertaining to their own social responsibility, especially in a postwar world that frowned upon dissent and public discourse. Most significantly, scientists such as Commoner who were concerned with these questions gravitated toward politics with the realization that only through political engagement could they command or reclaim the direction of national science policy.

Soon after the conclusion of World War II, the renowned physicist J. Robert Oppenheimer delivered a paper titled "Physics in the Contemporary World" at the Massachusetts Institute of Technology. Referring to the devastation the atomic bombs had inflicted upon Hiroshima and Nagasaki, Oppenheimer stated that "in some sort of crude sense which no vulgarity, no humor, no over-statement can quite extinguish, the physicists have known sin; and this is a knowledge which they cannot lose."[46] In this poignant statement, Oppenheimer—who had been the director of the Manhattan Project—recognized the gravity represented by the advent of nuclear power as a political entity every bit as much as a scientific one at the dawn of the Cold War. For some, the success of the Manhattan Project constituted a portal to an endless frontier on which well-funded science would systematically unlock the mysteries of human life and the universe. For others, according to Donald Worster, Oppenheimer's suggestion that the physicists now knew sin begged the implied question "whether they also knew the way to redemption."[47]

Not until after World War II did a small but organized group of scientists publicly raise doubts about the rationality and, more significantly, the controllability of such unbridled technological optimism. As the United States experienced a rapid transition to a highly technical society, many scientists insisted that they become more involved in the political arena. But by then, it was too late. The Cold War occupied the concentration of government and military, and leading scientists found themselves relegated from partners to subordinate technicians supplying weapons for the Cold War arms race. Military influence continued to dominate American science. Whereas directly after World War II scientists were enjoying the height of their political influence, the national security and arms race priorities of the Cold War channeled that influence dramatically during the 1950s. Domestic anticommunism and McCarthyism made the expression of dissent all the more difficult, especially for scientists who posed a particular threat of supplying information to the enemy; in sum, American scientists endured what the historian Jessica Wang called "an age of anxiety."[48] Since scientists working on particularly sensitive projects required military clearance, questions of scientists' national loyalty constituted a major restriction on scientific and political freedom. This dynamic had begun in the 1930s, and carried over into the secrecy surrounding the Manhattan Project and the race for the atomic bomb. American physicists acquired considerable political prominence during World War II, and the postwar demands related to national security guaranteed further visibility and influence. But those same conditions also drastically restricted physicists' freedoms. Scientists had dutifully accepted the need for wartime secrecy, but the doors never opened as that secrecy transitioned into Cold War secrecy in the guise of national security. As Commoner would later lament: "The basic difficulty with secrecy in science is that mistakes made in secret will persist."[49]

But just as the oppressive nature of McCarthyism and loyalty oaths inhibited scientists' freedoms, Lawrence Badash argues that they also created a context that helped the political maturing of American scientists.[50] This was true in Commoner's case. The first challenge to the scientists' sense of social responsibility emerged during the political debate over how best to manage nuclear power immediately after the war's conclusion. In 1946, the Atomic Energy Act established the Atomic Energy Commission to manage the postwar program to develop the military, scientific, and industrial potential of atomic and nuclear energy. The Act was passed almost a year after atomic bombs had been dropped on Hiroshima and Nagasaki, amid controversy as to whether the new agency should be put in the hands of civilians or the military. In an attempt to quickly push legislation through Congress in the fall of 1945, the May-Johnson Bill, which favored military control, was introduced in the House. Its Congressional and military supporters believed that maintaining the secrecy of the atomic bomb's construction could be preserved only through military control. Its supporters were surprised, however, by the fervent opposition of atomic scientists, who felt that extensive public hearings should be held on such an important matter. Commoner interpreted the scientists' efforts as being the last feature of their wartime military duty. That initial concern spread to the mainstream. *TIME* magazine asked: "Is the military about to take over U.S. science lock, stock, and barrel, calling the tune for U.S. universities and signing up the best scientists for work fundamentally aimed at military results?"[51]

In response to the growing tumult, the Senate ordered the creation of a special committee—headed by Senator Brien McMahon of Connecticut—to assess the position and recommend a course of action. After contentious hearings, the McMahon Bill ultimately compromised by affirming civilian control while situating "military applications" of atomic energy as its top priority.[52] While research into peaceful uses for atomic energy was a part of its stated purpose, the new Atomic Energy Commission's emphasis was on the development and manufacture of weapons as military need dictated. Nevertheless, the Commission was, at least in theory, under civilian control and the American voters could participate in the establishment of future policies.[53] This was a crucial debate, and one in which Commoner acquired important political skills and scientific connections. Before the end of his service, Commoner was appointed by the Navy to serve as a scientific liaison on West Virginia Senator Harley Kilgore's subcommittee to organize government support for science. Kilgore's subcommittee produced the first National Science Foundation Bill. Commoner, working in uniform, was still there when the question of atomic energy came up after the war, and, under Kilgore, organized the first hearings on the distribution of authority over nuclear power. This was the first time that the public learned there had been agitation among Los Alamos scientists over control of atomic energy. Commoner met and worked closely with the Los Alamos scientists before and during the hearings. For Commoner, it was a momentous event, one from which he learned a lot about science and political activism and made important connections with prominent scientists from across the country.[54]

Just as important, scientists were quite publicly major contributors to the successful war effort. While they lost the ear of policy makers as Cold War tensions rose—by the end of 1949, the Berlin crisis had frayed nerves, China had succumbed to the Maoist Revolution, the Soviet Union had detonated its first atomic bomb, and the arms race was on—they discovered that the public audience was more interested and more concerned than ever in what they had to say.[55] What ensued was a deliberate attempt by some scientists to reposition themselves and establish their relevance in the public discourse. The bomb changed the political landscape of science. Science had been a tool with which idealists felt Americans could realize greater progress, prosperity, and political stability. To many Americans—scientists, military, and public—the bomb was a continuation or confirmation of that sentiment, but others were notably more pessimistic, aware that the fruits of progress also threatened the future of humanity. Was science getting out of hand? Had technology evaded the guided control of the scientists and/or society? These were important questions, but because of the Cold War political climate, no one seemed willing to ask them openly.

But should scientists be held responsible for these concerns? An interesting element of the ensuing debate entailed scientists and intellectuals trying to extricate science and expertise from their uses. Science, many scientists argued, was still a neutral and value-free exercise in seeking knowledge and solving problems; society—not scientists—put scientific discovery to good or bad uses. Acquiring knowledge was intrinsically valuable, but what was done with that knowledge deserved moral, social, and political scrutiny.[56] This was a fairly reasonable claim; science remained the objective pursuit of knowledge, but outside interests (and money) had influenced which pursuits would receive priority. Technology and its applications, scientists argued, should therefore be the focus of any moral criticism, not the science that had produced it. While many scientists washed their hands of the damage their discoveries had wrought, others—Commoner prominent among them—felt that scientists should be more politically involved in determining how science should be used. Science might well be neutral, but scientists, unequivocally, were not. In essence, Commoner and other socially concerned scientists rejected the notion that science and technology could be separated, thereby insulating researchers from responsibility for the practical uses of the technologies they perfected.

Many scientists objected to the cloak of secrecy imposed upon their work, but in the anticommunist environment of postwar America, there was little room for dissent. Prominent among the dissenters was E. U. Condon, who suffered serious scrutiny from a subcommittee of the House Un-American Activities Committee. Condon, a notable quantum physicist from the 1920s and elder statesman of American physics, had been particularly critical of the secrecy imposed on science, and strongly advocated continued international scientific cooperation. On 1 March 1948, the subcommittee described Condon—at the time, the director of the National Bureau of Standards—as "one of the weakest links in our atomic security."[57] Condon was by no means a radical thinker, but he did believe that science functioned properly only in an open society. Secrecy could only retard research, and contradicted the goals of the scientific community. He argued for intellectual freedom through public writings and his membership in the American-Soviet Science Society, which dedicated itself to the exchange of scientific information between the two superpowers. Condon became a relatively easy target for anticommunists, and his case became "the scientists' cause célèbre until the Oppenheimer case overshadowed it."[58]

To many scientists, the integrity of the genuine search for knowledge—and the freedom to engage in that pursuit—had been irredeemably compromised by the lopsided financial support for science related to weapons research and nuclear physics. Commoner was particularly concerned with the declining prestige of science's integrity. As he cautioned in an unpublished paper titled "The Scientist and Political Power," the integrity of science was "the sole instrument that we have for understanding the proper means of controlling the enormously destructive forces that science has placed at the hands of man." Should the integrity of science be eroded, Commoner warned, "Science will become not merely a poor instrument for social progress, but an active danger to man."[59]

In identifying this danger, Commoner also recognized that the potential problems were social in nature. For example, whereas the discovery and production of thalidomide took place in the laboratory, the discovery of its deleterious social consequences—deformed babies—invariably took place outside the laboratory, "well after," Commoner was quick to point out, "the causative activity was in full swing."[60] In order to redeem the integrity of science, Commoner strongly believed that American science needed to refocus its energies on serving the public, not on realizing financial or military gain. In 1947, as Commoner settled into his botany position at Washington University in St. Louis, he sought ways of bringing science and science policy out of the laboratory and into public politics.

His opportunity arose in the early 1950s after a meeting with the mathematician Warren Weaver, whose reputation as a manager of science emerged during the1930s as a divisional director of the Rockefeller Foundation. One of the primary vehicles through which scientists expressed their concerns to the public was the American Association for the Advancement of Science (AAAS), which started raising questions about the relationship between science and society in concert with the government's growing control over science. Shortly after the Korean War, at the height of the Cold War and McCarthyism, Weaver actively sought to encourage the AAAS to engage in issues that examined the scientists' social responsibility. In 1951, he had been a key author of what became the Arden House Statement, designed to foster a broader network among scientists at a time when their specializations threatened to fracture the AAAS. He also sought to reinvigorate scientists' attention to the social effects of their work by emphasizing the notion that scientists worked for the public.[61] In 1953, in *Scientific American,* Weaver suggested that the intellectual climate in the United States had reached a low, and required immediate remedy.[62] He was not alone. Earlier that year, the physiologist Maurice B. Visscher had publicly insisted that "the paramount ethical problem facing scientists today is what moral stand they should take in the crisis of freedom of thought and expression."[63] To Weaver, financial support of basic research was crucial in order to let science develop freely. In July 1953, Weaver and Commoner met and agreed "that something needed to be done right away to reverse the trend of inaction among scientists—and to start developing the means of speaking out on the issues which are bedeviling us."[64] Weaver and Commoner had been in contact before; Commoner had received grants from the Rockefeller Foundation to support his research on the tobacco mosaic virus. Recognizing and encouraging Commoner's energy and enthusiasm for social issues, Weaver later visited Commoner in St. Louis and urged him to get involved to "work out a sensible program of social responsibility on the part of the AAAS."[65]

The AAAS was the largest national body that included scientists from a wide range of different subdisciplines, but in the trend of overspecialization, the meetings of individual societies were taking precedence over the annual year-end meetings of the whole association. Attendance at the St. Louis meeting in December 1952 was "disappointingly low (fewer than two thousand)" out of the 48,740 registered members.[66] Disparate scientific fields were, in effect, segregating themselves from each other. For this reason, Commoner felt the AAAS was declining as a vital forum for engaging with the larger, more social aspects of science. He recognized that a revitalized national association could be an exceptionally effective pulpit from which to raise awareness about the need to restore the integrity of science, and accepted Weaver's invitation. When they met in 1953, their central issue was the high degree of external control over science by government, military, and corporate interests and the climate of secrecy and conformity enforced by Cold War anticommunist politics. As Commoner noted in a letter to E. U. Condon, "The main jobs [for the AAAS] seem to be to stop the drive toward timidity and conformism engendered by the current investigational hysterics, and to ward off the crisis which appears to be facing scientists as a result of the government's tendency to cut off much of the support for basic research."[67]

Weaver and Commoner recognized that the AAAS was no longer serving its members if more and more people were staying away. They also noted that the AAAS had not taken up the broader social and political epistemological issues which the more specialized societies tended to ignore. First and foremost, they saw the scientists' struggle for autonomy and funds for basic research as a necessary political endeavor. Weaver and Commoner hoped that discussion of such issues might be a way of restoring some relevance to the struggling AAAS. While these initial goals did not make social responsibility a priority, Weaver and Commoner did appreciate that an extension of scientists' sovereignty over science would allow for the kind of recovery of scientific integrity that they sought. They also keenly recognized the importance of establishing broader and more sophisticated channels for communicating the social importance of science and science policy to the public. One of their stated ambitions was to acquaint the public with the facts and dangers of uncontrolled technological output and the importance of basic research, so that they could better understand the potential risks threatened by these new technologies. In a sense, scientists would use public interest to regain control of their discipline.

As Commoner recalled his conversation with Weaver in his letter to Condon, his friend and AAAS president (Weaver would succeed Condon as president at the end of 1953), he concluded by recommending that Condon use his presidency to appoint committees that would investigate scientists' freedom of inquiry and support for science in general. Because of the importance of these themes, Commoner counseled haste in their establishment, but also suggested "that the membership include some of the most important members of the AAAS in order to give the committee the strength that it needs and emphasize the importance which is placed on the committee's work." Commoner even suggested that Condon and Weaver be members of the committee, but that younger members also be invited in order to reach out to the younger ranks. As he confided to Condon in the same letter, "I sometimes despair at the sight of my contemporaries burying themselves under their immediate tasks, and giving no thought to the issues broader than their own narrow field. There is more spunk among the older people, and I think that a special effort should be made to bring into action some of the younger scientific workers. (Needless to say I would myself be honored to serve)."[68]

Commoner found himself increasingly drawn to activists within the AAAS, and soon aligned himself with the anthropologist Margaret Mead, another prominent and effective catalyst for social activism among scientists. In December 1955, just as Martin Luther King, Jr., began the black boycott of segregated buses in Montgomery, Alabama, the AAAS convened for its annual meeting in segregated Atlanta. While many members of the Anthropology Section had elected to boycott the Atlanta meeting, Mead attended in order to confront segregation on the spot. The AAAS had managed to win some concessions from the city in order to make all the meeting spaces accessible to all participants; several sessions were also held at Atlanta University, an African-American university. But when Commoner and Detlev Bronk, a distinguished physiologist and former president of the AAAS, tried to get a taxi from a downtown hotel to a session at Atlanta University, they discovered that white taxis could not take them there and black taxis were forbidden to carry white passengers. Standing in the rain and furious, Bronk shared his frustration with Commoner, and threw his support behind a AAAS Council antisegregation resolution spearheaded by Mead. The resolution committee, of which Bronk was a member, proposed that future meetings be held only in cities where "all members may freely meet for scientific discussions."[69] It continued: "American science does not place a regional educational mission above fundamental respect for the person and personality of human beings." The AAAS annual meeting did not return to the Deep South until 1990, when it was held in New Orleans.[70]

The antisegregation resolution was controversial and provoked heated debate in the Council meeting, but it constituted a critical plank in the post war construction of a movement for social action among scientists and the relationship between science and public issues. Also at the Atlanta meeting, the Council appointed a special interim committee on the social aspects of science to "assist [the Association] in the integration of science into the general sociological structure."[71] The University of Alabama biochemist Ward Pigman was appointed the first chair of the interim committee. When the biologist Jane Oppenheimer, one of the original committee members, resigned, Dael Wolfle recommended Commoner to Pigman as "a very able person who is much interested in AAAS activities." Wolfle continued: "I am sure that if [Commoner] has time to devote to the committee, he will be extremely helpful."[72] Over the next few months, Commoner recruited new members to the committee and helped Pigman to put together a draft on the committee's findings.

The committee's preliminary report, presented to the AAAS membership at the 1956 meeting and published in early 1957 in *Science* as "Social Aspects of Science," is perhaps the first postwar tract to deliberately outline how American scientists should approach their social responsibility. "Social Aspects of Science" noted that society had become "far more dependent on science than ever before," which constituted a "new scientific revolution." The revolution had occurred, the report contended, during World War II, as a result of accelerated growth in scientific activity and the subsequent increased use of scientific knowledge. During World War II, the world "experienced a series of classic examples of almost immediate conversion of a scientific advance to a process of large practical impact upon society: antibiotics, synthetic polymers, nuclear energy, transistor electronics, microwave techniques, electronic computers." This rapid "transformation of scientific experience to industrial operation" was new, the authors noted, and "probably unique in human history."[73] Yet, the committee expressed concern over the public's unquestioning acceptance of new scientific innovations, because "there are indications that the public interest in science is not commensurate with the important role of science in society."[74]

In addition to science's social position, the committee recognized a number of problems with the internal structure of the scientific community, citing unbalanced growth, inadequate funding for basic research, and difficulties in checking and critiquing new findings. Wartime science had put a premium on the physical sciences to such an extent that "growth has been based less on internal needs of science than on the interest of external agencies in possible practical results. In a sense," the report continued, "the speed and direction of the development of science has been determined by the users of science rather than the practitioners of science." This redirection of scientific interests naturally contributed to both the lack of funding for basic research and, ultimately, the difficulties in communication among scientists due to heightened emphasis on secrecy.[75] "Social Aspects of Science" reached a particularly dramatic conclusion: "that there is an impending crisis in the relationship between science and American society. . . . At a time when decisive economic, political, and social processes have become profoundly dependent on science, the discipline has failed to attain its appropriate place in the management of public affairs."[76] The magnitude of the impending crisis resonated in science's potential—both positive and negative—and the scientific community's waning influence on decision-making. It was imperative, the report insisted, that the new powers of science be used for "the maximum human good, for, if the benefits to be derived from them are great, the possibility of harm is correspondingly serious."[77] The committee finished by turning its attention to the responsibility of scientists and to the role of the AAAS more specifically. The impending crisis was a "matter that requires the persistent attention of all scientists. It exemplifies the pressing need that scientists concern themselves with social action." Drawing from Weaver's earlier calls for activism, the committee was adamant that the AAAS could not "continue in the face of crucial situations with closed eyes and a dumb mouth." That the AAAS recognized that scientists and their social responsibility was an important subject for discussion was the first step; "what is needed now is a way to meet it."[78]

But then what? Having outlined the problems in science as they stood and made recommendations on how to address them, the committee was now left—as it had stated in the final sentence of "Social Aspects of Science"—with the challenge of how to confront those problems in practice. Commoner and other members of the committee were convinced that trying out specific action was the only legitimate means through which they could test their findings in "Social Aspects of Science." They wanted to engage with a specific issue. Other members were less sure or less willing to engage in more focused activism. The report's positive reception resulted in the continuation of the committee's work, but not without some personnel changes. Wolfle invited the Ohio State University pharmacologist and assistant dean of the College of Medicine Chauncey D. Leake to accept the chair of the committee, replacing Pigman, who was becoming increasingly uncomfortable with the more radical positions advocated by Commoner, Mead, and Weaver. "Ward Pigman did the Association a real service a year ago at Atlanta in insisting that the committee be appointed," Wolfle wrote in his letter to Leake, "but he is not the best person to steer the effort through to useful conclusion."[79]

As the newly reformed Committee on the Social Aspects of Science worked to refocus its direction after the publication of "Social Aspects of Science," it found itself drawn into the maelstrom surrounding the dangers of radioactive fallout from nuclear weapons testing. In April 1957 the world-famous philosopher and missionary surgeon Albert Schweitzer issued a declaration of conscience regarding the threat of nuclear testing to humans and human health. His declaration was deliberately addressed not to any nation or government, but to the world's peoples. Schweitzer was intent that his opposition to nuclear testing not be marred by appearing to take a political position in the Cold War tensions. He sent his appeal to the Nobel Prize committee—which in 1952 had bestowed its prestigious Peace Prize on Schweitzer for his humanitarian activities—and, at Schweitzer's request, it was broadcast from Oslo on 23 April 1957 in fifty countries.[80] In his prepared statement, Schweitzer called on people around the world to rally together to demand an end to nuclear testing. "When public opinion has been created . . . among all nations, an opinion informed of the dangers involved in going on with the tests and led by the reason which this information imposes, then the statesmen may reach an agreement to stop the experiments." This kind of public opinion, Schweitzer argued, "stands in no need of plebiscites or of forming of committees to express itself. It works through just being there."[81]

In preparing his statement, Schweitzer sought direction from leading scientists to check and support his argument, and based much of his appeal on scientific information about fallout's hazards to air, animals, humans, and human genetics. After introducing the dangers posed by nuclear testing, Schweitzer debunked some myths about fallout and reassured people that the levels of radioactive fallout in the air presented only minimal hazards, since they were not strong enough to penetrate the skin. But the bigger danger came from drinking radioactive water or eating radioactive food "as a consequence of the increased radioactivity in the air."[82] "When we eat contaminated cheese and fruits," his statement continued, "the radioactive elements stored in them are transferred to us."[83] To support his argument, Schweitzer introduced data on levels of radioactivity in the Columbia River, into which the Hanford nuclear plant emptied its wastewater. While the radioactivity of the river water was insignificant, Schweitzer noted that "the radioactivity of the river plankton was 2,000 times higher, that of ducks eating the plankton 40,000 times higher, that of fish 15,000 times higher. In young swallows fed on insects caught by their parents in the river, the radioactivity was 500,000 times higher and in the egg yolks of water birds more than 1,000,000 times higher."[84]

Having established a plausible scientific argument for the hazards presented by fallout, Schweitzer turned to fallout's social and moral implications. "That radioactive elements created by us are found in nature is an astounding event in the history of the earth," Schweitzer insisted. "To fail to consider its importance and its consequences would be a folly for which humanity would have to pay a terrible price."[85] In effect, Schweitzer was implying that humans now had the capacity to make the planet unfit for life. Such a statement would typically be regarded as absurdly melodramatic, but Schweitzer pointed to the power of the hydrogen and cobalt bombs as the embodiments of potential destruction. Even without a war, testing of these superbombs could render the atmosphere dangerously contaminated. In an interview a couple of months before his appeal, Schweitzer warned that "danger of this magnitude is not easily grasped by the human mind. As day after day passes, and as the sun continues to rise and set, the sheer regularity of nature seems to rule out such terrible thoughts. But what we seem to forget is that, yes, the sun will continue to rise and set and the moon will continue to move across the skies, but mankind can create a situation in which the sun and moon can look down upon an earth that has been stripped of all life."[86] More significantly, Schweitzer called for the people's right to know what hazards these new weapons comprised. In addressing the world's populations and not governments, and providing accessible, digestible information, Schweitzer was pursuing a line of activism that Commoner would soon make his own. Nothing constructive could be achieved, Schweitzer was saying, until people had the necessary information on the basis of which a moral climate of opinion could be created. And, at the same time, that kind of informed public participation was urgently necessary.

Schweitzer's declaration of conscience was heard by millions of people around the world, but it was not aired in the United States. The following day, the *New York Times* put the story on its first page and included a substantial portion of his appeal on page 2. But Robert A. Divine speculates that Schweitzer's statement might have gone unnoticed in the United States had it not been for a widely circulated open letter of response from Atomic Energy Commissioner Willard Libby, who contended that Schweitzer's argument was not based "on the most recent information" on radioactive fallout.[87] In his open letter dated 25 April 1957, the day after the *New York Times* presented Schweitzer's declaration to an American audience, Libby correctly recognized that concern over fallout was based on perceptions of risk, and set out to allay those concerns. "There is no question that excessive dosages of radioactive strontium can cause bone cancer and leukemia," Libby conceded, but added that the average levels of exposure from testing were insignificant compared with natural radiations to which humans were exposed on a daily basis. He did not, however, make any reference to Schweitzer's contention that fallout's greatest harm came not from external exposure but from its concentration in the food chain, but rather deflected the debate toward questions of national security. "No scientist contends that there is no risk," Libby concluded. But, he added, "Here the choice seems much clearer—the terrible risk of abandoning the defense effort which is so essential under present conditions to the survival of the free world against the small controlled risk from weapons testing."[88] In the aftermath of the debate, the philosopher had made a scientific argument, and the scientist had made a political argument.

The public debate between leading philosopher and humanitarian and leading scientist reached a mainstream audience as *TIME, The Saturday Review,* and the *New York Times* presented Schweitzer's postulations and Libby's rebuttal to an interested readership. The popular attention to the question created a forum for further public debate, and before the end of May, Leake had written to Commoner suggesting that "this puts responsibility directly upon us [as the Committee on the Social Aspects of Science] to prepare if possible a preliminary statement on this matter which may be of such a sort as to be worthy of consideration by the Board of Directors as respective of AAAS opinion."[89] The American public was looking for more answers, and it was in this kind of a public forum that Leake and others firmly believed the AAAS should be exhibiting some leadership and direction. In his letter, Leake suggested that Commoner prepare a statement quickly, in order to be able to present it at the committee meeting to be held in Washington, D.C., at the AAAS headquarters on 21 June 1957.

Leake did urge some caution, however, stating that it would be wise to give very careful consideration to any statement that the committee offered to the board of directors. "We want to be sure that we keep our feet solidly on the ground," he warned Commoner. "There is a great deal of high feeling now with regard to a possible danger of radiation fallout from the testing of nuclear weapons. Unfortunately, there is confusion of opinion among scientists regarding the actual danger. This is a matter that has to be handled carefully, if the AAAS is to maintain its position of scientific integrity and wisdom of judgment."[90] What Leake did not want was a strong political statement that would very likely divide the AAAS membership. While the fallout problem constituted a prime example of what the Committee on Social Aspects of Science was supposed to address, Leake fully recognized the divisive nature of the question among AAAS members. In counseling Commoner to restrain his own feelings in the interest of publishing a AAAS statement that would be roundly accepted and seen as an authoritative scientific statement, Leake was being politically astute, even at the expense of compromising his opposition to aboveground nuclear weapons testing. To Leake, the AAAS represented American scientific authority, and a passive opposition to fallout—sensitive to the complexities inherent in the AAAS and global politics—from the AAAS was more valuable than no such statement at all. Commoner may not have been quite so conciliatory. Finding a position that accommodated the conservative views of the AAAS board of directors proved too difficult; as Commoner remembered, working with the AAAS board on a fallout statement was like "walking on eggshells all the time."[91]

By 12 June, Commoner had sent drafts to committee members for comment, and continued revisions until sending off a final draft to the AAAS board of directors in advance of their meeting on 6 July 1957. One of the key features of the report on the radiation problem was that imbalance in scientific growth constituted a serious problem. While physicists had charged forward in developing nuclear weapons and testing them, biologists had been poorly positioned to find and express concerns about the health risks to humans and to the environment. The report asked, "Why hasn't sufficient work, cost and difficulty notwithstanding, already been carried out" to ascertain the potential future threats posed by nuclear fallout. Speaking for the AAAS, the committee argued that part of the "responsibility for this failure must be accepted by scientists and the organizations of science." Government officials concerned with the practical uses of nuclear energy do not have "the training and insight to foresee the intricate biological problems that are the remote, but important, consequences of nuclear explosions and reactor operation. One can ask that such officials be receptive to advice, but the primary source of such advice must be the scientist." In addition to recommending that biologists participate more in assessing the potential health risks inherent in nuclear testing, the committee reiterated its belief that secrecy was a hindrance to science, arguing that "the security of the nation might be better served if the question of possible radiation hazards were open to full discussion in the normal channels of scientific and public communication."[92]

Overconfident of the board of directors' support, Commoner sent drafts of the fallout report to Robert Plumb at the *New York Times* and John Lear of *The Saturday Review* so that editors "may have an opportunity to consider it in advance of the release date." Commoner described the statement as "the first effort which the committee has made to carry out the mandate of the AAAS Council to develop a AAAS approach to social problems of scientific origin." Leading his media connections, Commoner suggested that the statement on fallout might "be of interest both as a commentary on the radiation problem itself and as a follow-up to the committee's report last Christmas." In his letter to Plumb, Commoner also hoped that the *Times* would be "interested in reproducing the committee's statement in full."[93]

On 6 July, however, the board of directors refused to authorize the report's public release under the auspices of the AAAS, finding it too long and "not quite satisfactorily worded."[94] It seemed as though the board's conservative nature would make passage of a AAAS statement on fallout particularly difficult. Remembering his early work in the AAAS, Commoner recalled that "the AAAS, as a whole, was very leery about politics."[95] Perhaps. But more likely the AAAS was leery about Commoner's politics. Indeed, the board was very used to playing politics through long-cultivated back channels; Commoner's approach was disconcerting precisely because it threatened to circumvent those channels.[96]

The report was sent back to the Committee on the Social Aspects of Science to be revised in time for the AAAS October board meeting. A couple of days after the 6 July meeting, Plumb telephoned Wolfle to inquire what decision the board had reached. Wolfle was outraged that the report had been distributed to the press prior to its approval, and in an angry letter to Leake, he wrote, "Would you prefer to tell the members of the committee or would you prefer to have me tell them that we think it better to have such statements held in confidence until they are ready for release, and that we very strongly prefer to release such statements simultaneously to all interested members of the press, and not to one or two favorites?"[97] This would not be the last time that Commoner would "scoop" an article.

Wolfle's ire and the difficulties in getting approval for a public statement on fallout from the AAAS board revealed the problems inherent in scientists' engaging in controversial issues. Effectively there were two approaches to controversial issues such as nuclear fallout. Scientists could make partisan statements, in which they could advocate actions that they considered desirable. When making partisan statements, however, the board cautioned the committee that the scientist should "do so as a citizen rather than as a scientist, and ordinarily this principle may preclude group action by scientific groups, societies, or associations."[98] The alternative was to present information and analysis of a variety of courses of action as analysts, without making value-laden conclusions. The lesson of these approaches would become the cornerstone of Commoner's future environmental activism, as he would use public education as a means of presenting scientific information to weigh in on difficult social issues. "I've made a career out of [the science information movement] by doing research and [sharing it with the public]," Commoner remembered, reflecting on his confrontation with the AAAS board over the fallout question.[99] But the distinction between the two alternatives was hardly concrete. By deciding that the fallout problem deserved consideration, Commoner and the Committee on the Social Aspects of Science were making a political or partisan decision. By simply engaging in the controversy, Commoner was taking a value-laden position.

Indeed, Commoner felt that he was following the more objective alternative in his various drafts of the AAAS statement on fallout, but the board saw only a confrontational polemic on nuclear testing. Further drafts intensified the division, and some committee members became reluctant to lend their names to the statement. In a letter to Leake, the distinguished analyst Lawrence Kubie, another committee member, was particularly critical. "As a strategic instrument representing the AAAS," he wrote, "it could not possibly be worse. . . . It preaches. It argues. It belabors the obvious."[100] Multiple drafts were prepared, and members could submit only a compromise draft of the statement that did not really satisfy any of them; in October, the board of directors again rejected the document. In his explanation, Wolfle, recognizing that the most recent draft "was a compromise," pointed out that the statement lacked focus, lacked a coherent audience, and was unclear with respect to its directives. "Is the United States Government being supported or attacked?" Wolfle asked. "Is the document addressed to scientists, and, if so, is it intended to influence their research or their activities as citizens? Because there was so much uncertainty and lack of clarity, the Board took no formal action with respect to the statement."[101] Traditionally, scientists were problem solvers and were devoted to the notion that objective problems had objective solutions. But in the fallout statement Commoner was embracing complexity and uncertainty, and insisting that scientists could not reach a solution on their own. He understood that made many scientists uncomfortable. In a letter to Leake, submitting the draft, he wrote:

> I am not at all pessimistic about the value of the statement as it now stands. . . . The statement has an important message, which to my knowledge has not been put before the public. It is true that we do not solve the problem of telling the government what it ought to do next; whether or not to stop testing, to concentrate on fusion processes, or what have you. We also make no attempt to settle the argument among the experts on biological hazards. It seems to me that no one can accomplish this right now. Indeed, this is the whole point—that we do not have information sufficient to make such decisions. If we can get that point across then scientists and the public generally can proceed to their own political conclusions as they see fit.[102]

But as the board of directors became more rigid, Commoner became increasingly frustrated. He claimed: "My original intention was to turn the AAAS into an effective agency in educating the public about politically sensitive, technological issues, as part of its mission. After a while, it was clear that this was an uphill fight and particularly around the whole fallout issue." Ultimately, Commoner would publish "The Fallout Problem" in *Science* under his own name, and not as an official AAAS statement. "It was urgent that it happen," Commoner insisted, "and I decided to do it on my own."[103] Organizing under the aegis of a larger organization was difficult, and reaching any kind of consensus on controversial questions such as fallout was near impossible. After the final revisions from the AAAS board made it clear that the AAAS would not take a definitive position on the fallout question, Commoner wrote to Leake, suggesting "it is clear . . . that one cannot expect any representative group of scientists not tied together by a more restricted set of beliefs to arrive at a policy-making decision." But to Commoner, that conclusion only indicated the extent to which the integrity of science had been compromised. Referring to the committee's own experience in trying to write a representative statement on fallout, Commoner continued: "Probably the chief reason for the present lack of agreement is the inadequate interchange of facts and ideas within the family of science and between scientists and other social groups."[104] As American scientists of the post-World War II era struggled with the kinds of epistemological questions that the new age of science posed for them, the Committee on the Social Aspects of Science raised strategic questions about how to recover the muted dialogue among scientists, and how to spark public interest in science and provide socially relevant information to nonscientists.

Ultimately the committee did not survive these questions, and it was dissolved after failing to produce a fallout statement. But in 1960 Commoner was invited to chair the AAAS's new venture into questions of social responsibility, the Committee on Science in the Promotion of Human Welfare, which included such eminent scientists as Robert Brode, Harrison Brown, and Margaret Mead. The new committee became commonly known as the Commoner Committee, and more successfully raised concerns about the widening gap between "hard" science and the social sciences, and "the conscious exploitation of science for military advantage."[105] A major failing of the Committee on the Social Aspects of Science had been its relative inability to establish a clear agreement that scientists needed to focus on political problems. The committee had located the problems it sought to address, but met resistance from within the AAAS in putting together an effective road map to address them effectively. The subsequent Commoner Committee proposed a very similar mission statement—"to develop an analysis of the problem of scientists' relations to the social issues created by scientific progress"—but as the fallout debate intensified, the AAAS and the public were increasingly willing to discuss the controversy.[106]

Scientists more prominent than Commoner were politically active in distributing information to the public, but Donald Fleming contends that the leading politico-scientists needed to be part of the new generation of scientists who had come of age during World War II. Established scientists such as Hermann J. Muller, Linus Pauling, and René Dubos had developed professional identities that made it difficult for them to engage completely in the political sphere. "Nothing could have been further from their self-conceptions than filling the role of general utility men for manipulating the lay response to science," Fleming argued.[107] Further, the experiences of Condon, Pauling, and Oppenheimer with the House Committee on Un-American Activities suggested that prominent scientists risked making public activism in science the target every bit as much as themselves. Since many of these older scientists had had a hand in creating the political and technological predicament after World War II, they clearly had a vested interest in restoring the integrity of science. But Weaver and others recognized that the future of the debate lay in the hands of the younger generation. In Commoner, they had found an ideal and tireless advocate for social responsibility.

Nevertheless, social activism came at a considerable cost. Inasmuch as the invasive influence of government, military, and corporate interests altered the practice of science, the politico-scientists found themselves compromising their own scientific ideals to an extent. In their trying to preserve the integrity of science during the early stages of the Cold War, the politico-scientists' reputation as pure researchers suffered. Just as the older generation of scientists had identities that prevented them from wholly engaging in the political arena, by 1960 Commoner's popular identity had become almost completely immersed in politics. In *Social Theory and Social Structure,* the sociologist Robert K. Merton argued that science and scientists functioned in accordance with a fixed set of norms, which he called the "ethos of science." This ethos protected and preserved the scientific community's standards, and ensured a climate in which good basic research could be conducted.[108] While Commoner and other politico-scientists worked to defend that ethos, their own reputations suffered as they were perceived to have breached the tightly held qualities of disinterestedness and objectivity in their pursuit of a heightened social responsibility.

In the conservative scientific community of the emerging Cold War, the politico-scientists were often considered the pariahs of established, disinterested science and traitors to the kind of integrity that they themselves claimed to defend. Indeed, in the twenty-first century, we know Commoner more for his political and environmental activism than for his research on the tobacco mosaic virus—for which he was awarded the prestigious Newcomb Cleveland Prize by the AAAS in 1953—or for his pioneering work on the role of free radicals, special molecules with unpaired electrons possessing a rather apt name, given Commoner's political persuasions. Commoner himself was quite aware of the "sacrifice" that he made, noting candidly in 1973 that "if I hadn't offended the Establishment, my work would have justified my being in the National Academy [of Sciences] a long time ago."[109] But to Commoner, this was a decision he made with little regret. When he entered Columbia in 1933, he knew he was going to be a biologist, but he was also aware that he was "intimately concerned with politics." By the time he graduated from Columbia and arrived at Harvard to do his graduate work, Commoner recalled, "I had it clear in my mind that I was going to do science and at the same time carry out activities that properly integrated science into public life. That was it; that was everything."[110]

2

Guarding the Public

I know of no safe repository of the ultimate powers of the society but the people themselves; and if we think them not enlightened enough to exercise their discretion, the remedy is not to take it from them, but to inform their discretion.
—Thomas Jefferson

"The greatest single cause of environmental contamination of this planet is radioactivity from test explosions of nuclear weapons in the atmosphere," Commoner wrote in 1964.[1] Because of that, he boldly claimed that "the Atomic Energy Commission made me an environmentalist."[2] The severity of the threat posed by radioactivity from nuclear tests also prompted Commoner to assert that the 1963 Nuclear Test Ban Treaty was "the first victorious battle in the campaign to save the environment—and its human inhabitants—from the blind assaults of modern technology."[3] Commoner was particularly optimistic about the symbolic relevance of the Test Ban Treaty and the growing effectiveness of the science information movement. The struggle over nuclear testing had been the politico-scientists' first major effort to engage the public with a universal scientific problem. "Seen in its true, environmental context," he claimed, "the power of nuclear technology is subject less to the control of the technologist than to the governance of the public will."[4] Not only was the Test Ban Treaty a significant political and environmental victory, it also constituted an impressive example of democracy's potency as a tool for social change.

Commoner had every right to be particularly proud of this key victory, as his development of a public information forum—first under the auspices of the AAAS, then with his Committee for Nuclear Information, and ultimately with the Scientists' Institute for Public Information—was arguably one of the most significant features of the campaign against nuclear testing.

Working in close collaboration with the anthropologist Margaret Mead—and inspired by the public advocacy of Nobel laureates such as Albert Schweitzer, P. M. S. Blackett, and Linus Pauling—he developed the science information movement while he served as the chair of the AAAS Committee for Science in the Promotion of Human Welfare. After outlining the program for public information, Commoner encouraged the growth of several grassroots information groups that provided information to the public to enable them to participate more actively in critical questions of science and its applications. The Greater St. Louis Citizens' Committee for Nuclear Information was among the most prominent and significant of these groups. Its scientists, led by Commoner, argued that the determination of what constituted acceptable risks was an inherently moral and public—rather than scientific—issue; in a free and democratic society, citizens should be appropriately informed in order to make these decisions. What "appropriately informed" meant was naturally open to debate, but Commoner insisted that public debate was imperative. He openly conceded that the nuclear test program had been an enormous success in solving exceedingly difficult problems in physics and engineering, but that Americans were not successful in solving "the resultant worldwide contamination from fallout."[5] If nuclear technology promised (or threatened) so much, surely a greater public understanding and endorsement of its inherent risks was necessary for the continuation of weapons testing. To Commoner, the absence of any such discussion constituted a very serious "crisis of democracy."[6]

This second chapter considers the social significance of the post-World War II science information movement, but also situates it and the controversy over control of nuclear power as one of the defining events of the modern environmental movement. Whereas the previous chapter examined how secrecy threatened to restrict scientific progress, this chapter outlines how that secrecy resulted in the accumulation of radioactive fallout in the food chain in a manner that galvanized the politico-scientists into action. The Washington University-based scientists and citizens who founded the Committee for Nuclear Information based their call for public information in part on the importance of the democratic process, but also in recognition of the environmental consequences that might be incurred if nuclear testing were to continue. As one of their main catalysts, Commoner warned ominously: "The first lesson to be learned from our experience with fallout is that given the enormous power and scope of modern physical science, and intense social pressure for its application, we are likely to put massive technological processes into operation before we understand their eventual biological consequences."[7] That lesson demonstrated the significance of the Committee for Nuclear Information's collaboration with public opposition to aboveground nuclear testing and constitutes a vitally important parable in our contemporary environmental understanding. Moreover, we can witness in the debate over nuclear weapons testing a practical example of scientists agonizing over their social responsibility. Whether scientists were supposed to be recognized authorities and specialists at the front of the triumphant march toward progress, or whether they should rein in the technological juggernaut when it seemed too risky, appeared to constitute a significant schism within the scientific community. No other technology provoked such a heated debate during the 1950s, nor did any other technology present such high stakes.

Just as important, Scott Kirsch notes that "the history of 'radiation safety' . . . [has] been largely a reactionary one, characterized by changing standards developed over time in response to new scientific knowledge of environmental health risks."[8] Reactionary history and the changing contexts of the awareness of environmental hazards are indicative of what Bruno Latour has called the "historicity" of scientific knowledge: "History not only passes but transforms."[9] As knowledge increases, our understanding of the past is altered. As a result, Kirsch observes in his work on the discovery of iodine-131 in nuclear fallout: "After 1962, ingested I-131 had posed the most serious radioactivity hazard to infants and children living downwind from nuclear testing *throughout* the previous decade."[10] Commoner's role in that history was to provide a voice of dissent and to engage in the active dissemination of scientific information as it was acquired. We might also take from this story a deeper understanding of the social confusion surrounding modernization. According to Ulrich Beck, "The more modern a society becomes, the more unintended consequences it produces, and as these become known and acknowledged, they call the foundations of industrial modernization into question."[11] To a degree, this phenomenon was responsible for the growing malaise of modernity, and as the unanticipated hazards of nuclear fallout became clear, they offered a lurid and ubiquitous introduction to a postwar world rife with sociopolitical tension and conflict and steeped in new poisons. Keeping the historicity of scientific knowledge in mind, however, the following account does not mean to highlight Commoner's prescience on the hazards of nuclear fallout, but rather to observe the success of his apparatus in action and to note the potential value of taking a more precautionary approach to new technologies.

With a flash in the desert, human history entered the atomic age. At 5:25:49 A.M. on 16 July 1945, at the Trinity test site at Los Alamos, New Mexico, American scientists detonated the first atomic bomb. The predawn sky was torn apart by a blinding burst of light. The mood within the test bunker was mixed. The test had been a success, but only after detonation did the observers recognize the full effect or power of the weapon upon which they had labored for several years. Quoting the *Bhagavad Gita* as he watched the mushroom cloud rise from ground zero, the Manhattan Project director, J. Robert Oppenheimer, lamented, "I am become death, the Shatterer of Worlds." Shaking Oppenheimer's hand in congratulation, test director Kenneth Bainbridge dryly stated, "Now we are all sons of bitches." General James Farrell later expressed concern "that we puny things were blasphemous to tamper with the forces heretofore reserved to the Almighty." Within a month, World War II would be over, as Americans would drop two atomic bombs on Japan, and the United States would try to reorganize its scientific and military complexes to restore prosperity after almost two decades of depression and war while simultaneously preparing for the next enemy on the horizon.[12]

Suggestions concerning what to do with the atomic program had been delivered in the 1946 Atomic Energy Act. While the Act had ensured that the Atomic Energy Commission (AEC) would function under civilian control, it also had compromised, recognizing military progress as its primary objective. Military need was perceived to have grown drastically in September 1949, as Americans discovered that the Soviet Union had developed and tested an atomic bomb. Prompted by a new Cold War arms race, the AEC was caught in a position where secrecy and uninhibited progress were both thought to be critical to national security. In militaristic terms, it was essential that the United States maintain its nuclear dominance, but to tap into that potential, the AEC needed to be able to develop nuclear technology without inhibiting regulatory impediments. Because the AEC was required to both develop and regulate nuclear power, it often felt handcuffed when it came to developing nuclear energy technology. As Commissioner Willard Libby stated, expressing the frustrations of many members of the AEC: "Our great hazard is that this great benefit to mankind will be killed aborning by unnecessary regulation. There is not any doubt about the practicability of isotopes and atomic power in my mind. The question is whether we can get it there in our lifetime."[13]

If its destructive capacities had horrified its creators, the atomic bomb's lingering side effect—fallout—would become a source of domestic tension during the Cold War. As nuclear testing began in Nevada and in the Pacific, the Atomic Energy Commission insisted that the dangers of radioactivity to Americans living downwind from the tests were minimal, and that accumulations of fallout within the body could never reach hazardous levels. In reassuring language, the AEC tried to quell concerns over the testing of hydrogen bombs in Nevada in 1952, stating that "these explosives created no immediate or long-range hazard to human health outside the proving ground."[14] But throughout the 1950s, while the AEC's specialists dismissed any danger related to radioactive fallout, a burgeoning movement within the scientific community argued otherwise. Determined to turn the science and politics of the Cold War arms race into public issues, scientists across the country demonstrated to the public that humans were consuming alarming amounts of strontium-90 and iodine-131, particularly dangerous sources of radioactivity that were chemically similar to calcium. One of the primary reasons for caution was the discovery that strontium-90 fell to earth much sooner than had been expected. Strontium-90 is a radioactive by-product of the fission of uranium and plutonium in nuclear weapons testing. Its half-life—the time it took for half of its atoms to disintegrate—was twenty-nine years. AEC scientists had confidently expected that it would remain in the stratosphere at least that long. However, on 26 April 1953, physicists experimenting with radioactivity at the Rensselaer Polytechnic Institute in Troy, New York, noticed a sudden surge in their "background" radiation counts. The surge, associated with a deluge of rain, was determined to be radioactive debris—fallout—from nuclear tests in Nevada thirty-six hours earlier that had blown across the country and been brought to earth by heavy rain. The hazards of nuclear weapons testing had become extremely palpable. Strontium-90 was a known hazard, but no one had ever fully investigated its danger, because it was not supposed to pose a threat from the stratosphere. Uncertainty and rapidly conducted experiments resulted in substantial differences of opinion among scientists which only exacerbated the debate, as scientists and citizens waited to learn about each new finding. That it had come down at all suggested that atomic science was again proving to be fallible and anything but omniscient.[15]

Because strontium-90 was a chemical relative of calcium, it followed a similar course through the biological food chain. Entering the human body through milk and calcium-rich vegetables, most strontium-90 passed right through the body, but trace amounts collected in bones and bone marrow and gave off radiation internally, threatening to cause bone cancer, cancer of soft tissue near bone, and leukemia. As radioactive fallout entered the soil, it accompanied calcium through the food chain—from soil, to plants, to animals—and into human bodies. Human—especially children's—bones were being fortified not only with calcium but also with a radioactive isotope, exponentially increasing one's susceptibility to cancer. Further, given its long half-life, significant quantities of strontium-90 could accumulate in human bones over a long period of time. Because of its capacity to contaminate food supplies upon which all Americans were dependent, the dangers of radioactive fallout presented a relatively universal risk.[16]

During the 1956 presidential campaign, the Democratic candidate and former governor of Illinois, Adlai Stevenson, introduced nuclear fallout as a campaign issue. In April 1956, Stevenson raised the suggestion that the United States "take the lead in halting further test explosions" in an address to the American Society of Newspaper Editors, an argument he raised again in Los Angeles as the Democratic nominee for president in a speech to the American Legion convention in September.[17] By the end of the month, Stevenson had raised weapons testing again at a speech in Minneapolis, stating that nuclear disarmament should be "the first order of business in the world today." Also in Minneapolis, Stevenson raised "the danger of poisoning of the atmosphere" as another reason for putting an end to atomic weapons testing.[18] It was the first time that fallout had been used as a political issue in a presidential campaign, and the first time that such public attention had been given to fallout as a potential health hazard. Stevenson had asked Dr. Evarts Graham, a lung surgeon at Washington University, to gather information on the dangers of fallout. Graham turned to his colleagues in science, including Commoner, to help compile the information Stevenson requested. Stevenson lost the election to the incumbent, Dwight D. Eisenhower, but public interest in putting a halt to atomic weapons tests was growing and scientists were just beginning to learn how effective they could be as disseminators of public information.[19]

The scientists' conclusions radically altered the official U.S. position on atomic fallout and led to the 1963 Nuclear Atmospheric Test Ban Treaty. More important, the Atomic Energy Commission's politics of secrecy and misinformation raised serious questions about the governance of nuclear technology and risk assessment. Even as late as 1963, no standards or limits had been laid out for acceptable doses of fallout radiation, and the government had been slow in developing any countermeasures to protect the public. Significantly, no government agency had kept the public informed of radiation's possible health hazards. Rather, the AEC had done its utmost to deny any danger. In October 1956, for example, President Eisenhower reassured Americans that "the continuance of the present rate of H-bomb testing, by the most sober and responsible scientific judgment . . . does not imperil the health of humanity."[20] Eisenhower's reassurance echoed the government literature that circulated. Pamphlets published by the AEC supported Eisenhower's statement that the various radioactive components presented very little risk to Americans. Accompanying the AEC's literature, a group of scientists who supported nuclear technology further publicized the necessity of bomb tests and inquiries into atomic energy.[21]

Edward Teller was among the most outspoken of these scientists and the foremost champion of nuclear technology's potential. As a part of the Manhattan Project, he had attended the first test at Los Alamos in 1945, but his enthusiastic reaction was in stark contrast with the more somber tone set by Oppenheimer and others in the bunker. "I was looking, contrary to regulations, straight at the bomb," Teller recalled. "I put on welding glasses, suntan lotion, and gloves. I looked the beast in the eye, and I was impressed."[22] After the war, Teller remained at Los Alamos, and became widely considered the "Father of the H-Bomb" after the detonation of the world's first thermonuclear bomb on 1 November 1952. In *The Legacy of Hiroshima,* Teller dismissed any inherent dangers of nuclear fallout. "Fallout from . . . testing is dangerous," he boldly stated, "only in the imagination."[23] Recent accounts have portrayed Teller as one of the great villains of twentieth-century American history because he very consciously contributed to the proliferation of nuclear fallout, but Teller simply saw himself as another politico-scientist, admittedly from the opposite side of the tracks than Commoner. A Hungarian refugee from Nazi Europe, Teller saw nuclear power as ultimately making a single world government inevitable; for Teller, such a world government needed to hinge on the democratic ideals of the West. The continuation of atomic research and testing was the only way to ensure that the West would be able to resist the postwar Communist threat. He actively used his position to promote the American nuclear program, less for his own immediate benefit—Teller was less interested in personal gain or in saving face when data on the health risks mounted against his position—than for national security. Given the tensions of the Cold War, he was convinced that a strong nuclear program was essential for Western survival and—ultimately—victory over Soviet Communism. For Teller, national security was a more immediate priority than public health, which he held was at less risk than many naysayers warned. His position in favor of testing made him a favorite scientist within military circles, who also supported continued testing and military expenditures.[24]

This tension between Cold War security and public information serves as one of the cornerstones of the dynamics that colored Cold War politics in the United States. The Communist threat demanded that greater emphasis be put on secrecy and civil defense, but the perceived cost to many was an inhibition of American freedoms, particularly of democracy and the freedom of expression. For many scientists and citizens, curtailing American democracy to preserve it seemed a perverse abuse of Americanism, and many confronted the Cold War administrations of the early and mid-1950s. J. Robert Oppenheimer, the former director of the Manhattan Project, had publicly fallen from grace after expressing concerns about policy directions pertaining to the development of nuclear technology. Attacked by 1950s cold warriors, Oppenheimer ironically fell victim because of his deference to social responsibility over federal service and national security. It appeared that the political mechanisms that had bestowed so much public attention and power on the scientific community could just as easily take them away.[25]

I discussed the E. U. Condon case in the previous chapter. Commoner was instrumental in getting Condon to join the Washington University faculty in 1956, and they became collaborators in promoting dissemination of nuclear information to the citizens of St. Louis. Commoner also came into close contact with the famed biochemist Linus Pauling. Pauling was an outspoken politico-scientist roughly a generation older than Commoner. In January 1952, the State Department had refused to issue Pauling a new passport. Pauling—who would be the unprecedented recipient of two Nobel Prizes, for chemistry in 1954 and for peace in 1963—was a strong and vocal critic of U.S. nuclear policy. In 1957, he organized a petition to the United Nations signed by scientists opposed to nuclear weapons; it ultimately collected 11,021 signatures from all over the world. Demanding a halt to weapons testing and advocating disarmament, the Pauling petition claimed that the danger to human health was one of its primary concerns. "Each nuclear bomb spreads an added burden of radioactive elements over every part of the world," it stated. "Each added amount of radiation causes damage to the health of human beings all over the world and causes damage to the pool of human germ plasm such as to lead to an increase in the number of seriously defective children that will be born in future generations."[26]

Similar in tone to Commoner's AAAS rhetoric about the role of the scientist, the petition also noted the scientists' authority in understanding the dangers that nuclear weapons presented. The petition was written in Commoner's office at Washington University in St. Louis, and the forms were printed in a St. Louis union shop and bore the union label. When Pauling was again called before the House Committee on Un-American Activities (HUAC), he refused to name anyone in the organization of this successful campaign. In this particular incident, Commoner might have been fortunate to escape the anticommunist sentiments of the period. HUAC did not pursue the St. Louis union label, which would have inevitably led back to Commoner's participation. But his close connection with both Condon and Pauling taught Commoner valuable lessons about how one might voice dissent without suffering political marginalization during an era of intolerance. His subsequent activism would be informed by—and in reaction to—the political climate that gave rise to Pauling's and Condon's cases.[27]

After the dissolution of the Interim Committee on the Social Aspects of Science, the AAAS board of directors created the Committee on Science in the Promotion of Human Welfare. In January 1959, AAAS Secretary Dael Wolfle wrote to Commoner, inviting him to be a member of the committee. "The Committee on Science in the Promotion of Human Welfare is in a fairly direct sense a descendant of the Committee on the Social Aspects of Science," he wrote. The AAAS was still concerned about questions dealing with the relationship between science and society, and the new committee was charged with assessing "the Association's present activities in terms of their effectiveness in fulfilling the Association's constitutional responsibility 'to improve the effectiveness of science in the promotion of human welfare.'"[28] Margaret Mead was also appointed to the committee, and she and Commoner formed an important working relationship that led to the realization of an effective science information movement.

After a few months of inactivity within the newly formed committee, Commoner was asked to take over as chair. Still sensitive about divisions within the AAAS concerning whether the Association should become more involved in politics, he was cautious about how best to move the committee beyond the obstacles faced by the Committee on the Social Aspects of Science. The AAAS remained a large and diverse organization, and one prone to conservatism. As Commoner confided to Mead upon accepting the chair of the new committee, "I think that there is still a serious problem of demonstrating that a committee such as ours can be of real value to the AAAS."[29] What was needed was a method of presenting scientific positions on social issues without antagonizing other scientists. Dividing scientists over political issues ultimately resulted in confusing the public as they received differing information from different camps. Further, trying to ensure that he avoided upsetting the AAAS board of directors and the membership in general, Commoner opted for defending the notion of scientific integrity. He regarded the integrity of science as "the system of discourse and procedures which science employs to discover and discuss the properties of the natural world."[30] As defenders of scientific truth, Commoner felt the committee could deflect most criticism by taking the moral high road, but this resulted in a repositioning of scientists and their social responsibility. Whereas Commoner and other politico-scientists had advocated rousing and stimulating public concern over issues relating to science and society, the new Commoner Committee moved away from direct political activism to serve as a more objective outlet for scientific information.

The cornerstone of Commoner's subsequent activism took on this premise: effective social activism needed to be unfettered and informed. The scientist's role, then, was to provide accessible information pertaining to difficult scientific questions to the public so that they could make informed decisions. At the height of the science information movement, Commoner reflected that "the scientist as the custodian of [scientific] knowledge has a profound duty to impart as much of it as he can to his fellow citizens. But in doing so he must guard against false pretensions, and avoid claiming for science that which belongs to the conscience."[31]

Commoner saw three parts to the politico-scientist platform. First and foremost, he insisted that scientists should not divorce themselves from social issues raised by their work. Given the prevalence of technology and the relative ubiquity of science and science policy in the postwar environment, scientists had a moral responsibility to participate in the social ramifications of their findings. While public policy decisions were not inherently scientific decisions, many of them were fundamentally reliant on a very important scientific factual basis. Scientists had a duty to help the public understand the complexities of the decisions that faced them as they related to science. Commoner called this "involuntary responsibility," the scientist's obligation to inform the public. Whereas university scientists had obligations to teaching and research—involuntary responsibilities—this kind of social engagement, to Commoner, constituted a third obligation.[32] A related second point involved the dissemination of scientific information. Commoner and Mead recognized a need for public information; scientists should no longer confine their efforts to advising political officials. Their social duty was to the public, not to the policy makers. The public needed to be more directly and completely informed by scientists about the technical aspects of social issues. As much as remaining responsible for their research and its applications, scientists were primarily responsible not to their funding agencies or employers, but to the American public and the world. Finally, scientists were not prophets. This last point was critical. While it was imperative that scientists provide information to the public, scientists should not take advantage of this role to dictate how nonscientists should interpret the moral or political elements of the scientific findings. Scientists were experts in interpreting the objective aspects of scientific findings; they were not experts in shaping policy decisions. In this respect, scientists should present data and information about the relative benefits and costs of a particular new technology—providing them equally to politicians and to citizens, for them to weigh the risk.

As Commoner understood it, the postwar technological revolution had created as many social puzzles as scientific ones. Scientists were well positioned to understand the causes of these problems, but their solutions—because they were social—demanded more public participation. But for that public participation to be productive and effective, citizens needed to understand the problem, to be able to weigh the pros and cons of differing positions, and to make informed decisions. Given the technical nature of the scientific causes of the social problems, scientists needed to find a way to filter through the technical language and translate it into lay terms. Commoner saw that two elements were essential to an effective methodology: clear information and a nonpartisan position. Combined, these two pillars could resurrect a faltering democratic system in relation to science and its application to society. On an issue as provocative as nuclear testing that combined both national security interests and public health concerns, clear, objective information could help the public to determine whether the health risk involved in preserving national security was acceptable or not. Objectivity, therefore, came to play a critical role in the political discourse of the science information movement. The intent and purpose of the information movement was to encourage the adoption of a particular position, but that activism was obscured by the mantle of objectivity, which produced a far more subtle and convincing line of rhetoric.

If there is a seminal document in the creation of the science information movement, it was "The Fallout Problem," which was Commoner's salvaging of the Committee on the Social Aspects of Science's attempt to establish a position on nuclear weapons testing for the AAAS. At the December 1957 AAAS meeting in Indianapolis, Commoner tested his nonpartisan approach to the dissemination of accessible information. He would publish the paper in *Science* in May 1958. In "The Fallout Problem," Commoner gave an overview of the long-range effects of worldwide fallout from nuclear weapons testing and outlined the relationship between scientific knowledge and public policy. "That governments find advantage in conducting test nuclear explosions may as well be taken here as a fact of political life. It is not our purpose at this time to debate the validity of this need." Rather, Commoner claimed, his job was to consider the possible health hazards of fallout. He proceeded to describe the science of fallout, defining terms and explaining what fallout was. Commoner then discussed why scientists disagreed—because there had been so little time to analyze the consequences of the new technology's intrusion into nature—and the source of public confusion—that the public relied on expert opinion, and experts were divided. Nowhere in "The Fallout Problem" did Commoner take any position on the fallout question. Rather, he concluded by turning the question over to the informed citizenry. With the proper information, they should act by following their consciences. "There is a full circle of relationships which connects science and society," he stated. "The advance of science has thrust grave social issues upon us. And, in turn, social morality will determine whether the enormous natural forces that we now control will be used for destruction—or reserved for the creative purposes that alone give meaning to the pursuit of knowledge."[33] Without taking a distinct position, Commoner challenged the public to "do the right thing."

Commoner's activism was never quite so objective, of course, but he did emphasize that the precautionary principle should be the driving force behind policy decisions, and in order for that to happen, the public needed to be more intimately involved. The first step, therefore, was making sure that the public was more aware of the stakes. "The power of science over our lives is now so complex," he warned at a Washington University lecture in 1960, "that we will do ourselves harm—blindly, unknowingly and sometimes disastrously."[34] In effect, politico-scientists needed a citizen constituency in order to help raise their concerns about the misguided nature of American technological enthusiasm. As Commoner noted later, this alliance of socially engaged scientists and informed citizens constituted "the one invention of our technological age which can conserve the environment and preserve life on earth."[35]

Moreover, in an era of anticommunist restrictions on the freedom of expression, Commoner's more passive rhetoric made a lot of sense, but with the hazardous implications of fallout so tangible, it must have been difficult to accept a more ambiguous political stance. After all, the public—even if it was confused—was looking to scientists to offer guidance through the proverbial minefield, and rather than guiding, Commoner was offering only a map with a list of possible destinations. Commoner defended this position against criticisms that it was a kind of political regression from "activist" politics by insisting that "the most vital missing element in our present political life is not so much leadership for 'good policies,'" but rather "that all of us, government and citizens alike, be given the means to know the facts, that we may bring before our personal and collective conscience the real depth of the troubles of our time."[36] Rather than trying to be the loudest advocate, Commoner offered a sense of order and calm in a storm of voices and contradictory opinions. What he was banking on for success was the populist appeal of public empowerment and the deference accorded to objective expertise.

Commoner continued to chair the Committee on Science in the Promotion of Human Welfare until 1964. Under his watch, the committee found a niche in defending the integrity of science and promoting the importance of public information, while the principles of "The Fallout Problem" served as a practical directive for all the subsequent work done by the Commoner Committee. But even as Commoner headed this new AAAS endeavor, he was shifting much of his energy toward a more grassroots variety of activism in opposition to nuclear weapons testing. After experiencing considerable frustration in trying to print the AAAS public statement taking a position against the testing of nuclear weapons, Commoner began gravitating toward more grassroots-oriented activism by cofounding the Committee for Nuclear Information. In April 1958, a group of concerned scientists and local women reformers founded the Committee for Nuclear Information to combat what they perceived to be a thin veil of government misinformation. They determined that the committee's primary directive should be to collect, evaluate, and make available to the public information concerning atmospheric nuclear testing. Washington University was a breeding ground for this kind of intellectual opposition. The university's chancellor, Arthur Holly Compton, an eminent physicist but no friend of Commoner's radicalism, contributed to the growth of activism in St. Louis by recruiting prominent chemists and physicists who had worked on the Manhattan Project. In so doing, Compton improved the prestige of the science faculty at Washington University, but he also unwittingly recruited scientists who knew sin firsthand (as Oppenheimer put it) and were more naturally inclined to share Commoner's belief that scientists should also be socially concerned citizens.[37]

Through its magazine and speakers' bureau, the Committee for Nuclear Information helped to pioneer the science information movement. Calling the Committee for Nuclear Information "the pioneer citizens' group in the field of nuclear education," the group's mission statement claimed that it did "not stand for or against particular policies. It presents the known facts for people to use in deciding where *they* stand on the moral and political questions of the nuclear age."[38] A 1962 brochure reiterated that the committee took "no position on political or military issues except the position that a free people must be an informed people."[39]

After some debate, the group's founders affirmed Commoner's recommendation that the group maintain a nonpartisan stance in the information they publicized, including possible endorsement of a nuclear test ban. But the committee's stated dedication to political neutrality and scientific objectivity was a point of some controversy among its founding members. For example, the physicist John Fowler, a Quaker, had a difficult time accepting the "information position." Quakers took positions, Fowler argued, and nuclear fallout was too serious a problem to risk nonpartisan politics. Commoner sympathized, and sought a compromise with Fowler. If Fowler would acknowledge that he was presenting neutral information as a scientist, he could share his position at the end as a citizen and voter, so long as emphasis was placed on the information and not his personal opinion. After some debate, the original committee members adopted a nonpartisan platform with the understanding that they would evaluate their progress under this rubric after a year.[40]

The rhetoric of impartiality ultimately served the committee well, and it was approved after its yearlong test. Their nonpartisan position proved to be an astute tactic that bolstered their public and political credibility as objective scientists. In order to realize their bigger goal of inciting a broader citizen participation and political mobilization through increasing concerns about radiation's potential harm, the Committee for Nuclear Information maintained a conscious tension between the importance of public information and their underlying political message. The decision to abstain from making any partisan statements was prompted in part by the notion that scientists were objective experts and should therefore adhere to a level of impartiality.[41] Their primary duty was to convey scientific facts to help the public make decisions on controversial social issues. But a second, and perhaps more critical, explanation for the Committee for Nuclear Information's nonpartisan approach stemmed from the political climate of the Cold War. As the Cold War carved out global political divisions, the scientific community became equally split. While many scientists appreciated the significance of national security, others continued to promote the importance of public health and intellectual freedom.

Moreover, intellectual freedom, by implication, also meant international cooperation and communication. The spirit of scientific sharing, however, conflicted with the overriding political tone of the American government during the Cold War. Prominent American scientists proposing to share scientific findings with their Soviet counterparts became easy targets for Senator Joseph McCarthy's tribunals. In such a polarized political arena, it was obviously difficult to demonstrate dissent without appearing to have Communist sympathies. The Committee for Nuclear Information avoided this pitfall by advocating a purer democracy and insisting they were impartial experts providing information and not political positions. By promoting the importance of an informed public, committee members positioned themselves as defenders of democracy, making it difficult to attack them without appearing to challenge the American affinity with democratic ideals. Further, their impartial position avoided most charges of radicalism.

Nevertheless, abstaining from taking political positions did not mean that the Committee for Nuclear Information avoided conflict. On the contrary, the committee charged that established governmental agencies were misleading the public and not doing their jobs properly. A regular target was the Atomic Energy Commission. In July 1957, the Joint Congressional Committee on Atomic Energy had observed that "information on fallout has evidently not reached the public in adequate or understandable ways."[42] Hoping to capitalize on this gulf between government and public, the Committee for Nuclear Information also faced several obstacles, most significantly and ironically the general public tendency to "leave it to the experts." How to effectively communicate nuclear information to a public that showed little interest in becoming involved in the debate proved to be a difficult process. But by situating the committee as an objective grassroots organization, Commoner and the other leaders hoped to forge a link to the public.

The Committee for Nuclear Information mounted a serious challenge to the Atomic Energy Commission and to the role that specialists had taken in informing the public about the potential hazards of nuclear fallout. Commoner and others worried that a nation seemingly engaged in a permanent Cold War might stress "national security" at the expense of a working democracy. Indeed, they interpreted the classification of information as just that sort of breach. Keeping scientific information from scientists constituted a breakdown in scientific progress, but keeping it from the public it was supposed to serve was even more problematic as it constituted a collapse in the structure of a functioning democracy. To counteract government secrecy, Commoner and others adopted a rhetoric that publicly promoted democratic principles, distributing accessible scientific information to the public in order to assist them in making moral judgments about radiation risks. Commoner in particular believed that a citizenry informed of the risks inherent in nuclear testing would share his concerns about radiation fallout and would object to the shortsighted machinations of its government so enthralled with the Cold War. In essence, he interpreted the public information movement as a movement for public empowerment and as a means of improving the lines of communication between the citizenry and their elected officials. Publicly distributed independent information became a powerful political tool.

Compared with Commoner's AAAS efforts in informing the public, the Committee for Nuclear Information, whose budget was a tiny fraction of the bigger organization's, was a far more successful enterprise. A lot of this had to do with the energy of its members and their dedication to their efforts, and just as much had to do with the creativity with which they engaged in getting information to the public. Through a series of outreach programs and well-advertised projects, the Committee for Nuclear Information (CNI) succeeded in establishing itself as a credible source for scientific information about nuclear technology. Between October 1958 and May 1959, CNI speakers addressed seventy-five organizations, including church, parent, student, and business groups. The biologist Florence Moog's fictional account of St. Louis one year after a nuclear war, for example, received considerable attention. Basing her account on hearings by the Joint Congressional Committee on Atomic Energy regarding the effects of nuclear war, Moog quantitatively speculated on what might happen to St. Louis in the event of a nuclear war. "Nuclear War in St. Louis: One Year Later" was very popular; more than a dozen publications worldwide reprinted the article, which was all the more poignant because it drew on the most recent scientific evidence to create a piece of science fiction. In December 1959, Dynamic Films approached CNI for film rights, but the movie was never made. As the CNI grew, the BBC, the *National Observer*, and *Audubon* magazine used it as a valuable resource for making sense of complicated nuclear issues, which they in turn passed on to their audiences. Moreover, committee members made regular appearances on local TV and radio programs, and other news services outside of St. Louis made regular use of *Nuclear Information,* the committee's monthly bulletin. While membership numbers remained modest, the committee's message enjoyed widespread attention.[43]

Members of the CNI were convinced that government information on nuclear testing and technology was either based on inaccurate data or, even more problematically, driven by sociopolitical—nonscientific—factors, and they were not wrong. Teller, in particular, was the subject of criticism from scientists on the CNI. Committee letters charged that Teller's work "failed to conform to the standards of validity which are customary in scientific work." In response, Teller accused committee scientists of "quibbling" over "small and irrelevant details."[44] But in insisting that dangers of fallout existed only in the imagination, Teller was twisting statistics on strontium-90 consumption to his own interests. He was correct in suggesting that the average level of strontium-90 was quite low. What his conclusion did not suggest, however, was that he had combined data from children and adults, which deflated the high levels of strontium-90 in children. Not only were children's bodies smaller, children also consumed more calcium—and therefore more strontium-90—than adults.[45]

Willard F. Libby was another AEC scientist who seemed to deliberately obfuscate questions of nuclear fallout. In June 1957, at the hearings of the Special Subcommittee on Radiation, Libby was challenged for statements he had made a couple of months earlier regarding the uniformity of fallout. In 1953, AEC publications suggested that fallout would be evenly distributed over the globe, implying that no area would suffer an excessive amount. By averaging the amount of fallout over the entire globe, the AEC anticipated a relatively low total of human exposure to fallout. By 1957, however, meteorologists were beginning to determine that fallout was concentrated in a band in the North Temperate Zone. Because the majority of the world's population lived in the North Temperate Zone, the total human exposure to fallout was clearly much greater than the AEC had predicted.[46] Libby dismissed the controversy by downplaying disagreements among scientists regarding how much fallout was indeed safe. He further defended nuclear testing against attacks by geneticists. Geneticists had become increasingly concerned that fallout from nuclear testing was posing mutative hazards to subsequent generations, but Libby casually insisted that "testing constitutes a small risk—very small compared to ordinary risks which can be tolerated."[47] In his open letter to Schweitzer regarding his appeal in the *Saturday Review,* Libby had admitted that fallout represented some risk, but was negligible, and that risk was an integral part of modern life. Risk was inherent in "our pleasures, our comforts, and our material progress," he argued.[48] That fallout raised the rate of leukemia by only 0.5 percent, as he suggested, seemed innocuous enough. In the same issue of the *Saturday Review,* the California Institute of Technology geochemist Harrison Brown conceded that Libby's increase seemed small, but pointed out that "when we say that 10,000 *individuals* are killed each year . . . the number suddenly seems very large."[49] This was a central aspect of the science information movement. The fraction 0.5 percent meant very little to the public, but 10,000 people was easier to comprehend. With accessible information, the public could form their own moral judgments about what constituted acceptable and unacceptable risks.

To concerned scientists, another troubling element of Libby's testimony and public writing was the comparison of risks. For Libby, the health risks from fallout were smaller than those taken by Americans every day when they boarded an airplane or drove a car, but what Libby failed to address was that some risks were voluntary and some were not. Eugene Rabinowitch, the editor of the *Bulletin of the Atomic Scientists,* objected to Libby's flippant comparison of risk from fallout to risks that people took voluntarily, stating that fallout was the product of "deliberate government action," and posed a ubiquitous threat to Americans and humans the world over.[50] Nobody had a choice to avoid the risk of fallout, while one could freely decide not to fly or drive or cross the street. Involuntary risk suggested a breakdown in the democratic process, if citizens could not express choice as to whether or not to accept a particular risk, nor receive the information necessary to make a choice in the matter. Libby's professional career was not beyond Commoner's scorn either. After Libby left the Atomic Energy Commission, he took a position in the Chemistry Department at the University of California, Los Angeles. In a letter to *Look* magazine editor Roland Berg, Commoner noted Libby's move to California instead of a return to his former position in Chicago. "Do you suppose," Commoner mused in a rather gratuitous swipe intended, perhaps, to inspire some comment in a future editorial, "that he chose to settle down in that part of the country which has the lowest fallout level?"[51]

For almost a decade, through persistent questioning of official findings, independent scientists had pushed the Atomic Energy Commission into a series of often embarrassing reversals. As radioactivity fell on America's fields, the possibilities that cattle were consuming strontium-90 raised alarms from independent scientists. On this score, government officials insisted that the risk of ingesting strontium-90 in addition to calcium was insignificant. Indeed, as late as 1953 the Atomic Energy Commission had asserted that strontium-90 constituted a minimal hazard that was limited to human "ingestion of bone splinters which might be intermingled with muscle tissue during butchering and cutting of meat."[52] By 1954, independent biologists had reminded the Atomic Energy Commission that most people received far more calcium—and with it, strontium-90—from milk, not splinters of bone in their hamburgers. By 1956, the Atomic Energy Commission had conceded that milk was the most significant source of strontium-90 in human food.[53]

To further emphasize strontium-90's danger, the committee engaged in one of their most innovative and highly successful campaigns, the Baby Tooth Survey, to determine whether children in St. Louis were being exposed to more strontium-90 by virtue of the nuclear weapons tests in Nevada. Because children, and especially infants, needed more milk than adults, it stood to reason that they were more likely to accumulate more strontium-90. Also, smaller bodies were at greater risk, a fact that roused both the concerns and the emotions of parents across the country. The analysis of baby teeth to measure the buildup of strontium-90, which began in December 1958, was inspired by the biochemist Herman M. Kalckar's August 1958 article in *Nature,* titled "An International Milk Teeth Radiation Census," which proposed a scientific study of baby teeth as a means of determining the extent to which fallout was being absorbed into human bodies. So far, Kalckar noted, only "erratic data existed, based on autopsy of bone samples derived mainly from adults." A radiation census of the type he recommended could "contribute important information concerning the amount and kind of radiation received by the most sensitive section of any population, namely, the children." "If a continued general trend toward a rise in radioactivity in children's teeth were attained," Kalckar posited, "it might well have important bearings on national and international policy." Recognizing the political sensitivity of the testing question, Kalckar insisted that "the results [of the study] should be conveyed to the public without interpretations which might give rise to either complacency or fear, but rather in a spirit that would encourage sober, continued, active concern."[54] Shortly after the article's publication, the Committee for Nuclear Information's vice president, the pediatrician Alfred S. Schwartz, proposed that the committee collect deciduous teeth for strontium-90 analysis after 1958 studies conducted by the United States Public Health Service found that levels of strontium-90 in St. Louis milk were surprisingly high, the highest of the ten cities they surveyed.[55]

In a press statement submitted for release on 21 December 1958, the Committee for Nuclear Information announced its plans to "collect 50,000 baby teeth a year to provide an important record of the absorption of radioactive strontium-90 by children." Echoing Kalckar's claim that a baby tooth survey would provide a unique and critical resource, the committee stated that "the importance of an immediate collection of deciduous, or baby, teeth lies in the fact that teeth now being shed by children represent an irreplaceable source of scientific information about the absorption of strontium-90 in the human body." Because strontium-90 had begun to fall to earth and contaminate food roughly ten years previously, "deciduous teeth now being shed were formed from the minerals present in food eaten by mothers and infants during . . . the first few years of the fallout era and therefore represent invaluable baseline information with which analyses of later teeth and bones can be compared."[56]

The Baby Tooth Survey was the first of its kind and was designed to produce the most comprehensive body of knowledge of strontium-90 absorption in children. Previous studies had been based on the analysis of bone samples, and a 1957 Columbia University study had indicated that one-year-old children possessed the highest levels. But those bone samples came from dead children, so the sample was naturally rather limited.[57] The Committee for Nuclear Information hoped that their study would offer more conclusive evidence as to whether strontium-90 was accumulating in children's bones and whether that posed a serious health hazard. Deciduous baby teeth offered a ready and accessible resource for determining levels of strontium-90 absorption. By applying the findings of strontium-90 in baby teeth, the committee expected to be able to determine the relative absorption in bone. Before proceeding, the committee elicited enthusiastic endorsements from both the Washington University and the St. Louis University schools of dentistry, both of which became instrumental in forming the scientific advisory group that guided the program. Initial grants from the American Cancer Society, the Leukemia Guild of Missouri and Illinois, and the United States Public Health Service helped to launch the Baby Tooth Survey.[58] Dr. Louise Zibold Reiss, an internist, volunteered full-time as the Baby Tooth Survey's director for the following three years. Predominantly organized and run by the Committee for Nuclear Information's women volunteers, the survey began locally in St. Louis, testing donated baby teeth for absorption of strontium-90. In order to obtain the necessary information on environmental factors that would contribute to the uptake of strontium-90, questionnaires were sent out to be returned with the teeth. The forms included questions concerning the child's date of birth, the date the tooth was lost, the mother's residence during pregnancy, the child's residence for the first year after birth, the duration of breast-feeding, the duration of formula-feeding, the kind of milk used in the formula, and other milk used during the first year. After the tooth and background information were received, children would be sent a button that read "I gave my tooth to science," an Operation Tooth Club membership card, and a new tooth form.

While the Baby Tooth Survey subcommittee sent out questionnaire forms and solicited support from the community, the Committee for Nuclear Information's publication, *Information,* worked to allay public panic regarding fallout hazards, while also effectively ensuring that the topic did not leave its newfound place of prominence. In February 1959, *Information* was devoted exclusively to "Milk and the Strontium-90 Problem," a statement published at the request of the St. Louis Dairy Council. In its statement, the Committee for Nuclear Information emphasized the gravity of the issue, but also insisted emphatically that milk was an essential part of a child's diet and that "nothing can be gained by reducing milk intake." The committee explained that "cutting down milk consumption would probably have no effect on strontium-90 absorption. The amount of strontium-90 absorbed by the body seems to depend on the ratio of strontium-90 to calcium in the diet, and not so much on the total amount of strontium-90 taken in."[59] In March, the committee focused on "Strontium-90 and Common Foods," addressing the relative lack of information on food products other than milk. The article commented on a three-year survey of wheat samples from Minnesota and the Dakotas. By October 1959, the committee's bulletin, now titled *Nuclear Information,* addressed food safety for children. In "Mothers Ask—What Should We Feed Our Kids?" the freelance writer Doris Deakin transcribed a discussion conducted by the St. Louis pediatrician-turned-housewife Miriam Pennoyer and a number of her neighbors, in which Pennoyer explained the connection between strontium-90 and milk, the connection between strontium-90 and bone cancer and leukemia, and general questions about radiation and radiation safety. One of the questions raised in "Mothers Ask" had to do with the disproportionately high levels of strontium-90 in St. Louis milk. While the science of the global distribution of nuclear fallout was still very much in its infancy in 1959, Pennoyer suggested, "We're finding that there are hot spots. The middlewest is one. We don't know why this is so. Maybe it's because of where we are, in relation to the bomb testing sites. Maybe it has something to do with the minerals in our soil. Or both. We're not sure."[60]

In its candor—both in answering questions and in not knowing all the answers—the Committee for Nuclear Information effectively positioned itself as a reputable voice in the fallout debate and an organization with an unfailing social conscience. Commoner's gamble that the committee could preserve its political neutrality had paid off. As William K. Wyant, Jr., noted in *The Nation,* in an article devoted to the success of the committee: "Ordinarily, a group that called itself the Greater St. Louis Citizens Committee for Nuclear Information would not be expected to last for any great period of time. Mortality among earnest and well-meaning organizations has been . . . great." What had helped the committee beat the odds, Wyant argued, was its decision not to take a political stand. "The view prevailed that what really was needed was information," he continued. "It was felt that too many people—the politicians, the military and the oracles speaking *ex cathedra* from the Atomic Energy Commission—were taking decisive attitudes on the basis of indecisive information, or none."[61] The committee's work in general, therefore, offered a public service, but also insisted upon broader public participation.

The very nature of the tooth campaign necessitated active public participation, and the committee could not be sure what kind of response it would receive. The response was considerable. By the spring of 1960, the survey had received 17,000 teeth. In late April 1960, Mayor Raymond Tucker of St. Louis declared Tooth Survey Week to initiate the committee's spring tooth drive. Support from the mayor, the St. Louis Dental Society, and the St. Louis Pharmaceutical Association provided plenty of publicity for the campaign; 10,000 teeth were collected in the following month alone.[62] Reiss tirelessly sought the cooperation of all the schools and school superintendents in the St. Louis district, and in October 1960, 250,000 questionnaire forms were published and distributed to children in the lower grades throughout the city.[63] Tens of thousands of small packages poured into the St. Louis post office and found their way to the Committee for Nuclear Information's offices, some addressed only to "The Tooth Fairy, St. Louis."[64] Some teeth, such as Gene Smith's of Decatur, Georgia, found their way to the mayor's office. The eleven-year-old wrote: "I always put my tooth under my pillow for a dime but had rather the scientists use this one."[65] Assuring the boy that he would forward his tooth to the committee, Mayor Tucker added: "I am enclosing a dime so that you will not suffer any financial loss by turning this tooth over to the scientists rather than putting it under your pillow."[66]

The comments from mothers sending teeth to the survey demonstrated that the Committee for Nuclear Information had struck a chord with the public. That nuclear fallout posed a particular threat to society's most innocent members—not to mention its future—compounded the problems of involuntary risk, and raised more public concern about the potential cost of the arms race in general. Some letters accompanying teeth expressed the love and anxiety parents felt for their children who might be at risk. Mrs. Doris Gould's letter claimed that "in my rare moments of leisure I take out those baby teeth and what memories they recall."[67] Mrs. Robert J. Masten reminded the committee that the teeth with which they had been entrusted constituted a "precious commodity," no doubt much in the spirit of Gould's nostalgia.[68] And while the study focused on St. Louis, teeth came in from all over the country. Mrs. Norman Steele of Wellesley, Massachusetts, was anxious to learn of the results. "The teeth which I have belonged to my son who died of cancer of the bone (osteogenic sarcoma) at the age of eleven a year ago," she wrote.[69]

Other notes were from children to the Tooth Fairy: "Dear Fairy, I would like to have a dime," wrote Jill in a small child's handwriting. "But do not take my tooth I am going to send it to siense [*sic*]."[70] Michael Pachulski of Grand Rapids, Michigan, sent a wad of Kleenex with a baby tooth in it. "If you can use it," he wrote, "I will be very happy." He continued: "I'm going to spread the word to all my friends."[71] Patty Hamley wrote to apologize that she would not be able to send any more teeth. "My reason is that the tooth I sent you was my last baby tooth," she wrote. "I will let my brother use the card you sent me. I will be proud to wear the pin, and will tell children about it."[72] A Mrs. Jenks enclosed one "I gave my tooth to science" button, "which has been through the washing machine. This has caused one broken heart and floods of tears at our house and I wonder if you could replace it."[73] Many of the children's letters expressed some parental concerns, such as Robert Roe's. "I drink about a quart of milk a day," the nine-year-old wrote in his letter.[74] Parents fortifying their children's bones with calcium must have been stunned and terrified to learn that they might actually be poisoning them instead. By the time of the Test Ban Treaty of 1963, the Baby Tooth Survey had collected data on 132,000 teeth; by 1966, it had collected more than 200,000.

In November 1961, Reiss published the Baby Tooth Survey's preliminary findings in *Science;* she presented strontium-90 absorption levels in St. Louis between 1951 and 1954, but concentrated on the viability of tooth collection and analysis as a legitimate means of analyzing strontium-90 accumulation in children. "The results reported show that deciduous teeth can be usefully employed as a means of monitoring strontium-90 in man," she wrote in her introduction.[75] By that time, 67,500 teeth had been cataloged and 1,335 teeth were used in the initial study. Reiss noted that 10 percent of the teeth received came from beyond the study area and another 15 percent came from children who were born elsewhere. Other teeth had developed outside the time parameters of the first study. Because tooth calcification begins after the twelfth week of pregnancy and is completed during the first year after birth, the Baby Tooth Survey was exceptionally particular about the teeth used in its analyses.

The study confirmed the committee's suspicions and fears that strontium-90 was increasingly present in children's bones. As the committee had predicted, the amount of strontium-90 began increasing after 1952, the year the first hydrogen bomb was detonated. Whereas levels of strontium-90 found in teeth from 1951 and 1952 contained roughly 0.2 micromicrocuries per gram, that number had doubled by the end of 1953 and tripled and even quadrupled in 1954. Interestingly, teeth from babies who had been fed formula typically contained higher levels of strontium-90 than teeth from babies who had been breast-fed. As Pennoyer had suggested in her October 1959 conversation with neighbors, mothers served as filters that reduced the amount of strontium-90 absorbed by their children.[76] The committee's published data showed that the baby teeth examined demonstrated a 300 percent increase in strontium-90 from 1951 to 1955, the result of increased nuclear testing. By even the most sober interpretations, more aboveground nuclear weapons testing meant greater exposure to radioactive fallout.

The Baby Tooth Survey continued until 1968, but from a public information standpoint, the call for baby teeth was an instant and inspired success. As Reiss commented in *Nuclear Information* in November 1961, "The Baby Tooth Survey has apparently lost its own milk teeth, and has become a growing institution with a bite!"[77] More effective than any advertising campaign, the Baby Tooth Survey served two purposes. First, it brought attention to the hazards of nuclear fallout to which the nation's children were particularly susceptible, and second, it required public participation by involving the public in the initial phase of the study and ensuring widespread interest in the committee's results. The overwhelming response to the requests for teeth, and the growing number of similar surveys around the country, suggested that Americans were becoming less willing to accept risk out of hand. The popular concern that developed over the potential health hazards inherent in aboveground nuclear testing—especially to children—marked one of the first stages of modern environmentalism in the United States. Americans wanted to learn more about the risks to which they and their loved ones were being exposed. The debate even came into play more prominently in the mainstream media. The widespread news coverage of the Baby Tooth Study occasionally confused the project's facts and details, but more often than not, national reports referred to strontium-90 as a "poison" from radioactive fallout that "attacks the marrow of the bone."[78] Though the committee continued to refrain from using such inflammatory language, concerns about radioactive fallout were becoming more widespread. Whereas Adlai Stevenson had barely caused a ripple among American voters in 1956 when he proposed a test ban, a more public debate over the costs and benefits of nuclear testing was front and center within a half-decade.

In no small measure because of increasing public awareness, Congress ordered a series of hearings on the potential hazards of nuclear fallout throughout the late 1950s and early 1960s. The May 1959 hearings, titled "Fallout from Nuclear Weapons Tests," became another opportunity for the Committee for Nuclear Information to make public their Baby Tooth Survey and the relevance of the politics of information to the public. Commoner was particularly intent on having his views included. Though he was not physically present at the hearings, Commoner submitted two previously published essays for the public record. The first, "The Hazard of Fallout—Nuclear Bomb Test Policy Should Be Decided by All," which originally appeared in the Washington University student magazine, *Student Life,* evaluated the growing dangers of fallout and strontium-90 and the existing scientific debate over the results, before concluding that decisions on fallout should rest with the public rather than with specialists. "[The scientific] discussion of the fallout hazard has . . . brought the issue before the public," Commoner wrote.

> Until a few years ago, the public had no way of knowing that the little information about fallout then allowed to reach the public press was uncertain, incomplete, or sometimes in error. . . . But it is fortunate that the issue has now reached the public generally. There is no scientific basis for judging the relative worth of the political gains which result from nuclear tests—and the human lives which they cost.[79]

Commoner's second submission was "The Fallout Problem," which had been published in *Science* a year earlier. Again, Commoner concluded by emphasizing the importance of an informed citizenry and the scientist's role in achieving it. Scientists, Commoner argued, were well positioned to explain to the public what consequences might result from a given policy. As informed citizens, he continued, scientists had the right and the obligation—shared by all informed citizens—to express an ethical opinion on the wisdom of continuing that policy. "But there is . . . no scientific way to balance the possibility that a thousand people will die from leukemia against the political advantages of developing more efficient retaliatory weapons."[80] Reiterating his conclusions from "The Hazard of Fallout," Commoner insisted that scientists were not equipped with any special competence with which to resolve moral judgments. These publications, enhanced by their nonpartisan appearance, were very much in keeping with his professed dedication to the information process, but Commoner also demonstrated the subtleties of his political activism. By pitting human lives against an apocalyptic government policy, he was influencing the way people thought about nuclear testing. In principle, if not entirely in practice, Commoner's perspective helped to frame the public debate.

Other findings presented during the hearings substantiated Commoner's concerns. Congress learned that "acceptable" levels of strontium-90 did not take into consideration the cumulative impact of the various other isotopes that were harmful. Indeed, government scientists conveniently neglected to consider the cumulative effects of other isotopes such as strontium-89, cesium-137, barium-140, and iodine-131, all present in a nuclear reaction and likely as harmful to humans as strontium-90. In 1959, at the spring subcommittee hearings, an Oak Ridge National Laboratory physicist, Karl Z. Morgan, advocated the drastic reduction of acceptable levels of strontium-90 in the human body. He argued that the allowable levels of strontium-90 should be cut in half to take into account the hazards of what amounted to a radiation cocktail.[81]

As scientists and the public reached a general level of acceptance that strontium-90 was indeed harmful, the Committee for Nuclear Information turned its attention to iodine-131, which also concentrated in milk. Though its half-life was only eight days, compared with strontium-90's twenty-nine years, iodine-131 accumulated in the more susceptible thyroid gland, rather than in bone. The small size of a child's thyroid moved the emphasis of the fallout debate from strontium-90 to iodine-131. Again the Atomic Energy Commission downplayed the threat, and again the Committee for Nuclear Information produced data that demonstrated flaws in the Atomic Energy Commission's position. In this instance, the Atomic Energy Commission argued that levels of radiation did not exceed established guidelines for external exposure. The Committee for Nuclear Information concurred, but "*only if the fallout which gives rise to this radioactivity does not enter the food chain.*"[82] In language that anticipated the ecological rhetoric of the environmental movement, one committee scientist criticized the Atomic Energy Commission for continuing to restrict "its concerns to 'persons.' Such a restriction exhibits a startling lack of appreciation of the basic ecological fact that 'persons' cannot exist alone. All living things are interdependent."[83] Adopting the rhetoric of ecology, the Committee for Nuclear Information challenged the Atomic Energy Commission to think more holistically. Fallout could enter the food chain and accumulate in human bodies in higher concentrations than occur from initial atmospheric exposure. The Atomic Energy Commission, therefore, was measuring only one type of exposure, ignoring the often more pertinent accumulations that resulted from secondary exposures.

In August 1963, at the Joint Committee for Atomic Energy hearings, the Committee for Nuclear Information presented the results from their recent studies that suggested that residents living downwind from the Nevada test site in Nevada, Utah, and Idaho had been exposed to fallout "so intense as to represent a medically unacceptable hazard to children."[84] At the same hearings, Gordon M. Dunning, deputy director of the Atomic Energy Commission's Division of Operational Safety, presented a direct rebuttal to the committee findings, arguing that committee "computations of probable iodine-131 exposure . . . 'are either statistically unreliable or cannot be supported by sound experimental measurements.'"[85] In the November 1963 issue of *Nuclear Information,* the committee published its own reply, which listed fourteen errors in Dunning's testimony and characterized the Atomic Energy Commission as "careless of the public welfare" and "less than candid."[86] At an impasse, in a letter to the Atomic Energy Commission, the Committee for Nuclear Information insisted that "either you or we are dead wrong."[87]

The impact of the Committee for Nuclear Information's campaigns was far-reaching. Politicians commented on the numerous letters received from housewives and mothers who wanted the Test Ban Treaty approved, and substantiated their positions with scientific explanations of how it would reduce the medical hazards from fallout.[88] Clearly, the public information message was being received loud and clear, and Commoner's faith in the public desire and ability to understand scientific information was well justified. It was further compounded by the signing of the Test Ban Treaty and by President Lyndon Johnson's address in October 1964, a year after it had been signed. In stark contrast to Eisenhower's dismissal of the hazards of fallout eight years earlier, Johnson stated that the Nuclear Test Ban Treaty

> has halted the steady, menacing increase of radioactive fallout. The deadly products of atomic explosions were poisoning our soil and our food and the milk our children drank and the air we all breathe. Radioactive deposits were being formed in increasing quantity in the teeth and bones of young Americans. Radioactive poisons were beginning to threaten the safety of people throughout the world. They were a growing menace to the health of every unborn child.[89]

Johnson's somber tone represented a drastic shift in the official response to nuclear fallout, but also a stark contrast to his presidential opponent Barry

Goldwater, who had advocated using nuclear weapons in Vietnam.[90] Johnson's reference to children's teeth and bones made a direct link to the work of the Committee for Nuclear Information and their Baby Tooth Survey.

Rather than marking a successful conclusion to the question of atmospheric nuclear weapons testing, the Nuclear Test Ban Treaty might be properly regarded as laying the groundwork for environmentalism and a much larger and more diverse means of galvanizing public activism. Margaret Mead would call this scientific endeavor to alert citizens to particular issues and furnish them with the appropriate information with which to evaluate the relative benefits and hazards of modern technology "a new social invention."[91] In 1963, Commoner and other committee members were among the catalysts for the creation of the Scientists' Institute for Public Information. Commoner determined the new institute's agenda by arguing that "scientists today are the first to live with the knowledge that our work, our ideas, and our daily activities impinge with a frightening immediacy on national politics, on international conflicts, on the planet's fate as a human habitation."[92] For Commoner, this new organization needed to establish "an *independent* and *active*" information movement similar, on a national scale, to the Committee for Nuclear Information's smaller operation.[93] Scientists, Commoner argued, represented the front line against ecological hazards, and the job of the Scientists' Institute for Public Information was to equip the populace with the knowledge necessary to combat those hazards.

The Nuclear Test Ban Treaty might also represent a palpable admission that the Cold War priority on national security over public health was inherently flawed and ironically counterintuitive. Over the course of a decade, activists had persuaded the public that the fallout hazard constituted too great a risk, and the American testing policy experienced a complete reversal. The subsequent ban of DDT and some of the other chemicals that were part of the post-World War II technological revolution further compounded this recognition. As Commoner reflected in *Science and Survival,* it became clear that "the government agencies responsible for the development of nuclear weapons embarked on this massive program before they understood the full biological effects of what they proposed to do. Great amounts of fallout were disseminated throughout the world before it became known that the resultant risks were so great as to require that nuclear testing be halted. The enactment of the Test Ban Treaty in 1963 is, in part, a confession of this failure of modern science and technology."[94]

As the debate naturally shifted from whether or not fallout represented a health risk to the extent of that risk, it exposed serious flaws in nuclear technology's potential, which hindered the progress of the atomic energy industry as well. Splitting atoms to boil water, Commoner maintained, was like "using a cannon to kill a fly."[95] The innovations that characterized the post-World War II technological revolution had solved very difficult physics and engineering questions, and had put at human disposal powers greater than any previously imagined. The danger, however, was that the biological consequences of these new powers had not been evaluated, and because of the potency of their innovations, more than ever scientists needed to be absolutely sure about what they were creating and how those creations worked. As in Commoner's analogy of the risk inherent in the development of the steam engine compared with that of a nuclear power plant, modern science and technology were simply too powerful to justify a trial-and-error approach.[96] Given the potential for disaster, Commoner preferred to err safely on the side of caution.

The notion that decisions on balancing benefits against social and environmental cost should be made by every citizen and not left to experts—in any environmental problem—became Commoner's overriding principle. When he stated in *The Closing Circle* that "the Nuclear Test Ban Treaty should be regarded . . . as the first victorious battle in the campaign to save the environment—and its human inhabitants—from the blind assaults of modern technology," he was referring not only to the result of the campaign but also to the process that realized that victory.[97] Democratic principles had endured as fundamental to American society, and the science information movement had taken advantage of that rhetoric. Moreover, when Commoner insinuated in the early draft of the Committee for Nuclear Information's founding statement that the country was experiencing a "crisis of democracy," he was pointing to the symbolic nature of what the withholding of nuclear information signified.

The political climate of the Cold War imposed priorities on public citizens in an undemocratic manner that excluded them from the decision-making process. Bruno Latour has observed that "when controversies flare up, the literature becomes more technical," a situation characterized by a shift from politics to expert opinion and a growing uncertainty among experts.[98] The science information movement's historical significance, then, is its deliberate confrontation with that tendency. That fallout posed an involuntary risk to many Americans suggests that the avenues along which Americans might participate in determining what constituted acceptable risks were closed to all but a very few. Without the necessary information, Commoner intoned, "citizens cannot with reason give their consent to any public policy."[99] What democracy currently exists on the nuclear issue can be directly attributed to the extent to which critics weakened government control over information. Without the dissent that followed, the quest for technological progress would have perpetuated public health risks and public exclusion from information and subsequent decision-making.

3

The New Jeremiad

If you can see the light at the end of the tunnel you are looking the wrong way.
—Barry Commoner

Due in no small measure to opposition to nuclear weapons testing from groups such as the St. Louis Committee for Nuclear Information, the 1960s became the Age of Ecology. In the early 1960s, synthetic pesticides quickly joined radioactive fallout as poisons known to be ubiquitous in the environment. By the end of the decade, the Santa Barbara oil spill and flames bursting from the Cuyahoga River in Cleveland spurred further public recognition of the postwar environmental decline and culminated in the first Earth Day, during which more than 20 million Americans took to the streets in protest and celebration. To many Americans it had become abundantly clear that the postwar landscape had been subjected to unparalleled environmental threats and that they were raising their families in a dangerous environment. As Adam Rome notes, "The insights of ecology gave countless citizens a new appreciation of the risks of transforming nature."[1]

If Commoner's activism against aboveground nuclear weapons testing contributed to the establishment of a link between the scientific community and a burgeoning environmental awareness, the 1960s helped to foster connections between those two institutions and the peace movement. The Vietnam War and the environmental crisis were both products of a dangerous technological logic. As Rome wrote, "In Vietnam, Americans destroyed towns to 'save' them; at home, Americans degraded the environment to make 'progress.'"[2] Another element of the public concern over nuclear weapons dealt quite practically with the dangers of nuclear war. While fallout constituted a legitimate domestic threat, the prospect of global war using nuclear weapons raised questions about the nature of civil defense, which had become a major industry in the late 1950s and early 1960s. People built fallout shelters in their suburban backyards, the very ones that their postwar affluence had made affordable. At school, American children futilely practiced atomic bomb drills by huddling under desks, and *Nuclear Information* saw fit to devote entire issues to questions of civil defense. This all led to a growing dissatisfaction with the ominous and omnipresent threat of war.[3]

Between such concerns over fallout and pressures of war readiness should the Cold War turn hot, links between the environmental movement and the peace movement were perhaps inevitable. Both seemed to demonstrate a relative disillusionment with American policy and its neglect of public participation. These connections became all the more apparent as the Vietnam War dragged on and became one of the most controversial events of an already controversial decade. At the heart of this connection was a more holistic critique of American social structures, which found its energy in leftist political thought. "Since the age of seventeen," Commoner recalled, "I was concerned with racial discrimination, labor problems, unemployment, so I didn't have to make a leap from environmentalism to the Peace Movement." Loath to see himself as strictly an environmentalist, Commoner insisted that his environmentalism was intimately related to a broad swath of other social issues, including peace, civil rights, and greater public control over the free market system.[4] Of his efforts to arrest aboveground nuclear weapons testing, Commoner declared: "Personally, I was not an environmentalist. What I was doing was . . . dealing with a hazard to people that happened to go through the environment, and sure it goes through the air, and gets in the grass and the cows eat it, and so on. It became clear after a while that this was something called ecology."[5] The environment became less a place or concept associated with nonhuman, organic life, and more one in which humans were participant organisms.[6]

Increasingly, as broader understanding of the risks of nuclear fallout galvanized concerns over environmental health, critics began to suggest that the emerging environmental crisis was the result of the pressures imposed on nature by the capitalist system. Another leading thinker and writer of this new strand was the anarchist social theorist Murray Bookchin. Writing under the pseudonym Lewis Herber, he published *Our Synthetic Environment* in 1962, arguing that the "pernicious laws of the market place are given precedence over the most compelling laws of biology."[7] Bookchin had been drawn to the postwar environmental crisis through his work on chemical additives in foods and—as Commoner had through his opposition to nuclear testing—had come to recognize that the postwar technological revolution had exacerbated a host of public health concerns and chronic diseases, such as heart disease, cancer, and asthma.[8] In his next book, *The Crisis in the Cities,* Bookchin identified the environmental crisis as a predominantly urban problem, again emphasizing the social elements of environmental deterioration.[9] Published a year after the groundbreaking 1964 Wilderness Act, *The Crisis in the Cities* made it clear that the new environmentalism had branched markedly from the more established conservation movement.

The philosopher Herbert Marcuse shared Commoner's and Bookchin's more holistic critique. In *One-Dimensional Man,* published in 1964, Marcuse described the postwar order as one driven by a militarized, waste-oriented economy. According to Roderick Nash, Marcuse believed that "capitalism . . . reduced both nature and people to raw materials with strictly utilitarian value."[10] Marcuse's subsequent call for "the liberation of nature" echoed his earlier criticisms of the unequal characteristics inherent in science, technology, and the capitalist system that organized them.[11] To radical leftists such as Bookchin, Marcuse, and Commoner, environment, peace, civil rights, labor, and feminism were inherently and consistently linked to each other: each consisted of a part of a larger critique of capitalist modes of production and power, and the unequal distribution of wealth and welfare. Pollution and the exploitation of public resources to generate private wealth were expressions of social inequity that would later galvanize the environmental justice movement that sought to blend social and environmental issues in its activism. To Commoner and other political radicals of the 1950s and 1960s, environmental health and equity were necessary components of a broader program of interests that sought to promote social progress, and their activism derived from the same social reform impulses that motivated the civil rights and peace movements.

For the first time, the 1960s moved these disparate movements in concert with each other, and in the process drew on and altered older thinking about the relations between people and the natural world. Prior to the 1960s, social concerns—the disparity of wealth distribution, the importance of public health and hygiene—were not widely considered environmental issues. "Environmentalism" in earlier centuries concentrated on nature protection and natural resource management. For the Romantics and naturalists in the eighteenth and nineteenth centuries, nature protection was an exercise in aesthetics. Industrialization was seen as a threat to nature's pristine or sublime aesthetic, but these concerns often had little proximity to the sociopolitical world of their surroundings, much less the health concerns with respect to urban squalor. Indeed, we might recognize modern strains of environmentalism in the activities of the early Jacksonian era urban reformers, but in antebellum America, their work was rather distantly removed from naturalism and nature protection.[12] Indeed, early interest in nature was distinctly personal or individual, rather than a social or communitarian effort to protect nature. Nature and civilization were perceived to be mutually exclusive notions, separated by the machine and reinforced by the growth of technological optimism that followed the Civil War.[13] By the time Americans welcomed the dawn of the twentieth century—the American Century—their blind faith that they could indefatigably exploit and reorganize nature to suit their interests was so ingrained that nature and culture were made to seem completely separate. Progress, efficiency, and utilitarianism became Progressive era catchwords. To the majority of Americans, human ingenuity maintained the confident air that nature could be completely and continually reshaped to suit human needs and interests.

During the nineteenth century, Transcendentalists from Ralph Waldo Emerson to John Muir incorporated an ethical dimension into nature protection rhetoric, arguing that Americans had an ethical duty to preserve God's creation and that nature itself had an intrinsic value beyond human use. In 1851 Thoreau had exulted that "in Wildness is the preservation of the World," and a generation later, Muir declared that wild nature possessed divine and mystical powers of inspiration and redemption, themes which would be secularized and reaffirmed for the post-World War II American public through the ecologist Aldo Leopold's seminal book, *A Sand County Almanac*.[14] While anti-industrialization acquired some following with the rise of the Industrial Revolution, it was not until the twentieth century that advocates of nature protection developed an appreciation for public health and human welfare as integral to an environmental ethic. In linking public health to environmentalism, health specialists such as Alice Hamilton were echoing the sentiments of urban health reformers from the mid-nineteenth century, but enjoyed the benefit of being able to demonstrate more completely the environmental effects of nineteenth-century urbanization and the Industrial Revolution.[15] Early twentieth-century nature preservationists also pointed to the dark plumes from smokestacks and resource depletion as too high a price for "progress." Over the course of the twentieth century, the social and the environmental began to discover their contemporary political partnership.[16]

During the 1960s a shift in environmental focus was completed from affirming life to fighting for survival in the wake of fallout and other poisons, which precipitated a transition from experiencing nature as an individual exercise to one that was necessarily social and communal. The intellectual expansion from aestheticism to a broader sense of environmentalism was a slow process, marked most noticeably by the human relationship with the physical environment, transforming from a private relationship or retreat to a decidedly public engagement, which preached inclusiveness in government, in courtrooms, and in classrooms. Just as the human body became a concentrated site of environmental decline, the environmental experience and the struggle for environmental protection became unmistakably social. Whereas Thoreau and Muir encouraged developing an intimate relationship with the nonhuman world, their efforts had been based on escaping civilization. To more socially oriented environmentalists such as Commoner, social and economic dependence on continual technological progress meant that escape from civilization was no longer possible, and that the more critical project was to integrate that intimate relationship with the nonhuman world *into* civilization. It was a project begun at the beginning of the twentieth century by Progressive era conservationists such as Gifford Pinchot, but after World War II, the battleground had changed markedly. Seeking to entice conservationists to the larger environmental struggle, Commoner noted in a 1966 paper, "The conservation movement was created in the United States to control [nineteenth-century industrial assaults on natural resources]. The same thing is happening today, but now we are mortgaging for future generations not just their lumber or their coal, but the basic necessities of industry, agriculture, and life itself: air, water, and soil. This is the new and larger task for the conservation movement."[17] This time, the stakes were much higher; one could not escape nuclear fallout by escaping civilization. Rather, it was time to confront civilization's unbridled development.

In this respect, Rachel Carson's *Silent Spring* might be regarded as the marriage of the aesthetic impulse with the more recent social environmentalist one, thereby constituting the dawn of the Age of Ecology. In *Silent Spring,* Carson, a confirmed nature lover most happy listening to birdsong and exploring tidal pools for marine life, blended her deep-seated appreciation for nature's splendors with an organized attack on the industrial invasion of new technologies. She deftly and convincingly outlined the technological shortcomings of the pesticide industry and the unforeseen risks about which Americans had not been consulted. "Lulled by the soft sell and the hidden persuader," she argued, "the average citizen is seldom aware of the deadly materials with which he is surrounding himself; indeed, he may not realize he is using them at all."[18] Just as pollution was beginning to garner public attention, thanks in no small measure to the fallout question, Carson demonstrated that health and the environment—and humans and nature—were intimately and inextricably linked. She had accurately charted for the popular audience an environmental ethic and, according to Maril Hazlett, "vested it in the human flesh: if humans did not treat nature more wisely, then they too risked death from the long-term effects of persistent chemical pesticides."[19] In so doing, Carson introduced human physiology as a topic for environmentalists to consider. "There is also an ecology of the world within our bodies," she asserted in *Silent Spring.*[20] Just as this interpretation of ecology demanded that science examine the bigger picture, Carson—like Commoner, Bookchin, and soon Marcuse—insisted that scientists and activists should adopt a more holistic scope of what constituted an environmental problem. Environmentalism shifted from Romantic sentiment to a social practice in harmony with the rise of popular ecology, and ecologists emerged, according to Donald Worster, "as the guardians of fragile life," their science ready to subvert the mainstream values that deemed humans dominant over nature. Ecology had become the subversive science.[21]

Like Commoner, Carson was exceptionally critical of science and the powers of shaping environments that it had assumed. "The 'control of nature' is a phrase conceived in arrogance," she boldly stated, "born of the Neanderthal age of biology and philosophy, when it was supposed that nature exists for the convenience of man." This outdated assumption, Carson warned, would inevitably result in an environment hostile to all life. "It is our alarming misfortune," she continued, "that so primitive a science has armed itself with the most modern and terrible weapons, and that in turning them against the insects it has also turned them against the earth."[22] But the intellectual foundations of twentieth-century science were not only hubristic; they were also dangerously misguided. As Carson noted in the serialized version of *Silent Spring*, which first appeared in *The New Yorker*, industrial science was corrupt, and the rapid rise of the pesticide industry after World War II suggested a new era "dominated by industry, in which the right to make money, at whatever cost to others, is seldom challenged."[23] Science was indisputably important, but it needed to be responsibly harnessed.

Industrial scientists did not take such criticisms lying down. The chemical industry mounted a vehement attack against Carson's work. Prior to *Silent Spring*'s publication in book form, the pesticide manufacturer Velsicol Corporation threatened a lawsuit if Houghton Mifflin published the book. In a letter to Houghton Mifflin, Velsicol charged that Carson's attack on the chemical industry portrayed American business interests in a negative light, and her critique risked reducing "the use of agricultural chemicals in this country and in the countries of western Europe, so that our supply of food will be reduced to east-curtain parity." Not only was *Silent Spring* inaccurate and libelous, Velsicol contended, but Carson was a Communist sympathizer.[24] Attacks against the book persisted after its publication, and Carson was summarily dismissed by her critics as a Communist, a hysterical woman (and often both), or as a woman embittered by her own—ultimately losing—battle with cancer and wholly incapable of understanding the scientific nuances of the pesticide industry.

In much of her language and her personality, Carson was a relatively conservative or reserved person, but behind her love for nature in *Silent Spring* rested a damning indictment of industrial capitalism. "For the first time in the history of the world," she charged, "every human being is now subjected to contact with dangerous chemicals, from the moment of conception until death." This was more than a lament at the loss of nature's aesthetic value; it was a distinct declaration of war that sought to bring together conservationists, outdoor recreationists, antitechnologists, public health advocates, and urban reformers. And it worked.[25]

Silent Spring's success was not lost on Commoner. "It was," he recalled, "the first evidence that there was a wide affinity for environmentalism among the American public."[26] Its popularity in serialized form in *The New Yorker* and its subsequent sales as a book made it perfectly clear that the Age of Ecology had begun and that the American public was anxious to learn more about the introduction of human-made health hazards into the environment. Concurrent with the publication of *Silent Spring* and the realization of the Nuclear Test Ban Treaty came a significant threshold at which Americans increasingly resisted environmental risk. The growing recognition that humans were susceptible through the flesh to the same invasions by industrial toxins as the landscape resulted in ever-rising standards of what constituted "acceptable risk." This shift in environmental values was most easily recognized in the growing opposition to aboveground nuclear testing, the 1961 thalidomide scare in America, the popular acceptance of *Silent Spring,* and the subsequent proliferation of campaigns to protect human and environmental health.

Another feature of *Silent Spring's* success not lost on Commoner was the validation of his science information movement as an effective activist tool. *Silent Spring* warned the public against leaving decision-making to experts or specialists. Much like Commoner, Carson was uncomfortable with the suggestion that science and specialists had all the answers. Indeed, both Commoner and Carson demonstrated that the common trend of "leaving it to the experts," a product of the Progressive era that persisted after World War II, was dangerously flawed. Commoner warned in *Science and Survival:* "The notion that . . . scientists have a special competence in public affairs is . . . profoundly destructive of the democratic process. If we are guided by this view, science will not only create [problems] but also shield them from the customary processes of administrative decision-making and public judgment." This was more than just a warning; Commoner insisted that such a misuse of science was so pervasive and the technical nature of information was so inaccessible to nonscientists that there already existed an "apparently insuperable barrier between the citizen, the legislator, the administrator and the major public issues of the day."[27] Carson was equally vociferous in insisting that dangerous technologies were being hidden behind complicated scientific jargon designed to confound public scrutiny. Parallel to Commoner's own advocacy, Carson insisted that responsible science was science made accessible and public, open to criticism and dialogue, and serving public rather than private interests. "We live in a scientific age; yet we assume that knowledge of science is the prerogative of only a small number of human beings, isolated priestlike in their laboratories," she stated in her 1952 National Book Award acceptance speech. "This is not true. The materials of science are the materials of life itself. Science is part of the reality of living; it is the way, the how and the why for everything in our experience."[28]

As with the debate over nuclear fallout, what was needed was clear, accessible science that the public could understand. At its most fundamental level, *Silent Spring* adhered to the principles of public information and translated science for the lay reader. Avoiding technical language, Carson presented the dangers of pesticide technology to the nonscientist in a compelling manner, making science accessible but also breaking down the boundaries between science and sentiment as a means of humanizing her argument. That *Silent Spring* raised public awareness and galvanized citizens to action is testament to the power of public information. In many respects, Carson's famous debate with industry scientists over the relative safety of DDT mirrored Commoner's struggle against fallout, which preceded it. Carson even drew on public concerns about radiation to advance her own argument, citing the buildup of strontium-90 in human bones and referring to chemical pollutants as the "sinister and little-recognized partners to radiation in changing the very nature of the world."[29] Later in *Silent Spring,* Carson continued: "We are rightly appalled by the genetic effects of radiation; how then, can we be indifferent to the same effect in chemicals that we disseminate widely in our environment?"[30] Indeed, Carson held the Committee for Nuclear Information in high esteem. In a 1963 letter to the committee, she wrote, "I have long admired your organization and have repeatedly referred to it as a model when I am asked about setting up a similar organization for the study of pesticide problems."[31]

Applying the principles of scientific information to environmental problems other than nuclear testing was a project Commoner had envisioned prior to the success of *Silent Spring,* and the Test Ban Treaty provided the context for that kind of transition. In introducing the May 1964 issue of *Nuclear Information,* the editor, Virginia Brodine, claimed that *Nuclear Information* was living up to its long-held intention to diversify the range of information it presented by moving beyond questions of nuclear technology. Brodine noted that the public's ignorance or confusion regarding scientific problems extended to "the use of chemical compounds for pest extermination; it is [also] true of the discharge of the wastes from our urban, industrial civilization into the air and water; just as it is true of many of the uses of nuclear energy."[32] In August 1964, Brodine told subscribers that *Nuclear Information* "outgrew [its] old name when we began to include other subject matter in addition to nuclear information." With that issue, *Nuclear Information* became *Scientist and Citizen*. The new name, she continued, "reflects our broadened interests and represents the purpose that has guided us from the first issue in 1958: To bring together the citizen who needs information and the scientist who has a responsibility to inform."[33]

The leading article in the August 1964 issue was "Water Pollution in Missouri," by the chemist James R. Whitley, which considered a number of kinds of water pollution, from mining runoff to urban waste disposal.[34] Water pollution had become a source of particular environmental concern when the fish kills on the lower Mississippi River in November 1963 gained national attention after the Louisiana Division of Water Pollution turned the investigation over to the U.S. Public Health Service. While there had been fish kills on the lower Mississippi in late fall the previous three years, the scale of the 1963 kill was alarming. Five million dead fish floated to the surface of the river, blocking the intakes to regional power plants and threatening public drinking water. "The bodies of turtles floated on the waters," *The New Republic* reported. "Tough 150-pound garfish and catfish weighing 70 pounds surfaced too weak to move. Crabs lay along the banks. Thousands of cranes and robins lay dead."[35] By April 1964, Public Health Service biologists had traced the fish kill to minute amounts—roughly half a microgram per gram of blood, .40 to .56 parts per million—of the pesticide endrin, which had entered the Mississippi from a Memphis waste-treatment plant owned by Velsicol, the same company that developed endrin and that had tried to prevent *Silent Spring*'s publication.[36]

The discovery not only further validated *Silent Spring* among skeptics—"How does Rachel Carson look now?" a reporter asked Public Health Service officials in Mississippi; "pretty good" was the response—but also served as occasion for greater public education on the fragility or vulnerability of the biosphere.[37] Disposal of chemicals designed to kill insects poisoned large numbers of fish and simultaneously threatened or potentially threatened drinking water resources in Arkansas, Mississippi, and Louisiana. The very low levels of endrin that had precipitated the massive fish kill in the Mississippi also sharpened and emboldened the ecological message. The high sensitivity of fish to various kinds of water pollution demonstrated in grand form the potential risks of pollution to humans. Public Health Service warnings concerning pollutant hazards to urban residents whose water came from the river ran rampant through the media and prompted the 1964 introduction of a Clean Water Bill in the Senate, sponsored by Senator Abraham Ribicoff of Connecticut and signed into law by President Lyndon Johnson in 1965.[38]

Momentum was very definitely on the environmentalists' side, and Commoner sought to capitalize on it. In "Fallout and Water Pollution—Parallel Cases," which appeared in the December 1964 issue of *Scientist and Citizen,* he compared the problems related to water pollution with his early work on fallout, and drew on the success of the fallout struggle to suggest that the lessons learned in that protest might be applied to the control of other contaminants. Problems of water pollution, Commoner noted, were similar to those of radioactive fallout insofar as both were "the unwanted result of the union between modern scientific knowledge and intense social demand for [the] use" of the technologies that produced them. At the same time, however, accurate assessment of the two problems could substantively contribute to remedying the bigger problem that linked them. Scientists and citizens working together, Commoner contended, needed "to learn how the objectivity of scientific investigation and the judgments of public opinion, properly interrelated, have now brought [nuclear] contamination to a halt."[39] Here was the lesson that needed to be more broadly applied to other environmental struggles.

In the wake of *Silent Spring* and the fish kills on the lower Mississippi, chemical pesticides became an important organizing issue for Commoner and other environmental scientists. Rachel Carson had been effective in articulating grounds for a passionate opposition to pesticides in addition to her scientific argument, which had made that issue pivotal to the growth of 1960s environmentalism. But pesticides were only a small part of a complex range of substances based on carbon chemistry and produced by a colossal petrochemical industry that over time became the target of a concerted campaign. Petrochemical products were distinctive in their use of purified raw materials found in petroleum and their energy-intensive chemical reactions with chlorine. The environmental problems posed by the production, use, and disposal of petrochemical products such as pesticides, fertilizers, detergents, PCBs, CFCs, and plastics varied, but cumulatively they dramatically changed the context of environmental protest. Since the petrochemical industry was "uniquely capable of producing materials not found in nature," Commoner noted in *The Closing Circle,* its products threatened the environment with "intrusion[s] into the ecosystem of a substance wholly foreign to it." Frequently these intrusions were of materials, such as plastic, that entered the market at expanded and unprecedented levels. The annual production of American plastics in 1960, for example, exceeded 6 billion pounds, and its growth curve rose more steeply than the Gross National Product between the end of World War II and 1965.[40] What to do with all this plastic presented a new problem; it did not break down in nature. "It therefore persists as rubbish or is burned—in both cases causing pollution."[41]

Broader awareness of the hazards of DDT—another petrochemical—resulted in heightened expectations from the public as to what constituted acceptable risk. In effect, the hazards of these new technologies constituted more imminent threats on a much larger scale. Commoner's main argument was that any amount of pollution could be expected to cause some damage, and that it was often nearly impossible to predict the extent or consequences of that damage. "Whenever the biological system exposed to a possibly toxic agent is very large and complex," he wrote in 1964, "the probability that any increase in contamination will lead to a new point of attack somewhere in this intricate system cannot be ignored."[42] The only way to prevent environmental deterioration as a result of toxic pollution, he contended, was to eliminate pollution from the environment; it could not be successfully managed.

Another important feature of the campaign against the petrochemical industry was control over its products' entry into the marketplace. Once integrated into the economic system, their removal was, on a practical level, next to impossible. "The costs of correcting past mistakes and preventing threatened ones are already staggering," Commoner lamented, "for the technologies which have produced them are now deeply embedded in our economic, social, and political structure."[43] The rapid rise of detergents synthesized from organic raw materials present in petroleum represented an alarming example of this trend. Like many other industries, the energy-intensive petrochemical production of domestic cleaning materials experienced revolutionary growth and transition in the decade following the end of World War II. With the expansion of suburban living spaces and home ownership came greater demand for materials with which to clean those homes and their amenities, marked most notably by the shift from organic soaps to synthetic detergents.

Detergent itself is an adjective and synonym for cleansing; soap, therefore, is a detergent. Synthetic detergents ultimately replaced organic soap because soap possessed some disadvantages that helped promote synthetic detergents as leading cleansers. In hard water with high mineral content, soap tended to form a deposit which did not wash away as readily as it did in softer water. In contrast, detergents were mixed with a variety of additives designed to soften hard water and ensure a more consistent clean without any deposit. Synthetic detergents had been invented during World War I in Germany, and were introduced into the United States marketplace by Procter & Gamble in 1933. Their sales, however, were limited by their exorbitant cost; in 1934, detergents cost four to five times as much as soap. As with DDT, World War II created a market for synthetic detergents. Synthetic detergent's displacement of laundry soap coincided with World War II because the U.S. Navy sought a cleanser that could be used effectively in saltwater. Further, this increased production of synthetic detergents made their price more competitive; in contrast, soap's raw material, fat, was dependent on agriculture, and its quality, availability, and price subsequently varied. In 1946, Procter & Gamble introduced Tide, "which was to initiate a revolution in the U.S. detergent industry." By 1953, synthetic detergents had replaced soap as the top-selling product by weight in the United States; in 1958, 72 percent of all detergents produced were synthetic, and they constituted more than 90 percent of all household packaged cleaning products.[44]

By the late 1940s, however, unprecedented levels of foam at sewage treatment plants, and even in rivers and lakes—some of which were sources of domestic water supply—were reported all over the United States. Only after billions of pounds of detergents were in use annually was it discovered that they constituted a serious environmental pollutant. "One aspect of this technological triumph received no attention in the research laboratories," Commoner explained, "the effects of dumping a huge amount of new synthetic substances (about 3.5 billion pounds per year in the United States in 1960) down drains into waste disposal systems."[45] Unlike soap, detergents resisted bacterial decay and accumulated in surface waters, resulting in foam coming from household faucets and other drinking water sources. Because they did not break down, detergents effectively choked water system bacteria. "The bacteria that act on organic wastes must have oxygen," Commoner stated in 1966, "which is consumed as the waste is destroyed. If the waste load becomes too high, the oxygen content of the water falls to zero, the bacteria die, the biological cycle breaks down, the purification process collapses, and the water becomes a foul and murky mess."[46] Synthetic detergents were typical of numerous other examples of how the approval and use of new technologies preceded any clear consensus of their impact on the environment and human health. Commoner wryly observed that such consequences were a natural symptom of our economic system, "since the purchases of detergents—and the consequent profits—result from their effectiveness as cleansers and not from their behavior in waste systems."[47] The historian William McGucken noted the paradox that "achieving human cleanliness entailed fouling the environment."[48] By the middle 1960s, the detergents scare had largely subsided after industrial scientists determined that their early detergents were synthesized from petroleum derivatives composed of branched molecules that were not biodegradable. Later detergents consisted of unbranched molecules that bacteria could break down. But to Commoner it remained "useful to ask why we got into trouble with the old detergents, and what we can learn from past difficulties to avoid new ones."[49] To Commoner, the problem was essentially a repetition of other environmental problems: detergents "were put on the market before their impact on the intricate web of plants, animals, and microorganisms that makes up the living environment was understood."[50]

Commoner's bone of contention with the synthetic detergent industry was the same as his objection to the earlier unquestioned assault on the environment by nuclear weapons testing: discoveries in the physical and chemical sciences failed to take into account their impacts on the life sciences. As he noted in *Science and Survival,* "Since the scientific revolution which generated modern technology took place in physics, it is natural that modern science should provide better technological control over inanimate matter than over living things."[51] Whereas ecology endorsed a more holistic understanding of the environment, industrial science worked in a more reductionist manner. In "The Integrity of Science," published in 1965, Commoner illustrated the dangers of this kind of reductionist approach, noting that the Soap and Detergent Association had admitted that no biological field tests had been conducted to determine how detergents would interact with the natural ecosystem.[52] "The separation of the laws of nature among the different sciences is a human conceit," Commoner concluded. "Nature itself is an integrated whole."[53] This disparity between the physicochemical sciences and the biological sciences was a direct consequence of the American science policy that followed World War II, as government funding supported nuclear physics and industry supported developments in the petrochemical industry. As the technological revolution raced ahead, few stopped to consider its impact. But to conclude that industrial science simply failed to do its biological homework is to miss the point. Paul Hirt argues that whereas ecologists promote "awareness of environmental limits to abundance," specialists—such as government silviculturalists or industrial chemists—strive precisely to "overcome limits and create greater abundance."[54] This emphasis on maximizing production invariably came at the expense of environmental health and sustainability. The new environmentalism insisted that new technologies needed to be governed by what was known—and cautious of what was not known—about life and its environment. In effect, this constituted a call for greater scrutiny in risk analysis.

Responding to this perceived need, Commoner opened his Center for the Biology of Natural Systems at Washington University in 1965. He outlined its role as an effort to "adapt our science to the urgent need for understanding the natural biology of the environment and so help to preserve the community of life from extinction at the hand of man."[55] Such an endeavor was urgently needed and critical. "Too often, today, we fail to perceive this system as a complex whole," Commoner lamented in *Science and Survival*. "Too often has this blindness led us to exaggerate our powers to control the potent agents which we have let loose on the environment. Only too often in the recent past has our unperceived ignorance led to sudden hazards to life—contamination of our streams with powerful but poorly understood biochemical agents; pollution of the air with powerful but poorly understood radiation."[56] By the later 1960s, Commoner's Center for the Biology of Natural Systems would engage with another poison that was infiltrating both air and water systems at an alarming rate.

In addition to his role as messenger, Mercury was the Roman god of commerce and was responsible for escorting the dead to the underworld.

After World War II, this dual role might have been perceived to be rather fitting, given the relative ubiquity of mercury use in industry and the severe health hazard it posed. Elemental mercury had been known to be toxic since Roman times, but its presence as an environmental pollutant dramatically increased after World War II from fossil fuel emissions—especially from coal-fired power plants—its use in paints and fungicides, its role in the production of chlorine in the chlor-alkali process, and its part in lithium enrichment for use in thermonuclear weapons.[57] As mercury use increased, so did the number of human ailments associated with it. In 1947, the "pink disease" that afflicted infants in the United States was connected to the use of mercurous chloride—calomel—in teething powders.[58] A little more than a decade later, a rash of cases of mercury poisoning related to the use of mercury compounds in fungicides used to treat flour and wheat occurred in Iraq (1960), Guatemala (1963–1965), and Pakistan (1969). In the late 1950s, the irresponsible dumping of mercury-contaminated waste into local waters resulted in widespread and high-profile poisoning tragedies in Minamata, Japan; hundreds of people were killed and as many as 20,000 were poisoned.[59]

Indeed, mercury pollution or contamination presents an especially poignant example of how the industrial processes after World War II emerged to create new, dangerous, and often unanticipated environmental problems. While mercury is a naturally occurring element and present throughout the environment, it rarely occurs independently in nature without human intervention. Rather, it is trapped in coal and other mineral deposits, and freed into air, soil, and water through such human activities as waste incineration and coal combustion. According to a 1997 Environmental Protection Agency report, coal-fired power plants in the United States were the predominant cause of mercury pollution in the environment.[60] The environmental hazard posed by mercury stems from an organic and lipid-soluble form of the element called methyl mercury, which is present in mercury vapors. Preventing mercury releases was especially difficult in manufacturing because whereas other toxic metals, such as lead and cadmium, were easily trapped with the fly ash in incinerator control systems, mercury was so easily vaporized that most of it passed through the control system, "out the incinerator stack, and into the air."[61] Once it escaped from the factory, methyl mercury accumulated in water and entered the food chain; unlike most elements of radioactive fallout, methyl mercury is almost entirely absorbed by humans' digestive systems.

In 1997, the Environmental Protection Agency estimated that about eighty-seven tons of mercury were deposited annually in the American environment, and that electrical power plants built from the 1940s to the 1970s were responsible for a sizable amount of those emissions.[62] While this number may appear somewhat inconsequential compared with the tonnage of other toxic substances released into the environment, studies indicate that a mere gram of mercury was sufficient to render fish from a twenty-acre body of water unsafe for human consumption.[63] Much as trace amounts of endrin were responsible for the fish kills on the Mississippi, mercury threatened similar hazards to fish and to humans. Summarizing the postwar recognition that mercury was polluting the environment on an unprecedented scale, Commoner observed: "That waste mercury would move through the aquatic ecosystem and accumulate in fish came as a sudden, unpleasant surprise."[64]

As mercury vapors billowed out of power plants and found their way into streams and lakes and up the food chain toward fish, and ultimately Americans' dinner tables, the ingestion of mercury became a prevalent source of mercury poisoning. Documented symptoms of mercury poisoning are widespread, ranging from psychological effects—such as irritability, anxiety, and depression—to sensory and motor effects—including loss of sensation in extremities, loss of hearing, abnormal reflexes, slurred speech, and the loss of fine motor coordination. More serious exposures to mercury also result in convulsions and seizures, comas, and death. As with radioactive fallout, children are generally at more risk than adults.[65]

After World War II, mercury became a widely used element in the manufacture of synthetic chemicals. In the late nineteenth century, it was introduced into chemical manufacturing to take advantage of its special electrical and chemical properties, and became a central tool in the manufacturing of chlorine. Chlorine was originally the unwanted by-product of the electrolytic chlor-alkali process; by the late nineteenth century, alkali was in high demand from manufacturers of glass, soap, paper, and textiles, but, according to Martha Moore Trescott, "markets had to be *created* [for chlorine], as with almost all of the products introduced by the electrochemicals industry."[66] Invention was the mother of necessity. During World

War I, chlorine was used as a war gas on the battlefields in 1915. The military industry quickly made more chlorine-based chemical weapons, including mustard gas.[67] After World War I, the petrochemical industry replaced the electrochemical industry that preceded it, and by the late 1920s and early 1930s, new organochlorine products began to appear, most notably polychlorinated biphenyls (PCBs), developed by Monsanto in 1929, and chlorofluorocarbon (CFC) refrigerants, introduced by Du Pont in the early 1930s.[68] In 1937, DDT's insecticidal qualities were discovered, and increased production of polyvinyl chloride (PVC) plastics, first marketed in 1936, ensured that chlorine manufacture remained profitable in the decades that followed World War II.

From being an unwanted by-product, chlorine became indispensable to the synthesis of organic chemicals, which were necessary in the production of the raw materials needed for new synthetic fibers, pesticides, detergents, plastics, and rubber, prompting Commoner to assert in *The Closing Circle* that "mercury poisoning is a feature of the 'plastic age.'"[69] Just as chlorine was essential to the manufacture of organic chemicals, mercury was critical to the manufacture of chlorine. To make chlorine, an electric current is passed through a salt solution via a mercury electrode. The biologist Joe Thornton notes that typically, "Most mercury is recycled, but significant quantities are routinely released into the environment through air emissions, water discharges, products, and waste sludges. [During the twentieth century], chlor-alkali production [was] the largest single source of mercury releases to the environment."[70] Between 1946 and 1969, Commoner noted, "Mercury consumption for this purpose has increased—by 3,930 per cent in the twenty-five year postwar period."[71]

While chlorine production was the second most prevalent source of mercury pollution after coal-fired power plants, mercury also found its way into the environment in unnaturally large quantities in a number of other ways. In *The Closing Circle,* Commoner showed that mercury use in mildew-resistant paints had grown 3,120 percent.[72] Mercury poisoning was typically associated with the Mad Hatter, a character made popular in Lewis Carroll's *Alice in Wonderland,* because mercury was used in the making of felt hats.[73] After World War II, mercury maintained its close connection to occupational hazards. Indeed, the first complaint that the Occupational Safety and Health Administration addressed under the 1970 Occupational Safety and Health Act pertained to levels of worker exposure to chlorine and mercury at an Allied Chemical Corporation chlor-alkali plant in Moundsville, West Virginia.[74]

By 1969, *Scientist and Citizen* had changed its name to *Environment*. Within a decade, Ralph Lutts notes, "What began as a mimeographed newsletter about fallout had turned into one of the nation's major sources of environmental information," and Commoner, whose face would appear on the cover of *TIME* magazine the following year, was widely recognized as one of the icons of the new American environmentalism.[75] In May 1969, *Environment* published a special issue devoted to mercury in the environment. The lead article, by the *Environment* editor Sheldon Novick, examined mercury in pesticides and fungicides. Whereas countries such as Sweden and Japan had banned the mercury pesticides and other means through which mercury might contaminate food, Novick expressed concern that in the United States there was "almost no information available about the extent of mercury contamination of food and of the general environment."[76] In "Birds Give Warning," Göran Löfroth and Margaret E. Duffy reported on the adverse effects of using Panogen, a fungicide containing methyl mercury, in large quantities. Commenting on cases in Sweden and Japan, they noted that birds were being poisoned after eating treated seeds or rodents who had eaten treated seed. Once again, toxic chemicals were extending their reach beyond the uses for which they were intended.[77]

"All this reminds us of what we have already been told by advertising . . . that we are blessed with an economy based on very modern technologies," Commoner would observe in *The Closing Circle*. "What the advertisements do not tell us—as we are urged to buy synthetic shirts and detergents, aluminum furniture, beer in no-return bottles, and Detroit's latest creation—is that *all this 'progress' has greatly increased the impact on the environment*."[78] Moreover, it contributed to a growing public sentiment that the technological optimism that immediately followed World War II was over—or, worse, had been a fallacy all along. Still, environmentally hazardous products flooded the market, and still American consumers rewarded companies that could offer the lowest prices, regardless of their products' environmental effects. So while awareness of environmental protection was growing across the United States, Americans continued to make only token and selective changes in their behavior.

It was within this context that the modern science of risk analysis was formulated. "In view of the large and unknown risks involved in multiple insults to the integrity of the environment," Commoner told the National Industrial Conference Board in 1966, "prudence suggests the withdrawal from our surroundings of as many synthetic pollutants as possible."[79] If risk analysis was designed to determine the potential threat of a new hazard, this new approach to environmentalism insisted that that new hazard not be introduced before the risk could be more fully and publicly assessed and considered. The basic idea was to prevent environmental damage until the benefits of a new technology could be weighed against its potential costs; waiting until a new technology was introduced into the environment was invariably too late. Commoner worried about the manner in which environmentalists typically found themselves reacting to existing problems rather than participating in preventing their introduction and proliferation.[80]

Throughout his campaign against aboveground nuclear testing, for example, Commoner was at the helm of criticisms directed toward the Atomic Energy Commission's rather insular treatment of risk analysis. Uncertainty in science and a perceived urgency in developing a national security agenda prompted the approval of numerous nuclear weapons tests on American soil that, later, would be recognized as a tangible health hazard to American citizens. While in some quarters the Cold War confrontation justified the risk involved in testing, decisions that put the military-industrial complex in firm control of the arms race relegated public input to the periphery. Calculating risk of this nature was not an equation that could be concocted by experts, but rather a question of social values and ethics that required far greater public participation. Using the Mississippi River fish kill as an example, Commoner claimed that "the very presence in the Mississippi River of substances known to be toxic to fish at low concentrations and to mammals at higher concentrations must be regarded as a definite risk to any biological population exposed to it. The only feasible way to judge the significance of this contamination is to estimate the risks, compare them with the benefits associated with the use of the pesticides, and strike a balance between risk and benefit that will be acceptable to the public."[81] By the mid-1960s, Commoner was beginning to recognize that risk analysis was the vital bridge across the great divide that separated the postwar technological revolution and the rising tide of ecological awareness.

When Commoner appeared on the cover of *TIME* in 1970, he was touted as the Paul Revere of ecology, the signaler of imminent danger. Within the article, he was also part of a group of ecologists whom *TIME* called the "new Jeremiahs." That Commoner should be labeled both "the Paul Revere of ecology" and a new Jeremiah—patriot whistleblower and harbinger of doom—in the same *TIME* cover story suggests some of the ambiguity and popular misunderstandings surrounding the emerging environmental movement, but it also implies the centrality of his role and message within a broader American cultural history. As the Paul Revere of ecology, Commoner, no stranger to environmental conflict and controversy, gained recognition as a messenger raising the alarm of the environmental crisis, and also as one of the founding fathers of the contemporary environmental movement.

The American Jeremiah—who engaged in a mode of public exhortation that sought to marry social criticism and spiritual renewal—has been a persistent figure in American intellectual history. In its original iteration, the American jeremiad sought to illuminate the relationship between religious apocalypse and the imminent Revolutionary War. In its twentieth-century incarnation, the jeremiad took on an ecological flavor, determined to draw the attention of Americans toward the great divide between environmental apocalypse and the need for a revolution in how they conceived of the environment and their place in it. In tones of biblical grandeur, the environmental crisis suggested that the Judgment Day was nigh. Sacvan Bercovitch described the jeremiad as an intellectual common ground for spirituality and revolution. With reference to the American Revolution, he argued that "the meaning of revolution was emphatically and unequivocally progressive."[82] Revolution promised a spiritual renaissance. In a sense, the *TIME* characterizaton of the new ecologists as the logical heirs of the American jeremiad made perfect sense because they were effectively trying to incite a spiritual revolution within the American population to refocus its principles around a more ecologically sustainable mode of life.

The jeremiad form foretold decline and doom, and was a popular method of revitalizing the social and spiritual mission. Just as the original Jeremiah's dire predictions warned of the destruction of Jerusalem, the new Jeremiahs warned of the ongoing destruction of the Earth's ability to sustain life; both lamented the human fall from grace and saw the human condition and attempts at redemption as almost hopeless. But while the jeremiad's message foreshadowed despair, there lingered a glimmer of hope to which audiences were meant to cling. This was a compelling rhetorical trick. Like the eighteenth-century evangelical leaders of the Great Awakening, Commoner and the other Jeremiahs aimed to lead their audiences to despair, but then redeem them through the narrowest of hopes. In publicly lamenting environmental decline and the dangers of postwar technological decisions, Commoner was very consciously adopting this powerful rhetoric to strengthen the urgency of his message. "*Any* change imposed on [the environment] for the sake of some economic benefit has a price," he wrote in *Science and Survival.*

> For the benefits of powerful pesticides we pay in losses of birdlife and fish. For the conveniences of automobiles we pay in the rise of respiratory disease from smog. For the widespread use of combustible fuels we may yet be forced to pay the catastrophic cost of protecting our cities from worldwide floods. Sooner or later, wittingly or unwittingly, we must pay for every intrusion on the natural environment.[83]

This was the jeremiad. Human folly had created an environmental crisis, the latter-day flood. The Second Coming was at hand, and humanity would need to seek redemption. But, in traditional jeremiad form, Commoner brought his audience back from the abyss. "We are still in a period of grace, and if we are willing to pay the price, as large as it is, there is yet time to restore and preserve the biological quality of the environment."[84] That price, he implied, involved a rejection of many of the technological products and production methods that significantly threatened human health.

Like any social movement, environmentalism was based upon a kind of moral persuasion that vigorously sought support through a variety of means. The jeremiad was a way of guilting people into behavioral change. Its success could be calculated by the popularity of the environmental leaders who adopted it. Popular scientists such as Commoner, Paul Ehrlich, René Dubos, and the ecologists LaMont Cole, Eugene Odum, and Kenneth Watt all used a rhetorical approach that mimicked previous jeremiads. Further, *Silent Spring* had been attacked for this kind of alarmism. In a particularly critical review in the *Saturday Evening Post, Newsweek*'s senior editor, Edwin Diamond, had blamed Carson for creating "a big fuss . . . to scare the American public out of its wits."[85] Even before the 1962 publication of *Silent Spring,* the apocalyptic warnings of environmental writers—particularly those who came from the scientific community—did to a certain extent emphasize the gloomy consequences of irresponsible environmental actions. Two highly influential environmental books from 1948 both tended toward the environmental jeremiad in their rhetoric. In

Road to Survival, William Vogt linked his jeremiad to the foibles of American free enterprise, which was divorced from biophysical understanding and social responsibility, and "must bear a large share of the responsibility for devastating forests, vanishing wildlife, crippled ranges, a gullied continent, and roaring flood crests."[86] In contrast, Fairfield Osborn firmly believed that free enterprise was inherently capable of correcting its own systemic abuses, but he, too, descended into a jeremiad in *Our Plundered Planet,* exhorting Americans to be cautious of "technologists [who] may outdo themselves in the creation of artificial substitutes for natural subsistence." The only proper approach, Osborn contended, was to accept "the necessity of cooperating with nature."[87]

Not surprisingly, the prospect of nuclear Armageddon spurred popular fiction and cinema. Nevil Shute's *On the Beach* and Walter M. Miller's *A Canticle for Leibowitz* are among the great literary works of the horrors associated with the nuclear age, while Stanley Kubrick's *Dr. Strangelove* brought the terrors of atomic holocaust to the silver screen.[88] Even Linus Pauling's 1957 petition for a nuclear test ban—written in Commoner's Washington University office—adopted the tone of a jeremiad in warning against potential dangers of not controlling nuclear weapons, culminating in "a cataclysmic nuclear war."[89] Late in 1960, the ecologist Paul Sears sent Chauncey Leake a document titled "A Statement of Conviction About Overpopulation," asking him to present it to the AAAS board. The document, signed by thirty-eight Nobel Prize winners, contained a similar ominous tone, warning that "unless a favorable balance of population and resources is achieved with a minimum of delay, there is in prospect a Dark Age of human misery, famine, under-education and unrest which could generate growing panic, exploding into wars fought to appropriate the dwindling means of survival."[90] Sears's 1935 classic on soils, *Deserts on the March,* was also imbued with gloomy prognostication for the future.[91]

Carson, therefore, had not exactly opened the floodgates, but as *Silent Spring* gained widespread attention, the jeremiad grew louder and bolder. To the most stringent of Jeremiahs, the end of history was indeed at hand. Garrett Hardin lamented the "tragedy of the commons," in which natural resources were being depleted with no chance of being replenished, and warned about the dangers of population growth in much the same tone as Paul Ehrlich would in his 1968 bestseller, *The Population Bomb*. In 1972, the Club of Rome, a group of highly esteemed MIT scientists, projected that "if the present growth trends in world population, industrialization, pollution, food production and resource depletion continue unchanged, the limits of growth on this planet will be reached within the next hundred years. The most probable result will be a rather sudden and uncontrollable decline in both population and industrial capacity."[92] But while the siren calls of the new jeremiad brought considerable attention to the environmental cause, the project over the next decade would be to decipher the different messages in the jeremiad and make sense of environmental decline in America.

The environmental jeremiad became a powerful form of rhetoric wielded by a select group of charismatic politico-scientists who came to be recognized as the shamans of the spring.[93] Their knack for public engagement was instrumental in their relative success; these were not awkward lab scientists in lab coats, but articulate spokespeople advocating that ecological awareness was essential to human survival. The rise of the environmental jeremiad also marked an important development among the politico-scientists. Not only was the jeremiad politically engaged, it also demonstrated the development of a new language that was better suited to its audience. This development was absolutely critical to the growing public interest and literacy in ecology, and the urgency of the jeremiad. Ehrlich, in particular, was adept at offering such cataclysmic warnings both in his writings and in interviews. In one particularly famous interview that appeared in *Look* magazine the day before Earth Day, Ehrlich said: "When you reach a point where you realize further efforts will be futile, you may as well look after yourself and your friends and enjoy what little time you have left." For Ehrlich, in reference to overpopulation, "that point for me is 1972."[94] According to the journalist Stephen Fox: "In his endless round of lectures, interviews, and TV appearances, Ehrlich—with his thundercloud visage and deeply resonant voice—seemed the very personification of the Voice of Doom."[95]

Ehrlich was convinced that overpopulation had become such a significant problem that by 1968 it was already too late to prevent disaster. "The battle to feed all of humanity is over," he began in *The Population Bomb*. "At this late date nothing can prevent a substantial increase in the world death rate."[96] According to Ehrlich, famine and devastation were inevitable. Part of his success in *The Population Bomb* was this apocalyptic—jeremiad-like—tone that forced his readers to consider the issue of global overpopulation. After condemning humanity to damnation, Ehrlich offered a modicum of hope. "Many lives could be saved," he suggested, "through dramatic programs to 'stretch' the carrying capacity of the earth by increasing food production. But these programs will only provide a stay of execution unless they are accompanied by determined and successful efforts at population control."[97] He founded Zero Population Growth, an organization promoting smaller families in the United States, and outlined the necessity for population control in his 1968 bestseller. *The Population Bomb* was an immediate success. Over three decades later it was still the most popular environmental book ever published, selling over 3 million copies in the first decade.[98] *The Population Bomb* was well written, which contributed both to its commercial success and to its persuasiveness. Ehrlich was committed to promoting the authority of science to combat the environmental crisis, and his ability to communicate his position effectively helped his cause. Readily adopting the role of Jeremiah allowed Ehrlich to promote the scientist as the intellectual and moral leader in the fight against the environmental crisis.[99] This authority gave even greater immediacy and significance to his message. The success of the book, his subsequent popular appearances, and his felicitous public speaking style made Ehrlich an instant celebrity, and his position all the more popular.

But while this energy propelled American environmentalism to new heights, it also provoked some interesting tensions surrounding the appropriation of scientific disciplines. Professional ecologists found their discipline under siege by political activists. Peter J. Bowler observes that "many people now see ecology as a science whose subject matter must necessarily lead its practitioners to side with environmentalists. The very word 'ecological' has come to denote a concern for the environment."[100] During the 1960s, ecology became a commonplace feature of the American lexicon; Commoner, Ehrlich, Carson, and other "ecologists" became household names; and shortly after Earth Day, Commoner would present his "Four Laws of Ecology."[101] Ecology and environmental politics evolved to the point that they were almost inseparable in the public imagination, and central to the new social project of ingraining environmental values into the popular American consciousness. Indeed, to these champions of ecology, ecology was more than just a tool for implementing environmental values; ecology, they asserted, would *inspire* environmental values.[102]

But few of these popular scientists—Commoner among them—had had any formal training in ecology. For Commoner and others, ecology was an idea masked in the authority of science rather than a science in practice. Stephen Bocking writes: "In contrast to assumptions that ecology provides a holistic view of nature, in practice ecologists focus on nutrient and energy flows, or on predation and competition, applying perspectives that can be highly reductionistic. . . . What is especially striking, then, in the ecology invoked by non-ecologists, is that while it trades on the authority of science, it does not correspond to ecology as practiced by scientists."[103] Why was Commoner so successful at co-opting ecology? In part, because he was outside the discipline, he was likely well positioned to recognize ecology's social significance and better able to synthesize—even beyond recognition—its principal tenets to make them accessible to a larger audience.[104] But Commoner and Ehrlich were also exceptionally charismatic and already had an eager audience. They had a pulpit from which they could expound upon this modification of the popular ecological gospel. Even if they did not hold up scientifically, the interconnected webs of life that characterized popular ecology were evocative, provocative, and effective in drawing out the environmental jeremiad on the fragility of life while also implying a level of scientific authority.[105]

Nevertheless, the frequent adoption of the jeremiad came at some cost to the environmental movement and to the scientific authority from which it drew. As the sociologist Deborah Lynn Guber notes, "By downplaying environmental progress and by using exaggerated doomsday warnings to motivate public awareness and concern, the environmental movement has sacrificed its own credibility by giving in to the politics of chicken little."[106] The political scientist Walter A. Rosenbaum warned that too much publicity and too many dire warnings posed the danger that "Americans may become desensitized to the problem or begin to suspect that the constant emphasis exaggerates the issue."[107] Moreover, through the use of the environmental jeremiad, Commoner and others were contradicting the guiding principles of the science information movement; whether it was precipitated by their rhetoric or the visible state of environmental decline, the public came to see these popular scientists as prophets. Commoner fought this—it was, ironically, another instance of a lay audience turning to expert authority—but the public was enraptured with the compelling ecological rhetoric presented by these charismatic scientists, many of whom did not subscribe to the tenets that had driven Commoner's own commitment to science and social responsibility.

According to the critic Charles Rubin, another of the consequences of the jeremiad was the acquisition of a "public taste" for largesse and omens of ecological disaster. Citing Carson's *Silent Spring* and Commoner's *The Closing Circle,* Rubin argued that writing on environmental issues became

> the intellectual equivalent of a gothic romance, with a large cast of characters, involuted relationships, and a lurking menace. But the public's ability to appreciate the delicate balances and interrelationships of political and social structures has undergone a corresponding debasement, evident in rampant sloganeering, shameless emotionalism, and mindless panic and pessimism whenever "what is wrong with our society" comes under discussion. In this realm, only the crudest morality tales satisfy. Carson and Commoner have alerted us to matters that may well demand our attention. But they have done so at the cost of our ability to give that attention in a thoughtful way.[108]

But to suggest that Commoner and Carson were responsible for creating a context for "rampant sloganeering" and "shameless emotionalism" is more than a little misguided. In articulating their critique of industrial practices, they impressed upon the public the gravity of the situation, grounded their concerns in scientific evidence, and presented them in a style that adhered to their faith in the power of public information. By the 1960s, there were also scientific bases for environmental concern; Carson's fears about pesticides were certainly justified by the Mississippi River fish kills, for example. Further, Commoner and the other ecological scientists contended, the longer society ignored their warnings, the more jeremiad-like they would—by necessity—become.[109]

Indeed, to Commoner and the other Jeremiahs, the state of the environment—from air pollution to soil and water contamination—combined with consumerism as the prevailing public characteristic, warranted a little public alarmism. "We have compiled a record of serious failures in these recent encounters with the environment," Commoner insisted in a 1966 address based heavily upon work that appeared in *Science and Survival.*

> This record shows that we do not yet understand the environment well enough to make new intrusions on it, on the large scale that is now possible, with any reasonable expectation of accurately predicting the consequences. But we can ignore the biology of the environment—and tolerate our present ignorance of it—only at our peril. Pollution by detergents, pesticides, herbicides, radioisotopes, and smog is dangerous, in my view, because it represents a blind intrusion into aspects of the

complex biology of the environment which are still poorly understood. Apart from their known hazards these pollutants represent a huge gamble. The odds are unknown, but the stakes are enormous.[110]

Here, in a nutshell, was the significance of risk analysis. Surely the stakes—human health and the health of our environment—were too high to justify ignoring the potential risk of forging ahead without greater recognition of the extent and the impact of those intrusions.

Indeed, Commoner's activism was carefully calculated. He had learned during his undergraduate years at Columbia in the 1930s the importance of finding a rational way of approaching problems and of publicizing them.[111] Distinct from other jeremiads, Commoner's method was more deliberate and more premeditated, and, perhaps, less overtly jeremiadic. In his prose, Commoner maintained a calm tone designed to engage his readers rather than incite them. His main priority remained a deep-seated belief that access to information constituted a vital form of public empowerment. The necessity of public participation and the perceived political power of an informed citizenry became his standard theme. If the jeremiad moved Americans toward numbing fear of environmental problems, then it was hardly the right technique to promote public participation.

Or maybe it was. There was certainly a time in which the jeremiad was exceptionally persuasive—as evidenced by Ehrlich's mainstream celebrity—and scientific information relating to the environment was unquestionably dire. The environmental momentum cultivated in the 1960s became the central focus of the greatest environmental celebration in human history. At its core, Earth Day paid homage to the ecological imagination, made public its declarations of the importance of more sustainable industries and lifestyles, and sought to educate the American public in achieving these new goals. Earth Day was a teach-in and, in that guise, a prime example of the power of public information. Just as ecology preached a more holistic approach to environmental problems, Earth Day appealed to a more inclusive sense of movement. Issues of clean air, clean water, and safer foods were not concerns over which the new social environmentalists held any kind of monopoly; these issues also appealed in many ways to the conservative, silent majority, who had been alienated by much of the 1960s social activism. In fact, Earth Day and subsequent environmental activism illustrated some of the difficulties of bringing divergent interests under the same tent. The more people sought to identify with environmentalism, the more difficulty arose in trying to define the movement or to reconcile different priorities. Was environmentalism about natural resource conservation? Public health? Wildlands protection? And even within these disparate categories, rationale for their defense varied significantly. If Earth Day was a celebration of environmentalism's ascendance, it would also mark the beginning of the rifts that would divide the movement.

4

When Scientists Disagree

We have met the enemy—and he is us.
—Pogo

No singular event more amply illustrates the promise and the chaos of modern environmentalism than the first Earth Day. According to Harold Sprout, "Not since the Japanese attack on Pearl Harbor has any public issue received such massive support in all the news media, local as well as national."[1] The organizers of Earth Day sought to define the celebration as a "commitment to make life better, not just bigger and faster, to provide real rather than rhetorical solutions" to the environmental crisis.[2] As broadly as possible, Earth Day intended to demonstrate the extent to which American values regarding the environment had changed—particularly in relation to the increased rejection of American standards of acceptable risk—while also articulating the scope of this cultural shift in American society.

Earth Day also reaffirmed Commoner's connections between peace and environmentalism. The Vietnam War was still very much a source of fractious sentiment in the United States, and antiwar activists were prominent among the Earth Day celebrants. Balloons and banners across the country boldly stated, "war is the worst pollution," "war is not healthy for children and other living things," and "Earth—love it or leave it."[3] An Earth Day commentator trying to assuage differences between antiwar and environmental activists concluded that "most people don't want the world to go up in smoke—or under in smog."[4] Commoner was far more explicit in making the connection. In an Earth Day talk at Brown University, he charged that the herbicide attacks on Vietnamese forests and agricultural fields constituted "the first ecological warfare conducted by the U.S. since the attacks on American Indians."[5] In the days preceding 22 April, Earth Day coordinator Denis Hayes's Washington, D.C., office was deluged with requests for information, slogans, and banners. When one visitor asked for a bumper sticker, one of Hayes's young staff members reportedly replied: "We don't have any bumper stickers. You want to know why? They go on automobiles."[6] Indeed, Earth Day marked a popular association between environmental health and conservationist principles. By no stretch of the imagination did Earth Day revelers share a uniform notion of what environmentalism was or what the day stood for, but there did appear to be a general acceptance that environmental health—broadly defined—was inherently connected to human physical and spiritual health, defined equally broadly. And certainly, Earth Day represented a forum in which the ecological message could be applied holistically. Hayes, a twenty-five-year-old Harvard law student, presented an expansive interpretation of the environmental crisis and Earth Day's ambitions at a press conference in Washington, D.C., when he exclaimed: "Ecology is concerned with the total system—not just the way it disposes of its garbage."[7]

When Senator Gaylord Nelson of Wisconsin conceived of Earth Day in November 1969, he could not have imagined the extent to which Americans would heed his call for a nationwide environmental teach-in on college campuses. Nelson would submit that Earth Day ultimately represented "truly an astonishing grass-roots explosion."[8] Congress stood in recess, the National Education Association estimated that 10 million public school children participated in teach-in programs, and citizen groups in more than 2,000 communities across the United States took to the streets.[9] In all, some 20 million Americans participated in public Earth Day activities across the country, making the first Earth Day the largest single-day public demonstration in American history. In New York City, Fifth Avenue was closed to traffic between 59th and 14th streets for two hours after noon, and 14th Street between Third and Seventh avenues, "left free for pedestrians between noon and midnight, became an ecological carnival."[10] Despite a notable absence of smog in Los Angeles as a result of cooler than average temperatures, hosts of students and activists attacked air pollution across the city. University of Southern California students buried an automobile engine—one of many buried across the country—as the Tommy Trojan statue witnessed the proceedings from behind a gas mask.[11] At an antipollution rally in Atlanta's Hurt Park, a sign reading

"Fight Dirty" reportedly "summed up the thousands of words spoken throughout Georgia . . . in observance of Earth Day."[12] Thousands congregated on the Washington Monument grounds at the Sylvan Theater for several hours of speakers and folk songs, concluding with a performance by the folksinger and environmental activist Pete Seeger, Earth Day's honorary chairman.[13] Just outside the nation's capital, fifteen housewives bicycled to the Potomac River and held a stand-up picnic at a nearby dump after picking up piles of dead fish from the shore.[14] At the University of New Mexico in Albuquerque, students collected signatures on a big plastic globe, which they called the "enemy of the earth award" for twenty-eight state senators accused of weakening recent antipollution legislation.[15] In St. Louis, the United Auto Workers led a parade through the city center featuring a smogfree, propane-powered car, and in Tacoma, Washington, high school students rode down the highway on horseback.[16] Fifteen hundred students in Louisville Kentucky, crowded into the concourse at Atherton High School in a demonstration designed to illustrate the problems of overpopulation, which ended with pushing, grabbing, and pinching. In Madison, University of Wisconsin students braved freezing weather to greet the dawn with biblical readings and an apology to God for environmental abuse, while just up the road, high school students in West Bend paid to take part in the destroying of a car, the proceeds going to a school antipollution group.[17] Even a goat in Centralia, Washington participated, wearing a sign reading "I eat garbage, what are you doing for your community?"[18] In addition, elementary and high school students across the country participated in collecting litter and cleaning community and city parks, streets, and landmarks.

Earth Day deserves careful attention as a key event in the reification of American environmentalism. Historical accounts that "periodize" American environmentalism often recognize Earth Day as that key moment when the movement became "modern." The suggestion is that conservation impulses and urban reform issues became allied under the same roof. But such contentions regarding Earth Day's role in the history of American environmentalism tend to limit the larger evolution of American environmental values. Samuel P. Hays correctly asserts: "Earth Day was as much a result as a cause."[19] Indeed, Earth Day 1970 might be recognized as the coming-out party for modern environmentalism in the United States, inasmuch as the event demonstrated a considerable public interest in issues of environmental health. According to the political scientist Walter Rosenbaum, "In the early 1970s, environmentalists mobilized for political action in a uniquely congenial climate of opinion; perhaps at no time in this century was the American public more receptive to the environmental gospel."[20] That congenial climate could never have been realized without the publication of Rachel Carson's *Silent Spring* in 1962, Commoner's public information efforts in his opposition to nuclear weapons testing in the years preceding the 1963 Test Ban Treaty, and the growing recognition of the dangers inherent in the rampant technological optimism that consumed American culture.

Environmentalism's political power had a resounding impact in the White House, too. If he was nothing else, President Richard Nixon was a cagey political survivor; his political reemergence after losing the 1960 election to John Kennedy was testament to that. Very early in his presidency, Nixon recognized that his administration would have to appear supportive of environmental protection. While the silent majority that had put Nixon in power remained wary of the counterculture embodied in the antiwar movement, the New Left, and Black Power, polls indicated that they were concerned about the environment. Indeed, concern about the environment and support for Earth Day did not split along traditional lines of generational or political persuasion. In the days leading up to the April 1970 festivities, the Georgia Comptroller General and Republican candidate for governor, James L. Bentley, had sent out $1,600 worth of telegrams at taxpayers' expense, warning that Earth Day might be a Communist plot, because the date chosen for the event was Lenin's birthday.[21] But on the left, the journalist and social commentator I. F. Stone called Earth Day a "gigantic snowjob" that diverted public attention from the ongoing war in Southeast Asia.[22] Another leading leftist voice, *Ramparts* magazine, concurred, calling Earth Day "the first step in a con game that will do little more than abuse the environment further."[23] Capitalizing on the popular concern over the state of the environment—and without the risk of alienating his core constituency—Nixon had signed the first Endangered Species Act in 1969 and the National Environmental Policy Act in 1970, co-opting an issue commonly held by prominent Democratic rivals such as senators Edmund Muskie and Henry Jackson. He also devoted considerable energy to the environment in his 1970 State of the Union address, calling environmentalism the new "selflessness" and announcing that "the great question of the '70s is: shall we surrender to our surroundings or shall we make our peace with nature and begin to make reparations for the damage we have done to our air, to our land, and to our water?"[24]

Indeed, emblazoned over Commoner's portrait on the cover of *TIME* magazine in February 1970 was "Environment: Nixon's New Issue." But while Nixon offered his tacit approval of Earth Day, he spent a routine day in his White House office, unable to get an invitation to speak; an article in the *Chicago Tribune* the following day wryly noted: "Nixon seemed almost the only public figure in the country not making a speech."[25] Meanwhile, outside the Department of the Interior, 2,500 demonstrators protested that department's controversial oil leases, chanting "Off the oil!" "Stop the muck!" and "Give Earth a chance!"[26] In Denver, antinuclear activists bestowed the Colorado Environmental Rapist of the Year award on the Atomic Energy Commission, while at the University of Alaska, Interior Secretary Walter Hickel was booed off the stage before he could finish outlining administration support for the Alaska Pipeline.[27] A "Herblock" cartoon in the *Washington Post* on 23 April 1970 satirized the administration's environmental policies, portraying an official presenting the administration's position on air pollution from the back of a car belching exhaust fumes over a distressed onlooker. Beside the government official in the car were fat cats representing the auto and oil companies.[28] For all the environmental legislation the Nixon administration supported prior to Earth Day and in the years following, and as much as Nixon liked the notion of comparing himself to Theodore Roosevelt as a Republican champion of efficiency, progress, and conservation, 22 April 1970 found the Nixon administration under siege by environmental activists all over the United States.[29]

Sharing the Nixon administration's astute observation that the environment was an issue they needed to appear to support, the American business community, often the target of environmental protests, also endorsed Earth Day. The Scott Paper Company pledged $36 million to control pollution at its plant in Washington state, and suggested it might spend an additional $20 million on its plant in Winslow, Maine.[30] Dow Chemical and the Ford Motor Company sponsored speakers at the University of Michigan teach-in; New York's Consolidated Edison provided an electric bus to New York mayor John Lindsay to facilitate his transportation between scheduled events; and Monsanto reasserted its promise to become one of the industrial leaders in pollution control technologies.[31] Much of this corporate environmental benevolence was met with less than sincere gratitude from activists who saw such outreach as nothing more than another example of the Janus-faced nature of American industry and corporate "greenwashing." In Miami, yellow dye was dumped into sewage treatment plants to track the progress of wastes into waterways.[32] Also in Florida, activists dumped a dead octopus and several fish at Florida Power & Light's headquarters to protest the company's thermal pollution in Biscayne Bay, and a group called the Environmental Vigilantes deposited used crankcase oil in the reflecting pool outside the Standard Oil of California building on Market Street in San Francisco. They acknowledged their act was "indefensible—and indistinguishable from the corporate policy of Standard Oil Company of California,"[33] but that was the point. By polluting the physical environment, American business interests were increasing their wealth by socializing the costs of their industries. The petrochemical industry, for example, made money only because it could pollute. The extent of those social costs depended on society's evaluations of the risk, and Earth Day indicated that the American public was starting to consider the size of the bill too great.[34]

Even the media took the opportunity to criticize American business. The *Washington Post* reported on the introduction of Hopfenmaier's new public relations kit, demonstrating its support for Earth Day, at its rendering plant in Georgetown. As the manager spoke, "the big Hopfenmaier smokestacks on the Georgetown waterfront were belching their regular emission of contaminants, produced in the plant by 'cooking' livestock remains for use as fertilizer and soap by-products." In another display of environmental compassion, Washington-based Pepsi Cola Bottling Company's marketing director, James P. Anderson, outlined the company's new antilitter campaign and kit, which contained litter bags, bumper stickers, "a brochure on a 28-minute beautification movie starring Lassie," and a letter to bottlers from Pepsi president James B. Sommerall asserting that "you can be a leader in the civic activities of your community by participating in local antilitter programs." According to the *Washington Post,* however, "about half of yesterday's Pepsi production in Washington was packaged in the nonreturnable bottles and cans of the type ecologists say contribute heavily to the nation's mountains of refuse."[35] Already, many environmental activists seemed unwilling to accept industrial and legislative compromises in place of more large-scale action and prevention.

But as the Nixon administration and other politicians, corporate and industrial interests, and (not least) the media jostled for public attention on Earth Day, there emerged a growing concern that the message might be watered down. Robert Gottlieb observed, "What became most disconcerting to the traditional conservationists was the intense media coverage of Earth Day and the sense of discovery, especially by the media, that a new issue and a new movement had emerged full-blown with little connection to earlier conservationist and protectionist movements."[36] Similarly, many environmentalists worried about the longevity of environmental concern expressed by the participants in Earth Day. Frank Renshaw, the chairman of a teach-in sponsored by five Cincinnati colleges, declared: "We hope that each participant, supplied with some of the facts about environmental problems in his own backyard, will commit himself to a program of action." The University of California zoologist Kenneth Watt shared Renshaw's hope, but also expressed a deeper concern. Speaking at Swarthmore College, Watt urged students to maintain the day's momentum. "The history of movements like this is not very promising," he warned. "We had great movements on civil rights and the Vietnamese war. The problems are still with us but the movements have died away."[37] An Earth Day editorial comment in the *Chicago Tribune* echoed Watt's concern. "After the last speech has been made and the last car buried today," it averred, "we hope that Earth day will be followed by a quiet determination by everybody to enlist for the duration in this war. . . . This will take more than speechmaking, or listening to speeches, or publicity stunts. People, not machines, are the prime cause of our environmental troubles."[38] Their concerns were ultimately well founded. Eight days after Earth Day, Nixon announced his decision to send American troops into Cambodia, and within a week four students had been killed at Kent State University in Ohio. Americans and the media turned their attention elsewhere.[39]

Commoner expressed a different source of dissatisfaction with the Earth Day proceedings. "What surprised me most," he wrote in *The Closing Circle*, "were the numerous, confident explanations of the cause and cure of the crisis." As Americans marched together throughout the country, it seemed that every environmentalist had a different explanation for the rise of the environmental crisis. Some blamed affluence; others blamed poverty. Still others blamed human nature, capitalism, socialism, religion, or technology. Commoner continued: "Having spent some years in the effort simply to detect and describe the growing list of environmental problems—radioactive fallout, air and water pollution, the deterioration of the soil—and in tracing some of their links to social and political processes, the identification of a single cause and cure seemed a rather bold step." The environmental crisis was much more complicated than that, but during Earth Week, Commoner "discovered that such reticence [to accept complex answers] was far behind the times." In cleaning up litter and marching for clean air and water, Americans seemed uninterested in the origins of the problem. "It seemed to me," Commoner reflected, "that the confusion . . . was a sign that the [environmental crisis] was so complex and ambiguous that people could read into it whatever conclusion their own beliefs—about human nature, economics, and politics—suggested."[40]

Reflecting in 1985 on the inchoate outburst of sentiments toward the environment, Commoner recalled that "there was damned little organization at first; everybody was sounding off in one direction or another. What really held it together was the very simple moral statement that future generations depend on the environment and we have been blind as to what's happening to it."[41] And here was the strategic problem the environmental movement faced in the wake of Earth Day: "Like a Rorschach ink blot, Earth Week mirrored personal convictions more than objective knowledge."[42] As Commoner found himself at the vanguard of a new environmental movement, he saw it as his duty to articulate the origins and the stakes of the environmental crisis and to confront the Babelian state of American environmental concern. Just as American environmentalism was enjoying the height of its success, internal rifts threatened to tear apart its tenuous alliances and growing political power. These internal rifts revolved around dictating priorities for future action, and foreshadowed not just future divisions but also the subsequent move away from Commoner, his environmental politics, and his apparatus for activism.

Commoner was one of the most active figures involved with the Earth Day teach-ins, lecturing on four university campuses in Rhode Island and Massachusetts. The day before Earth Day, he was at Harvard University, where he outlined his agenda and motivations for the Earth Day celebrations.

"Everyone now knows that the environmental crisis is upon us," he began. "What is not so clear," he continued, "is how we got into this mess and what we need to do to get out of it."[43] Earth Day was an important event, therefore, because it offered the opportunity to chart a path out of the environmental crisis. "I have come here because there is something I want to say about the environmental crisis," Commoner told Brown University students attending his Earth Day lecture. "But I have also come here to learn."[44] For Commoner, the teach-in element of Earth Day was critical to the continued success of environmental protection, conceptually and from a policy standpoint. While issues of environmental health transcended generational barriers, Commoner recognized the vitality of the student movements of the 1960s and hoped to channel that energy into activism for the environment. Averting the environmental crisis was also a long-term and complicated mission; there was no quick fix. Students constituted a fundamentally important constituency, Commoner told them:

> It is marvelously fitting—and to me deeply moving—that the nation's new fight for survival is being led . . . by the youth. For young people and future generations are the real victims of impending ecological catastrophe. You were born under the shadow of the bomb. You are the first generation in the history of man to carry strontium-90 in your bones and DDT in your fat; your bodies will record in time the full effects of environmental destruction on mankind. It is you who face the frightful task of seeking humane knowledge in a world which has, with cunning perversity, transformed the power that knowledge generates into an instrument of catastrophe.[45]

Like countless other professors, politicians, and activists, Commoner pointed to the gravity of environmental decline and offered encouragement for the struggle to come. "The grinding oppression of environmental deterioration . . . degrades the hope of our citizens in the future and their will to secure it," but grassroots activism to restore environmental health and enforce antipollution ordinances promised to "give tangible meaning to the spirit of environmental revival."[46] There was hope. But Commoner was also determined to outline the course that he felt was most important. Indeed, it was on Earth Day that he introduced a more comprehensive explanation for the environmental crisis, which would become the foundation for *The Closing Circle*. "I should like to propose a thesis which, I believe, may provide some useful insights into [the environmental crisis]," he told his Brown University audience. "The thesis is this: environmental pollution is not to be regarded as an unfortunate, but incidental, by-product of the growth of *population,* the intensification of *production,* or of technological progress. It is, rather, an intrinsic feature of the very technology which we have developed to enhance productivity."[47] Radioactive fallout; the production of photochemical smog; new detergents, insecticides, and fertilizers; and countless other synthetic chemicals and carcinogens released into the environment were all testament to Commoner's position.

The problem seemed to arise from a misguided sense of scientific priority. Citing sewage removal in an NBC interview that aired before Earth Day, Commoner claimed: "If we look at the ecological facts, it's perfectly clear that organic wastes belong in the soil; that is where nature can accommodate them into the cyclical process. . . . If we can put a man on the moon it's within our power to collect the organic matter of sewage, handle it in a way to prevent the spread of disease and get it back in the soil."[48] And this was a problem: in 1970, the United States could land a man on the moon, but could not maintain a healthy environment for its citizens. "The environmental crisis, together with all of the other evils that blight the nation—racial inequality, hunger, poverty, and war—cry out for a profound revision in our national priorities," Commoner insisted on Earth Day. "None can be solved until that is accomplished. But, tragically, the nation remains immobilized by the cost of the Vietnam War and the huge military budget, by the talent- and money-gulping space program, by the disastrous cuts in the federal budget for research support, by the reduction in funds for the cities and education."[49]

But if Commoner's Earth Day message and his speeches and interviews before and after Earth Day were consistent with the holistic nature of the environmental critique he had developed through the 1960s, only one message consistently filtered through public and media discourses: Barry Commoner did not consider current population growth to be a real ecological problem. This was a gross misstatement and oversimplification of Commoner's position, but it was his attack on population control advocates in the United States that stuck in the popular interpretation of his ecological activism. The basis of Commoner's talk at Harvard University the day before Earth Day was a disavowal of population as the *source* of the environmental crisis. "In my opinion," he declared, "population trends in the U.S. cannot be blamed for the deteriorated condition of the environment."[50] Commoner contended that the real source of environmental pollution was the proliferation of new, polluting technologies since World War II. "In most cases the increases [in pollution] in the last 20 to 25 years have been in the order of 500 to 1,000%," whereas the concurrent changes in population were a more modest 40 to 45 percent. "Of course," he continued, "if there were no people in the country there would be no pollution problem, but the fact of the matter is that there simply has not been a sufficient rise in the U.S. population to account for the enormous increase in pollution levels."[51]

Over the following year, people all over the United States wrote to Commoner, criticizing his opposition to population control. "Your April 22 speech at Brown University has recently come to my attention," wrote Ruth Troetschler of Los Altos, California, "and I was surprised that you, a scientist with long-term environmental concerns, should have indicated that we do not have a population problem."[52] Mrs. Lynne H. Perry of Austin, Texas, asked: "Isn't it rather foolish and dangerous to publicly sanction the continuation of indiscriminate breeding, to be unconcerned about the addition of millions more tomorrow when we haven't yet managed to cope effectively with the problems of the numbers we have now?"[53] Dr. L. E. Marshall of Estherville, Iowa, charged that Commoner's public efforts to quell concerns about population growth in America constituted "*overt, dangerous, irresponsibility*" that was helping the country "about as much as bubonic plague."[54] Even the supportive letters suggested that the population question was culturally divisive, and supporters of Commoner's position tended not to fully appreciate the sophisticated nature of his larger message. Sister Veronita Ruddy of Bloomington, Illinois, asked Commoner to "accept my congratulations for being one of the few scientists who is not being influenced by the propaganda of Planned Parenthood on the subject of over-population."[55]

Commoner did oppose the suggestion that the environmental crisis in the United States was attributable to overpopulation—"it is a serious mistake to becloud the pollution issue with the population for the facts will not support it," he told his Harvard University audience the day before Earth Day—but he never dismissed overpopulation as a legitimate and very serious problem on a global scale and especially in the developing world.[56] What Commoner specifically rejected was the notion that population control would solve the environmental crisis. Even on this last point, though, he faced considerable opposition. By Earth Day, the ecologist Paul

Ehrlich was the leading proponent of human population growth as a cause of—and population control as a solution to—the environmental crisis. Recognizing the environmental movement's lack of priorities, Ehrlich emphasized the ecological significance of global overpopulation as the catalyst for the existing environmental crisis and an appropriate priority for environmental organizations.

In his very popular book *The Population Bomb* (1968), Ehrlich had taken a neo-Malthusian approach to the environmental crisis, arguing that overpopulation posed an ecological strain on the Earth's carrying capacity and food production limits. His argument was a modern adaptation of the British economist and demographer Thomas Malthus's essay on population, which predicted an inevitable food supply crisis based on the world's multiplying population. Published anonymously in 1798, Malthus's *An Essay on the Principle of Population as It Affects the Future Improvement of Society* was widely read. The crux of the treatise was the difference in scale between population growth and growth of food production. Whereas population increased geometrically (1,2,4,8,16), Malthus pointed out that food production could only increase arithmetically (1,2,3,4,5). At some point, then, something had to give. More food production required not only more land, but also more efficient technologies—fertilizers and pesticides—in order to maximize yields. Agricultural land was stressed, and industrial output and productivity needed to increase continually. It was an impossible cycle. Modern-day Malthusians such as Ehrlich believed the post-World War II technological revolution was a response to population pressures. Pollution was the result of population growth. Malthus hypothesized that demographic strains on natural resources—of which food was far and away the most significant—was ultimately limited, and would be alleviated by what he called positive checks: famine, disease, or war, which would reduce population size to a more suitable equilibrium with resources.[57] In 1968, 170 years later, at a time when an American audience was never more eager to learn about the impending environmental crisis, Ehrlich presented arguably the loudest and most persuasive treatise on the ecological problems of human overpopulation.

In 1967, Ehrlich had given a speech at the Commonwealth Club in San Francisco, where David Brower of the Sierra Club heard him, and asked him to write a short book on the population explosion. *The Population Bomb* was published the following year, issued in paperback by Ballantine and the Sierra Club, and sold 3 million copies over the next decade.[58] Having developed an objective appreciation of the problem of overpopulation in his research, Ehrlich traced his emotional discovery of the problem to a trip to Delhi, India, where he discovered the "*feel* of overpopulation."[59]

> The streets seemed alive with people. People eating, people washing, people sleeping. People visiting, arguing, and screaming. People thrusting their hands through the taxi window, begging. People defecating and urinating. People clinging to buses. People herding animals. People, people, people, people. As we moved slowly through the mob, hand horn squawking, the dust, noise, heat, and cooking fires gave the scene a hellish aspect.[60]

To Ehrlich, the causes of environmental deterioration were symptoms of an obvious chain of ecological effects: "Too many cars, too many factories, too much detergent, too much pesticide, multiplying contrails, inadequate sewage treatment plants, too little water, too much carbon dioxide—all can be traced to *too many people.*"[61] According to Ehrlich, rises in pollution were a result of more people consuming more products and creating more waste. Population increases resulted in pollution increases. His solution was to control national and global populations: "We must have population control at home . . . by compulsion if voluntary methods fail. We must use our political power to push other countries into programs which combine agricultural development and population control."[62] Not addressing overpopulation could have serious consequences, Ehrlich warned in a quintessential jeremiad. "There are only two kinds of solutions to the population problem," he argued. "One is a 'birth rate solution,' in which we find ways to lower the birth rate. The other is a 'death rate solution,' in which ways to raise the death rate—war, famine, pestilence—*find us.*" Naturally the former solution was preferable, but its implementation presented logistical difficulties.[63] While Ehrlich traced the environmental crisis to too many people, he concluded by suggesting that overpopulation was both a catalyst and a symptom of environmental decline. "In the long view, the progressive deterioration of our environment may cause more death and misery than any conceivable food-population gap."[64]

By 1970, the National Wildlife Federation had adopted a resolution that supported restricting the American population to its current level, and the Sierra Club, which had published *The Population Bomb,* also supported numerous population control programs. Indeed, the reaction to Commoner's opposition to population control in the United States and Ehrlich's growing popularity—he was a regular guest on Johnny Carson's Tonight Show—suggested that overpopulation concerns had won the day. While Commoner barnstormed the Northeast on Earth Day, Ehrlich spoke to 10,000 people gathered at Iowa State University. One Earth Day report even noted the number of population control balloons seen in New York City. As people celebrated Earth Day on the streets, balloons bobbed above the crowd, many of them beseeching families to "stop at two."[65]

Commoner had long kept up with concerns about the global human population crisis, and was well aware of its existence. But to Commoner, mandatory birth control enforcement as a means of reducing the global birthrate was neither pragmatic nor moral. And he was also fairly confident that such a program would not work. In June 1968, Commoner wrote an article titled "The Population Problem" for Planned Parenthood. Therein, Commoner drew connections between population control and social progress, noting that "improvement in living conditions is closely tied to an interest in limiting family size. People are more likely to want large families when living conditions are difficult, because it means that there will be more children available to work . . . and help support the family." Conversely, as living standards improve, "people are more willing to limit family size."[66] This basic principle—that social progress is a key determinant in reducing birthrates—was not Commoner's invention, but it has become the cornerstone of our understanding of the demographic transition, which suggested that death rates, and then birthrates, would decline in industrialized states as affluence increased and industrialism matured.

Commoner acknowledged that a significant portion of the world's population did not get enough to eat, but he also linked developing world population growth to the expansion of Western industrial capitalism. In his Earth Day talk at Brown University, he recognized that many countries in the world suffered from overpopulation, but noted that this was a result of "the exploitation of the human and natural resources of the underdeveloped world by the technologically advanced nations." Citing Nathan Keyfitz's demographic analysis of the effects of colonialism, Commoner argued that "the development of industrial capitalism in western nations in the period 1800–1950 resulted in the development of a one billion excess world population, largely in the tropics, as a result of exploitation of these areas for raw materials (with the resultant need for labor) during the period of colonialism."[67] But whereas improved living conditions—roads, communications, engineering, agricultural and medical services—were important steps toward realizing the demographic transition in colonial regions, Commoner noted that the resultant wealth "did not remain in the colony." Moreover, the developed world's subsequent adoption of synthetic materials after World War II "replaced tropical raw materials with synthetic ones," resulting in a diminished market for the underdeveloped world's natural resources.[68] As Commoner the historian summarized, after decolonization the former colonial powers cut the developing world loose. The increased population in the developing world benefited from modern medicines and agricultural technologies such as insecticides, fertilizers, and machinery—further reducing the death rate—but lacked the markets to secure higher standards of living in the postcolonial period, thereby maintaining high birth rates and inhibiting the crucial second phase of the demographic transition. Rather than declining, human population exploded.

Commoner stated that the wealth derived from colonial exploitation assisted in completing the demographic transition in the colonizing nation, and not its colony. "Thus colonialism involves a kind of demographic parasitism," he argued, "The second population-balancing phase of the demographic transition in the advanced country is fed by the suppression of that same phase in the colony." To Commoner, this parasitism was responsible for the inequitable rate of development among the nations of the world. "As the wealth of the exploited nations were [*sic*] diverted to the more powerful ones," Commoner told the International Convocation on the World Population Crisis in 1974, "their power, and with it their capacity to exploit increased. The gap between the wealth of nations grew as the rich were fed by the poor."[69] And now the world felt itself gripped in a potentially devastating population crisis. Commoner concluded on Earth Day: "The population explosion is a cost of the western industrial society that we are so proud of."[70] The previous December, at an American Association for the Advancement of Science symposium titled "Is There an Optimum Level of Population?," Commoner had charged: "The population crisis is the huge hidden cost of the wealth accumulated in the advanced nations as a result of the Industrial Revolution. If the advanced nations are now confronted with the urgent need to pay this long-delayed debt, there is at least the moral consolation that it is their own."[71]

Because Commoner felt that the population crisis in the developing world was the result of colonial exploitation, he reacted vociferously to the neo-Malthusians' more draconian solutions to overpopulation. He rejected Ehrlich's suggestion that coercive birth control policies might need to be instituted, and he was particularly disgusted by the lifeboat ethics proposed by more radical neo-Malthusians such as Garrett Hardin. In articles in *Bioscience* and *Psychology Today,* Hardin had constructed a tenuous philosophical discussion on how the developed world might be justified in turning its back on the underdeveloped countries and their population problems as a means of ensuring their own survival. The Earth and its resources were like a lifeboat, and too many people threatened to sink it; in order to save the lifeboat, the developed world might sensibly refuse to help the underdeveloped populations unless they adopted drastic measures to reduce their numbers. In *The Closing Circle,* Commoner referred to Hardin's population positions as "faintly masked . . . barbarism."[72]

Commoner insisted that "the so-called 'lifeboat ethic' would compound the original evil of colonialism by forcing its victims to forego [*sic*] the humane course toward a balanced population—improvement of living standards—and to reduce their birthrate while still far short of that goal, or if they refuse, to abandon them to destruction."[73] Commoner's own solution to the population crisis was radically different. "If the root cause of world population crisis is poverty," he argued in 1974, "then to end it we should abolish poverty. And if poverty is the grossly unequal distribution of the world's wealth among the nations of the world, then to end poverty, and with it the population crisis, we need to redistribute that wealth, among nations and within them."[74] In effect, Commoner urged scholars, environmentalists, and policy makers to extend their examination of the population crisis beyond the scope of the ecological problems to which it contributed, in order to recognize that human population growth was—in his reading—a feature of a larger system of human oppression. To Commoner, the relationship between the subjugation of nature and the subjugation of increasing numbers of people was an essential facet of drawing ecological questions into the social limelight.

And it mattered how the public responded to the population crisis. In light of Earth Day's success and the momentum environmentalism enjoyed in the early 1970s, there were grounds for being optimistic that more environmental progress would be realized. But to Commoner, the neo-Malthusian solution to population growth was not progress, but rather a big step in the opposite direction. On a panel with Ehrlich and his fellow neo-Malthusian Garrett Hardin at the December 1970 meeting of the American Association for the Advancement of Science, Commoner argued that "saying that none of our pollution problems can be solved without getting at population first is a copout of the worst kind."[75] Commoner's more extensive critique came the following year in *The Closing Circle,* where he stated that Ehrlich had succumbed to the temptation of finding a simplistic solution to a complicated problem. "Since the basic problems are themselves biological," he argued, "there is a temptation to short-circuit the complex web of economic, social, and political issues and to seek direct biological solutions."[76] Commoner was convinced, however, that such reductionist attempts would ultimately fail. "In the long run," he insisted, "effective social action must be based on an understanding of the origin of the problem which it intends to solve."[77] Because he was convinced that polluting technologies and the free market that produced them caused the environmental crisis, developing biological solutions—as advocated by Ehrlich—to social problems was misguided.

Commoner wrote *The Closing Circle* partly in response to his portrayal in the 2 February 1970 issue of *TIME,* in which he had been touted as the "Paul Revere of ecology," with "a classroom of millions."[78] As a result, Commoner had become a household name, and in response to the celebrity and authority that *TIME* afforded him, he wrote *The Closing Circle* to justify his standing. He took advantage of the opportunity to explain his own positions more carefully, and in so doing, mounted a harsh criticism of Ehrlich's neo-Malthusian argument.[79]

More significant than the "population explosion" to which Ehrlich alluded, Commoner claimed, was that the Earth had experienced a "civilization explosion."[80] The widely accepted occurrence of an environmental crisis, he wrote, "tells us that there is something seriously wrong with the way in which human beings have occupied their habitat, the earth."[81] Commoner argued that the environmental crisis emerged as a result of poor technological decisions coming out of World War II. The war led to "not only a great outburst of technological innovation, but also an equally large upsurge in environmental pollution."[82] Commoner believed that Ehrlich's biological interpretation of the causes of the environmental crisis failed to appreciate the socially irresponsible uses of technology and the related overconsumption of material resources in the developed world, which, if left unchecked, would continue to present increased social and environmental problems. To Commoner, the pollution from ill-conceived technologies was the natural expression of the free economy, driven at all costs to increase productivity, output, and profit. In response to this conundrum, Ehrlich's population thesis had argued that the only way to limit output was to reduce population. To Commoner, this solution was "equivalent to attempting to save a leaking ship by lightening the load and forcing passengers overboard. One is constrained to ask if there isn't something radically wrong with the ship."[83] Suggesting that a better solution would be more public access to and control over industrial and environmental decisions, Commoner concluded that the rampant proliferation and dissemination of polluting technologies was directly related to the capitalist system. Capitalism promoted a growth-at-all-costs free enterprise system that excused environmental waste in the name of increased profit margins. In *The Closing Circle,* Commoner promoted more environmentally responsible commerce through incentives and penalties on polluting industries. At its most basic level, Commoner wanted to transform modern technology "to meet the inescapable demands of the ecosystem."[84] This strategy necessarily required radical changes in the capitalist system.

However, for all the fire that Commoner flung at Ehrlich, the neo-Malthusians, and free market capitalism, *The Closing Circle* was, first of all, a book about ecology and how ecology might help the public to make sense of the environmental crisis. In spite of its growing popularity through the 1960s, ecology had not yet developed a series of cohesive, simplifying generalizations—laws—as more traditional scientific disciplines such as physics had done. Commoner's introduction of an informal set of laws of ecology was arguably the centerpiece—certainly the best-remembered and most often repeated aspect—of *The Closing Circle*. Commoner posited that the laws of ecology could be reduced to four:

1. Everything is connected to everything else.
2. Everything must go somewhere.
3. Nature knows best.
4. There is no such thing as a free lunch.

Commoner's Four Laws of Ecology are a social and historical phenomenon embedded in the culture of crisis that pervaded the 1970s. They were not incontrovertible scientific fiats, but rather an articulate road map for Americans seeking to understand the environmental crisis. Rather than representing an infallible interpretation of the workings of complex ecosystems, Commoner's laws—blending popular, holistic interpretations of ecology with some biological truisms—served as a useful synthesis that was accessible to a lay audience and advanced Rachel Carson's contention that humans and nature constituted what the sociologist Ulrich Beck has called "a *solidarity of living things*."[85] Commoner's laws were not scientific in nature, but rather generalizations that applied most effectively to the foibles of unchecked technological progress.[86]

Much of the research in *The Closing Circle* was not new—chapters on nuclear fallout and Lake Erie were similar to material that had been worked into *Science and Survival*—but like *Silent Spring* and *The Population Bomb, The Closing Circle* vaulted its author into the public limelight. The celebrity status of the post-Earth Day ecologists on the front line of modern environmentalism helped keep the movement in the mainstream, but the public dissension in the ranks between Commoner and Ehrlich threatened to obfuscate the movement's overriding message. The pollution versus population dispute between Commoner and Ehrlich emerged as one of a series of antagonistic debates within modern environmentalism, illuminating the histories of environmental philosophy and politics as well as the continuing divisions within the contemporary movement. That public disagreement—outlined in *The Closing Circle*—would demonstrate that environmentalism represented less a set of policies than a movement that sought to redefine human values in order to address the existing environmental crisis, but it also illustrated the precarious balance between disparate priorities. The dispute stemmed from Commoner's distinctly humanist (and socialist) approach to the environmental crisis, whereas Ehrlich's interests lay predominantly in the naturalist (and more liberal) sphere. While Ehrlich interpreted the crisis as principally biological or ecological in nature, Commoner explained the environmental crisis as having social origins firmly rooted in the irresponsible exploitations of technology by capitalism and colonialism.

While Commoner and Ehrlich championed pollution and population, respectively, as explanations for the environmental crisis, still other "jeremiads" pointed toward affluence, poverty, religion, and human nature, among others.[87] The diversity of interests within the modern environmental movement—from wilderness preservation to urban health policies—precluded the progress of a unified "environmental" agenda. Among these divisions, the humanist-naturalist split was the most fundamental, but it was also representative of the changing landscape of American environmentalism after World War II. Whereas the prewar conservation movement had been predominantly shaped and led by white elites, the new environmental leadership had acquired considerable momentum from a variety of minority groups. This phenomenon manifested itself not only in a broadening of the mainstream agenda from conservation to a wider sense of environmentalism, which incorporated more social concerns, but also in the new movement's leading philosophers. Indeed, by the first Earth Day, many of the most vocal, articulate, and charismatic leaders of the movement did not come from the Anglo middle class. Commoner and Ehrlich—both of Jewish, immigrant descent—were the most prominent examples of this trend, but lawyers from immigrant backgrounds, such as Ralph Nader (Lebanese) and Victor Yannacone (Italian) also represented a burgeoning of more radical concern and activity on environmental issues.[88] Their emergence in the conservation movement resulted in a significant shift in environmental priorities, from land use policies to public health. This trend allowed the prominence of Commoner's more humanist environmental politics and *TIME's* making Commoner its appointed leader of modern environmentalism in America.

But the new and more diverse environmental movement was hardly uniform, as the debate between Commoner and Ehrlich made clear. Born 29 May 1932, Ehrlich grew up with naturalist tendencies, catching butterflies and frogs near his Maplewood, New Jersey, home.[89] A mentor at the American Museum of Natural History in Manhattan encouraged him to do butterfly research, so he studied zoology at the University of Pennsylvania. After earning his B.S. in 1953, Ehrlich pursued graduate studies in biology at the University of Kansas, finishing his Ph.D. in 1957. He received a fellowship from the National Institutes of Health and continued his entomological research at the Chicago Academy of Sciences, eventually taking a position at Stanford in 1959. He was promoted to Bing Professor of Biology by 1967, the year before *The Population Bomb* was published. While still at college, Ehrlich had been influenced by one of the major trends in the naturalist writing of the late 1940s, which warned of the imminent environmental crisis and the dangers posed therein by human population growth. At college, he read Osborn's *Our Plundered Planet* and Vogt's *Road to Survival,* both of which argued persuasively that overpopulation and the abuse of natural resources would lead to widespread famine and impoverishment.[90] Ehrlich was convinced that overpopulation represented the most significant threat to the environment. While overpopulation introduced an unmistakably human element into his environmental message, his concerns maintained a naturalist flavor. Aside from the social repercussions, too many people compromised the vitality of the Earth's ecosystems. Urban expansion reduced habitat for various plant and animal species.

Commoner and Ehrlich were the products of divergent politics, influences, and perspectives. The combination of Commoner's early fascination with nature and his immersion within the radical social activism in New York nurtured his more humanist and socialist solutions to resolving the environmental crisis. Similarly, Ehrlich's liberal and suburban upbringing influenced his penchant for naturalism.[91] Whereas Commoner's politics were overtly socialist, Ehrlich's were far more ambiguous. His population control policy suggestions appealed to such divergent political agendas as Chinese population policy, New Left opposition to consumerism, and conservative diatribes on Mexican immigration and high birthrates among minorities. Commoner criticized Ehrlich and others who advocated simple population control, because he felt they were missing the real cause of environmental decline. "The favorite statistic is that the U.S. contains 6 to 7 percent of the world population but consumes more than half the world's resources and is responsible for that fraction of the total environmental pollution," Commoner told his pre-Earth Day audience. "But this statistic hides another vital fact: that not everyone in the U.S. is so affluent. For that reason the simple test of the slogan 'Consume Less' as a basis for social action on the environment would be to tell it to the blacks in the ghetto. The message will not be very well received for there are many people in this country who consume less than is needed to sustain a decent life."[92] To Commoner, the overpopulation perspective blamed humanity's consumption and reproduction for the environmental crisis, but ignored the corporate interests that disproportionately plundered natural resources and spewed pollutants into the environment.

With characteristic panache, Commoner insisted that "pollution begins not in the family bedroom, but in the corporate board-room."[93]

Reading between the lines, Commoner interpreted in Ehrlich's message—likely more spitefully than accurately—a social Darwinist argument in favor of population control.[94] In 1803, Malthus had revised and significantly expanded his essay on population. This second essay has had a much larger impact on contemporary thought, largely because of Malthus's severe attack on the poor. Malthus saw that lower classes tended to reproduce far faster than the middle and upper classes, and argued that the poor ought not to be entitled to any kind of relief, claiming that any assistance would only result in their producing more offspring, meaning more poverty. In a strange reversal of traditional understandings, Malthus believed that poverty could be attributed to too much charity, rather than not enough. In so doing, he attacked England's Poor Laws; he opposed any notions that advocated egalitarianism on the grounds that excessive population growth among the poor would only dilute the middle classes of society. Several generations before the philosopher Herbert Spencer coined the phrase, Malthus was effectively referring to a socioeconomic "survival of the fittest." Certainly Ehrlich's population control colleague, Garrett Hardin, was not above such arguments, but sometimes Ehrlich's rhetoric came in line with these less savory arguments in favor of population control, especially when he talked about involuntary population control. Commoner particularly objected to Ehrlich's suggestion that coercion might be necessary in order to arrest the world's population growth because of its social implications, which "would condemn most of the people of the world to the material level of the barbarian, and the rest, the 'fortunate minorities,' to the moral level of the barbarian."[95] Ehrlich recognized this problem. "I agree with Commoner when he worries about the political implications of what I'm saying," he told Anne Chisholm. "I worry about them myself."[96]

Because of their divergent humanist-naturalist beliefs, Commoner and Ehrlich differed on whom they thought the environmental movement should be courting. Ehrlich's naturalism clearly catered to middle-class outdoors enthusiasts, who already comprised the majority of the movement. In contrast, Commoner's humanism was more attractive to the urban middle class and carried more weight or credibility among minorities and groups whom environmental politics had heretofore marginalized. Commoner raised the public's awareness of the relationship between living

FIFTY CENTS
FEBRUARY 2, 1970
TIME
Environment: Nixon's New Issue
ECOLOGIST BARRY COMMONER
The Emerging Science of Survival

Top: Warren Weaver, ca. 1955. Courtesy of the Rockefeller Archive Center.
Bottom: Commoner with physiologist and former AAAS president Detlev Bronk at the council session of the AAAS annual meeting in Atlanta in December 1955, where they supported the antisegregation platform spearheaded by the anthropologist Margaret Mead (at left). Photo courtesy of Barry Commoner.

Commoner measuring the effect of light on the free radicals formed during photosynthesis in the alga *Chlorella* at Washington University in 1956. Behind him is Dr. Jack Townsend, a Washington University physicist and "electronics wizard," who built the electron spin resonance machine in the foreground. At the time, this spectrometer was unique in its ability to tolerate water, and paved the way for Commoner's innovative work on free radicals. Photo courtesy of Barry Commoner.

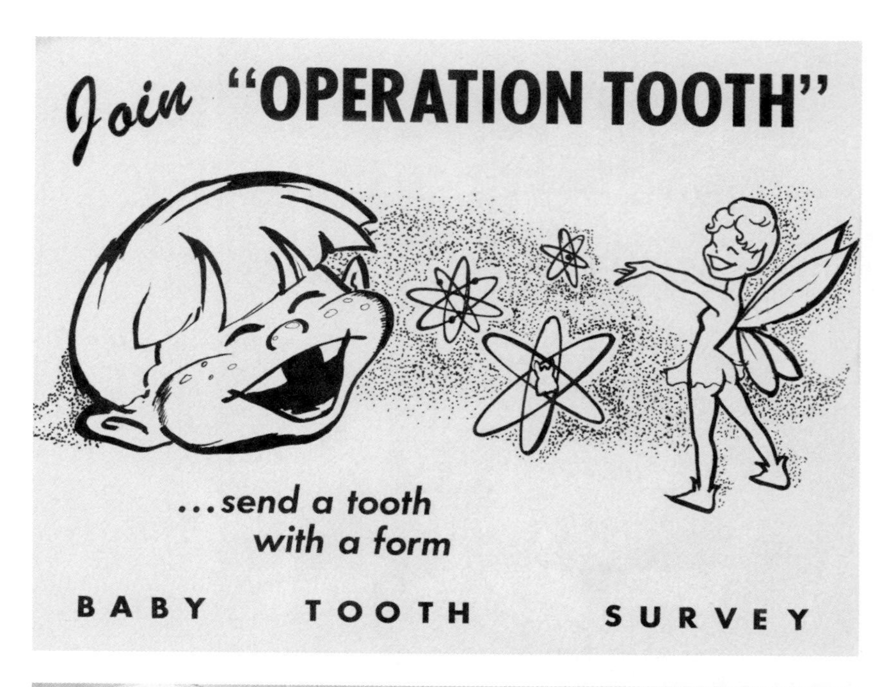

This card shows that I
am a member of the

OPERATION TOOTH CLUB

with full privileges, and
am entitled to wear the
membership button.

Because science needs my teeth when they fall out, I will continue sending them to "Operation Tooth".

Signature

Top: Committee for Nuclear Information Baby Tooth Survey poster. Western Historical Manuscripts Collection, University of Missouri-St. Louis.
Bottom: Button and membership certificate for the Operation Tooth Club, sent to children who provided baby teeth for the Committee for Nuclear Information's Baby Tooth Survey. Western Historical Manuscript Collection, University of Missouri-St. Louis.

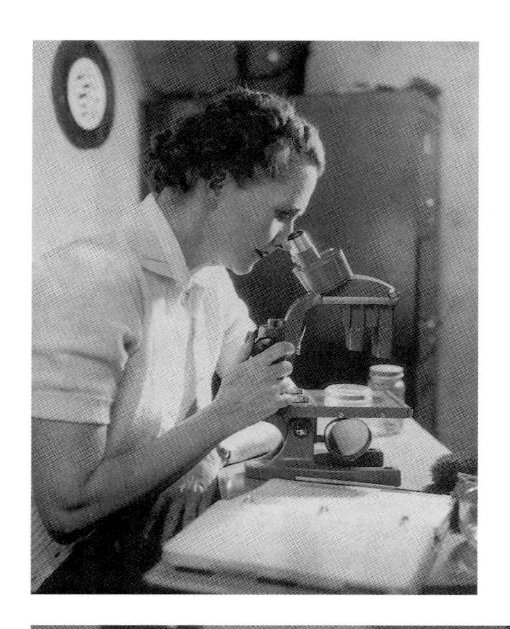

Top: Rachel Carson. Photo from the Brooks Studio; used by permission of the Rachel Carson Council, Inc.
Bottom: Commoner at a 1968 Las Vegas press conference on nuclear bomb tests; Atomic Energy Commission representatives at left, and the future editor of *Environment*, Sheldon Novick, at right. Photo courtesy of Barry Commoner.

© 1970 by Herblock in the *Washington Post*.
Opposite, top: Paul Ehrlich in his greenhouses at Stanford University, April 1972. Photo © Ilka Hartmann, 2006.
Opposite, bottom: Commoner at a conference on lead pollution in St. Louis, May 1971. Photo courtesy of Barry Commoner.

Get the leadout
Conference on lead poisoning in St. Louis

Top: Commoner at the 1970 Committee for Environmental Information annual meeting at the Ethical Culture Society in St. Louis. Behind him is the folk singer and environmental activist Pete Seeger. Western Historical Manuscript Collection, University of Missouri-St. Louis.
Bottom: Participants in a course on problems of environment and development given by Commoner and the staff of the Center for the Biology of Natural Systems at Washington University, under the sponsorship of the United Nations Environmental Program, for graduate students from developing countries, July 1976. Photo courtesy of Barry Commoner.

spaces and the environment. Whereas the mainstream conservation movement had previously concentrated its efforts on wildlife and wildland preservation, Commoner advocated a more social interpretation of the immediacy of the environmental crisis. While Ehrlich saw his population critique as an addition to the existing environmental paradigm, Commoner envisioned environmentalism as part of a more holistic social revolution. Commoner wanted the environmental movement to be socially progressive. He interpreted a healthy environment as a necessary condition for promoting a more egalitarian society.

At the time of its publication, *The Closing Circle* was arguably the most comprehensive work on the environmental crisis and its causes. While Commoner ultimately narrowed his critique to a single cause—the profit-first mentality of the capitalist economy seeking reductions in costs of production by making use of cheaper, but polluting, technologies—his exposé claimed to have established hypotheses and tested them. Commoner was the first to admit that even science was subjective, but *The Closing Circle*'s tone seemed more rational and, perhaps, less of a jeremiad, than works such as *The Population Bomb,* even if his conclusions insisted upon radical changes in environmental activities and political and economic systems. In presenting such overtly political and social statements, Commoner reinforced his long-standing faith in public participation and the role of scientific information. The environmental crisis represented more of a social than a scientific problem. Any solution to the crisis was most fundamentally political, so the scientific community's primary duty was to disseminate scientific knowledge to enable and empower the public so that it was sufficiently informed to make its own value judgments. It was a familiar refrain.

If Ehrlich approved of Commoner's environmental and social concern, he was critical of Commoner's conclusions, his science, and his dismissal of the dangers of overpopulation. Moreover, he became infuriated by the manner in which his views on *The Closing Circle* were publicized. In December 1971 Ehrlich and the physicist John P. Holdren wrote a very critical review of *The Closing Circle* for the *Bulletin of the Atomic Scientists,* which was to appear in the spring. In their review they called the book "inexplicably inconsistent and dangerously misleading."[97] The crux of their critique rested on Commoner's complete reduction of demographic factors to an inconsequential aspect of the environmental crisis. Ehrlich and Holdren introduced a formula by which to measure the various factors of pollution. They argued that environmental impact (pollution) was the product of population, affluence, and technology; the number of people, the quantity of goods people consume, and the technologies people employ to produce the goods.[98] They presented the compact formula as

$$I = P \bullet A \bullet T$$

Essentially, this simple equation dictated that an increase in population *or* in consumption *or* in polluting technologies would result in an increase in environmental impact. According to Ehrlich and Holdren, the differences between Commoner and Ehrlich, therefore, depended upon the emphasis given to each of the three factors. Ehrlich and Holdren stressed population and affluence, while Commoner highlighted the significance of technology, arguing that population and affluence were intimately linked to technology. Using their formula, Ehrlich and Holdren argued that Commoner's adherence to technology as the only significant factor of the equation to the environmental crisis was problematic. "Obviously," they contended, "*the actual magnitude of the environmental deterioration engendered by an adverse change in technology depends strongly both on the initial levels of population and affluence.*"[99] Ehrlich and Holdren also accused Commoner of bad science, stating that "*examination of the basic mathematics alone, irrespective of the definitions and analysis behind the numbers Commoner presents, shows that the relationships are not what he claims.*"[100] They concluded by defending their population control position, alluding to Commoner's analogy of saving a leaking ship. "If a leaking ship were tied up to a dock," they posited, "and passengers were still swarming up the gangplank, a competent captain would keep any more from boarding *while* he manned the pumps and attempted to repair the leak."[101] But while Ehrlich calculated population and technology as independent variables in his equation—and one just had to assess the relative weight of each in the formula—Commoner contended that population and technology were not independent variables at all. Rather, they were dependent on forms of social organization and control that existed beyond the constraints of the IPAT formula.

Ehrlich and Holdren distributed drafts of their review widely among scientists, journalists, and environmentalists with an accompanying letter that indicted Commoner and his ideas as being dangerous.[102] The *Bulletin* informed Commoner that it intended to publish the review, titled "One-Dimensional Ecology," in its April 1972 issue and invited him to submit a rejoinder. Commoner accepted the invitation, but insisted that his rebuttal appear in the same issue. Because Commoner could not meet the April deadline, *Bulletin* editor Richard S. Lewis delayed publication of "One-Dimensional Ecology" and Commoner's response until the May issue. In the interim, Commoner's own journal, *Environment,* "scooped" the *Bulletin* by printing the Ehrlich and Holdren review and Commoner's response in its April edition. Ehrlich and Holdren were outraged. In a published communication to the *Bulletin,* they wrote that they "were shocked to discover that Barry Commoner and *Environment* had pirated 'One-Dimensional Ecology' and published it without your knowledge or ours. We cannot imagine how Commoner could ethically have done this." They expressed indignation that *Environment* would publish an "uncorrected preprint . . . circulated with a letter stating that it was a 'preliminary copy,' that it was 'not for publication.'" To add insult to injury, *Environment* had removed Ehrlich and Holdren's title.[103]

Commoner clearly violated standard academic ethics in printing "One-Dimensional Ecology" in *Environment* without permission and prior to its publication in the *Bulletin.* And while he openly defended the decision to scoop the review as his duty—part of his involuntary responsibility—as a public citizen to spread information,[104] the larger rationale seemed to stem from his intent to defend his position more publicly after Ehrlich and Holdren had circulated their draft so widely. Publication of his rebuttal in the *Bulletin* would hardly have reached the same audience as the draft; because *Environment* had a larger audience, perhaps Commoner justified his decision as a means of self-defense. Indeed, the draft's copyright did appear to be in dispute. *Environment* editor Sheldon Novick wrote to *Environment*'s Science Advisory Board in defense of his decision to publish the review: "The Ehrlich-Holdren article had been published without a proper copyright notice, in a manner which placed it in the public domain, and which left me free to republish it if I wished."[105]

But if ego was privately at the heart of the bitterness—and in that department, both Commoner and Ehrlich were exceptionally well endowed—principle was the public rationale. Ehrlich began transcribing telephone communications with Lewis and *Environment* scientific director Kevin

Shea, and zealously solicited support from leading scientists and activists around the country as a means of enhancing and publicizing his position as the wronged and aggrieved party in the debate. In the meantime, by distributing his review of *The Closing Circle* so widely, he had very consciously launched a concerted attack on Commoner to which Commoner could not easily respond. His shock at Commoner's parry was, at best, contrived. For his part, in his complicity in the theft of Ehrlich and Holdren's paper, Commoner deliberately avoided the high road. And his confrontational manner only intensified the dispute. Just over a month later, at the United Nations Conference on the Human Environment in Stockholm, Commoner and many of his followers—students and international scientists who criticized family planning as a plot to reinforce the hegemony of the white and industrialized northern countries—crashed a population session and prevented Ehrlich from presenting his argument.[106]

In spite of the ugliness that pervaded their encounter, however, one is inclined to find something admirable in the disparate motivations—though not the methods—that brought both combatants to the fray. Both Commoner and Ehrlich recognized what was at stake in their dispute. Ehrlich very sincerely wanted to quell the public argument, fearing that any public disagreement between the two would "'split the environmental movement' and reduce the chances of effective action toward environmental improvement."[107] To Ehrlich, there seemed "little purpose in deluding the public about the need to grapple simultaneously with overpopulation, excessive affluence, and faulty technology," but to Commoner, silencing the debate was unconscionable and in violation of his commitment to public discourse and even the freedom to express dissent.[108] Population control would not resolve the environmental crisis; of this Commoner was sure. Making it a priority would impede real environmental improvement, especially if population growth was mitigated by several other social factors and not strictly a biological phenomenon. Moreover, Commoner was concerned that substantial attention to population questions would divert attention from what he considered to be the more pressing environmental issues: polluting technology and a capitalist means of production that endorsed growing world poverty and a concentration of wealth.

And while Commoner handled the situation poorly—and even tried to silence Ehrlich in Stockholm—he did genuinely believe in the importance of public discourse and the value of disagreement. A false conformity, he argued, would do an even greater disservice to the environmental agenda; there was a big difference between discourse and compromise. Commoner defended *Environment*'s decision to print "One-Dimensional Ecology" for a broader audience by insisting that "if there is in fact a real and important difference between my views of the origins of the environmental crisis and Ehrlich's, then *both of us are obliged to express them openly;* otherwise the mechanism by which science generates the truth—open discussion—is thwarted and our obligations, as scientists, to inform the public, evaded."[109] There is little question that he could have absorbed criticism more diplomatically and that his posturing inevitably hurt his position more than it helped, but Commoner was a hardened political warrior and was reluctant to compromise or cede any ground. What had long been one of his heroic characteristics became, in this instance, a blinding weakness.

Commoner did not jump over the line with both feet, but criticisms from outsiders suggested that he did come rather close to finding himself on the wrong side of the divide between critical intellectual and ideologue. On the wrong side of that separation, Donald Worster has argued, social critics "become prisoners of ideology rather than masters of it."[110] Indeed, Commoner and Ehrlich both suffered publicly and professionally as a result of their protracted dispute. Letters to both the *Bulletin* and *Environment* indicated that audiences—professional and popular alike—were tiring of the debate. "Perhaps I am the only reader who feels this way," one letter began, "but I think that Ehrlich and Commoner deserve each other, and should spare the rest of us their tedious controversies."[111] An appeal for peace between Commoner and Ehrlich, and a renewed alliance between their humanist and naturalist positions in their combined efforts to protect the environment, came from a rather unlikely source. In a letter to the editor of *Environment* in June 1972, the folksinger Pete Seeger offered a proverbial olive branch. In response to "Dispute," published a couple of months earlier, Seeger began by applauding both Ehrlich and Commoner, appreciating the interchange but hoping that it would not turn vindictive. "Commoner has convinced me," he wrote, "that technology and our private profit politics and society must be radically changed and quickly. But I'm still working hard for Zero Population Growth, because . . . it's a big world problem." Seeger rejected the false dichotomy presented in the humanist-naturalist debate and insisted that he was on both sides. "The world is the concern of everyone," he added. Seeger's interest in linking and promoting population and pollution control globally was that such a movement would serve as "one of the world's greatest educational drives." Seeger saw the need for limits, but they did not need to come singularly from one place. While he appreciated the critical significance of a more egalitarian society, he also confessed that he wanted his descendants "to have room to walk on a lonely beach, or climb a wilderness mountain, or yodel and make noise occasionally for the fun of it. . . . The less crowded this earth will be, the better for them."[112]

Seeger was right to address the manufactured division between humanists and naturalists. His comments in *Environment* demonstrated that the chasm between naturalist and humanist interests was largely conceptual, and that, from an activist standpoint, both were relatively compatible. After all, Rachel Carson's seminal work, *Silent Spring,* which warned against the dangers of DDT, contained both humanist and naturalist messages, and in this respect, *Silent Spring*'s significance in the history of American environmentalism can hardly be understated.[113] Carson lamented DDT's assault on birds and nature, but she also wrote vigorously on the dangers it presented to humans, effectively balancing the impact of both social and biological factors. But this is not to say that the Commoner-Ehrlich debate was moot. Carson had the luxury of writing when environmentalism had not yet effectively broken into the mainstream. As in many other social movements, harmony prevailed within the environmental movement, as the philosopher Andrew Feenberg has noted, "precisely in proportion to the burden of exclusion carried by those brave enough to join."[114] Environmentalists discriminated between their priorities only after they had entered the mainstream. The Commoner-Ehrlich debate, therefore, was historically significant because it marked the first serious fracture within the movement since the energy instilled in it by *Silent Spring* and Earth Day. Commoner's and Ehrlich's disparate opinions rested on the relative significance they afforded to biological and social factors, but also on their interpretations of science's role in establishing a cure. For Commoner, every feature of the environmental crisis was the symptom of social problems relating to capitalism; scientists could search for a panacea, but the ultimate decisions belonged to the public. For Ehrlich, population growth was the product of biological processes that had gone out of control; scientists needed to use their authority to lead attempts to reduce its growth.

Back when the Committee for Nuclear Information was engaging the Atomic Energy Commission in the debate over aboveground nuclear weapons testing, Commoner was particularly concerned about the impact that debate might have on the public and especially on its trust in science. While he was adamant that citizens not entrust experts with all the decision-making powers, he maintained considerable faith in science done properly. During the often ugly struggle against nuclear weapons, Commoner was conscious that his attack on the eminent scientists of the Atomic Energy Commission might confuse and thereby alienate the public from that crucial topic, and he worked very carefully to ensure that the public was both adequately involved and informed. For Commoner, the dangers of the post-World War II technological revolution signified not just the need to reengage scientists in a dialogue, but now also to include the public. It was no longer possible to argue privately within the scientific community over issues that had more social implications than scientific ones. Commoner firmly believed that scientists needed to be a good deal more open in their disagreements and disabuse citizens of their belief that they could leave these problems to the experts. "Citizens are sometimes disturbed by a disagreement among scientists," claimed an editorial in the May 1962 issue of the Greater St. Louis Citizens' Committee for Nuclear Information's bulletin, *Nuclear Information,* on just that issue. "They look toward science as a means of getting at objective truth." But disagreement, the editorial continued, was a healthy part of the scientific process: "open publication and criticism is the way in which science gradually improves its knowledge and in time develops a body of information which is accepted by all scientists."[115] The editorial, titled "When Scientists Disagree," sought to allay public concerns about the growing levels of conflict and confrontation among scientists with respect to issues pertaining to nuclear fallout. By 1962, the Committee for Nuclear Information's battle against the Atomic Energy Commission for control over nuclear information was at its height. The committee interpreted public scientific debate as a valuable "process which can guide laymen in their effort to find and understand the best scientific information available."[116] Prompted by increasing government secrecy on atomic issues, the mounting disagreement within the scientific community about the potential hazards of nuclear testing struck a chord with the public, which escalated its concern over the Atomic Energy Commission's authority on questions of atomic responsibility.

One of the interesting features of the Commoner-Ehrlich debate was the manner in which they treated their respective positions as vital to the success of the public information movement. In a sense, Commoner and Ehrlich were engaged in a kind of ecological brinksmanship, in which neither could back down without his position being deemed the less consequential. Further, the politico-scientists were effective at learning and conforming to press standards of newsworthiness. And controversy is a necessary component. So was the power of the sound bite. Commoner and Ehrlich were both dynamic, charismatic, and distinguished scientists. And both had learned how to effectively communicate to all kinds of audiences. Ironically, then, the Commoner-Ehrlich debate showcased two politico-scientists at the height of their powers. Just before the fall. In the end, the media got in the way. In scrambling to present stories on this delicious controversy between two of the most prominent ecologists, the media simplified their arguments to the extent that they no longer really represented their respective positions. Ehrlich never suggested that population was the sole explanation for the environmental crisis and that minorities or particular religious groups should be further marginalized by mainstream population concerns, and Commoner never implied that the Earth could hold an infinite number of humans and their growing consumption. But media oversimplification was the devil's bargain of the politico-scientists' entry into the mainstream. Their arguments were far more nuanced and complicated, but in using the media to convey their message, they had, to an extent, been hoist with their own petard. Ultimately the debate contributed to an increased distrust of scientists and their warnings. Commoner would appreciate the irony: after two decades of attacking establishment science and insisting that the public should not trust specialists when it came to social and moral judgments, he found himself a victim of his own advice.

5

Biological Capital

> We must not delude ourselves with an idea that the past is recoverable. We are chained and pinioned in our moment. . . . What we recover from the past is an image of ourselves, and very likely our search sets out to find nothing other than just that.
>
> —Bernard DeVoto

If Commoner won the battle, he lost the war. Over the three decades since the Commoner-Ehrlich debate, a wide variety of scholars has come to support Commoner's position that social factors are the best indicators of population growth, and that increased affluence and higher levels of education—especially among women—are the most effective methods of reducing high birthrates. But for all that, Commoner very clearly lost the war. After Earth Day, after the protracted dispute over population, the mainstream environmental movement turned away from the radical social critique—presented by 1960s luminaries such as Commoner, Herbert Marcuse, and Rachel Carson—in favor of a more politically centrist path that tended to separate environmental decline and other pressing social issues. To a degree, this made sense as a means of bolstering the environmental message without diluting it and, arguably, made it more digestible to more people in the middle—or mainstream—strata of society. But to Commoner, it suggested the failure of a social movement that, in 1970, seemed poised to incite significant social change. The result was stratification and marked division between disparate social movements that Commoner had spent the 1960s trying to unite. As a result of losing the war, Commoner's message was relegated to a marginal place in the environmental discourse just at the moment that its prescience seemed almost incontrovertible.

To many, the 1970s was a period most aptly interpreted by "Doonesbury"'s characters, who, at decade's end, toasted "a kidney stone of a decade."[1] During the 1970s, the euphoria that followed World War II dissipated into tension, angst, and crisis, punctuated by the Watergate scandal, defeat in Vietnam, the oil embargo, and severe economic depression. Noting the popular response to such unsettling events, Tom Wolfe proclaimed the 1970s the "Me Decade," characterized by self-exploration, fragmentation, and separation; Christopher Lasch called it a "culture of narcissism," which involved living in the moment and for self, not predecessors or posterity.[2] "After the political turmoil of the sixties," wrote Lasch, "Americans . . . retreated to purely personal preoccupations."[3] A sort of spiritual hedonism swept American culture and helped to insulate Americans from the crises that pervaded public and political life. In a strange sense, it was a perfect and yet impossible condition for the burgeoning environmental consciousness that had progressively become an integral feature of the American mainstream through the 1960s. On the one hand, the narcissist demanded a clean and beautiful environment; on the other, there existed a popular disconnect between present, past, and future that rendered almost hopeless any efforts for effective, long-term environmental protection. The immediacy of the crises that struck the 1970s belied their historical origins, and public and policy makers alike exhibited little vision in scrambling for short-term fixes to bigger problems. Nowhere was this more apparent than in the popular response to the energy crisis and the continuing demand for cheap energy, pervasive since the economic boom after World War II.

The debate over the magnitude of environmental risks predated the 1970s, but it became a defining feature of the environmental landscape during a decade dominated by a series of crises. The decade began, of course, with Earth Day and the widespread recognition of an environmental crisis that demanded public and policy attention. After the unprecedented success of the first Earth Day, Denis Hayes and other Earth Day organizers targeted "the Dirty Dozen," the twelve congressmen with the worst environmental records; during the fall 1970 elections, seven of the twelve lost their seats and the environmental movement presented itself as a legitimate and powerful new force in Washington, D.C. This victory was followed by strong legislation to clean air and water, control pesticides and pesticide use, and protect endangered species.[4] The energy crisis in 1973 gave credibility to the warnings of environmentalists as oil shortages caused mass hysteria in the press and at the gas pump, but it also muted the broader environmental agenda and left Americans clamoring for cheap fuel and electricity, not responsible energy use and conservation. By the middle of the decade, America found itself consumed in a dire economic crisis, and the environmental momentum gained by successes early in the decade was dead. The primary significance of Commoner's activism during the 1970s, then, was to reassert and demonstrate the social and historical significance of the environmental crisis. Commoner had spent the 1950s and 1960s working to provide information about various environmental hazards; during the 1970s he battled against spreading social apathy fueled by cultural fragmentation to illustrate the inherent interconnectedness between environmental decline, economic failure, and social disillusionment. Most poignantly, Commoner emphasized the direct relationship between environmental protection and economic sustainability.

"We are living in a false prosperity," he warned in 1970. "Our burgeoning industry and agriculture has produced lots of food, many cars, huge amounts of power, and fancy new chemical substitutes. But for all these goods we have been paying a hidden price." That price was the destruction of the ecological system that supported not only human existence but also—ironically—the very industries that threatened it. "What this tells us," Commoner surmised, "is that our system of productivity is at the heart of the environmental problem."[5] Whereas Commoner had previously courted the public with his information and sometime jeremiads, he very consciously recognized that government and business needed to have environmental destruction explained in economic terms in order to be swayed by the gravity of the situation. Even before Earth Day, Commoner was conscious of this, and in a 1969 address at the eleventh annual meeting of the National Association of Business Economists, he translated the environmental crisis into economic terms:

> The environment makes up a huge, enormously complex living machine—the ecosphere—and on the integrity and proper functioning of that machine depends every human activity, including technology. Without the photosynthetic activity of green plants there would be no oxygen for our smelters and furnaces, let alone to support human and animal life. Without the action of plants and animals in aquatic systems, we can have no pure water to supply agriculture, industry, and the cities. Without the biological processes that have gone on in the soil for thousands of years, we would have neither food, crops, oil, nor coal. This machine is our

biological capital, the basic apparatus on which our total productivity depends. If we destroy it, our most advanced technology will come to naught and any economic and political system which depends on it will founder. Yet the major threat to the integrity of this biological capital is technology itself.[6]

The message was ecological, but it was also unmistakably and profoundly economic. And it was a damning indictment of the industrial forces behind the technological revolution. Commoner summarized these ideas in *The Closing Circle.* "Environmental problems seem to have an uncanny way of penetrating to the core of those issues that most gravely burden the modern world," he told his readers. "There are powerful links between the environmental crisis and the troublesome, conflicting demands on the earth's resources and on the wealth created from them by society."[7]

In economic terms, nature was a resource and pivotal to enterprise. But economists suggested that we also consider nature to be capital in order to make sense of the full relationship between economic systems and the natural environment. Indeed, in essence, nature is the world's basic capital or wealth. Not only does nature sustain human life, it also drives human economies with its resources. One of the most fundamental tenets of capitalism, however, is that societies should not consume their capital base to pay for current expenses. In order to realize real growth, economies need to separate wealth from income and live off of income rather than wealth; enterprises that consumed their capital and called it profit invariably went bankrupt.[8] During the 1970s, Commoner argued that, in principle, American technological systems threatened to unwittingly commit this gross blunder.

The transition of wealth or growth from one market to another belied the social costs hidden behind new, polluting industries, often registered in public health concerns and rising unemployment. Economic theory had no place for these kinds of costs. But because all industrial nations were pursuing a traditional economic model, Commoner warned that they were rapidly degrading and dissipating their economy and life-sustaining resource base, consuming capital assets, and counting it as profit. In economic terms, here was another iteration of the ongoing controversy over environmental risk.

In many respects, Commoner's explanation for the continuation of high levels of pollution and ecological destruction was strictly economic: it paid. "Soap companies significantly increased their profit per pound of cleaner sold when they switched from soap to detergents; truck lines are more profitable than railroads; synthetic plastics and fabrics are more profitable than leather, cotton, wool, or wood; nitrogen fertilizer is the corn farmer's most profit-yielding input; power companies claim that capital-intensive nuclear plants improve their rate of return; and as Henry Ford II has said, 'minicars make miniprofits.'"[9] Industrial pollution was widely recognized as the cost of postwar affluence; it represented jobs, productivity, and reduced prices of consumer goods and services. Because the petrochemical industry could manufacture synthetic fertilizers in huge quantities—which lowered production costs—synthetic fertilizers quickly came to dominate the market. Pollution controls, sustainable energy consumption, and greater efforts to ensure workplace safety and health were frequently marginalized because they reduced the scale of profits enjoyed by such high-polluting industries. Pollution, inefficient energy use, and the trivialization of worker safety became popularly accepted as the price of progress, but in reality they cumulatively constituted a critical example of the false prosperity that would drive 1970s America into an economic crisis. Controls, Commoner argued, were necessary to ensure that the economic system did not destroy the environment, thereby cannibalizing itself in the process.

More to the point, the real costs of pollution were not appearing accurately on the balance sheet. While private industries belched carcinogens into the environment, for example, the public suffered rising cancer rates.[10] Until fairly recently, economic theory made little room for environmental factors, but the rapid increase in environmental problems since World War II necessarily revised how exchanges took place in economic systems. In classical economic theory, the exchange of goods, services, and wealth is mutual and voluntary between the exchanging parties, but the technological boom after World War II created—or, rather, augmented—a context for external impacts that extended far beyond the control or interests of the exchanging parties. In *The Closing Circle,* Commoner stressed the significance of externalities: the infliction of involuntary, nonbeneficial, or indeed detrimental repercussions on another industry or the environment or the public. "Mercury benefits the chloralkali producer but harms the commercial fisherman," he observed.[11] With its pollution and unanticipated costs, the technological revolution had introduced a series of "external diseconomies," the external or third-party effects of commerce.[12] As early as 1966, Commoner saw this disconnect between the apparent and real costs of new technologies. "Many of our new technologies and their resultant industries have been developed without taking into account their cost in damage to the environment or the real value of the essential materials bestowed by environmental life processes," he told the National Industrial Conference Board. "While these costs often remain hidden in the past, now they have become blatantly obvious in the smog which blankets our cities and the pollutants which poison our water supplies. If we choose to allow this huge and growing debt to accumulate further, the environment may eventually be damaged beyond its capacity for self-repair."[13]

Air pollution was indeed an excellent example of external diseconomies. Concerns about air pollution were a prevalent part of the environmental crisis. The proliferation of carbon monoxide, sulfur oxides, hydrocarbons, nitrogen oxides, and particulate matter in ambient air posed—individually and in combination—serious health hazards. According to the political scientist Walter Rosenbaum, resulting property damage was also enormous.[14] A 1972 Environmental Protection Agency study estimated that the total annual toll of air pollution on Americans could approach $20 billion within five years. Of that sum, $7.6 billion consisted of destruction of materials and vegetation; almost $8 billion was associated with residential property damage; and health costs would exceed $9 billion. The Environmental Protection Agency study also acknowledged the conservative nature of its estimate by noting that its calculations anticipated the introduction of stringent air pollution abatement programs across the country. Those abatement programs did not materialize in the Environmental Protection Agency's five-year time frame.[15]

To Commoner, these externalities hid the true damage of the environmental crisis. "Environmental degradation represents a crucial, potentially fatal, *hidden* factor in the operation of the economic system," he argued in *The Closing Circle*.[16] Coal-burning power companies were among the greatest polluters of air. Pointing to the disparity between their rising profits as demand for electricity increased and the growing social and environmental costs, Commoner argued: "If power companies were required to show on electric bills the true cost of power to the consumer, they would have to include the extra laundry bills resulting from soot [from burning coal], the extra doctor bills resulting from emphysema, the extra maintenance bills due to erosion of buildings [from acid rain]." These were hidden expenses. "Their true account books are not in balance," Commoner continued, "and the deficit is being paid by the lives of the present population and the safety of future generations."[17] As a result of these kinds of externalities, Commoner argued, "the costs of environmental degradation are chiefly borne not by the producer, but by society as a whole."[18] If the public was involuntarily involved in paying these external costs, then surely they deserved a place in the debate over how such social and environmental costs should be determined. Commoner noted in *The Closing Circle:* "A business enterprise that pollutes the environment is therefore being subsidized by society; to this extent, the enterprise, though free, is not wholly private."[19] Because it was cheaper to produce nonreusable plastic containers for drinks than it was to use glass and then collect it for reuse, most bottling companies switched to plastic. Because it was cheaper to produce and purchase synthetic fertilizers rather than relying on the older systems of composting for nitrogen fixation, more synthetic fertilizers entered into water systems and introduced contamination problems "downstream." And here was the final stage of external diseconomies as they related to economic growth and the environmental crisis. More and more of the wealth accumulated in the hands of a select group of producers, while more and more of the environmental risk—the red ink on the balance sheet—was outsourced to the public in the form of pollution, health risks, and increasing waste disposal problems.

This question of external diseconomies also resonated among labor groups and served as further incentive for an alliance between labor and environmentalism. In their firsthand and long-term exposure to environmental pollutants during their manufacture, workers themselves had long been subsidizing a significant portion of the costs of production. Health risks associated with mining and factory work had long been established.[20] And occupational risks increased after World War II. In the mid-1970s, for example, vinyl chloride, the raw material used to make polyvinyl chloride (PVC), was linked to angiosarcoma of the liver, an unusual form of cancer that occurred in strikingly high numbers among workers in a number of polyvinyl chloride plants.[21] Further, polyvinyl chloride's relative ubiquity by the 1970s—it was present in tile floors, automobile upholstery, wallpaper, plumbing, and clothing—suggested that the health risks incurred in its production constituted an acceptable price, given its centrality to economic growth.[22] At the same time, however, it was clear that those who profited from the environmental risk were not those most directly exposed to the health hazards.

Assaults on the chemical industry and other industries resulted in the inadvertent propagation of the myth that there existed a natural conflict between environmentalism and the economy, and one had to be sacrificed for the benefit of the other.[23] Typically, it seemed that attempts to curtail economic growth resulted in job losses, a downward-spiraling economy, and labor's distrust of environmentalism. According to Robert Gottlieb, "The slogan 'No work, no food—Eat an environmentalist,' first heard in steel-producing communities during the 1973–75 recession and later in timber-producing regions, symbolized the potential fissures between environmental and worker constituencies."[24] Commoner acknowledged this problem in *The Closing Circle*. "The attempt to meet the real, social costs of environmental degradation, either through increased prices or reduced wages," he argued, "would appear to intensify the long-standing competition between capital and labor over the division of wealth produced by the private enterprise system and worsen the already intolerable incidence of poverty."[25] If industries were prevented from polluting, the argument went, jobs would be lost and the economy would suffer. The record certainly indicated as much. When Congress abandoned the supersonic transport project in 1971, environmentalists hailed an important environmental victory, but it came in opposition to the unions who supported the potential growth in jobs.[26] Similarly, in 1970, when environmentalists blocked the construction of a huge BASF chemical plant at Hilton Head, South Carolina, their success ensured the preservation of an area renowned for its natural beauty, but perpetuated high unemployment, a less publicized feature of the area.[27] At the same time, in Oregon, some unions and corporate interests organized together to oppose the "environmental McCarthyism" of local conservation groups determined to keep Oregon green.[28] Such incidents—and countless others across the country—placed labor and environmental interests on opposite sides of environmental decisions, but Commoner insisted that "these manifestations of an apparent built-in antagonism between labor's goals and concern for the environment are misleading."[29]

For Commoner, workplace health hazards such as the production of polychlorinated biphenyls (PCBs) were instrumental to the rise of the environmental crisis. "To a significant extent," he wrote in *Environment* in 1973, "the environmental crisis is an extension of problems that were once confined to the workplace to the community as a whole; likewise, the burden of these problems, which was once borne almost exclusively (and still most heavily) by the worker, is now shared by the entire population."[30] When the externality came home to roost, the public rose up in arms. The disconnect between labor and environmentalism stemmed more from a conceptual distance between the two interests than from any kind of economic division of interests once the real costs of production had been assessed.

PCBs were first produced commercially in 1929, but went into large-scale production after World War II, when they were used in electrical insulators, in heat-exchange and hydraulic systems, in plastics, tires, some textiles, and carbon paper. Like mercury and other toxic pollutants, PCBs resisted degradation and entered into the ecological food chain. In their chemical structure, PCBs resembled DDT, and ecologists were concerned that they were likely to pose similar dangers to the ecosystem. By the early 1930s, the relationship between the manufacture of PCBs and workers' health had already been established. Early workers in manufacturing plants experienced skin diseases such as chloracne—which resembled severe acne and covered their bodies with pustules—along with other ailments such as liver failure. Moreover, early public health specialists observed that PCBs were so stable that they could be carried home on workers' clothing, which frequently caused chloracne among workers' wives and children. "By the end of World War II," Commoner stated, "it was known, from *the workers' experience* that PCBs were so toxic that industrial techniques ought to be controlled in order to *avoid* exposure."[31]

In 1966, PCBs were identified in Baltic Sea fish, inciting a widespread concern about their health and environmental effects. By 1969, the Food and Drug Administration established acceptable limits for PCBs in foods, and in 1970, the Monsanto Company declared it had withdrawn PCBs from sale for uses which might lead to food contamination or other forms of ecological harm. Sales of PCBs in the United States dropped from a high of 75 million pounds in 1970 to about 35 million pounds in 1971. But from the PCB workers' standpoint, those controls were a long time coming. "Although the hazard from PCB was first discovered in the work place, in 1933, the problem was given relatively little scientific attention . . . until 30 years later, when it was first recognized as an *environmental hazard*." As Commoner suggested, the consequence was an environmental focus that tended to exclude human health from the spectrum of environmental concerns. "We seem to be better informed about the detailed biological effects of PCBs on quail and minnows than we are about their effects on human beings," he continued.[32]

In many respects, Commoner saw the new technologies that developed after World War II as being responsible for both the weakening of labor and the tension between labor and environmentalism. That transition entailed a shift toward an economy that used energy—and not laborers—to do its work, thereby marginalizing labor's bargaining position. This new shift emphasized the problem of externalities by reducing internal expenses but increasing external expenses—those borne by society at large—in pollution and unemployment. While the "gospel of efficiency" had been the cornerstone of conservation practices at the beginning of the twentieth century, private industry had become the staunchest convert to efficiency by the second half of the century.[33] Efficiency experts such as Frederick Taylor, Charles Bedaux, and Henry Ford learned that more efficient production translated into greater profits. During the first half of the twentieth century, workplace techniques, habits, and materials were revolutionized in the name of efficiency, progress, and profit.

However, greater workplace efficiency and productivity—and profits—often tended to result in greater and less efficient consumption of petroleum and other fossil fuels for energy. As Commoner outlined in his keynote address at the American Institute of Planners' annual conference in 1972:

> Automobile engines have been redesigned to operate at increasingly higher compression ratios; electric power, generated in very large power plants, has increasingly replaced geographically-spread home heating directly by fuel; materials, such as aluminum and certain chemicals, the production of which is intensely power-consumptive, have increasingly replaced more power-sparing materials; railroad freight haulage has been displaced by truck freight, which uses six-times more fuel per ton-mile than the railroads.[34]

To Commoner, this was a rampant example of the economic system devouring its wealth and calling it profit. It was also responsible, he claimed, for the series of crises that dotted the 1970s: "Each effort to solve one crisis seems to clash with the solution of the others—pollution control reduces energy supplies; energy conservation costs jobs. Inevitably, proponents of one solution become opponents of the others. Policy stagnates and remedial action is paralyzed, adding to the confusion and gloom that beset the country."[35] It should come as no surprise that Commoner considered the clash between pollution, energy, and jobs to be part of a larger, interconnected whole. All four Laws of Ecology dictated as much: everything was, after all, connected to everything else.

To Commoner, the successive crises constituted a breakdown in what he called the three basic systems "that, together with the social or political order, govern all human activity." The first of these systems was the ecosystem, "the great natural, interwoven, ecological cycles that comprise the planet's skin, and the minerals that lie beneath it," which provided all the necessary resources to support human life and activity. The second system was the production system, which consisted of the human network of agricultural and industrial processes. The production system translated the ecosystem's resources into goods and services—food, manufactured goods, transportation, and communication, for example—which made up the real wealth that sustained society. Finally, there was the economic system, wherein those products were exchanged and real wealth was transformed into earnings, profit, credit, savings, investment, and taxes. Just as significantly, Commoner argued, the economic system "governs how that wealth is distributed, and what is done with it."[36] The three systems were intimately connected. As Commoner put it in *The Closing Circle,* "Wealth . . . is . . . produced by human actions which are guided by science, mediated by technology, governed by an economic system, and exerted through the ecosphere."[37]

As Commoner saw it, the dependencies between the three basic systems followed a directional logic: the economic system depended upon the production system and the production system depended upon the sustainable resource capacity of the ecosystem. But free market capitalism had tried to reverse this logic. Because capitalism thrived on perpetual growth, the economic system imposed continual and increasing demands upon the production system, which in turn stressed the ecosystem. Such inefficient consumption of nonrenewable resources broke with the kind of economic sustainability and security that Commoner advocated, but it was suggestive of the economic confidence—or arrogance—that had propelled the

American economy during the postwar years. By the 1970s, however, that confidence was on the wane.

Since the end of World War II, the American economy had been buoyed by unparalleled, rampant prosperity unprecedented in its history. Indeed, such was the boom and sense of confidence that during the 1960s President Lyndon Johnson had tried to fight the Vietnam War without raising taxes. For a time, it seemed as though the bullish economy would sustain Johnson's efforts, but by the time he left office in 1969, his defiance of economic logic posed difficult problems for the Nixon administration.[38] After more than two decades of economic growth and prosperity, the bottom fell out in the 1970s and the economy was in an acute crisis, which precipitated the onset of stagflation, manifested by a series of related factors: productivity was in decline; unemployment was on the rise, and so were interest rates and inflation, in part a result of Johnson's tax-free war; and trade deficits, unbalanced budgets, and a growing national deficit were stalling the national economy. Sagging productivity, galloping inflation, and stifling unemployment—especially among minorities and the millions of baby boomers now entering the workforce—constituted a difficult challenge for the new Nixon administration, and it proved quickly that it was not up to the challenge.

The socioeconomic and environmental hazards inherent in the inefficient consumption of energy hit home to Americans with the onset of the 1973 energy crisis. According to Walter Rosenbaum, "On the eve of the 'energy crisis' of 1973, per capita American energy use exceeded the rest of the globe's per capita consumption by seven times and remained twice the average of that in European nations with comparable living standards."[39] In October 1973, Americans experienced a "crude awakening." Angered by Nixon's devaluation of the American dollar—which had already resulted in higher oil prices and contributed to worldwide inflation—and the American support for Israel during the Yom Kippur War, Arab leaders of the Organization of Petroleum Exporting Countries (OPEC) imposed an embargo on shipments of oil to the United States. In December 1973, OPEC raised the price of oil to $11.65 a barrel, almost four times the cost prior to the Yom Kippur War. The oil embargo lasted from 16 October 1973 to 18 March 1974; Americans contended with what Nixon called "a very stark fact: We are heading toward the most acute shortage of energy since World War II."[40]

Nixon's statement revealed a dire miscalculation of the global economic climate by his administration. American policy dictated that Arab oil exporters needed American capital and technology more than Americans needed their oil. After all, an attempted embargo in 1967 had supported this point of view; amid regional instability and embargoes, the oil still got through.[41] What had changed by 1973? In short: domestic oil production peaked in 1970. In the spring of 1971, the *San Francisco Chronicle* printed a cryptic one-sentence announcement: "The Texas Railroad Commission announced a 100 percent allowable for next month."[42] The Texas Railroad Commission was effectively a government-sanctioned cartel that matched domestic oil production to demand. In 1971, Texas wells began pumping oil at full capacity, but domestic oil fields could no longer keep up with American demand. In 1960, Americans consumed 9.7 million barrels of oil a day; by 1970, that number had grown to 14.4 million, and it had climbed to 16.2 million in 1974.[43] Said Byron Tunnell, chairman of the Texas Railroad Commission, after it reached the decision to pump at full capacity: "We feel this to be an historic occasion. Damned historic, and a sad one. Texas oil fields have been like a reliable old warrior that could rise to the task, when needed. That old warrior can't rise anymore."[44] The strength of domestic wells had allowed the United States to stockpile a surplus capacity of about 4 million barrels of oil a day between 1957 and 1963. By the 1970s, that surplus had dropped to 1 million barrels a day, and the United States was forced to become a major oil importer. American demand for oil, extraction at full capacity at home, and growing dependence on an unstable and volatile part of the world for the nation's lifeblood prompted former Commerce Secretary Peter Peterson to claim wryly: "Popeye is running out of spinach."[45] It certainly seemed the case. In 1967, 19 percent of oil for American consumption came from overseas; by 1972, that figure had risen to 30 percent, and to 38 percent two years later.[46] Oil imports more than doubled between 1967 and 1973—from 2.2 million barrels a day to six million barrels a day—and the increasing importation of Arab oil, not to mention the enormous quantities of dollars held by Arab oil countries, contributed markedly to the devaluation of the dollar in 1971 and again in 1973.[47]

As a result, the Nixon administration's position dramatically underestimated the American dependence on foreign oil.[48] According to Bruce Schulman, "The world's great superpower seemed suddenly toothless, helpless, literally and metaphorically out of gas."[49] The oil embargo precipitated a series of events that demonstrated the centrality of oil to the American economic system. Because production industries were so energy-intensive, it became apparent that inflation was driven by the price of energy. The price of gasoline, heating oil, and propane climbed markedly, as did the prices of many petrochemicals, such as fertilizers and pesticides that were made from petroleum products. Gasoline prices—combined with the shortage of gasoline—depressed car sales, and the automotive industry experienced a serious decline. According to a 1975 issue of *Survey of Current Business,* a Department of Commerce publication, within a year of the embargo, the $5.3 billion decline in gross auto product during the fourth quarter of 1974 accounted for more than 25 percent of the decline in real Gross National Product. In simpler terms, the battered auto industry was pinched by the oil embargo and contributed to the spreading economic alarm by laying off over 100,000 autoworkers.[50] Increased fuel prices raised transportation costs and the price of agricultural chemicals, both of which contributed to inflated grocery bills. Costs for heating went through the roof.[51] "Suddenly," Commoner recalled after the fact in *The Poverty of Power,* "energy problems were problems of inflation and unemployment; energy had become firmly enmeshed in the deepening economic crisis."[52] The energy crisis brought the country to its knees. As Secretary of State Henry Kissinger told *Business Week* late in 1974—ironically, a year after receiving the Nobel Prize for Peace—forceful action against Middle Eastern countries withholding oil might be justifiable in preventing "some actual strangulation of the industrialized world."[53] A few weeks earlier, *Newsweek* had quoted a "top U.S. official" as saying that "if the oil-producing nations drive the world into depression in their greed, the West might be forced into a desperate military adventure."[54]

Commoner was very quick to pick up on the energy crisis as a theme that could be exploited to emphasize his larger concerns about social, economic, and technological systems in America. "We live in a time of unending crisis," he told the Council on Foundations in early May 1974, less than two months after the oil embargo was lifted.[55] The energy crisis, he noted, came on the heels of racial discrimination, urban decay, poverty, the hazards of automation, the environmental crisis, the population crisis, and the growing demand for food worldwide. "And, overshadowing all," Commoner added a few months later at a public convocation sponsored by the Fund for Peace, "war and the threat of war."[56] "Usually we attempt to solve each crisis in its own terms," Commoner claimed, but he insisted that the energy crisis was special: "It sharply illuminates the complex web of connections among all these problems that has made it so difficult to solve each of them separately."[57]

According to Daniel Yergin, after World War II, oil had become "the lifeblood of the world's industrial economies," and its apparent shortage during the crisis sparked a series of debates about energy production in the United States.[58] "There are no easy answers to these questions," Commoner conceded:

> But there is one way to begin to look for them. And that is to recognize that energy problems will not be solved by technological sleight-of-hand, clever tax schemes, or patchwork legislation. The energy crisis and the knot of technological, economic, and social issues in which it is embedded call for a great national debate—to discover better alternatives to the deeply faulted institutions that govern how the nation's resources are used.[59]

Energy was the "red thread" that connected the ecosystem, the production system, and the economic system, Commoner told a teach-in at Fresno State University in April 1976.[60] Reliance on fossil fuels—foreign or domestic—had to be curbed. As the oil embargo made abundantly clear, nonrenewable fossil fuels would become increasingly costly as reserves were depleted, and their escalating prices would cause inflation.

But was there really an oil shortage in the United States? Commoner was not convinced. While American oil companies and the Department of Energy insisted that the shortage was real, and that oil magnates were genuinely serving their country by importing oil from the Middle East, Commoner drew on oil extraction studies to argue that oil companies had stopped looking for American oil because it was cheaper to buy it from Saudi Arabia.[61] Just as profitability had driven American industries to embrace postwar technological innovations, profitability created the context for American dependence on foreign oil. The major oil companies got a higher rate of return on their investment by producing and refining oil abroad. Due to declining oil supplies in the United States, domestic exploration became more and more costly as drilling turned up more and more dry holes. While the maxim "nothing ventured, nothing gained" hinted that more expenditure would result in more successful wells in the United States, for the oil companies it was a zero-sum game. Major oil companies invested less in exploration in the United States owing to the inexpensive and easily accessible oil supplies in the Middle East and Venezuela, where the extraction of oil cost nearly one-tenth what it would cost at home (owing to exploration expenses). As the energy crisis evolved into a prominent feature of the mid-1970s, disdain toward the oil companies grew as they continued to enjoy multibillion-dollar profits throughout the energy crisis, as demand for domestic oil outstripped supply and prices soared.

For their part, the major oil companies were caught between a rock and a hard place. On the one side, the American public seemed to be experiencing withdrawal symptoms and criticized the oil companies for not supplying enough oil. On the other side, the Arab nations were imposing strict limitations on the amount of oil the companies could extract and where it could go. While the oil companies wanted to alleviate the oil shortage in the United States, it was clear that the exporting countries in the Middle East would not hesitate to nationalize their oil fields and leave the oil companies—and the United States—high and dry.[62] At the same time, however, tax incentives made the importation of oil even more profitable for the major oil companies. So while Nixon encouraged conservation and Americans fretted over energy shortages, major oil companies reported fourth quarter profits in 1973—at the height of the embargo—that were 57 percent higher than the previous year.[63]

In an attempt to alleviate their public relations crisis, American oil companies engaged in a vigorous advertising campaign to persuade American consumers that they were actively engaged in resolving the energy crisis. In *TIME,* Texaco told readers it had spent half a billion dollars on exploratory drilling in the continental United States.[64] In *Business Week*, the Sun Oil Company told of its offshore drilling tracts, and its success rate in finding gas and oil. "And that's what this country needs," the ad concluded.[65] Long-term commitment to locating American oil reserves and civic duty were also priorities of the two-page Exxon ad that appeared in *Business Week* the week before.[66] But public opinion polls increasingly showed little popular support or sympathy for the oil companies, which most Americans blamed for the crisis.[67]

In essence, the energy crisis illustrated a decline in popular technological enthusiasm that accompanied it. James Patterson noted: "Cheap oil has been a key to American prosperity and economic growth in the postwar era, enormously benefiting major industries such as automobiles and utility companies, accelerating large-scale social transformations such as the spread of suburbanization, and stimulating the consumerism that lay at the heart of postwar American culture."[68] But as oil prices soared, Americans found themselves at a crossroads. "The energy crisis signalizes a great watershed in the history of human society," Commoner told his Fund for Peace audience. "What we do in response to it will determine, I believe, for the United States and for every nation in the world, whether our future continues the progress toward humanism and democracy, or ends in catastrophe and oppression."[69] The response was underwhelming.

And here was a critical, missed opportunity. Response to the energy crisis could have resulted in a reversal in American policy similar to that regarding the hazards of fallout or DDT. There existed a small window of opportunity to impress upon industry, policy makers, and the public the value of adopting greener and more sustainable modes of production. Indeed, the aftermath of the energy crisis seemed a unique chance to persuade these disparate interests that alternative modes of production and consumption were not only feasible, but indeed preferable, environmentally *and* economically. Ultimately, though, the cold reality of American overconsumption never struck a chord with the public. Rather than constituting the kind of crisis that required direct and immediate attention, as had the information on fallout or Carson's message in *Silent Spring,* the other side of the energy crisis might be better understood in relation to the conclusion of the Great Depression and the economic boom brought on by World War II. This, too, it was hoped, would pass. And, to an extent, it did. By the middle of 1976, gas and electricity consumption had returned to pre-embargo levels, and the United States was importing a greater proportion of its oil than it had in 1972.[70] Here, in a microcosm, was the resounding defeat of Commoner's social activism against fallout, population, and the environment: American optimism was incapable of recognizing limits.

The historian David Nye has suggested that the energy crisis was as much a cultural crisis as it was a question of energy shortage. He argued that Americans perceived the crisis as a series of cutbacks by energy suppliers rather than as a problem of overconsumption. National public opinion polls supported his contention. When asked whether the United States should increase energy production or conserve energy use, Americans consistently and overwhelmingly preferred the former. Efforts to approve and build the Alaska Pipeline in order to transport oil from Alaska's North Slope to American markets seemed to environmentalists a palpable example of American denial of overconsumption. In an even more grotesque state of denial, the Interior Department in late 1973 announced it would issue a new environmental impact statement on oil leasing and drilling in the Santa Barbara Channel, which, four years earlier, had been the site of a calamitous spill. Outside of Santa Barbara, the announcement created barely a ripple. The fragmentation described by such cultural analysts as Tom Wolfe and Christopher Lasch was already deeply ingrained. The subsequent response to the energy crisis provided strong evidence for Nye's claim, as policy and public interest focused on locating new sources of energy rather than on cutting usage. In spite of being a very legitimate scare, the energy crisis resulted in very few changes in American energy consumption habits.[71]

Because of the complexity and dynamism of the multitude of factors that drive economies, it is impossible to predict the outcome of social, political, and economic decisions. Optimism and the courage or willingness to gamble on favorable outcomes have long driven the American boom-and-bust economy, often at the expense of the environment. According to Donald Worster, during the Great Depression, "Risk was treated . . . almost as a positive value, as a needed spur to success. Without risk, there could be no gain."[72] But if the environmental crisis signaled anything, it was the folly inherent in embracing uncertainty. In *The Poverty of Power,* Commoner noted the contradiction between the gravity of the crisis and the hopeful optimism of the American public: "On the East Coast, gasoline was so hard to find that motorists spent hours in long lines of cars (their idling engines uselessly burning gasoline) waiting to buy a few days' supply."[73] This missed opportunity was not for lack of effort from critics of American energy policy. While the energy shortage received plenty of attention from all kinds of environmental groups, they found themselves engaged in a reactive response to the promotion of nuclear power rather than a concerted public debate on the merits of limiting energy consumption. Rather, energy consumption had to be reconceived in a manner that did not exhaust or pollute the ecosystem.

That message did not resonate in the halls of political power. While the United States was becoming increasingly dependent on foreign oil to satiate its power consumption needs, the energy crisis was evidence that its access to oil could be severed. This realization led to Nixon's 7 November 1973 declaration and the White House's subsequent efforts to produce American "energy self-sufficiency" by 1980. "Today the challenge is to regain the strength we had earlier in this century—the strength of self-sufficiency," Nixon told the nation in a broadcast from the White House. "Let us unite in committing the resources of this nation to a major new endeavor. An endeavor that in this bicentennial era we can appropriately call Project Independence."[74] Nixon promoted Project Independence as similar in scope and ambition to the Manhattan Project and the Apollo space program, but notions of energy self-sufficiency as defined by the Nixon administration alarmed environmentalists, as it was tantamount to renewing the raid on domestic resources with reckless abandon rather than reducing consumption, improving efficiency, and developing clean and renewable sources of energy. While his address touched ever so briefly on conservation measures, the thrust of the new Nixon policy sought to stimulate the rapid development of coal production and the widespread proliferation of nuclear reactors.[75] Both provoked the ire of environmentalists because of the belief that further fuel exploration would accelerate the nation's energy demands and distract public attention from the reality of limited energy reserves. Compared with oil, coal could be easily and relatively inexpensively located, but the ecological impact of coal mining was increasingly taking its toll on the American landscape.[76] Further, the burning of coal emitted methyl mercury and sulfur dioxide, which Commoner called "an especially pernicious pollutant" because of its tendency to attack the lungs and its influence on acid rain.[77]

Much as coal use was seen as an ecological pariah that threatened to devastate the American landscape and then poison its people with its emissions, the encouragement of nuclear power plants provoked a similar firestorm. Project Independence indicated that Nixon used the energy crisis as a means of promoting nuclear power as a solution to American energy demands. Through the 1970s, administration support for nuclear power had gained ground, but with the advent of Project Independence, Commoner accused Nixon of "using [the] hysteria over energy shortages to get that particular camel into the tent."[78] In June 1973, Nixon appointed Dixy Lee Ray, head of the Atomic Energy Commission, to lead a task force assigned to outline a research and development plan for the energy future of the United States. "That," Commoner declared bitterly, "is like asking the chief fox to work out a research problem in the chicken house."[79]

The report was submitted on 1 December 1973 and closely followed Nixon's guidelines. It insisted that "every effort short of administrative controls, if possible, must be made to reduce energy consumption and to increase the technical efficiency of the energy system," but nowhere in the report was there any indication of what those acceptable efforts were.[80] Predictably, of the five parts of the program to acquire and maintain energy self-sufficiency, Ray promoted "validating the nuclear option." She noted: "A self-sufficiency based on fossil fuels can only be temporary," and lauded the promise of nuclear power as an alternative that "must be ensured and accelerated."[81] Commoner told Larry DuBois, in a July 1974 *Playboy* interview, that the Atomic Energy Commission was "leading us blind into a cave of tigers, and I think it's totally irresponsible."[82] Two years later, in *The Poverty of Power,* Commoner outlined what he perceived to be the absurdity inherent in pursuing a nuclear policy to stem the tide of the energy crisis. His argument rested on the simple fact that as an energy source, nuclear fission was inefficient and dangerous. It constituted too high a risk to warrant serious pursuit. "The use of nuclear radiation for the relatively mild task of boiling water violates the familiar caution against attacking a fly with a cannon," Commoner argued in a now celebrated analogy. "The fly is likely to be killed, but at the cost of considerable unnecessary damage."[83] So, too, with nuclear power plants.

Greater dependence on nuclear power was also the realization of a thirty-year-old ambition of many American nuclear scientists. As one study suggested: "For [American nuclear scientists], the transition to civilian atoms represented an indispensable social legitimation of their scientific interests, the irrefutable historic justification of the primacy of nuclear physics in the field of science and technology."[84] Robert Righter took the idea even further: "The idea of redemption (or guilt) for the destructive power of the atomic bomb played a part in the scientific community's dedication to nuclear power."[85] Indeed, hearkening back to J. Robert Oppenheimer's charge that the nuclear physicists had known sin, the prospect of nuclear power ensuring American energy self-sufficiency surely constituted some kind of redemption, though its rise in prominence had already peaked by the time of Nixon's endorsement. Growing commercial acceptance of nuclear power as a viable alternative for generating electricity came on the heels of the Nuclear Test Ban Treaty. In December 1963—less than a month after the ban on atmospheric nuclear weapons testing—Jersey Central Power and Light purchased a boiling water reactor for a plant in Oyster Creek, New Jersey. After the 1956 Suez crisis and increasing American dependence on foreign oil, nuclear energy had emerged as a powerful bargaining chip designed as an economic deterrent to keep oil prices artificially low.[86] In retrospect, it was a bluff—nuclear power did nothing to reduce American demand for foreign oil and never came close to assuring domestic energy self-sufficiency—but American utilities companies ordered 235 nuclear plants through 1974, and, at the behest of the Atomic Energy Commission, Project Independence advocated a return to nuclear power.

Nor was nuclear energy as environmentally safe as its proponents advocated. While it did not emit the kinds of air pollutants that sullied oil and coal use, nuclear power produced radioactive waste that raised serious disposal problems. Commoner highlighted the gravity and scale of this problem in *The Poverty of Power:* "The waste produced by a billion-watt nuclear power plant . . . is equivalent in radioactivity to about 2500 tons of radium. In contrast, the total amount of radium used thus far in the world for medical and scientific purposes—all of it handled in very small amounts and elaborately contained and shielded—probably amounts to a few pounds." The waste's high radioactivity posed dangerous problems, and its release into the environment was potentially lethal. "The radiation from the wastes produced by a city's nuclear power plant . . . would be sufficient to kill 100 times the city's population." Storage of such toxic materials also required critical attention. "Nuclear wastes are persistent," Commoner explained. "Their radioactivity will remain at a very harmful level, and will need to be meticulously isolated from people and the environment for about 200,000 years."[87] This was an especially precarious legacy to pass on to future generations. With no easy solution for disposing of radioactive waste, the nuclear power system adopted temporary storage facilities as an interim solution, but these spaces quickly became overloaded. "Our nuclear cup runneth over," Commoner observed critically.[88]

The year 1974 became the magic date for interest in nuclear reactors. Only thirteen were ordered after that year, and none after 1978. Moreover, more than 100 orders for plants were canceled between 1974 and 1982, even though several were already under construction.[89] Electrical energy too cheap to meter—Atomic Energy Commission chair Lewis L. Strauss's 1954 promise—never materialized. Questions of efficiency, safety, and waste disposal plagued the nuclear power project in large part because nuclear power sought to defy the parameters of Commoner's three basic systems rather than accept those restrictions. While a degree of technological enthusiasm drove the economic argument in favor of nuclear power, its production and the disposal of nuclear waste exacerbated stresses on the ecosystem. Further, nuclear power promised to preserve levels of consumption, even if those levels were unsustainable in the long term. An economic system that propelled an ecosystem was doomed to break down.

In part, the failure of the nuclear power industry was a result of bad timing. Ironically, a temporary drop in American electricity consumption after the energy crisis eliminated the need for new power plants.[90] But falling demand also coincided with stricter environmental regulations, and the cost of building nuclear plants that adhered to mounting safety concerns became exorbitant. Industry and government officials often blamed these escalating costs on a surprisingly powerful antinuclear movement. In his study of opposition to nuclear power in California, Thomas Raymond Wellock argues: "Far from being pesky but harmless gnats, the antinuclear movement halted nuclear construction by modifying the underlying values of state energy regulation."[91] Commoner most certainly agreed. Indeed, in *The Poverty of Power*, he pointed to environmental activism as the primary explanation for the demise of nuclear power. "The factor which correlates most significantly with the increase in capital costs is the length of the period in which the [Atomic Energy Commission] and state agencies consider whether to license the construction of the plant. . . . [Government and industry] argue that environmentalists have delayed the licensing procedure by raising questions about the safety and environmental effects of the plants, and that capital costs increase because of interest charges and the costs of inflation incurred during the added time."[92] Moreover, after the Supreme Court upheld a California law that blocked nuclear power plant construction in the state until the United States "has approved a demonstrated technology or means for the permanent or terminal disposal of high-level wastes," the Wall Street Journal ruefully recalled a Commoner interview from the mid-1970s in which "he more or less boasted that his movement would succeed in stopping nuclear power through harassment tactics that would delay nuclear power plants, escalate their costs and make them uneconomical to build."[93]

This marked another important environmental victory and an important victory for the usefulness of scientific information. The nuclear power industry developed in tandem with the growing environmental consciousness that carried through the 1960s. Concerns about radiation and recognition that environmental risks needed to be properly considered were widespread. So were protests against local sitings of reactors for a variety of environmentally motivated reasons, including the loss of scenery; thermal pollution from power plant discharges, which were found to be responsible for dramatic fish kills in rivers across the United States between 1962 and 1967; and bigger questions about reactor safety.[94] In their efforts to alleviate public concerns and shore up support for nuclear power, utility companies' costs skyrocketed. For example, after the Yankee Nuclear Power Corporation in Vermont ordered a reactor on the Connecticut River, electricity prices in Vermont quadrupled.[95] In effect, the economic woes experienced by the nuclear power industry—particularly in light of environmental activism—represented a classic example of external diseconomies in practice. As Commoner had observed in reference to the petrochemical industry: "When environmentally required changes in technology are imposed upon these highly productive enterprises, these activities do *not* thereby gain in productivity."[96] By adding environmental protection to the balance sheet, nuclear power was priced out of the market.

To Commoner, alternative energies were cheaper, safer, and cleaner. Solar energy, he advocated, could "easily compete with nuclear reactors as a source of electricity."[97] In 1973, a report on the viability of solar power was prepared for Dixy Lee Ray as part of a comprehensive federal energy research and development program. It suggested that an aggressive research and development program in solar technologies could yield 21 percent of the nation's electrical demand—roughly 5.5 percent of the total energy budget—by 2000. The report recommended a budget of $1 billion for this research and development. Ultimately, Ray's final recommendation budgeted $200 million for solar technology, half the amount the subpanel claimed was needed for a "minimum viable" research program. But Ray treated the funds as a sizable contribution, stating: "Because solar energy systems are capital intensive and practical systems have not been fully developed, Federal involvement in the program is warranted."[98] And then the subpanel report seemed to temporarily disappear. The Atomic Energy Commission initially refused to give the report to Senator Henry M. Jackson of Washington, presidential assistant Peter Flanigan, and Senator James Abourezk of South Dakota, who received it only after demanding it and citing the Freedom of Information Act.[99] Whether a cover-up occurred or not, it was clear to Commoner that a more concerted effort was needed to develop affordable technology to procure solar energy and to make it the centerpiece of the American energy policy.[100]

"The supplies of oil, natural gas, and uranium are limited and rapidly becoming more demanding of capital and higher in price as the readily exploited deposits are depleted," Commoner wrote. "Expanded use of these fuels would worsen environmental deterioration and, in the case of nuclear power, create new and unmanageable hazards. It is now accepted as inevitable that future energy supplies, unlike present ones, must be renewable and less harmful to the environment."[101] For Commoner, as for many environmentalists, solar energy was the answer. "In effect, the sun is a huge, essentially eternal nuclear reactor, assembled by the play of cosmic forces rather than by the hand of man," Commoner commented in *The Poverty of Power*.[102] By 1979, Commoner saw solar energy as "emerging as a potentially creative force in the economy, while nuclear power has become an economic cripple."[103] The road to environmental and economic recovery ran through an imperative change in the direction of American energy policy. "We have a surprisingly clear path to follow," he stated in the introduction to *The Poverty of Power:*

> It begins with the *sources* of energy, the fossil and nuclear fuels on which we now depend, and the huge but still largely unused source—the sun. Here we need to learn why those energy sources on which we now rely are so poorly adapted to the purposes to which we put them; why they have begun to seriously disrupt both the environment and the economic system. Then we need to look at the *uses* of energy in the production system and discover why that system has been so designed as to waste energy so blatantly. Here we will find powerful links between the ways we use and misuse energy, capital, and labor. And only at that point will it become evident that our current crisis is a symptom of a deep and dangerous fault in the economic system.[104]

Commoner noted that debate over the relative merits of solar energy and nuclear energy was strangely inverted. "Solar energy," he commented in his 1979 book, *The Politics of Energy,* "the oldest source exploited by human society . . . was usually regarded as an impractical, exotic product of advanced science." At the same time, nuclear energy—"certainly an exotic way to boil water"—Commoner observed bitterly—was promoted as the more traditional stalwart, championed by prominent scientific and government figures.[105]

And Commoner was not alone. Prior to the energy crisis, the scientific trade press had devoted a number of optimistic articles to solar energy's potential.[106] One book, written by reporters from the Research News section of *Science,* claimed that with substantially more research and development funding from the government, solar energy could be competitive before 1980.[107] But while specialists were becoming more enthusiastic, the mainstream media paid little attention.[108] After the energy crisis, solar energy gained greater popular support. One 1976 Gallup poll reported that solar power ranked first among Americans as a long-term solution to energy self-sufficiency, and second only to coal in the short term.[109] To Commoner, it was clean and cheap. "Solar energy can not only replace a good deal, and eventually all, of the present consumption of conventional fuels—and eliminate that much environmental pollution," he argued in *The Poverty of Power,* echoing the Atomic Energy Commission's solar subpanel findings, "but [it] can also reverse the trend toward escalating energy costs that is so seriously affecting the economic system."[110]

In the wake of the environmental crisis and the energy crisis, why had energy conservation (which only delayed the inevitable) and solar power (which sought to confront it) not caught on? In his *Playboy* interview, Commoner reminded readers, "Don't forget that in plumping for solar energy we're bucking an enormously powerful, well-heeled atomic energy machine. Don't forget that the oil companies now own not the sun but uranium supplies."[111] For Commoner, a shift toward solar energy would take power—political and electrical—out of the hands of the wealthy and distribute it more equitably. As Commoner was also keenly aware, nuclear power required centralization and hierarchy, while solar energy could be easily distributed and controlled more locally and democratically.[112] Commoner's final chapter in *The Poverty of Power* turned into a blistering critique of private enterprise and the capitalist system. Commoner had been working toward such a conclusion throughout the book, but the conclusion made his overt advocacy of a more socialist economic system perfectly clear. This was a risky approach, and Commoner admitted he had some reservations about directly promoting socialism in *The Poverty of Power.* To most Americans still experiencing the Cold War, socialism was a pejorative term, and not one that would help win converts for Commoner's critique of American energy policy. But the environmental crisis, the energy crisis, and the economic crisis, Commoner contended, demonstrated that the capitalist enterprise was leading to imminent disaster. By the 1970s, even industry was claiming that consumers should consume less and put more money into savings so that business could access that capital to grow. Such economic realities, however, threatened a decreasing standard of living. To Commoner, this was especially egregious, because as living standards were lowered, poorer members of society would be the first to suffer job losses and strains on their purchasing power. While economic crises hit everyone, they invariably hit the lower sectors of the economic scale hardest.

According to Commoner, Americans would have to chart a new course to blend a newly conceived economic socialism with the political democracy that was so fundamental a characteristic of Americanism. He recognized that repressive regimes in Cuba, China, and the Soviet Union were hardly glowing endorsements for the adoption of socialist economic principles in the United States, but he also noted that "no existing example of a socialist society . . . is consistent with . . . the economic democracy of socialism." Nevertheless, he believed Americans were capable of meeting the challenge. "It is appropriate, in 1976," he continued, using rhetoric that mimicked but countered Nixon's rationale for Project Independence, "to remind ourselves that such radical political innovation is a 200-year-old, if long-neglected, tradition in the United States."[113]

The Poverty of Power was roundly complimented for the lucidity of Commoner's explanation in lay terms of the complicated Second Law of Thermodynamics. Whether or not journalists, economists, scientists, engineers, or Department of Energy employees commented positively on the strength of Commoner's argument in the book, they almost unanimously praised the quality of his chapter on the Second Law of Thermodynamics in their reviews. And he had, of course, alluded to socialism in *The Closing Circle,* intimating that "the socialist system may have an advantage over the private enterprise system with respect to the basic relationship between economic processes and ecological imperatives."[114] While the capitalist system required perpetual growth, the socialist economy—in theory, anyway—did not. His argument in *The Poverty of Power* was less restrained. As the review of *The Poverty of Power* in the *Philadelphia Inquirer* aptly commented: "It was clear from *The Closing Circle* that sooner or later Commoner was going to have to come right out with it. . . . Society would never be saved with the capitalist system."[115] Fearing the inevitable reprisals, Commoner was quick to note that leading economists such as John Kenneth Galbraith were arguing the same thing. Reflecting on the woes of the energy crisis and the imminent and related economic crisis, which he blamed on private industry, Galbraith had claimed in 1975 that "the word socialism is one we can no longer suppress."[116]

Not everybody was convinced. On a CBS panel hosted by Walter Cronkite in late 1971, when Commoner asserted that "the entire operation of the economic system depends on the integrity of the environment [and] at present, the way we run our production is suicidal," he was rebuked by Herbert Doan of the Dow Chemical Company. "Mr. Commoner winds up [*The Closing Circle*] by advocating . . . that socialism must be a more easy way to control the environment than the free enterprise system we live in. This brings me to the point of saying that Mr. Commoner has within him the ability to speak some utter nonsense."[117]

Within environmental circles Commoner's socialist message was also often a problem. Even prior to *The Poverty of Power,* his linking of environmentalism with socialism provoked stern criticism. Paul Ehrlich, among others, worried that advocating this alliance between environmentalism and socialism would do no favors to the mainstream environmental movement. "There is no point in waving a red flag in front of the bulls," Ehrlich commented in 1971.[118] But consistent with his dedication to public information, Commoner insisted on forging ahead, arguing that the free enterprise system was hardly free or private anyway. This was certainly the case with nuclear power, he noted, which constituted "a lopsided partnership between the private and public sectors, in which the rewards have been private and the huge risks—the hazards to life, the waste of billions of dollars, the rising cost of power, the impending collapse of the nuclear-power program, and the ensuing economic chaos—have been assigned to the public."[119] Because society was already paying the environmental costs—in poor health as a result of air and water contamination, for example—the public ought to have a more socialized means of controlling these costs. This inequity would come to the fore in the following decades with the rise of the environmental justice movement. Returning to his attack on the capitalist system, Commoner remarked: "When engineers want to understand the strength of a new material they stress it to the breaking point and analyze how it responds. The energy crisis is a kind of 'engineering test' of the United States' economic system, and it has revealed a number of deep-seated faults."[120] This was the poverty of power.

At the end of *The Closing Circle,* Commoner offered a prescription for solving the environmental crisis. It was a solution steeped in altering wasteful economic and technological practices. "If we are to survive economically as well as biologically, industry, agriculture, and transportation will have to meet the inescapable demands of the ecosystem," he warned.

> This will require the development of major new technologies including: systems to return sewage and garbage directly to the soil; the replacement of many synthetic materials by natural ones; the reversal of the trend to retire land from cultivation and to elevate the yield per acre by heavy fertilization; replacement of synthetic pesticides, as rapidly as possible, by biological ones; the discouragement of power-consuming industries; the development of land transport that operates with maximal fuel efficiency at low combustion temperatures and with minimal land use; essentially complete containment and reclamation of wastes from combustion processes, smelting, and chemical operations (smokestacks must become rarities); essentially complete recycling of all reusable metal, glass, and paper products; ecologically sound planning to govern land use including urban areas.[121]

His list was comprehensive, and the social restructuring necessary to realize these changes was significant, but Commoner argued that because the environmental crisis was the product of social and economic mismanagement, a social and economic reorganization was essential to any attempt to cure society's environmental ills. Not surprisingly, the American industrial network embraced Commoner's faith in science and technology's potential, but it and policy makers charted a wide course around his suggestions aimed at making industry more responsible. "Not surprisingly," because the enduring American legacy of growth at all costs is staged to continue, generating the most fundamental environmental problems of the twenty-first century. To echo William Cronon, who suggested that the persistent neglect of nature in our history is itself a historical artifact, one might be compelled to argue that the neglect of nature in our economy is an equally compelling historical artifact.[122]

6

The "Other" Environmentalism

It may be that we are situated at the beginning of a historical process of habituation. It may be that the next generation, or the one after that, will no longer be upset at pictures of birth defects, like those tumor-covered fish and birds that now circulate around the world, just as we are no longer upset today by violated values, the new poverty and a constant high level of mass unemployment. It would not be the first time that standards disappear as a result of their violation.

—Ulrich Beck

Less than five years after publicly insisting that ecological systems could never be reconciled with the rapacious nature of the capitalist system and that the only solution was a kind of economic socialism, Commoner ran for president of the United States. For a longtime radical, it appeared a strange move, but for Commoner it was part of a rational evolution. As he insisted in an interview shortly after the 1980 campaign: "What I have been doing in recent years is to look for the reasons for such problems as the energy crisis and the environmental crisis. I've ended up concluding that the reasons have to do with the governance of production decisions: who decides how we use our resources; what we produce and how we produce it." He did not say it outright, but he certainly intimated that the manner in which risk was assessed and distributed was central to his critique. Risk assessment, or the priorities that went into assessing risk, were frequently the source of environmental and energy problems, and they were intimately connected to the means and modes of production. The crucial issue, Commoner had determined, was the democratic social governance of the means of production; those most subjected to environmental pollution risks should have a more prominent place at the table. "I'm involved in politics," Commoner concluded, "because it's become crystal clear that the issues I've been concerned with—nuclear issues, environmental issues, energy issues—are not going to be solved simply by protest."[1] Commoner had frequently referred to himself as a congenital optimist, but this was a rather striking reversal of his earlier faith in the scholar's obligation to dissent. Or was it? For almost three decades, he had put his faith in an informed public; by 1980 he had concluded that the big change he considered necessary could occur only from inside and that public pressure from outside was not enough. At the same time, was there a better venue for raising public awareness than a presidential campaign? Commoner was sixty-three; reporting on his presidential candidacy, *Newsweek* described him as "a rumpled, somewhat owlish figure, his eyes popping wide with enthusiasm behind his ever-slipping horn rims."[2]

In April 1980—ten years after the first Earth Day—Commoner accepted the Citizens' Party presidential nomination at a chaotic convention in Cleveland. He was one of the founders of the new party, brought to life the previous summer by a group of dissident left-leaning philanthropists and social activists, including the author Studs Terkel, the Gray Panthers leader Maggie Kuhn, and the Steelworkers insurgent Ed Sadlowski. The Indian-rights activist and founder and president of Americans for Indian Opportunity, LaDonna Harris from Oklahoma, was the vice presidential candidate. The idea behind the Citizens' Party, Commoner told *Newsweek*, "was to provide an alternative for the growing number of dispirited Americans fed up with the major parties."[3] Commoner compared the Citizens' Party's creation to the rationale behind the birth of the Republican Party in the nineteenth century, during which Americans "elected all the presidents whose names you don't remember" in the years leading up to the Civil War. Commoner argued that these presidential candidates "were carefully chosen as nonentities because none of the political parties wanted to discuss slavery in a national campaign for fear of losing the election. . . . The creation of the Republican Party was really almost forced on the country by the abdication of politics by the Whigs and the Democrats."[4] By the end of the 1970s, as Commoner laid out at the end of *The Politics of Energy*, the major parties seemed to be deliberately avoiding the socioeconomic issues that had given rise to the energy crisis and the environmental crisis.[5] The Citizens' Party offered a voice to the poor, to labor, and to minorities who were alienated from mainstream American politics.

In December 1979, an organizing committee had filed papers with the Federal Election Commission to establish the Citizens' Party. From the outset, the Citizens' Party wrestled with the difficulties of adhering to a strict internal democracy. Its founders insisted that the new party needed to distinguish itself by establishing a strong sense of democracy within the membership, and that all local parties should have input in drafting the national party platform. This contributed to the convention's bedlam. Position papers and resolutions were sent in from all over the country, and the convention sought the input of all the party's members through a mail-in voting system, which Commoner later called "an insane idea, which utterly failed."[6] Laudable as such high notions of internal democracy were in theory, in practice they turned out to constitute organizational nightmares. The party's late start also contributed to its difficulty in raising funds; the Commoner-Harris ticket appeared on the ballot in thirty states and received 234,294 votes, well behind the Republican Ronald Reagan, the Democratic incumbent Jimmy Carter, the upstart independent John Anderson, and the Libertarian candidate Edward Clark. The long-range hope was that the Citizens' Party would receive 5 percent of the vote, which would entitle it to federal matching funds, but its grassroots principles and idealistic commitment to internal democracy failed to mesh with its top-down creation, which limited its appeal in the black and low-income communities from which it had hoped to gain strength. Before the November election, Commoner had expressed high hopes that the Citizens' Party would become an established third party, but after its poor showing he drifted away from it and eventually became a key adviser to the Reverend Jesse Jackson's Rainbow Coalition campaign in 1984, explaining that white leadership could not advance the kind of politics that was likely to change the American political landscape. Commoner helped Jackson mobilize the sizable underclass that felt increasingly alienated.[7]

Mobilizing those most oppressed by environmental pollution had always been a primary feature of Commoner's new apparatus. Public information and risk analysis were specifically designed to give marginalized voices the technical tools with which to engage in public debate. Indeed, when Commoner claimed in *The Closing Circle* that "the costs of environmental degradation are chiefly borne not by the producer, but by society as a whole," he presaged the sociologist Ulrich Beck's concern that the production of wealth resulted not only in the unequal distribution of goods but also in the unequal distribution of environmental hazards.[8] The unequal distribution of environmental risks would become the concerted focus of his activism during the 1980s and 1990s. The costs of environmental degradation were most disproportionately borne by the poor.[9] This was especially egregious, for as Commoner had pointed out in *The Closing Circle,* pollutants that inhibited human health also inhibited social progress.[10] Poverty also suggested that problems of environmental health and safety were imposed most significantly upon communities of color, exacerbating the uncomfortable existence of an institutional racism in the United States and prompting Commoner to charge that "there is a functional link between racism, poverty, and powerlessness, and the chemical industry's assault on the environment."[11] New petrochemical plants invariably sprang up in poorer neighborhoods such as those throughout "Cancer Alley," an eighty-five-mile, pollution-ridden industrial corridor between New Orleans and Baton Rouge.[12] According to Commoner, this was easily explained in economic terms. In making risk-benefit calculations, some economists proposed that the value of a human life be based on a person's lifelong earning power. "It then turns out that a woman's life is worth much less than a man's, and that a black's is worth much less than a white's," Commoner observed in 1987. "In effect, the environmental harm is regarded as smaller if the people it kills are poor—a standard that could be used to justify situating heavily polluting operations in poor neighborhoods."[13]

However, the number-crunching and economic analysis of the previous chapter left out a vital component: the prescription of social costs resulting from environmental damage was flawed because the assessment of social costs assumed that all Americans shared those costs equally. But while some environmental hazards such as nuclear fallout did not discriminate against where they fell, others such as air pollution from power facilities, manufacturing plants, or waste incinerators posed problems that were more local in nature. The placement of such facilities—invariably in poorer communities—contributed to an unequal distribution of exposure to risk among Americans that adhered to class and color lines.[14] Subsequently, society's politically disempowered groups—those who invariably risked greater exposure to environmental pollutants and the resultant health hazards, and typically had the least access to health care—suffered the most severe environmental consequences, because they did not have the necessary franchise or organization to promote their social values and implement change. Through the 1980s, these disempowered groups found a grassroots voice through the burgeoning movement for environmental justice, which found a national voice through the Rainbow Coalition.

This chapter sets out to chart this "other" environmentalism and Commoner's participation. The sociocultural divide that broadly fractured American society by race and class also existed when it came to how Americans organized to protect the environment. To poorer communities and to communities of color, mainstream environmental organizations were not in tune with the socioeconomic conditions outside of the white middle class, and their national priorities and environmental activisms indicated as much. It often seemed as though the protection of trees and birds was more important than the protection of human health and human lives. In New York City, for example, asthma morbidity and mortality rates were not only significantly higher than the national average, but studies indicated that those numbers were greater in the city's poorer neighborhoods. Further, asthma was more concentrated in nonwhite communities, "with hospitalization and death rates among blacks and Latinos up to five times higher than those of whites."[15] Such urban realities prompted many environmental justice activists to challenge the mainstream environmental organizations "to get off the stick of preserving birds and trees and seals and things like that and talk about what's affecting real people."[16]

The reality was never so black-and-white, but such tensions and perceptions opened a very palpable chasm between groups that generally shared related goals. The tension ultimately arose over the appropriation of the ecological language developed in the years leading up to the first Earth Day. It was this language that articulated the stakes of the environmental crisis. Naturally enough, that postwar language was shaped and dominated by the intellectual and scientific elites, who were prominent among the earliest and loudest broadcasters of the environmental crisis to a public audience. "Ecology," "sustainability," and "quality of life," not to mention "beauty, health, and permanence," entered the popular lexicon as the defining terms of this environmental language.[17] While the confluence of science and environmental ethics was one of the prevailing features of the new environmentalism, that approach typically concentrated its initial efforts on mapping the scientific implications of environmental decline: what pollution and despoliation meant to ecological sustainability and human health.[18] Critics of this mainstream approach would censure its apparent and "enduring ambivalence toward modernity, urbanism, and cultural diversity."[19] Since the first Earth Day, "social justice" and "power relations" have been added to the environmental vocabulary. The sophistication of an alternative race- and class-based ecological language or persuasion grew markedly during the Age of Ecology, and found its most provocative advocates in the burgeoning environmental justice movement, which elucidated the intimate connections between environmental problems and social injustice and the complexities of power politics in environmental decisions. If words such as "sustainability" originally referred to ecosystem health, the new language used them in connection with human and community *survival,* which constituted a substantial difference in how Americans imagined ecology and the environment. Environmental justice's struggle against mainstream environmentalism was over the general acceptance of its contributions to that language. Risk and whose risk were central to that discussion.

Implicit in this discussion of risk was a growing awareness that the human body was, itself, a landscape threatened with pollution. Commenting on the growth of American environmentalism, Christopher Sellers claims that "the body—at once human and animal—has emerged as arguably the most critical middle ground where fin-de-siècle relations between nature and culture are being actively remade as well as rethought." As Americans discovered how radioactive fallout, DDT, and other toxic pollutants were affecting not just the physical environment but also human health, rigid distinctions between nature and culture were blurred. This ecological awakening—the realization that harming nature also harmed human health—is the defining feature of what we might call "modern" environmentalism. "The human body," Sellers insists, "still serves as synecdoche for 'nature' writ large," and that nature included all Americans.[20]

This notion became a prominent feature of Americans' responses to pollution and draws a very clear historical narrative from Commoner's 1960s activism to contemporary environmental justice activism. More important, it provides for a critical expansion of the language of American environmentalism. Indeed, in seeking to push back the historical roots of the environmental justice movement, we might engage in a little intentional historicism. While the history of the environmental justice movement typically traces its origins to the 1980s, we might sensibly note that the language of environmental justice—introduced into the environmental lexicon in the 1980s and 1990s—is vividly present in 1960s civil rights and social justice movements. Also, issues that preoccupied the civil rights movement—rats in tenements, urban poverty, asthma, pediatric cancer, struggles for access to and governance over urban space—are now recognized as environmental issues. The big point is this: minorities may have felt marginalized within mainstream environmentalism, but they were by no means absent from the history of environmental activism.

The substance of the political and historiographical tension between mainstream environmentalism and the environmental justice movement has much to do with perspective, and points to the significance of pluralism as a prominent feature of the American landscape. Pluralism, Louis Menand tells us, "is an attempt to make a good out of the circumstance that goods are often incommensurable."[21] Because people understand the world differently and seek different ends, different people establish different—and often conflicting—priorities. While this truism obviously applies across the spectrum of human endeavors, it is no less applicable to divergent interpretations of the American environmental consciousness. Interest groups that are bigger, or richer, or enjoy better access to political channels have a disproportionate advantage when it comes to pursuing their agenda in the political arena. This power has the effect of muting related or minority perspectives and arriving at an artificial or contrived consensus. This is the substance of power relations, and a critical explanation for Commoner's vehement opposition to Ehrlich's population control advocacy. Pluralism suggests or embraces the notion that different groups are related but independent of each other. It advocates that there is no one vocabulary, but multiple vocabularies. How pluralism works in theory and in practice, of course, is a different matter. Typically, however, the social positionality of grassroots environmental justice advocates altered the context of the environmental struggle in which they engaged, thereby necessitating the adoption of a vocabulary distinct from the one already established by other groups. And that shift in focus was pluralism's central—though often contentious—dialectical contribution to American environmentalism.[22] It is also within this interface that Commoner's importance to the history of American environmentalism becomes most apparent.

"The emergence of the concept of ecology in American life is potentially of momentous relevance to the ultimate liberation of black people. Yet blacks and their environmental interests have been so blatantly omitted that blacks and the ecology movement currently stand in contradiction to each other."[23] So wrote the *Black Scholar* publisher and sociologist Nathan Hare in April 1970 as Earth Day activists filled urban centers across the country. While Hare embraced the significance of ecology, he lamented the movement's omission of interests that pertained to people of color and their particular environmental problems. He cited Robert Rienow's 1967 study, *Moment in the Sun: A Report on the Deteriorating Quality of the American Environment,* which he argued was representative of the environmental literature emerging in the 1960s; it made no reference to African-Americans. Further, while "suburbia" received considerable attention, "slums" and "ghettos" did not appear in Rienow's index.[24] To Hare, the suggestion existed that some places warranted more environmental protection than others. Moreover, while population control policy suggestions appealed to a significant portion of the environmentally concerned, leading African-Americans opposed zero population growth, which they saw as a serious challenge to their political survival. Hare argued that the population explosion was less of a problem than the population implosion, the increasing concentration of people on relatively small proportions of the United States' land surface.[25] This increased urbanization resulted in crowding and environmental problems, many of which were specific to communities of color, who were invariably poorer and less mobile. To Hare, the new environmentalists in suburbia were blind to the urban-living environmental issues most immediately relevant to communities of color.[26]

Many mainstream environmentalists agreed. As early as 1967, Sydney Howe, the president of the Conservation Foundation, complained that "we are now a racially segregated profession. . . . Conservation must be of and for increasingly urban environments and their people."[27] But even the biggest ecological celebration in history failed to adequately build that bridge. Earth Day coordinator Denis Hayes had tried to demonstrate that civil rights, poverty, antiwar, and environmental interests all shared the same platform. Earth Day's goal, he insisted, "is not to clean the air while leaving slums and ghettos, nor is it to provide a healthy world for racial oppression and war."[28] But this message failed to galvanize broader acceptance of a more pluralist environmentalism, because it was drowned out by messages such as Earth Day creator Senator Gaylord Nelson's assertion that "the most critical issue facing mankind" was the environmental crisis, which made "Vietnam, nuclear war, hunger, decaying cities, and all other major problems one could name . . . relatively insignificant by comparison."[29] While the spirit of Nelson's statement might not have tangibly differed from Hayes's—the dangers of ecological degradation contributed to war, famine, oppression, and poverty—its suggestion could not have been worse in terms of marginalizing the groups that Hayes hoped to bring into the tent. Whereas Hayes recognized that the ambivalence peripheral groups might have felt toward the big celebration that threatened to turn attention away from their own activisms, Nelson's rhetoric catered to more ecocentric interests.

Communities of color might have sympathized with Hayes's initial contention as an attempt to embrace the holistic nature of environmental problems, but the popular strength of Nelson's more traditional statement carried the day. For the vast majority of African-Americans, access to political empowerment—achieved through acquiring economic empowerment—was the ultimate means of solving the environmental problems endemic to their poorer and more oppressed communities, and the message they received was that mainstream environmentalism was not yet ready to address those concerns.[30] Minority activists such as Freddie Mae Brown of Black Survival in St. Louis, Arturo Sandoval of La Raza in Albuquerque, and Charles Hayes, a prominent African-American union leader in Chicago, spoke to large Earth Day audiences, but they received far less media coverage and attention than did more mainstream activists.[31] As a result, black media sources confirmed the relative absence of widespread African-American support for Earth Day. The April issue of *Ebony,* the most widely circulated African-American periodical, focused on the continuing civil rights struggle, putting a photograph of the late Martin Luther King, Jr., on its cover, and making no mention of Earth Day in its pages. Neither of the national weekly editions of the *Pittsburgh Courier* or the *Baltimore African American* carried much coverage of the event, and Urban League President Whitney Young commented that "the war on pollution is one that should be waged after the war on poverty is won."[32] The message seemed clear: the struggle for civil rights—and not environmental integrity—was of primary importance to African-Americans.

Moreover, African-American leaders distrusted the growing environmental movement and interpreted the nation's widespread celebration of the first

Earth Day as a manifestation of the white desire to escape from the civil rights discourse. Mutual divisions between the civil rights movement and the environmental movement existed throughout the 1960s.[33] The civil rights movement initially regarded the environmental movement as a rival for federal funds and resources to which it felt it had a moral priority.[34] By the 1970s, African-American leaders complained that the environmental movement (as it was originally articulated) ignored the role of poverty in creating environmentally marginalized spaces for the vast majority of African-Americans. The environmental movement was, in their opinion, ecocentric, and threatened to move the national discussion away from the civil rights discourse, which advocated fuller access to the political economy.[35]

But rhetoric aside, in practice African-Americans and other minority groups were consciously and actively engaged in environmental activism, even if it did not go by that name. Claiming sovereignty over the places where their families worked, lived, and played was obviously a social struggle, but it was also inherently environmental. As Matthew Gandy argues, "The origins of urban environmental struggles [during the 1960s] reveal a radical fusion of grassroots demands for greater community control over urban space with a powerful emphasis on social justice." Moreover, Gandy's perceptive examination of the Young Lords of New York City presents compelling evidence that these second-generation Puerto Ricans were engaged in environmental justice activism throughout the 1960s.[36]

To Commoner, civil rights and environmental protection were inseparable. "To resolve the environmental crisis," he predicted in *The Closing Circle,* "we shall need to forego [*sic*], at last, the luxury of tolerating poverty, racial discrimination, and war."[37] He told the 1972 United Nations Conference on the Human Environment in Stockholm, "A peace among men must precede the peace with nature."[38] But Commoner also rejected the argument that environmental issues were so innocuous that they served to divert people from more serious, controversial issues, insisting that "as a political issue, environmental protection is neither innocuous nor unrelated to basic questions of social justice."[39] He equated environmental hazards with obstacles relating to social progress: "One thing that does clearly emerge from nearly all statistical studies of the effects of air pollution on health," he wrote in *The Closing Circle,* "is that they are most heavily borne by the poor, by children, by the aged and infirm."[40] Commoner was not telling African-Americans anything they did not already know. While he anticipated environmental justice's tangible influence on mainstream American environmentalism by more than a decade, the issues that defined that movement were already prevalent in civil and minority rights discourse.

Much Earth Day environmental rhetoric implied that all Americans were equally guilty of overconsumption, but Hare and others argued that such contentions were oblivious to the fact that consumption and affluence were not evenly distributed throughout the country's population. Commoner made the same comment in front of an Earth Day audience at Brown University. "Since the wastes generated by . . . intense consumption pollute our environment, the eco-activist is advised to 'consume less,'" Commoner, said. "In the absence of the added statistic that in the United States the per capita consumption by blacks is much less than that of the white population, such observations are not likely to make much sense—to blacks, or to anyone who is concerned with social justice."[41] Because he believed in the inherent relationship between poverty, inequality, and environmental degradation, Commoner criticized the environmental movement's lack of foresight in attempting to make alliances with minority groups; "ecological crusades" against overconsumption made environmentalism irrelevant to advocates of social justice, especially when the production of polluting industries took place within their communities. On Earth Day, Commoner described a recent incident to his audience at Brown University: San Jose State College students buried a brand-new car as a symbol of environmental rebellion. The burial reflected the mainstream environmental movement's contention that excessive consumption was responsible for the environmental crisis, but it also suggested that the environmental movement had some ground to cover if it wanted to speak to and for the entire spectrum of the American population. Black students picketed the event, arguing that the $2,500 paid for the car could have been put to far better use in the ghetto.[42]

For Commoner, the division between African-Americans and environmentalism, much like the division between labor and the environment, was grossly overstated, or was not as real as it seemed. Precisely because of their frontline experiences with urban health issues such as lead poisoning and air pollution, Commoner insisted that "blacks need the environmental movement, and the movement needs blacks."[43] Commoner acknowledged the kind of marginalization expressed by critics such as Hare and actively sought ways of including African-Americans within the mainstream context. "In many ways," he argued on Earth Day, "blacks are the special victims of pollution."[44] Commoner suggested that a white suburbanite could "escape from the city's dirt, smog, carbon monoxide, lead, and noise when he goes home," but that ghetto dwellers—predominantly minority populations—lived in it.[45] "To middle class Americans," Commoner asserted, "survival is not a familiar issue. They have not yet learned how to face such a soul-shaking threat; witness our continued failure to appreciate that the existence of ready-armed nuclear weapons means that doomsday may be tomorrow. For blacks, the issue of survival is 200 years old."[46] In the burgeoning environmental justice movement, Commoner saw the urgency that was absent in mainstream environmentalism.

After the 1980 presidential election, Commoner left Washington University and returned to New York City, taking his Center for the Biology of Natural Systems with him to Queens College, where he had first taught before World War II. Early in 1980, the college's president and provost had traveled to St. Louis and offered to set up the Center at Queens under very favorable terms: a hard-money budget including three permanent tenured lines for personnel, adequate quarters, and the full support of the university administration. Approaching retirement age, Commoner accepted their offer, and early in 1981, three eighteen-wheel trucks moved the Center for the Biology of Natural Systems' equipment east.[47]

It would be wrong to suggest that Commoner was chased from Washington University, but it was clear that conflicts with the university administration motivated his departure. Commoner later recalled that the university had no intention of supporting his Center without him.[48] In its fifteen years in St. Louis, the Center for the Biology of Natural Systems, under Commoner's leadership, had experienced remarkable success in raising grant money, which meant the Center (and Commoner) enjoyed considerable independence from the university. At the same time, however, Commoner had frequently clashed with the university over his very public—and often confrontational—stances against industry and, especially, the Vietnam War. In many respects, the move to Queens College was a homecoming, but Commoner did not go home to New York to retire. Indeed, he showed no signs of or interest in slowing down. Being based in New York City provided fuller opportunities to engage in environmental and energy problems, especially those pertaining to urban environments and the urban poor. At Queens College, in Flushing, Commoner and the Center confronted a series of urban environmental issues, especially targeting urban waste disposal and related health issues. As Douglas H. Strong put it, Commoner "remained dedicated to solving the 'real problems' of urban and rural communities."[49] That is to say, he continued to examine and address the social implications of the environmental crisis.

Commoner's return to New York coincided with a new urban crisis: New York City's waste management problems. In *The Closing Circle,* Commoner had attributed the environmental crisis to the wasteful and sometimes toxic nature of new technologies developed since World War II. The petrochemical industry in particular had capitalized on the production of new materials that rendered redundant or too expensive the older, organic, recyclable materials they replaced. But after disposable diapers and beer bottles and plastic wrap and milk containers were disposed of, they did not instantly vanish. They accumulated. Until 1970, burning trash had been a popular method of urban waste disposal—apartment buildings often had their own incinerators to burn residents' trash—but the 1970 Clean Air Act Amendments raised emission standards higher than all but a few incinerators could meet. Americans turned to dumping their trash. When the odors became bad, they dug holes and covered the trash over in landfills.[50]

It seemed, however, as though waste disposal techniques were another example of what Commoner called the Band-Aid approach to environmental problems. Rather than solving the puzzle, industry sought a technological fix. Burying trash superficially solved the odor problem, but landfills posed serious environmental problems. In addition to exuding a stench, many landfills became repositories for unwanted pesticides and other chemicals, waste motor oil, and used cleaning fluids and solvents, which invariably leached out of the landfill and threatened underground water supplies and nearby surface waters. "Moreover," Commoner pointed out in his 1990 book, *Making Peace with the Planet,* "the landfill's organic waste putrefies and ferments, producing inflammable methane and other gases, some of them quite noxious, that pollute the surrounding air."[51] Rather than simply contaminating the soil in which it was buried, trash threatened the air and water. It was like applying a Band-Aid to a gaping wound.

The quantity of solid waste also constituted a serious management problem in many urban centers, and intensified the existing health hazards, especially among poorer communities. Landfills were situated on cheap land close to urban centers, invariably next to poor and minority neighborhoods. But the problem continued to escalate. By 1991, a Department of Sanitation study estimated that New York City produced more than 24,000 tons per day of solid waste, not counting medical and construction waste or sewage sludge.[52] The problem with landfills was that, like fossil fuels, they were a nonrenewable resource; once they had been filled to capacity, their usability was exhausted. As more and more landfills were closed, more distant and more expensive new sites became necessary. Commoner explained in *Making Peace with the Planet*, "Like any other nonrenewable resource, landfills became progressively more expensive."[53] As mountains of waste accumulated, the cost of depositing trash in landfills—the "tipping fee"—rose dramatically, making waste disposal uneconomic and inciting many urban centers to find alternative methods of managing their solid waste.

The solution was a return to an old idea: burning the garbage. In 1978, New York City Mayor Edward I. Koch proposed the construction of a new kind of incineration plant at the Brooklyn Navy Yard, which would turn waste into steam or electricity. These "resource recovery plants" proposed to solve two problems at once: disposal of waste *and* production of electric power. But Commoner was unconvinced. The waste incineration industry consisted of the same corporate giants—Combustion Engineering, Westinghouse, Bechtel, and Babcock & Wilcox—that had pioneered the U.S. nuclear power industry before its collapse, and had now turned their attention to selling trash incinerators as a means of recouping a fraction of their losses. Commoner was also quick to point out that incinerators and nuclear power plants had one important feature in common: both produced pollution that did not exist before the plant was switched on. "Just as nuclear power failed because it created an environmental hazard—radiation—so incinerators turned out to be gravely hampered by the same sort of self-generated environmental hazard, in this case dioxin."[54]

Incineration shrank the size of the mountains of garbage, but waste incineration policies failed to appreciate the validity of Commoner's Second Law of Ecology, that everything must go somewhere. Commoner surmised: "Once regarded as a 'proven technology' that created no environmental hazard, incinerators are now known to emit enough highly toxic compounds to create a risk of cancer and other diseases that is at best borderline, and more often unacceptable according to existing guidelines."[55] Chief among these hazards were the dioxins that escaped from the emissions of chlorine-containing compounds such as plastics and other synthetic materials. Commoner called the new generation of incinerators "dioxin-producing factories."[56] Dioxin is a name given to a number of toxic by-products of the burning of chlorinated wastes, and is generally regarded as the most potent cancer-inducing synthetic chemical.[57] As Commoner warned in a keynote address at the second Citizens' Conference on Dioxin in St. Louis, on 30 July 1994, "Dioxin and dioxin-like substances represent the most perilous chemical threat to the health and biological integrity of human beings and the environment."[58] Environmental Protection Agency documents acknowledged that in addition to causing cancer, dioxin disrupted hormone systems related to sexual development; attacked the nervous system; and damaged the developing immune system, leaving exposed children more susceptible to infectious diseases.[59]

On 18 May 1995, the Center for the Biology of Natural Systems released a comprehensive study on dioxin that demonstrated an eerie connection between dioxin and nuclear fallout. Dioxin, the study argued, created a toxic chemical fallout problem because the dust could travel more than 1,000 miles through the air before settling. Like strontium-90 falling to earth thousands of miles from test sites, dioxin, emitted from 1,329 North American sources, was an imminent threat beyond the immediate vicinity of its source. According to Commoner and Mark Cohen, the primary authors of the report, the greatest risk of human exposure to dioxin came—as with radioactive fallout—through the food chain, as dioxin contaminated dairy foods and beef even though they were produced great distances from the sources of dioxin emissions. Commoner's interest in these findings was clear; by maximizing public concern, he hoped to garner enough public support to reduce or eliminate dioxin emissions in the United States.[60]

Dioxin had been detected as a highly toxic impurity in chlorinated herbicides such as 2,4,5-T, but was discovered as an environmental pollutant in 1973, when it was found in fish contaminated with the defoliant Agent Orange during the Vietnam War. In 1976, a pesticide plant accident in Seveso, Italy, spread dioxin and other contaminants through the community, resulting in abnormally high rates of cardiovascular disease and cancer.[61] At Love Canal, New York, in 1979, the discovery that the town had been built over a chemical waste dump—into which 130 pounds of dioxin had been dumped in the 1940s—forced residents to move out of their homes. Similarly, dirt roads and horse arenas in Times Beach, Missouri, were sprayed with 2,000 gallons of dioxin-contaminated oil for "dust control" on 26 May 1971. Fourteen years later, after the Environmental Protection Agency issued its first formal cancer risk assessment for dioxin, the town was evacuated and destroyed when it was found that the quantity of dioxin on the land still considerably exceeded the established cancer risk.[62] Commoner had long warned that the petrochemical industry produced toxins that broke out of the closing circle. Here, at Times Beach, that dire warning was made palpable. Much of the polyvinyl chloride (PVC) plastics that are found in medical products, toys, food packaging, plumbing, and vinyl siding was thrown in the trash and incinerated. Commoner told his keynote audience at the second Citizens' Conference on Dioxin, "Toxic waste is not simply a matter of poor housekeeping or bad management; it is an *inescapable* part of chlorine-based chemical production."[63]

To Commoner, it appeared that the designers, operators, and regulators of trash incinerators represented the next generation of deceitful industrialists. As well as dioxin, the new incinerators emitted mercury vapors and other heavy metals into the environment. While the waste industry insisted upon the safety of their factories and denied that they created dioxin in the combustion process—they promoted their resource recovery plants as state-of-the-art technology—a 1984 Environment Canada study unequivocally demonstrated that dioxin was indeed released by trash-burning incinerators.[64] Commoner concluded, "Clearly, trash-burning incinerators have serious environmental problems. But they reveal a failing that is even worse: the incinerator industry has been building these devices without fully understanding how they operate, at least with respect to their impact on the environment."[65] Lois Gibbs of the Citizens' Clearinghouse for Hazardous Waste remarked: "State of the art really just means industry's latest experiment."[66]

In response to these dangers, the debate over the Brooklyn Navy Yard incinerator took on the elements of an environmental justice struggle. While the emission of dioxin constituted an objective health hazard, the location of the site in the poor and minority-dominated neighborhood of Williamsburg raised the ire of numerous local groups. Commoner and the Center for the Biology of Natural Systems provided considerable technical aid to the local residents. According to Gandy, "Commoner, in advance of the emerging consensus against chlorine, succeeded in politicizing the science of waste incineration to an unprecedented extent and enabled community activists to utilize the latest advances in international toxicology and public health research."[67] In addition to its studies on dioxins and furans, the Center also considered local and national environmental problems, including asthma, intensive recycling, and ethanol's replacement of gasoline in automobiles.[68]

To Commoner, environmental injustice remained inherently connected to the political economy. "To the economist, a person exists to work and to earn money. Therefore, they call the value of a life the expected lifetime earnings of that person." As a result, the argument continued, the health of the poor was a smaller expense than the health of the wealthy, and environmental responses could proceed based upon economic value: extensive (and expensive) cleanup in more affluent communities, and less spending in poorer neighborhoods. "Of course, the American people do not believe that it is fair, right, or moral that poor people should be exposed to more pollution than rich people," Commoner continued. "Yet, the strange thing is, that is exactly what we have been doing. New York City's proposed trash burning plant is not slated to be built on Park Avenue."[69] Naturally, the real estate in Williamsburg was cheaper than comparable real estate on Park Avenue, and this harkened back to Commoner's earlier point about public values. The fact that the land was more affordable did not mean that local residents were more open to being subjected to air pollution. But that fell outside the scope of the economic investment. Indeed, according to Gandy, "The processing and disposal of waste products presents us with one of the sharpest geographical indices of social power etched into the urban landscape."[70]

Politics and economics tied these issues together: the problem of waste disposal resulted in corporate interests pushing to relax environmental regulations on air pollution, environmental cleanup, and other impediments to their profitability.[71] As Commoner noted in *Making Peace with the Planet,* "A reduction in the [official] cancer risk would have powerful consequences not only reducing the cost of the cleanup in [Times Beach] and many of the Superfund sites, but also enhancing the environmental acceptability of trash-burning incinerators, weakening the claims of Vietnam veterans who were exposed to Agent Orange, and affecting the outcome of numerous court cases."[72] But a reduction in official risk did nothing to reduce the real risk to which people were exposed. This kind of debate also threatened to limit the options available to resolve the problem. It was like looking at a gaping wound from a different angle so as to make it appear that the Band-Aid fit better. What this debate obscured was an examination of the alternatives.

And, as far as Commoner was concerned, there were alternatives. In his speech to the New Jersey Environmental Federation, he described two recycling studies conducted by the Center for the Biology of Natural Systems which, he indicated, offered some hope for a sustainable solution. In East Hampton, New York, residents conducted a ten-week pilot study, during which they separated their garbage into four groups: food garbage; paper; bottles and cans; and nonrecyclable plastics and other waste. The study demonstrated that with existing recycling technology, the East Hampton residents could recycle 84 percent of their trash.[73] Commoner also noted that in Seattle, Washington, residents had achieved 60 percent without even trying to compost their food wastes. "So it is clear that recycling can substitute for incineration to do the only thing that incineration is good at, which is to get rid of 70 percent of the trash. You can get rid of more of it by recycling."[74] And recycling could also be cost-effective. While the East Hampton study suggested that recycling was 35 percent cheaper than incineration even if expensive hazardous waste was dumped cheaply and locally, the Center for the Biology of Natural Systems' pilot recycling program in Buffalo, New York, showed that recycling was more economically beneficial to the local community. If communities purchased an incinerator, the study argued, money left the local community and ended up in the pockets of multinational corporations. Intensive recycling, in contrast, created more local jobs, and, in Buffalo's case, the local economy would receive a $12 million boost it would not enjoy with the purchase of an incinerator.[75]

But just as federal agencies funded research on solar energy just enough to suggest they were serious—but not nearly enough for it to yield any tangible results—state and municipal authorities set modest goals for recycling that would not damage the profitability of waste incinerators, those online and those contracted to be built. Commoner argued that the most significant obstacles to successful recycling programs were state laws that set modest recycling goals. In New Jersey, for example, the state required all counties to establish programs that recycled 25 percent of their trash. "What's the significance of this?" Commoner asked. "You have to ask, what happens to the other 75 percent?"[76] He continued, in *Making Peace with the Planet,* that 80 percent of trash could be recycled or incinerated, "but obviously not both."[77] In sum, Commoner's critique of state laws charged that states which aimed to recycle a quarter of their garbage were essentially guaranteeing that much of the remaining three quarters would be incinerated even though the majority of it could be recycled. "I tell you the New Jersey law . . . [is] a sly method for ensuring that incinerators will be built," Commoner told his New Jersey audience.[78] Indeed, as he noted in *Making Peace with the Planet,* "the only insurmountable hindrance to recycling is building an incinerator."[79] But while there existed an ecological allure to the inclusion of recycling in an integrated waste management program, Commoner argued that the compromise between recycling and incineration was not sufficient to prevent further environmental degradation. However, if the goal was "to give people a sense of ecological virtue, then any token amount of recycling . . . will do."[80] Commoner also recognized that the reluctance to adopt a more vigorous approach to recycling had as much to do with the cost of the incinerators that environmentalists and officials were trying to phase out. That it would take twenty to thirty years to pay off the cost of the incinerators constituted another external diseconomy, this time the continued hazard to human health.

Commoner noted with some frustration in *Making Peace with the Planet* that the human capacity to understand the environmental crisis had not resulted in any kind of remedy. "For the first time in the 4-billion-year history of life on this planet," he lamented, "living things are burdened with a host of alien man-made substances that are harmful to them."[81] The vast majority of these pollutants had become even more prevalent in animal tissue than they were twenty years earlier, when Earth Day first imposed itself on the popular consciousness. The corporate aversion to alternative technologies—solar energy or recycling, for example, in which they had little or no stake—was the hub of the enduring nature of the environmental crisis. Risk and access were intimately linked. Without access to decision-making, the American public was more exposed to environmental hazards imposed by business interests, and that exposure weighed disproportionately on the poor.

In a short piece that first appeared in *Greenpeace* in 1989, Commoner reflected on the environmental legislation that accompanied the American environmental awakening around Earth Day and asked the "important and perhaps embarrassing question: how far have we progressed toward the goal of restoring the quality of the environment?"[82] His answer the following year, in *Making Peace with the Planet,* was not positive: "The campaign to clean up the environment has largely failed," he wrote, "but not for lack of effort."[83] Commoner assessed the modest—and slowing—progress made since the energetic period immediately after Earth Day, but also pointed to a number of important and unequivocal successes. "Pollution levels of a few chemicals—DDT and PCBs in wildlife and people, mercury in the fish of the Great Lakes, strontium-90 in the food chain and phosphate pollution in some local rivers—have been reduced by 70 percent or more. Levels of airborne lead have declined more than 90 percent since 1975." These exceptions to a less heartening trend, he argued, helped explain what did and did not work. "Every success on the very short list of significant environmental quality improvements reflects the same remedial action: *production of the pollutant has been stopped.*" DDT and PCBs had been banned; mercury had been eliminated from the manufacture of chlorine; lead had been removed from gasoline; and the cessation of atmospheric nuclear testing had resulted in a reduction of strontium-90 in the environment. "The lesson is plain: pollution prevention works; pollution control does not."[84] In successful cases, instead of legislating limitations on the release of these toxins, governments restricted their production or use.

In contrast, controls on other pollutants had been much less effective and were, Commoner contended, "ultimately self-defeating."[85] Gradual reduction of pollutants did not seem to work, and multiple entry points into the environment inevitably made control measures next to impossible. Between 1975 and 1981, the Environmental Protection Agency recorded that sulfur dioxide emissions, a major contributor to acid rain, had declined by 19 percent, but then remained constant. Between 1975 and 1985, nitrogen oxides emissions from automobile exhausts and power plants that were converted into photochemical smog increased by 4 percent, and in 1987, carbon monoxide, which caused respiratory problems, still exceeded Environmental Protection Agency standards in a number of cities including New York.[86] "The few real improvements," Commoner argued, "have been achieved not by adding control devices or concealing pollutants (as by pumping hazardous chemical wastes into deep water-bearing strata) but simply by eliminating the pollutants."[87]

There were two related lessons here. The first suggested that compromise and control were not as effective as prevention. The only real successes had occurred when the relevant technologies were changed to eliminate the pollutant. As a result, the second lesson indicated that reforming production processes—democratizing the governance of the means of production—was the only effective method of resolving the environmental crisis. For Commoner, American environmentalism had been concentrating on treating the symptoms of pollution, not preventing the disease.

In his keynote address at the second Citizens' Conference on Dioxin in St. Louis on 30 July 1994, Commoner told his audience:

> The history of dioxin is a sordid story of devastating sickness inflicted, unawares, on chemical workers; of callous disregard for the impact of toxic wastes on the public; of denial after denial by the chemical industry; of the industry's repeated efforts to hide the facts about dioxin and, when these become known, to distort them. . . . We need to learn what must be done, now, not merely to diminish, but to *end* the menace of dioxin and its many toxic cousins to life.[88]

To that end, Commoner embraced the environmental justice impulse. Environmental justice advocates, he argued in a 1987 article in *The New Yorker,* were better positioned to fight for environmental health, because for them, "The front line of the battle against chemical pollution is not in Washington, it is in their own communities. For them, the issues are clear-cut and are not readily compromised . . . the corporations are on one side and the people of the community on the other, challenging the corporations' exclusive power to make decisions that threaten the community's health." Commoner was less charitable toward the major environmental organizations, which, for a variety of reasons during the 1980s, had shifted much of their resources into lobbying and litigating. For Commoner, this could result only in compromise. "The national organizations deal with the environmental disease by negotiating about the kind of Band-Aid to apply to it," he wrote in *The New Yorker.* In contrast, "The community groups deal with the disease by trying to prevent it."[89] Prevention was the key to environmental justice because those neighborhoods were the final refuges from many pollution hazards. As Commoner told his New Jersey

Environmental Federation audience, the grassroots environmental movement "exemplifies the cutting edge of environmentalism," and was largely responsible for curbing the advances of the nuclear/incineration industry by asking for facts, seeking the truth, and insisting that their backyards were not sinks for pollutants.[90]

For Commoner, the grassroots struggle to participate equally in community and environmental decision-making processes was part of a much larger engagement to reclaim public sovereignty over quality-of-life issues and concerns. In sum, the environmental justice movement seemed to be fighting for social and democratic governance of production, which had been at the heart of Commoner's own activism since before World War II. It was also in this particular struggle that Commoner saw the blending of social and environmental activisms that he felt was pivotal to the survival and success of American environmentalism. American environmentalism needed to find itself more in concert with the civil rights movement, the peace movement, the feminist movement, the antiwar movement, and the labor movement. At the same time, these other interests needed to imagine the political landscape more holistically. Together, Commoner wrote in a 1987 article in *The New Yorker,* this larger movement for social governance "constitute[s] not only the major aspects of public policy but its most profound expression: human rights; the quality of life; health; jobs; peace; survival. . . . Here environmentalism reaches a common ground with all the other movements, for each of them also bears a fundamental relation to the choice of production technologies."[91]

In 1990, Commoner began writing *Making Peace with the Planet* as an analysis of environmental improvements in the twenty years since the first Earth Day. "Since the early 1970s," he wrote:

> the country has been governed by basic laws that were intended to eliminate air and water pollution and to rid the environment of toxic chemicals and of agricultural and urban wastes. National and state environmental agencies have been established; about a trillion dollars of public and private money have been spent; local organizations have proliferated. Environmental issues have taken a permanent place in the country's political life.[92]

But ozone depletion, global warming, the ongoing contamination of groundwater and oceans, increasing smog in urban centers, the continuing problems of storing more radioactive waste, and the widespread chemical contamination of food, water, and human bodies suggested that in spite of all that legislation and effort to reverse environmental destruction, the American environmental consciousness was, in the journalist Mark Dowie's words, "losing ground."[93] Both Commoner and Dowie saw an emerging hope, however, in the environmental justice movement, which advocated prevention rather than control, and promoted, generally, a zero tolerance approach to toxins and other pollutants. Some chemicals could not be controlled. As the biologist Joe Thornton points out, "If Love Canal taught us a lesson, it should be this: pollutants do not stay where we put them."[94]

"Control" was part of the conservationist vocabulary. It made sense. One did not want to prevent resource extraction; one only wanted it to be properly managed so that resources were not wasted or depleted. "Prevention," on the other hand, was part of the new environmental language, which applied to questions of human health and community empowerment. The languages were fundamentally different and almost required a conflict of interests, especially when it came to the more dangerous chemical pollutants. But here was the significance of pluralism. The political scientist David Schlosberg has argued that "there is no such thing as environmentalism. Any attempt to define the term in a succinct manner necessarily excludes an array of other valid definitions. 'Environmentalism' is simply a convenience—a vague label for an amazingly diverse array of ideas that have grown around the contemplation of the relationship between human beings and their surroundings."[95]

The catch, or the problem, or the source of tension between the nationally based, mainstream environmental organizations and the environmental justice movement stemmed from their use of the same language and disagreement over its ownership. For local environmental justice advocates, compromise was rarely a part of their environmental vocabulary when it came to arresting hazardous pollutants that made their children ill and threatened their communities. There is no victory in limiting risk, they would argue, when risk should rightly be abolished or removed. Problems arose, then, when control of environmental pollutants was adopted even when local residents considered control an empty victory.

The ongoing political marginalization of poor and minority interests from decision-making processes was consistent with the stratification of American power. That environmental justice activism provoked the ire of corporate and governmental agencies was hardly surprising, given its hard-line message and tactics. But this was a power game and, as Commoner noted, environmental justice "represents social (as contrasted with private) governance of the means of production—an idea that is so foreign to what passes for our national ideology that even to mention it violates a deep-seated taboo."[96] The thrust of environmental justice's campaign to protect human lives and communities from dangerous pollutants helped to expand the American environmental consciousness. Health and quality-of-life questions had been front and center at the first Earth Day, but the environmental justice movement ensured that these questions developed tangible rather than abstract meaning.

Conclusion

If We Would Know Life

Come, my friends,
'Tis not too late to seek a newer world.
—Alfred, Lord Tennyson

On 17 February 1965, at the fourth Mellon Lecture at the University of Pittsburgh's School of Medicine, Commoner gave a paper titled "Is Biology a Molecular Science?" He criticized molecular biology and the new cult of DNA, which promised to unlock the secret of life, and concluded his remarks with the assertion "If we would know life, we must cherish it—in our laboratories and in the world."[1] It was a simple statement, but one that would resonate through most all of his activism and take on especially poignant significance by the end of the twentieth century. Commoner's environmental apparatus—dissent, information, and public risk analysis—had been designed precisely to avoid the hubris inherent in the notion that human science and technology were impervious to the laws of nature. At the beginning of the twenty-first century, however, that remained a lesson learned only in retrospect.

Early in 2002, Commoner would reiterate his conviction that life must be cherished in an article in *Harper's* that put him back in the center of a public and scientific maelstrom. As the Human Genome Project conceded that it would not uncover enough genes to account for the complexity of our inherited traits, as activists all over the world—and especially in Europe—had taken to the streets to oppose the continued development of biotechnology and genetically modified food products, Commoner closed another circle by returning to the discipline in which he had started his career, cautioning against renewed technological optimism, pointing to the limits of DNA analysis, and reviving his faith in the science information movement. "Biology once was regarded as a languid, largely descriptive discipline, a passive science that was content, for much of its history, merely to observe the natural world rather than change it," he wrote. "No longer."[2] In many respects, biotechnology is a fitting conclusion to this study, because it encapsulates the spectrum of Commoner's larger social and scientific concerns and the problems that propelled him into the vanguard of American environmentalism.

For forty years, Commoner's criticisms of the petrochemical industry focused on the manner in which its products barged unwelcome into the chemistry of living things and polluted people, animals, and ecosystems. While most of the chemicals manufactured or released as waste by the petrochemical industry resembled the structure of chemical components found in nature, they were sufficiently different to be hazardous to life. To Commoner, the connection to twenty-first century genetic engineering was clear: we were in the process of committing the same tragic error, but this time with the secret of life. According to Stephen Fox, "Commoner resisted genetic theory, because it applied models from physics and chemistry to living cells, thereby wiping out the vital distinction between animate and inanimate matter. Without that distinction in place, modern technology was free to manipulate inanimate nature with a blithe disregard for any implications for living creatures."[3] But Commoner's attack was not based on such a strictly conservationist or philosophical concern over the social repercussions of what constituted inanimate matter. To Commoner, the politics and economics of scientific research had dubbed genetic theory as the new field that warranted unconditional support, but by the turn of the century genetic theory was still prone to disaster because it did not "take into account *all* the relevant data and [was] based on an arbitrary exclusion of certain essential facts."[4] In many respects, then, Commoner's critique was a reiteration of his long-held concern about technological progress creating or stumbling into unanticipated problems. Enthusiasm for the potential of technology, he argued, constituted the protean source of social and scientific mismanagement that "too often . . . has led us to exaggerate our power to control the potent agents which we have let loose in the environment."[5] The promise of genetic engineering represented another example of profit supplanting uncertainty in the determination of the risk.

With typical flair, Commoner noted in 1967: "It should now be clear that the power given to man by modern science is based on seriously incomplete knowledge and carries with it the grave risk of acting in ignorance. The notion that we must unquestioningly use the power that science endows has now become an unreliable guide to modern life."[6] Out of the laboratory and into the farmer's field (and, indeed, the frying pan), genetic engineering immediately became an environmental issue. To critics, the new science brought dark and ominous implications to American food production and consumption. Commoner referred to biotechnology as "an endless invasion into life. . . . We don't know what's going to happen but something will happen and I think we need to be afraid."[7] As difficult as it was to escape the hazards of nuclear fallout, the relative ubiquity of molecular biology's fruits (and vegetables and animals, for that matter) could potentially pose an equally unavoidable threat. Its capacity to selectively transfer genes from one *species* to another was an incredible feat of technology that far surpassed any innovation of Mendelian selective breeding. The science of the genome has been adopted by the food industry to grow bigger, faster, cheaper crops. Flavr Savr tomatoes, for example, were designed to ripen more slowly, so they would last longer after being picked; corn and soybeans were made tolerant of pesticides; canola, papaya, cotton, and countless other crops were "improved" in one way or another. As we have already witnessed in the production of automobiles, plastics, and synthetic chemicals generally, bigger, faster, cheaper does not always mean better, healthier, and more environmentally sound. Nor does it imply careful analysis of unforeseen environmental costs.

Armed with the weapons necessary to break the genetic code, molecular biology appeared, in Commoner's words, "poised to assume godlike powers of creation, calling forth artificial forms of life rather than undiscovered elements and subatomic particles."[8] The molecular biologists' conceit eerily mirrored a similar aura of omnipotence that had surrounded the antagonists of Commoner's first environmental campaign. After World War II, as the scientific supremacy of nuclear physics evolved into a Cold War arms race, physicists were increasingly disparaged for introducing the potential for global annihilation and the unanticipated fallout hazards that accompanied nuclear weapons testing.[9] Physicists successfully smashed the nucleus of the atom, but they found that they were unable to predict the properties of the whole nucleus by studying its parts. This oversight had been the ecological failing of the petrochemical industry as well, as it produced chemicals that reacted poorly in the environment. The results were alarming, and were indicative of what Pnina Abir-Am regarded as part of the "ongoing historical process of 'progressive colonization' by the so-called exact sciences."[10] Fallout poisoned Americans indiscriminately; DDT was more effective than it was supposed to be; and at the end of the twentieth century, after thirty years of heightened environmental awareness, American air and water systems experienced dangerously high levels of toxicity. Commoner argued that only through examining matter in its natural environment could relationships with other organisms be properly understood. The human condition was inextricably linked to biological systems. Everything was indeed connected to everything else.

Commoner's insistence on the importance of cherishing life struck at the very nerve center of environmental concern. It preached caution and warned against unmitigated technological enthusiasm, the products of which had galvanized Commoner, Rachel Carson, and a new environmental movement to protest the proliferation of chemical pollutants. To cherish life also meant to abandon the fallacy that humans could completely dominate or control nature. This line of thinking was the crux of conservationist thought and had developed a strong following since the Progressive era. Further, cherishing life also challenged the unquestioning application of science. The pursuit of knowledge was a worthy goal, but its utility seemed to have been perverted from improving human welfare to promoting industrial progress and equating welfare with levels of consumption. In this capacity, Commoner spoke as a scientist, criticizing the hubris of his own discipline. Most important, however, cherishing life offered a powerful directive on how societies and people should interact. How could we work to protect nature if we were unable to treat each other more humanely? In this vein, working for peace and against poverty, for civil and women's rights and against tyranny, intersected with more traditional environmental interests as part of the same mission. In essence, cherishing life meant striving toward a more egalitarian world.

In 1997, just as he readied himself to refocus his energy on genetic theory, Commoner turned eighty. In recognition of his birthday, a symposium was held in New York City to celebrate him as an international leader in the environmental movement. Invited speakers from around the world—friends, colleagues, and fellow activists of all stripes—spoke about Commoner's influence and contribution. Peter Montague, the director of the Environmental Research Foundation, championed Commoner as "the father of grassroots environmentalism," charting the influence of his career on grassroots environmentalism in the United States. Montague pointed out that Commoner "developed many of the fundamental ideas that today propel the burgeoning movement of grassroots environmental activism." These included such tenets as the public being the guardians of moral wisdom and having a right to know the risks inherent in policy decisions; specialists possess no special moral authority and have an obligation to make alliances with citizens; pollution must be prevented, because it cannot be successfully managed; and the understanding of risk is political in nature, not scientific.[11]

Commoner's longtime fellow activist, Virginia Brodine, followed Montague and reflected on the significance of the Committees for Nuclear and Environmental Information. While Montague addressed Commoner's influence on grassroots activism, Brodine talked specifically about the power of the science information movement as a mode of public empowerment. That movement, Brodine contended, was buoyed by Commoner's clarity of purpose. "What carried . . . the whole organization along more than anything else was Barry Commoner's unwavering confidence in the importance of information and the ability of the public to understand and use it."[12] After Brodine, the labor leader Tony Mazzocchi recalled the environmental and occupational health work in which Commoner had engaged, demonstrating the relationship between labor and the environment. He was followed by Ralph Nader, who attacked "junk science," and the dangerous relationship between science and corporate money.

Cumulatively, the papers presented in celebration of Commoner's birthday painted a picture of Commoner's activism since World War II. His mode of dissent—the insistence on the importance of open discourse—reflected the period. As the Cold War imposed a cultural and political conformity that polarized American society and ghettoized disparate social concerns such as those for the environment and social justice, Commoner struggled to create a forum for public discourse and dissent. He framed his position in American values, particularly the centrality of democracy to the American condition and the scientist's responsibility to the public, and proceeded to draw connections between social and environmental problems that developed after World War II. The message was unashamedly holistic. As Nader observed, Commoner refrained from limiting his criticism of environmental issues to particular risk or hazard levels. Rather, "He asks much more fundamental questions as to what is the utility of the petrochemical industry and why do we even have a fossil fuel-based industry projected into the next century? What is the nature of industrial organizations that has to be changed so that we develop different kinds of incentives for different kinds of environmentally benign technologies?"[13] The bigger questions provoked bigger challenges to American political and economic systems.

Commoner gave the final address that day: a paper titled "What Is Yet to Be Done," a none-too-subtle reference to Lenin's celebrated essay. Commoner's was a lighthearted speech, but one laced with a solemn sense of purpose that in more than fifty years of activism had not waned. "The environmental crisis expresses the relation between science and society in a special way," he told the gathering. "It illustrates the overriding importance of action."[14] The themes he presented were familiar and wide-ranging. "The environmental crisis arises from a fundamental fault," he claimed:

> Our systems of production—in industry, agriculture, energy, and transportation—essential as they are, make people sick and die. As the Surgeon General would say, these processes are hazardous to your health. But that is only the *immediate* problem. Down the line, these same production processes threaten a series of global human catastrophes: higher temperatures; the seas rising to flood many of the world's cities; more frequent severe weather; and dangerous exposure to ultraviolet radiation. The nonhuman sectors of the living ecosystem are also affected by the crisis: ancient forest reserves are disappearing; wetlands and estuaries are impaired; numerous species are threatened with extinction.[15]

But the environmental crisis was a human event, caused by what people do, and the ultimate measure of its impact was the threat to human health and well-being. If environmentalism was devoted to human welfare, Commoner argued, then the northern exploitation of the southern world needed to be addressed. "We, who are environmental advocates, must find a way—for the sake of the planet and the people who live on it—to join a historic mission to end poverty wherever it exists. That," he concluded, "is what is yet to be done."[16]

From the late nineteenth century to World War II, Americans witnessed "the transformation of science from a mostly amateur and individualized undertaking to a complex, professionalized, and largely government-sponsored endeavor."[17] The organizational and financial advantages of such a transformation were obvious. The danger, however, was that expertise might trump public interest and culminate in the cloistering of scientific knowledge and, as a result, policy and decision-making. These fears came to fruition during the Cold War as concerns over national security condoned secrecy. By the beginning of the 1960s, outgoing President Dwight D. Eisenhower warned against the impending powers of the emerging military-industrial complex. In his study of the postwar science establishment, Stuart W. Leslie called it the military-industrial-academic complex in order to emphasize the complicity of independent research.[18] From its earliest stages, Commoner's career sought to reconnect professionalized science with the public interest. If it sounded like a crusade, that is because—in a sense—it was. As the 1960s ushered in a period of receptivity to environmental protection, Commoner couched his rhetoric in that burgeoning language.

In so doing, Commoner influenced the direction of the modern environmental movement and helped foster its sophisticated concern for public health and the human body as an environmental landscape needing protection. The marriage of natural resource conservation and public health was frequently divisive, but it also generated a new and innovative arsenal as well as novel directions for environmental activism—economics, class politics, and globalization, for example—and presented the prospect of further coalitions that transcended race, class, and national boundaries. That is the optimistic conclusion, anyway. And it is one that sees the contemporary debates over genetic engineering and global warming as the greatest environmental threats since nuclear weapons, but also as having the potential to unite the disparate factions of American environmentalism. Conservationists, environmental justice advocates, radical environmentalists, and human health advocates express grave concerns about genetic engineering and global warming. A common front might indeed restimulate American environmentalism. But that is the optimistic conclusion. Though he was ever the congenital optimist, Commoner acknowledged that the scale and the scope of environmental deterioration were becoming more—rather than less—worrisome.

Indeed, Commoner's historical significance and the tragedy of this narrative stem from the breadth of environmental issues he addressed that remain not just historical artifacts but ongoing contemporary problems.

And at a point when the direction of the contemporary environmental movement is at best unclear, perhaps Commoner's career warrants more careful attention. The apparatus he brought to his activism and the manner in which he sought to define the relationship between environmental issues and a more comprehensive movement for social justice might be worth another—more careful—look. During the latter half of the twentieth century, Commoner represented a durable, stalwart, and remarkably consistent position that American society needed to revise the manner in which it accepted or rejected risk. He saw this revision as being integral to any program that might offer social and environmental sustainability over the long term, but he also insisted it was a critical and missing element of a functional democracy. As a prominent and early dissenting voice in the discourse on postwar technological influence, Commoner helps shed light on the moral and political intricacies of American society *inside* the environmental crisis.

Notes

Introduction: The New Apparatus

1. Barry Commoner, *The Closing Circle: Nature, Man, and Technology* (New York: Knopf, 1971), 11.

2. Rachel Carson, *Silent Spring* (Boston: Houghton Mifflin, 1962).

3. This suggestion is put forward by Theodore M. Porter in *Trust in Numbers: The Pursuit of Objectivity in Science and Public Life* (Princeton, NJ: Princeton University Press, 1995), 16. See also Edmund Russell, *War and Nature: Fighting Humans and Insects With Chemicals From World War I to Silent Spring* (New York: Cambridge University Press, 2001). Russell posits the theory that "war and nature coevolved: the control of nature expanded the scale of war, and war expanded the scale on which people controlled nature." See page 2.

4. Commoner, *The Closing Circle,* 129.

5. Barry Commoner, *Science and Survival* (New York: Viking Press, 1966), 3.

6. Samuel P. Hays, *Beauty, Health, and Permanence: Environmental Politics in the United States, 1955–1985* (Cambridge: Cambridge University Press, 1987), 4–5.

7. Lydia Saad and Riley Dunlap, "Americans Are Environmentally Friendly, but Issue Not Seen as Urgent Problem," *Gallup Poll Monthly* 415 (April 2000), 12–18.

8. Arthur Ekirch, Jr., *Man and Nature in America* (New York: Columbia University Press, 1963), 189.

9. While the average fuel rate (miles per gallon) for vehicles on American roads has increased substantially since 1973 (from 11.9 miles per gallon in 1973 to 16.9 miles per gallon in 2000), recently there has been a distressing move to larger vehicles. The ratio of passenger cars to total vehicles declined from 80 percent in 1977 to 64 percent in 1995. See George Martin, "Grounding Social Ecology: Landscape, Settlement, and Right of Way," *Capitalism Nature Socialism* 13 (March 2002), 3–30. Bigger vehicles invariably mean greater fuel consumption, so while passenger cars have continued to become more fuel-efficient, the average fuel rate for all vehicles has fluctuated only mildly since 1991. See the Department of Energy Web site statistics: http://www.eia.doe.gov/emeu/aer/txt/ptb0209.html. Further, while per vehicle fuel consumption is lower than before the oil crisis, it has

climbed back to the 1980 rate, a disturbing rise associated with the increasing popularity of sport utility vehicles. See John Cloud and Amanda Bower, "Why SUV Is All the Rage," *TIME* (24 February 2003), 35–42. See also Keith Bradsher, *High and Mighty: The Dangerous Rise of the SUV* (New York: Public Affairs, 2003).

10. Hal K. Rothman, *The Greening of a Nation? Environmentalism in the United States Since 1945* (Orlando, FL: Harcourt Brace College, 1998), 210.

11. For cancer rates among children, statistics are available from the National Cancer Institute. See http://seer.cancer.gov/csr/1975_2001/sections.html. For the growing asthma rates among children, see the American Lung Association Web site, http://www.lungusa.org/.

12. Michael Shellenberger and Ted Norhaus, "The Death of Environmentalism: Global Warming Politics in a Post-Environmental World," online at http://www.thebreakthrough.org/images/Death_of_Environmentalism.pdf.

13. Barry Commoner, "A Reporter at Large: The Environment," *The New Yorker,* 15 June 1987, 46–71. Quotation is from page 46.

14. Ibid., 54–56.

15. Barry Commoner, "The Scholar's Obligation to Dissent," commencement address, University of California at San Francisco Medical Center, 10 June 1967 (Barry Commoner Papers, LoC, box 493), 7.

16. Cass R. Sunstein, *Why Societies Need Dissent* (Cambridge, MA: Harvard University Press, 2003), 6.

17. Ibid., 5.

18. Commoner, "The Scholar's Obligation to Dissent," 6.

19. Donald Worster, *Under Western Skies: Nature and History in the American West* (New York: Oxford University Press, 1992), 17.

20. Sylvia Noble Tesh, *Uncertain Hazards: Environmental Activists and Scientific Proof* (Ithaca, NY: Cornell University Press, 2000), 81–99.

21. Ulrich Beck, *Risk Society: Towards a New Modernity,* translated by Mark Ritter (London: Sage, 1992).

22. Frederick Buell, *From Apocalypse to Way of Life: Environmental Crisis in the American Century* (New York: Routledge, 2003), 193.

23. Thomas P. Hughes, *American Genesis: A Century of Invention and Technological Enthusiasm* (New York: Viking Press, 1989), 4.

24. Brian Balogh, *Chain Reaction: Expert Debate and Public Participation in American Commercial Nuclear Power, 1945–1975* (New York: Cambridge University Press, 1991). See also Thomas Raymond Wellock, *Critical Masses: Opposition to Nuclear Power in California, 1958–1978* (Madison: University of Wisconsin Press, 1998), 4.

25. Donald Worster, *Nature's Economy: A History of Ecological Ideas,* 2nd ed. (New York: Cambridge University Press, 1994), 22.

26. Donald Fleming, "Roots of the New Conservation Movement," *Perspectives in American History* 6 (1972), 7–91. Scientists had long been politically active, but

after World War II, they became more prominently visible and the channels through which their politics were conveyed became more public.

27. In so doing, chapter 1 walks a tightrope between competing historiographies in science and technology. In *Beyond the Laboratory: Scientists as Political Activists in 1930s America,* Peter J. Kuznick argues that "the 1930s proved to be a critical period for the scientists. Never again would science exude the benign, thaumaturgic innocence of these prewar years." In addition, Kuznick notes that during the Depression, scientists were confronted with the public's growing distrust of science and technology. In contrast, Thomas P. Hughes argues that "the attitude of Americans toward technology was one of enthusiasm until after World War II, when the temper of the times changed markedly." In discussing technological dissent prior to World War II, Hughes refers to "a reflective minority [that] lamented the rise of the grim industrial city, poison gases, and bombing raids, the monotony of the assembly line, and the unemployment caused by the replacement of workers by machines." Peter J. Kuznick, *Beyond the Laboratory: Scientists as Political Activists in 1930s America* (Chicago: University of Chicago Press, 1987), 2; and Hughes, *American Genesis,* 443. I posit that World War II marks a critical turning point in American environmental history as a result of the new and polluting technologies that flooded the market and the physical environment, but that "scientists" were not altogether caught off guard, as Commoner's own training and subsequent activism would suggest.

28. Barry Commoner, quoted in Andrew Szasz, *EcoPopulism: Toxic Waste and the Movement for Environmental Justice* (Minneapolis: University of Minnesota Press, 1994), 153.

29. Commoner, *Science and Survival,* 29.

Chapter 1: In the Thunderclap's Wake

1. Lizabeth Cohen, *A Consumers' Republic: The Politics of Mass Consumption in Postwar America* (New York: Knopf, 2003), 6. Cohen argues that "in the aftermath of World War II a fundamental shift in America's economy, politics, and culture took place, with major consequences for how Americans made a living, where they dwelled, how they interacted with others, what and how they consumed, what they expected of government, and much else." Cohen, *A Consumers' Republic,* 8.

2. For quotations, see Beard's introduction to J. B. Bury, *The Idea of Progress* (New York: Macmillan, 1932), xxii, xx. See also Charles A. Beard (ed.), *A Century of Progress* (New York: Harper & Bros., 1933), 3–19.

3. David M. Potter, *People of Plenty: Economic Abundance and the American Character* (Chicago: University of Chicago Press, 1954).

4. Robert Righter, *Wind Energy in America: A History* (Norman: University of Oklahoma Press, 1996), 149.

5. In *The Affluent Society,* the economist John Kenneth Galbraith criticized the American pursuit of private consumption at the expense of social consumption, the infrastructure necessary for a humane society; the social theorist Herbert

Marcuse noted the relationship between mass consumption, mass culture, and mass complacency in *One-Dimensional Man;* and the historian Daniel Bell lamented the decline of the "public household" and social solidarity in favor of personal consumption. John Kenneth Galbraith, *The Affluent Society* (Boston: Houghton Mifflin, 1958); Herbert Marcuse, *One-Dimensional Man: Studies in the Ideology of Advanced Industrial Society* (Boston: Beacon Press, 1964); and Daniel Bell, *The Cultural Contradictions of Capitalism* (New York: Basic Books, 1976). See also Christopher Lasch, *The Culture of Narcissism: American Life in an Age of Diminishing Expectations* (New York: Norton, 1978); and C. Wright Mills, *White Collar: The American Middle Classes* (New York: Oxford University Press, 1951).

6. Elmo Richardson, *Dams, Parks, and Politics* (Lexington: University Press of Kentucky, 1973), 201.

7. Jared Diamond, *Guns, Germs, and Steel: The Fates of Human Societies* (New York: Norton, 1997), 247–248. In addition to economic advantage, social value and prestige, compatibility with vested interests, and the ease with which a new technology's advantages can be discerned composed Diamond's four factors that influence the social acceptance of technological innovations.

8. Barry Commoner, *The Closing Circle* (New York: Knopf, 1971), 177.

9. Barry Commoner, "Fallout and Water Pollution—Parallel Cases," *Scientist and Citizen* 6 (December 1964), 2–7. Quotation is from page 2.

10. Mary Douglas and Aaron Wildavsky, *Risk and Culture: An Essay on the Selection of Technical and Environmental Dangers* (Berkeley: University of California Press, 1982), 3. According to the sociologist of science Steven Shapin, "Good order and certainty in science have been produced at the price of disorder and uncertainty elsewhere in our culture." Shapin was discussing the tensions of knowledge acquisition during the seventeenth century, but his observations bear particular relevance to postwar environmentalism, where new innovations created the context for widespread and unprecedented environmental decline and further questions. Steven Shapin, *The Scientific Revolution* (Chicago: University of Chicago Press, 1996), 164.

11. While we might appreciate that science and technology are ubiquitous features of public life in the United States, many observers have suggested that federal science and technology policy developed as part of a general and coherent postwar consensus inspired by presidential science adviser Vannevar Bush's seminal publication *Science, the Endless Frontier* (Washington, DC: U.S. Government Printing Office, 1945). For a good summary of Bush's life and work, see G. Pascal Zachary, *Endless Frontier: Vannevar Bush, Engineer of the American Century* (New York: Free Press, 1997). More recent scholarship has argued that that dialogue was indeed far more complex. See, for example, David M. Hart, *Forged Consensus: Science, Technology, and Economic Policy in the United States, 1921–1953* (Princeton, NJ: Princeton University Press, 1998); Patrick J. McGrath, *Scientists, Business, and the State, 1890–1960* (Chapel Hill: University of North Carolina Press, 2002); Jessica Wang, *American Science in an Age of Anxiety: Scientists, Anticommunism, and the Cold War* (Chapel Hill: University of North Carolina Press, 1999); Peter J. Kuznick, *Beyond the Laboratory: Scientists as Political Activists in*

1930s America (Chicago: University of Chicago Press, 1987); A. Hunter Dupree, *Science in the Federal Government: A History of Policies and Activities to 1940* (Cambridge, MA: Belknap Press of Harvard University Press, 1957); Daniel J. Kevles, "The National Science Foundation and the Debate Over Postwar Research Policy, 1942–1945," *Isis* 68 (March 1977), 5–26; and Michael A. Dennis, "A Change of State: The Political Cultures of Technical Practice at the MIT Instrumentation Laboratory and the Johns Hopkins University Applied Physics Laboratory, 1930–1945," Ph.D. dissertation, Johns Hopkins University, 1991.

12. Donald Fleming, "Roots of the New Conservation Movement," *Perspectives in American History* 6 (1972), 7–91. See pages 40–43. Rae Goodell calls these politically engaged scientists the "visible scientists"; Ralph E. Lapp refers to the "new priesthood"; and Joel Primack and Frank von Hippell discuss what they term "public interest science." In contrast, Kuznick rejects titles and simply calls them scientists who became involved. Rae Goodell, *The Visible Scientists* (Boston: Little, Brown, 1977); Ralph E. Lapp, *The New Priesthood: The Scientific Elite and the Uses of Power* (New York: Harper & Row, 1965); Joel R. Primack and Frank von Hippell, *Advice and Dissent: Scientists in the Political Arena* (New York: Basic Books, 1974), 3–9; and Kuznick, *Beyond the Laboratory.*

13. Richard C. Lewontin, *Biology as Ideology: The Doctrine of DNA* (Toronto: Anansi Press, 1991), 3.

14. David DeLeon (ed.), *Leaders From the 1960s: A Biographical Sourcebook of American Activism* (Westport, CT: Greenwood Press, 1994), 313.

15. Barry Commoner, conversation with author, 25 August 2005.

16. Barry Commoner, interview with author, 15 November 2001. Chief among studies that examine American scientists as activists prior to World War II is Kuznick, *Beyond the Laboratory.* See also Charles William Heywood, "Scientists and Society in the United States, 1900–1940: Changing Concepts of Social Responsibility," Ph.D. dissertation, University of Pennsylvania, 1954.

17. Elizabeth Hodes, "Precedents for Social Responsibility Among Scientists: The American Association of Scientific Workers and the Federation of American Scientists, 1938–1948," Ph.D. dissertation, University of California at Santa Barbara, 1982, 59. In 1950, Senator Joseph McCarthy attacked the American Association of Scientific Workers as a Communist movement. Though Commoner escaped censure, the group was weakened.

18. Kuznick, *Beyond the Laboratory,* 2. For Thimann, Elliott, and the American Association of Scientific Workers, see ibid., 227–252.

19. Hodes, "Precedents for Social Responsibility Among Scientists," 258. See also Christopher Lewis, "Progress and Apocalypse: Science and the End of the Modern World," Ph.D. dissertation, University of Minnesota, 1991, 300–352.

20. Barry Commoner, interview with author, 22 November 2002. For readings on the Jewish experience in the United States, see Hasia R. Diner, *A New Promised Land: A History of Jews in America* (New York: Oxford University Press, 2003), and *In the Almost Promised Land: American Jews and Blacks, 1915–1935* (Westport, CT: Greenwood Press, 1977); Jennifer Lee, *Civility in the City: Blacks, Jews,*

and Koreans in Urban America (Cambridge, MA: Harvard University Press, 2002); and Carey McWilliams, *A Mask for Privilege: Anti-Semitism in America* (Boston: Little, Brown, 1948). For the relationship between religious ethos and environmental persuasion, see Donald Worster, "John Muir and the Roots of American Environmentalism," in Worster's *The Wealth of Nature: Environmental History and the Ecological Imagination* (New York: Oxford University Press, 1993), 184–202; and Mark Stoll, "Green Versus Green: Religions, Ethics, and the Bookchin-Foreman Dispute," *Environmental History* 6 (July 2001), 412–427.

21. See Douglas H. Strong, *Dreamers and Defenders: American Conservationists* (Lincoln: University of Nebraska Press, 1988), 223. See also Danny Kohl, "Barry Commoner's Science: An Anecdotal Overview," in *Barry Commoner's Contribution to the Environmental Movement: Science and Social Action,* edited by David Kriebel (Amityville, NY: Baywood, 2002), 45–56.

22. See Merritt Roe Smith, "Technology, Industrialization, and the Idea of Progress in America," in *Responsible Science: The Impact of Technology on Society,* edited by Kevin B. Byrne (San Francisco: Harper & Row, 1986), 1–20; and Leo Marx, "Does Improved Technology Mean Progress?," *Technology Review* 90 (January 1987), 32–41, 71.

23. Robert V. Bruce, *The Launching of Modern American Science, 1846–1876* (Ithaca, NY: Cornell University Press, 1987), 3.

24. Walter Lippmann, *Drift and Mastery* ([1914] Englewood Cliffs, NJ: Prentice-Hall, 1961), 151.

25. See Philip P. Wiener (ed.), *Values in a Universe of Chance: Selected Writings of Charles S. Peirce* (Garden City, NY: Doubleday, 1958), 113–136.

26. Charles A. Beard and Mary R. Beard, *The Rise of American Civilization,* new ed., rev. and enl. (New York: Macmillan, 1930), 52–121. For a good overview of the intellectual instability of the period, see Louis Menand, *The Metaphysical Club: A Story of Ideas in America* (New York: Farrar, Straus, and Giroux, 2001).

27. The 1910 U.S. Census listed the American urban population at 42,166,120, and the rural population at 49,806,146. The 1920 Census listed the urban population at 54,304,603, and the rural population at 51,406,017. "Urban" referred to communities of more than 2,500 people. U.S. Bureau of the Census, *Statistical Abstract of the United States, 1940* (Washington, DC: Bureau of the Census, 1941), 8. See also Robert H. Wiebe, *The Search for Order, 1877–1920* (New York: Hill and Wang, 1967). This transition from an agrarian society to an urban one was also largely powered, of course, by huge numbers of immigrants who poured into the United States—mostly from Europe—until just before World War I.

28. Lewis Mumford, *The City in History: Its Origins, Its Transformations, and Its Prospects* (New York: Harcourt, Brace & World, 1961), 478–480, 563–567. For the rise of American science and technology, see Bruce, *The Launching of Modern American Science, 1846–1876.* For surveys of the history of American technology during the Gilded Age, see Ruth Schwartz Cowan, *A Social History of American Technology* (New York: Oxford University Press, 1997), 67–219. For technological optimism, see Thomas P. Hughes, *American Genesis: A Century of Invention and Technological Enthusiasm, 1870–1970* (New York: Viking Press, 1989); John F.

Kasson, *Civilizing the Machine: Technology and Republican Values in America, 1776–1900* (New York: Grossman, 1976); Daniel T. Rodgers, *The Work Ethic in Industrial America* (Chicago: University of Chicago Press, 1978); Howard P. Segal, *Technological Utopianism in American Culture* (Chicago: University of Chicago Press, 1985); and Joseph M. Petulla, *American Environmental History,* 2nd ed. (Toronto: Merrill, 1988), 175–196. See also Brooke Hindle and Steven Lubar, *Engines of Change: The American Industrial Revolution, 1790–1860* (Washington, DC: Smithsonian Institution Press, 1986). For the transformation of the American city, see Martin V. Melosi, *The Sanitary City: Urban Infrastructure in America From Colonial Times to the Present* (Baltimore: Johns Hopkins University Press, 2000); Jane Jacobs, *The Death and Life of Great American Cities* (New York: Random House, 1961); Sam Bass Warner, Jr., *The Urban Wilderness: A History of the American City* (New York: Harper & Row, 1972); Edwin G. Burrows and Mike Wallace, *Gotham: A History of New York City to 1898* (Oxford: Oxford University Press, 2000); William Cronon, *Nature's Metropolis: Chicago and the Great West* (New York: Norton, 1991); and Theodore Steinberg, *Down to Earth: Nature's Role in American History* (New York: Oxford University Press, 2002), 157–172.

29. Hughes, *American Genesis,* 3.

30. Cowan, *A Social History of American Technology,* 165.

31. Hughes, *American Genesis,* 1.

32. Perry Miller, "The Responsibility of Mind in a Civilization of Machines," *The American Scholar* 31 (Winter 1961–1962), 51–69. Quotation is from page 55.

33. See, for example, Samuel P. Hays, *Conservation and the Gospel of Efficiency: The Progressive Conservation Movement, 1890–1920* (Cambridge, MA: Harvard University Press, 1959). For a good synthesis of the Progressive era confidence in the human capacity to dominate nature, see John Opie, *Nature's Nation: An Environmental History of the United States* (New York: Harcourt Brace, 1998), 243–264.

34. Opie, *Nature's Nation,* 435.

35. For the rise of industrial science, see Hughes, *American Genesis,* 7; Cowan, *A Social History of American Technology,* 149–171; David F. Noble, *America by Design: Science, Technology, and the Rise of Corporate Capitalism* (New York: Knopf, 1977); George Wise, *Willis R. Whitney, General Electric, and the Origins of U.S. Industrial Research* (New York: Columbia University Press, 1985); Leonard S. Reich, *The Making of American Industrial Research: Science and Business at GE and Bell, 1876–1926* (New York: Cambridge University Press, 1985); David Hounshell and John Kenly Smith, *Science and Corporate Strategy: DuPont R&D, 1902–1980* (New York: Cambridge University Press, 1988); and John Servos, "The Industrial Relations of Science: Chemical Engineering at MIT, 1900–1939," *Isis* 71 (December 1980), 531–549.

36. Thorstein Veblen, *The Higher Learning in America: A Memorandum on the Conduct of Universities by Business Men* (New York: B. W. Huebsch, 1918), 1–58. Cited in Stuart W. Leslie, *The Cold War and American Science: The Military-Industrial-Academic Complex at MIT and Stanford* (New York: Columbia University Press, 1993), 8.

37. Daniel J. Kevles, "Cold War and Hot Physics: Science, Security, and the American State, 1945–56," *Historical Studies in the Physical and Biological Sciences* 20 (March 1990), 239–264; and Allan Needell, "Preparing for the Space Age: University-Based Research, 1946–1957," *Historical Studies in the Physical and Biological Sciences* 18 (1987), 89–110. Both Kevles and Needell cite the Korean War as the point when American universities were integrated into the military-industrial complex.

38. President's Scientific Research Board, *Science and Public Policy* (Washington, DC: Government Printing Office, 1947), vol. 1, 10.

39. Daniel J. Kevles, *The Physicists: The History of a Scientific Community in Modern America* (Cambridge, MA: Harvard University Press, 1995), 341.

40. Ibid., 395.

41. See J. Stefan Dupré and Sanford A. Lakoff, *Science and the Nation: Policy and Politics* (Englewood Cliffs, NJ: Prentice-Hall, 1962), 9; and Martin Brown (ed.), *The Social Responsibility of the Scientist* (New York: Free Press, 1971), 1–2.

42. William O. Douglas, *Freedom of the Mind* (Chicago: American Library Association, 1962), 2.

43. Leslie, *The Cold War and American Science,* 1. See also Peter J. Westwick, *The National Labs: Science in an American System, 1947–1974* (Cambridge, MA: Harvard University Press, 2003); Paul Forman, "Behind Quantum Electronics: National Security as a Basis for Physical Research in the United States, 1940–1960," *Historical Studies in the Physical and Biological Sciences* 18 (1987), 149–229; McGrath, *Scientists, Business, and the State, 1890–1960;* Hart, *Forged Consensus;* and Wang, *American Science in an Age of Anxiety.*

44. Barry Commoner, *Science and Survival* (New York: Viking Press, 1966), 27. My emphasis.

45. Ibid., 28–29.

46. J. Robert Oppenheimer, *Physics in the Contemporary World* (Portland, ME: Anthoensen Press), 11.

47. Donald Worster, *Nature's Economy: A History of Ecological Ideas,* 2nd ed. (New York: Cambridge University Press, 1994), 342.

48. Wang, *American Science in an Age of Anxiety.*

49. Commoner, *Science and Survival,* 48.

50. Lawrence Badash, "Science and McCarthyism," *Minerva* 38 (2000), 53–80.

51. *TIME,* quoted in Paul Boyer, *By the Bomb's Early Light* (Chapel Hill: University of North Carolina Press, 1994), 145.

52. The McMahon Bill of 20 December 1945 became the 1946 Atomic Energy Act and is reprinted in full in Philip L. Cantelon, Richard G. Hewlett, and Robert C. Williams (eds.), *The American Atom: A Documentary History of Nuclear Policies From the Discovery of Fission to the Present,* 2nd ed. (Philadelphia: University of Pennsylvania Press, 1991), 77–91.

53. Richard G. Hewlett and Oscar E. Anderson, *A History of the United States Atomic Energy Commission: The New World, 1939–1946* (University Park: Penn-

sylvania State University Press, 1962), 428–455. See also Robert Jungk, *Brighter Than a Thousand Suns: A Personal History of the Atomic Scientists,* translated by James Cleugh (New York: Harcourt Brace, 1986), 221–238; Brian Balogh, *Chain Reaction: Expert Debate and Public Participation in American Commercial Nuclear Power, 1945–1975* (New York: Cambridge University Press, 1991), 21–59; George T. Mazuzan and J. Samuel Walker, *Controlling the Atom: The Beginnings of Nuclear Regulation, 1946–1962* (Berkeley: University of California Press, 1985), 3–4.

54. Commoner, interview with author, 28 December 2005.

55. See Eric Goldman, *The Crucial Decade and After: America, 1945–1960* (New York: Vintage Books, 1960); Spencer R. Weart, *Nuclear Fear: A History of Images* (Cambridge, MA: Harvard University Press, 1988), 128–151; and Allan M. Winkler, *Life Under a Cloud: American Anxiety About the Atom* (Oxford: Oxford University Press, 1993), 57–83.

56. Philip Kitcher, *Science, Truth, and Democracy* (Oxford: Oxford University Press, 2001), 85–91.

57. *Report to the Full Committee of the Special Subcommittee on National Security of the Committee on Un-American Activities* (Washington, DC: House Committee on Un-American Activities, Special Subcommittee on National Security, 1 March 1948), 1.

58. For Condon's case as the "cause célèbre," see Alice Kimball Smith, *A Peril and a Hope: The Scientists' Movement in America, 1945–47* (Chicago: University of Chicago Press, 1965), 424. For an overview of Condon's position on the importance of intellectual freedom, see E. U. Condon, "Science and Our Future," *Science* 103 (5 April 1946), 415–417. Condon promoted international cooperation because he claimed that "the outcome will be world friendship and cooperation, not atomic war and the destruction of civilization." Quotation on page 417. For more on Condon, see Jessica Wang, "Science, Security, and the Cold War: The Case of E. U. Condon," *Isis* 83 (1992), 238–269, and *American Science in an Age of Anxiety,* 130–152. For academic blacklisting during the Cold War, see Ellen Schrecker, *No Ivory Tower: McCarthyism and the Universities* (New York: Oxford University Press, 1986), 265–282. Commoner believed that Condon was "persecuted, largely because people thought his wife [Emilie Honzik] was a communist." Commoner, interview with author, 22 November 2002.

59. Barry Commoner, "The Scientist and Political Power," unpublished manuscript, August 1962 (Barry Commoner Papers, LoC, box 14). Quotations are from pages 4 and 2–3.

60. Commoner, *Science and Survival,* 24. For the thalidomide scare, see Richard E. McFayden, "Thalidomide in America," *Clio Medica* 11 (1976), 79–83; and Rock Brynner and Trent Stephens, *Dark Remedy: The Impact of Thalidomide and Its Revival as a Vital Medicine* (Cambridge, MA: Perseus, 2001).

61. Warren Weaver, "AAAS Policy," *Science* 114 (2 November 1951), 471–472. For accounts of the preparation of the Arden House Statement, see also Bruce V. Lewenstein, "Shifting Science From People to Programs: AAAS in the Postwar Years," in Sally Gregory Kohlstedt, Michael M. Sokal, and Bruce V. Lewenstein,

The Establishment of Science in America: 150 Years of the American Association for the Advancement of Science (New Brunswick, NJ: Rutgers University Press, 1999), 103–165; and Dael Wolfle, *Renewing a Scientific Society: The American Association for the Advancement of Science from World War II to 1970* (Washington, DC: AAAS, 1989), 48–57.

62. Warren Weaver, "Fundamental Questions in Science," *Scientific American* 189 (September 1953), 47–51.

63. Maurice B. Visscher, "Scientists in a Mad World," *The Nation* (24 January 1953), 69–71. Quotation is from page 69. Visscher had also been the architect of the AAAS 1948 Committee on Civil Liberties for Scientists. See Wang, *American Science in an Age of Anxiety,* 197–204.

64. Commoner to E. U. Condon, 5 August 1953 (Barry Commoner Papers, LoC, box 343).

65. Commoner, interview with the author, 22 November 2002. For a good biographical sketch of Weaver, see Mina Rees, "Warren Weaver," in *Biographical Memoirs* 57 (1987), 493–530. For Weaver in his own words, see Warren Weaver, *Scene of Change: A Lifetime in American Science* (New York: Scribner's, 1970), and "Confessions of a Scientist-Humanist," in *What I Have Learned: A Collection of Twenty Autobiographical Essays by Great Contemporaries From the Saturday Review* (New York: Simon and Schuster, 1968), 298–309. See also Robert E. Kohler, *Partners in Science: Foundations and Natural Scientists, 1900–1945* (Chicago: University of Chicago Press, 1991), 265–303.

66. Lewenstein, "Shifting Science From People to Programs," 113. For AAAS membership numbers between 1848 and 1998, see Kohlstedt et al., 174–175.

67. Commoner to E. U. Condon, 5 August 1953 (Barry Commoner Papers, LoC, box 343).

68. Ibid.

69. Quoted in Carleton Mabee, "Margaret Mead's Approach to Controversial Public Issues: Racial Boycotts in the AAAS," *The Historian* 48 (1986), 191–208. Quotation is from page 199.

70. Lewenstein, "Shifting Science From People to Programs," 122.

71. Ward Pigman to Dael Wolfle, 5 November 1955 (Catherine Borras, Committee Files, AAAS Archives, box 10).

72. Dael Wolfle to Ward Pigman, 22 June 1956 (Catherine Borras, Committee Files, AAAS Archives, box 10).

73. "Social Aspects of Science," *Science* 125 (25 January 1957), 143–147. Quotations are from page 143.

74. Ibid., 144.

75. Ibid.

76. Ibid., 143.

77. Ibid., 146.

78. Ibid., 147.

79. Dael Wolfle to Chauncey D. Leake, 14 February 1957 (Catherine Borras, Committee Files, AAAS Archives, box 10).

80. "Schweitzer Urges World Opinion to Demand End of Nuclear Tests," *New York Times,* 24 April 1957, 1. The Norwegian state radio wanted to send a reporter to Schweitzer's hospital in Lambaréné, in French Equatorial Africa, to make a recording of the speech he had sent, but the eighty-two-year-old Schweitzer claimed to be too weak to read the appeal himself.

81. "Excerpts from Message by Schweitzer," *New York Times,* 24 April 1957, 2.

82. Ibid.

83. Albert Schweitzer, "Appeal to End Nuclear Tests," *Bulletin of the Atomic Scientists* (June 1957), 205.

84. "Excerpts From Message by Schweitzer," 2.

85. Ibid. Reprinted in *The Saturday Review* (18 May 1957), 17–20; and *Bulletin of the Atomic Scientists* (June 1957), 204–205. See also the preface to Schweitzer's appeal by Norman Cousins. Norman Cousins, "The Schweitzer Declaration," *The Saturday Review* (17 May 1957), 13–16.

86. Cousins, "The Schweitzer Declaration," *The Saturday Review* (18 May 1957), 13–16. Quotation is from page 14.

87. Willard F. Libby, "An Open Letter to Dr. Schweitzer," *The Saturday Review* (25 May 1957), 8–9, 36–37. Quotation is on page 8. Reprinted in the *Bulletin of the Atomic Scientists* (June 1957), 206–207. See Robert A. Divine, *Blowing on the Wind: The Nuclear Test Ban Debate, 1954–1960* (New York: Oxford University Press, 1978), 122.

88. Libby, "An Open Letter to Dr. Schweitzer," 37.

89. Chauncey D. Leake to Commoner, 24 May 1957 (Barry Commoner Papers, LoC, box 310).

90. Chauncey D. Leake to Commoner, 5 June 1957 (Barry Commoner Papers, LoC, box 344).

91. Commoner, interview with author, 17 July 2003.

92. "Statement on the Radiation Problem: Revised by Dael Wolfle, Following Discussion by the Board of Directors on 6 July 1957" (Barry Commoner Papers, LoC, box 344).

93. Commoner to Robert Plumb, 2 July 1957 (Barry Commoner Papers, LoC, box 344). See also Commoner to John Lear, 3 July 1957 (Barry Commoner Papers, LoC, box 344).

94. Chauncey Leake to Dael Wolfle, 8 July 1957 (Catherine Borras, Committee Files, AAAS Archives, box 10).

95. Commoner, interview with author, 17 July 2003.

96. I am grateful to Amy Crumpton for helping to clarify numerous confusions pertaining to the relationship between the Committee on the Social Aspects of Science and the AAAS board of directors.

97. Dael Wolfle to Chauncey Leake, 17 July 1957 (Catherine Borras, Committee Files, AAAS Archives, box 10).

98. Dael Wolfle to Chauncey Leake, 9 July 1957 (Barry Commoner Papers, LoC, box 344).

99. Commoner, interview with author, 17 July 2003.

100. Lawrence Kubie to Chauncey Leake, 10 September 1957 (Barry Commoner Papers, LoC, box 344).

101. Dael Wolfle to members of the Committee on the Social Aspects of Science, 30 October 1957 (Barry Commoner Papers, LoC, box 297).

102. Commoner to Leake, 2 October 1957 (Barry Commoner Papers, LoC, box 344).

103. Commoner, interview with author, 17 July 2003.

104. Commoner to Leake, 23 November 1957 (Barry Commoner Papers, LoC, box 297).

105. Donald W. Cox, *America's New Policy Makers: The Scientists' Rise to Power* (Philadelphia: Chilton Books, 1964), 237.

106. Statement of Purpose (Committee on Science in the Promotion of Human Welfare, AAAS Archives, box 1).

107. Fleming, "Roots of the New Conservation Movement," 40.

108. Robert K. Merton, *Social Theory and Social Structure,* rev. and enl. ed. (Glencoe, IL: Free Press, 1957), 552.

109. Commoner quotation is in Goodell, *The Visible Scientists,* 67. For scientists and politics, see Mary Jo Nye, "What Price Politics?: Scientists and Political Controversy," *Endeavour* 23, 4 (1999), 148–154.

110. Commoner, interview with author, 15 November 2001.

Chapter 2: Guarding the Public

1. Barry Commoner, "Fallout and Water Pollution—Parallel Cases," *Scientist and Citizen* 6 (December 1964), 2–7. Quotation is from page 2.

2. Barry Commoner, interview with author, 15 November 2001.

3. Barry Commoner, *The Closing Circle* (New York: Knopf, 1971), 56.

4. Ibid., 65.

5. Commoner, "Fallout and Water Pollution—Parallel Cases," 2.

6. Barry Commoner, "Committee for Nuclear Information founding statement draft," 16 April 1958 (Committee for Nuclear Information records, Western Historical Manuscript Collection, University of Missouri-St. Louis, file 56).

7. Commoner, "Fallout and Water Pollution—Parallel Cases," 2.

8. Scott Kirsch, "Harold Knapp and the Geography of Normal Controversy: Radioiodine in the Historical Environment," *Osiris* 19 (2004), 167–181. Quotation is from page 170. See also Kirsch, *Proving Grounds: Project Plowshare and the Unrealized Dream of Nuclear Earthmoving* (New Brunswick, NJ: Rutgers University Press, 2005).

9. Bruno Latour, *Pandora's Hope: Essays on the Reality of Science Studies* (Cambridge, MA: Harvard University Press, 1999), 306.

10. Kirsch, "Harold Knapp and the Geography of Normal Controversy," 169.

11. Ulrich Beck, *World Risk Society* (Cambridge: Polity Press, 1999), 119.

12. Dan O'Neill, *The Firecracker Boys* (New York: St. Martin's Press, 1994), 11–12.

13. Cited in George T. Mazuzan and Samuel J. Walker, *Controlling the Atom: The Beginnings of Nuclear Regulation, 1946–1962* (Berkeley: University of California Press, 1985), 60. See also Brian Balogh, *Chain Reaction: Expert Debate and Public Participation in American Commercial Nuclear Power, 1945–1975* (New York: Cambridge University Press, 1991); and Thomas Raymond Wellock, *Critical Masses: Opposition to Nuclear Power in California, 1958–1978* (Madison: University of Wisconsin Press, 1998).

14. Atomic Energy Commission, *The Thirteenth Semiannual Report of the Atomic Energy Commission* (Washington, DC: Government Printing Office, 1 January 1953), 124.

15. The account of radioactive debris falling on Troy is given in Commoner, *The Closing Circle,* 50. See also Herbert M. Clark, "The Occurrence of an Unusually High-Level Radioactive Rainout in the Area of Troy, N.Y.," *Science* 119 (7 May 1954), 619–622.

16. Good sources on the objective hazards of fallout from nuclear weapons testing can be found online at U.S. government Web sites. See especially the Centers for Disease Control and Prevention, http://www.cdc.gov/nceh/radiation/fallout/default.htm; and the Department of Energy, http://tis.eh.doe.gov/ohre/new/findingaids/radioactive/index.html, 2004.

17. For Stevenson's campaign speech, see Walter Johnson (ed.), *The Papers of Adlai E. Stevenson,* vol. 6: *Toward a New America, 1955–1957* (Boston: Little, Brown, 1976). Quotation is from page 440.

18. Ibid., 248–249.

19. For an account of Stevenson's antitesting platform, see Robert A. Divine, *Blowing on the Wind: The Nuclear Test Ban Debate, 1954–1960* (New York: Oxford University Press, 1978), 86–88.

20. Associated Press dispatch from Washington, D.C., 24 October 1956. Also cited in Barry Commoner, *Science and Survival* (New York: Viking Press, 1966), 14.

21. For literature on nuclear fallout sponsored by the Atomic Energy Commission, see Gordon M. Dunning and John A. Hilcken (eds.), *Symposium [on] the Shorter-Term Biological Hazards of a Fallout Field, Washington, D.C., December 12–14, 1956* (Washington, DC: U.S. Government Printing Office, 1958); and J. Laurence Kulp and Arthur R. Schulert (eds.), *Strontium-90 in Man and His Environment* (Palisades, NY: Geochemical Laboratory, Lamont Geological Observatory, Columbia University, 1961). See also Christopher J. Jolly, "Thresholds of Uncertainty: Radiation and Responsibility in the Fallout Controversy," Ph.D. dissertation, Oregon State University, 2004.

22. Cited in John Langone, "Edward Teller: Of Bombs and Brickbats," *Discover* 5 (July 1984), 62–68. Quotation is from page 65. See also O'Neill, *The Firecracker Boys,* 12.

23. Edward Teller, *The Legacy of Hiroshima* (Garden City, NY: Doubleday, 1962). Cited in Virginia Brodine, "On Scientific and Political Disagreement," *Nuclear Information* (July 1962), 19.

24. For more on Teller, see Gregg Herken, *Brotherhood of the Bomb: The Tangled Lives and Loyalties of Robert Oppenheimer, Ernest Lawrence, and Edward Teller* (New York: Henry Holt, 2002); Herbert F. York, *The Advisors: Oppenheimer, Teller, and the Superbomb* (Stanford, CA: Stanford University Press, 1989); Stanley A. Blumberg and Gwinn Owens, *Energy and Conflict: The Life and Times of Edward Teller* (New York: Putnam, 1976); Edward Teller, *Memoirs: A Twentieth-Century Journey in Science and Politics* (Cambridge, MA: Perseus, 2001); and Edward Teller, Wendy Teller, and Wilson Talley, *Conversations on the Dark Secrets of Physics* (Cambridge, MA: Perseus, 2002). For an account and description of the creation of thermonuclear explosions, see Richard Rhodes, *Dark Sun: The Making of the Hydrogen Bomb* (New York: Simon & Schuster, 1995). Teller was not alone in his political worldview and the role of nuclear weapons therein. In fact, it was a relatively common view held by many scientists—including Teller's fellow Hungarian Eugene Wigner—who had arrived in the United States before World War II. For more, see Donald Fleming and Bernard Bailyn (eds.), *The Intellectual Migration: Europe and America, 1930–1960* (Cambridge, MA: Belknap Press of Harvard University Press, 1969).

25. In response to a 1954 survey conducted by *Fortune* magazine, Commoner called the Oppenheimer investigation an "unpardonable treatment of [an] outstanding American" that was "motivated by outright partisan political objectives and victimizes the nation as well as Oppenheimer." Wire correspondence from Commoner to Francis Bello, science editor for *Fortune* magazine, 17 April 1954 (Barry Commoner Papers, LoC, box 2). For more on Oppenheimer's loyalty case, see Herken, *Brotherhood of the Bomb;* Harold P. Green, "The Oppenheimer Case: A Study in the Abuse of Law," *Bulletin of the Atomic Scientists* 33 (July 1977), 12–16, 56–61; and Lincoln Wolfenstein, "The Tragedy of J. Robert Oppenheimer," *Dissent* 15 (1968), 81–85. See also multiple contributions in *Bulletin of the Atomic Scientists* 10 (May 1954), 173–191.

26. Linus Pauling, "An Appeal by American Scientists to the Governments and People of the World," *Bulletin of the Atomic Scientists* 13 (September 1957), 264–266. Quotation is from page 264.

27. Barry Commoner, interview with author, 22 November 2002. In addition to Condon, the Cold War attacks on the scientific community at Washington University targeted the engineer Alexander Suss Langsdorf. In 1956, Langsdorf, who in 1958 would be the committee's first president, had been accused of Communist Party membership, a charge that was never substantiated.

28. Dael Wolfle to Commoner, 30 January 1959 (Barry Commoner Papers, LoC, box 341).

29. Commoner to Margaret Mead, 27 May 1959 (Barry Commoner Papers, LoC, box 341).

30. Barry Commoner, "The Integrity of Science," *Science Journal* (April 1966), 75–79. Quotation is from page 75.

31. Barry Commoner, "The Scientist and Political Power," unpublished manuscript, August 1962 (Barry Commoner Papers, LoC, box 14), 10.

32. Commoner, interview with author, 15 November 2001.

33. Barry Commoner, "The Fallout Problem," *Science* 127 (2 May 1958), 1023–1026. Quotations are from pages 1023 and 1026.

34. "Dr. Commoner Cites Scientists' Dilemma," *St. Louis Globe-Democrat,* 13 October 1960, 4.

35. Commoner, *Science and Survival,* 120.

36. Commoner, "The Scientist and Political Power," 12.

37. Barry Commoner, interview with author, 20 November 2003.

38. For the mission statement, see any issue of *Nuclear Information.*

39. Committee for Nuclear Information brochure, 1962. Cited in Allen Smith, "Converting America: Three Community Efforts to End the Cold War, 1956–1973," Ph.D. dissertation, American University, 1995, 173.

40. Commoner, interview with author, 22 November 2002. See also William Cuyler Sullivan, Jr., *Nuclear Democracy: A History of the Greater St. Louis Citizens' Committee for Nuclear Information, 1957–1967,* College Occasional Papers no. 1 (St. Louis, MO: Washington University, 1982).

41. Women's reform work also tended to base its activism on education principles, and was ultimately open to nonpartisan politics. Indeed, the League of Women Voters was a model for nonpartisan politics. For the relationship between scientists and women reformers on the Committee for Nuclear Information, see Smith, "Converting America," 133–175. For more on women's activism against nuclear testing, see Amy Swerdlow, *Women Strike for Peace: Traditional Motherhood and Radical Politics in the 1960s* (Chicago: University of Chicago Press, 1993).

42. Cited in Sullivan, *Nuclear Democracy,* 20.

43. Florence Moog, "Nuclear War in St. Louis: One Year Later," *Nuclear Information* (September 1959), 1–4. For a detailed discussion of "Nuclear War in St. Louis," see Sullivan, *Nuclear Democracy,* 28–29. Sullivan argues that "Nuclear War in St. Louis" should be ranked with Nevil Shute's *On the Beach* and Walter M. Miller's *A Canticle for Leibowitz* as the great literary works on the horrors associated with the nuclear age.

44. Cited in Richard Dudman, "Washington University Teacher Attacks Teller's Atomic Fallout Views; Accused of 'Fighting Windmills,'" *St. Louis Post-Dispatch,* undated [March 1958].

45. Barry Commoner, review of *The Legacy of Hiroshima, Chemical & Engineering News* (28 May 1962), 86 & 148.

46. Commoner, *Science and Survival,* 16. The Atomic Energy Commission also backtracked on various studies that analyzed the potential for genetic mutation resulting from fallout.

47. *The Nature of Radioactive Fallout and Its Effects on Man,* hearings before the Special Subcommittee on Radiation of the Joint Committee on Atomic Energy, 5 June 1957, 1222.

48. Willard F. Libby, "An Open Letter to Dr. Schweitzer," *The Saturday Review* 40 (25 May 1957), 8–9, 36–37. Quotation is from page 37.

49. Harrison Brown, "What Is a 'Small' Risk?" *The Saturday Review* (25 May 1957), 9–10. Quotation is from page 10.

50. Divine, *Blowing on the Wind,* 123.

51. Commoner to Roland Berg, 23 March 1959 (Barry Commoner Papers, LoC, box 431).

52. Atomic Energy Commission, *Thirteenth Semi-Annual Report.*

53. Commoner, *The Closing Circle,* 52.

54. Herman M. Kalckar, "An International Milk Teeth Radiation Census," *Nature* 182 (2 August 1958), 283–284. Quotation is from page 283.

55. See W. K. Wyant, Jr., "50,000 Baby Teeth," *The Nation* (13 June 1959), 535–537. See also *Nuclear Information* (24 December 1958). The Committee for Nuclear Information papers seem to exhibit some inconsistencies as to when Schwartz introduced the notion of organizing a baby tooth analysis campaign in St. Louis. In the 24 December 1958 issue of *Nuclear Information,* Schwartz is credited with having raised the Baby Tooth Survey idea in the early summer of 1958, before Kalckar's *Nature* article. In Yvonne Logan's account of the history of the Baby Tooth Survey, Schwartz brought Kalckar's article to the committee in the fall of 1958. See Yvonne Logan, "The Story of the Baby Tooth Survey," *Scientist and Citizen* (September–October 1964), 38–39. The Baby Tooth Survey subcommittee consisted of several male scientists during its initial stages, but subsequent meetings were composed almost exclusively of nonscientist women activists, with the exception of Dr. Louise Reiss, who chaired the subcommittee. See Baby Tooth Survey subcommittee minutes (Committee for Nuclear Information records, Western Historical Manuscript Collection, University of Missouri-St. Louis, file 194).

56. Committee for Nuclear Information press release, 20 December 1958 (Barry Commoner Papers, LoC, box 431).

57. J. Laurence Kulp et al., "Strontium-90 in Man," *Science* 125 (8 February 1957), 219–225.

58. The Committee for Nuclear Information, in conjunction with the Washington University dental school, won a $197,000 grant from the Public Health Service to measure the levels of radiation. See Smith, "Converting America," 156. For a detailed analysis of how the Committee for Nuclear Information was funded, see Sullivan, *Nuclear Democracy.*

59. "Milk and the Strontium-90 Problem," *Information* (February 1959), 1–2, 4.

60. Doris Deakin, "Mothers Ask—What Should We Feed Our Kids?," *Nuclear Information* (October 1959), 1–4. Quotation is from page 3.

61. Wyant, "50,000 Baby Teeth," 535.

62. See Louise Z. Reiss, "Baby Tooth Survey—First Results," *Nuclear Information* (November 1961), 1–6. Account of the collection of teeth is on page 2.

63. "Baby Tooth Survey Forms Going Out," *St. Louis Post-Dispatch,* 23 October 1960, 3. See also "Baby Tooth Survey Opens," *The Observer,* 9 November 1960, 7B.

64. Logan, "The Story of the Baby Tooth Survey," 39.

65. Gene Smith to Committee for Nuclear Information, 12 May 1960 (Committee for Nuclear Information records, Western Historical Manuscript Collection, University of Missouri-St. Louis, file 197).

66. Raymond Tucker to Gene Smith, 17 May 1960 (Committee for Nuclear Information records, Western Historical Manuscript Collection, University of Missouri-St. Louis, file 197).

67. Mrs. Doris Gould to the Committee for Nuclear Information, 17 April 1960 (Committee for Nuclear Information records, Western Historical Manuscript Collection, University of Missouri-St. Louis, file 197).

68. Mrs. Robert J. Masten to Committee for Nuclear Information, 11 May 1960 (Committee for Nuclear Information records, Western Historical Manuscript Collection, University of Missouri-St. Louis, file 197).

69. Mrs. Norman Steele to Commoner, 17 November 1959 (Barry Commoner Papers, LoC, box 431).

70. Jill to Committee for Nuclear Information, undated (Committee for Nuclear Information records, Western Historical Manuscript Collection, University of Missouri-St. Louis, file 197).

71. Michael Pachulski to Committee for Nuclear Information, undated (Committee for Nuclear Information records, Western Historical Manuscript Collection, University of Missouri-St. Louis, file 197).

72. Patty Hamley to Committee for Nuclear Information, 9 June 1961 (Committee for Nuclear Information records, Western Historical Manuscript Collection, University of Missouri-St. Louis, file 197).

73. Mrs. Jenks to Baby Tooth Survey, 8 January 1962 (Committee for Nuclear Information records, Western Historical Manuscript Collection, University of Missouri-St. Louis, file 197).

74. Robert Roe to Committee for Nuclear Information, 17 April 1960 (Committee for Nuclear Information records, Western Historical Manuscript Collection, University of Missouri-St. Louis, file 197).

75. Louise Z. Reiss, "Strontium-90 Absorption by Deciduous Teeth," *Science* 134 (24 November 1961), 1669–1673. Quotation is from page 1669.

76. Tables of strontium-90 levels can be found in ibid., 1670, and Reiss, "Baby Tooth Survey—First Results," 4. For Pennoyer's discussion of breast-feeding versus formula, see Deakin, "Mothers Ask—What Should We Feed Our Kids?," 3.

77. Reiss, "Baby Tooth Survey—First Results," 3.

78. May 1960 local stories (Committee for Nuclear Information records, Western Historical Manuscript Collection, University of Missouri-St. Louis, scrapbooks). See also Wyant, "50,000 Baby Teeth"; and "Fallout: Moment of Tooth," *Newsweek* (25 April 1960), 70. Wyant, whose article was published in *The Nation,* was a *St. Louis Post-Dispatch* journalist. In *American Science Policy Since*

World War II, Bruce L. R. Smith argues that the dissolution of postwar scientific consensus occurred around 1966. Although the Committee for Nuclear Information and other grassroots antitesting groups were modest in size, they did set the stage for broader expressions of dissent, which found their feet in the early 1960s. Note, for example, the impact of Rachel Carson's *Silent Spring* (1962). See Bruce L. R. Smith, *American Science Policy Since World War II* (Washington, D.C.: Brookings Institution, 1990).

79. Barry Commoner, "The Hazard of Fallout—Nuclear Bomb Test Policy Should Be Decided by All," in *Fallout from Nuclear Weapons Tests,* hearings before the Special Subcommittee on Radiation of the Joint Committee on Atomic Energy, 5–8 May 1959, 2170–2176. Quotation is from page 2175. Previously published as "The Hazard of Fallout," *Student Life* (Washington University, 19 December 1958).

80. Commoner, "The Fallout Problem," in *Fallout from Nuclear Weapons Tests, 2572–2577.* Quotation is from page 2576. Previously published as "The Fallout Problem," *Science* 127 (2 May 1958), 1023–1026.

81. Karl Z. Morgan, "Maximum Permissible Exposure of the Population-at-Large to Sources of Ionizing Radiation," in *Fallout from Nuclear Weapons Tests,* 1614–1633. See especially page 1631. See also J. B. Reynolds and Barry Commoner, "Hearings Reveal New Facts," *Nuclear Information* (May–June 1959), 6. Reynolds and Commoner noted that these other isotopes had rather short lifetimes, and were important only during explosions and for a short time thereafter.

82. Committee for Nuclear Information, Technical Division, "Local Fallout: Hazard from Nevada Tests," *Nuclear Information* (August 1963), 1–13. Quotation is from p. 2.

83. Quotation from William O. Pruitt, Jr., "Comments From Other Scientists," *Nuclear Information* (November 1963), 11.

84. *Fallout, Radiation Standards, and Countermeasures,* hearings before the Joint Subcommittee on Research, Development, and Radiation of the Joint Committee on Atomic Energy, 21 August 1963, 602.

85. Atomic Energy Commission, "Iodine 131 in Fallout," in *Fallout, Radiation Standards, and Countermeasures,* 1103. Also cited in Committee for Nuclear Information, Technical Division, "Hazard from Nevada Tests: A Reply to the Atomic Energy Commission," *Nuclear Information* (November 1963), 1.

86. Allen Smith, "Democracy and the Politics of Information: The St. Louis Committee for Nuclear Information," *Gateway Heritage* (Summer 1996), 2–13. Quotation is from page 11.

87. Eric Reiss to AEC Deputy Director Gordon Dunning, 4 November 1963 (Committee for Nuclear Information records, Western Historical Manuscript Collection, University of Missouri-St. Louis, file 278).

88. See Sullivan, *Nuclear Democracy.*

89. President Lyndon B. Johnson, televised address, 12 October 1964. Also cited in Commoner, *Science and Survival,* 14–15.

90. For Goldwater, see James T. Patterson, *Grand Expectations: The United States, 1945–1974* (New York: Oxford University Press, 1996), 558; and Allen Matusow, *The Unraveling of America: A History of Liberalism in the 1960s* (New York: Harper & Row, 1984), 148–150.

91. Commoner, *Science and Survival,* 120.

92. Cited in "Closing the Information Gap," *Nuclear Information* (March–April 1963), 12.

93. "Science and Human Welfare," *Science* 132 (8 July 1960), 68–73. The Scientists' Institute for Public Information was created in 1963, but Commoner had implored the American Association for the Advancement of Science to create such an organization in "Science and Human Welfare."

94. Commoner, *Science and Survival,* 19.

95. Commoner, interview with author, 22 November 2002. Commoner was referring to the analogy he presented in his *The Poverty of Power* (New York: Knopf, 1976), 99.

96. Commoner, *Science and Survival,* 28–29.

97. Commoner, *The Closing Circle,* 56.

98. Bruno Latour, *Science in Action* (Cambridge, Mass.: Harvard University Press, 1987), 30.

99. Barry Commoner, "Committee for Nuclear Information founding statement draft," 16 April 1958 (Committee for Nuclear Information records, Western Historical Manuscript Collection, University of Missouri-St. Louis, file 56).

Chapter 3: The New Jeremiad

1. Adam Rome, "'Give Earth a Chance': The Environmental Movement and the Sixties," *Journal of American History* 90 (September 2003), 525–554. Quotation is from page 526.

2. Ibid., 547.

3. See *Nuclear Information* (March 1962, July 1962, October 1962, December 1962; February 1963, May 1963, July 1963, September–October 1963; February 1964, March 1964, and June–July 1964).

4. Barry Commoner, interview with author, 17 July 2003.

5. Barry Commoner, interview with author, 15 November 2001.

6. Samuel P. Hays, *Beauty, Health, and Permanence: Environmental Politics in the United States, 1955–1985* (Cambridge: Cambridge University Press, 1987), 13–39.

7. Lewis Herber, *Our Synthetic Environment* (New York: Knopf, 1962), 26. During the summer of 1961, Bookchin arranged to send his chapter on the potential hazards of needless exposure to ionizing radiation to Commoner for review and comment. He noted that "my views on fallout have been influenced by your remarkable article in *Student Life* (December 19, 1958) and by your contributions

to *Nuclear Information.*" Seeking Commoner's comment, Bookchin asserted that "I do not believe that we are socially or morally prepared to enter the 'nuclear age.' . . . I doubt there is anything that will keep us from so doing, but, if enter we must, I would like to see us tread with the utmost caution. I do not know if you share my views about modern man's social and moral qualifications for using nuclear energy at the present time, but it seemed to me that you argue admirably for prudence in such matters." Murray Bookchin to Commoner, 15 July 1961 (Barry Commoner Papers, LoC, box 4). Commoner replied that he was pleased to learn of Bookchin's efforts to write *Our Synthetic Environment.* "The [relationship between the environment and public health] is very much in need of the public's informed attention," he encouraged. Commoner to Murray Bookchin, 3 August 1961 (Barry Commoner Papers, LoC, box 4).

8. Lewis Herber, "The Problems of Chemicals in Foods," *Contemporary Issues* 3 (1952), 206–241. Bookchin's critique of capitalism in *Our Synthetic Environment* concentrated on this earlier interest in the petrochemical industry.

9. Lewis Herber, *The Crisis in Our Cities* (Englewood Cliffs, NJ: Prentice-Hall, 1965). See also Murray Bookchin, *The Limits of the City* (New York: Harper & Row, 1974). For summaries of Bookchin's intellectual contributions to the remaking of American environmentalism, see Robert Gottlieb, *Forcing the Spring: The Transformation of the American Environmental Movement* (Washington, DC: Island Press, 1993), 87–88; and Roderick Nash, *The Rights of Nature: A History of Environmental Ethics* (Madison: University of Wisconsin Press, 1989), 164–166. For a strong critique of Bookchin's positions, see Andrew Light (ed.), *Social Ecology After Bookchin* (New York: Guilford Press, 1998). For an interesting comparison of Commoner's and Bookchin's theories, see James O'Connor, *Natural Causes: Essays in Ecological Marxism* (New York: Guilford Press, 1998), 283–285.

10. Nash, *The Rights of Nature,* 166.

11. Herbert Marcuse, *Counterrevolution and Revolt* (Boston: Beacon Press, 1972), 59.

12. For further reading on nineteenth-century urban reform, see Sam Bass Warner, Jr., *The Urban Wilderness: A History of the American City* (New York: Harper & Row, 1972); Charles Sellers, *The Market Revolution: Jacksonian America, 1815–1846* (New York: Oxford University Press, 1991); Sean Wilentz, *Chants Democratic: New York City and the Rise of the American Working Class, 1788–1850* (New York: Oxford University Press, 1984); Stuart M. Blumin, *The Emergence of the Middle Class: Social Experience in the American City, 1760–1900* (Cambridge: Cambridge University Press, 1989); Carroll Smith-Rosenberg, *Religion and the Rise of the American City: The New York City Mission Movement, 1812–1870* (Ithaca, NY: Cornell University Press, 1971); Amy Bridges, *A City in the Republic: Antebellum New York and the Origins of Machine Politics* (Cambridge: Cambridge University Press, 1984); and John Duffy, *A History of Public Health in New York City, 1625–1866,* vol. 1. (New York: Russell Sage Foundation, 1968).

13. Leo Marx, *The Machine in the Garden: Technology and the Pastoral Ideal in America* (New York: Oxford University Press, 1964).

14. Aldo Leopold, *A Sand County Almanac and Sketches Here and There* (New York: Oxford University Press, 1949). For the Thoreau quotation, see Henry David Thoreau, "Walking," in his *Collected Essays and Poems* (New York: Library of America, 2001), 239. For Muir's discussion of nature as "the [holy] temple . . . consecrated by the heart of man," see John Muir, *The Yosemite* (New York: Century, 1912), 261–262. For Thoreau, see Walter Harding, *The Days of Henry David Thoreau* (New York: Knopf, 1965); and Nash, *The Rights of Nature.* For Muir, see Donald Worster, "John Muir and the Roots of American Environmentalism," in Worster's *The Wealth of Nature: Environmental History and the Ecological Imagination* (New York: Oxford University Press, 1993), 190–196; Stephen Fox, *The American Conservation Movement: John Muir and His Legacy* (Boston: Little, Brown, 1981); Michael P. Cohen, *The Pathless Way: John Muir and the American Wilderness* (Madison: University of Wisconsin Press, 1984); Dennis C. Williams, *God's Wilds: John Muir's Vision of Nature* (College Station: Texas A&M University Press, 2002); and Roderick Nash, *Wilderness and the American Mind,* 4th ed. (New Haven, CT: Yale University Press, 2001), 122–181.

15. For Alice Hamilton and American environmentalism, see Gottlieb, *Forcing the Spring,* 47–51.

16. For more comprehensive discussion of the evolution of American ideas about nature and nature protection, see Nash, *Wilderness and the American Mind* and *The Rights of Nature;* and Donald Worster, *Nature's Economy: A History of Ecological Ideas,* 2nd ed. (New York: Cambridge University Press, 1994).

17. Barry Commoner, "A Scientist Views Pollution," address before the National Industrial Conference Board, New York City, 15 December 1966 (Barry Commoner Papers, LoC, box 493), 17.

18. Rachel Carson, *Silent Spring* (Boston: Houghton Mifflin, 1962), 157.

19. Maril Hazlett and Michael Egan, "Technological and Ecological Turns: Science and American Environmentalism," paper presented at the History of Science Society annual conference, Cambridge, MA, 22 November 2003.

20. Carson, *Silent Spring,* 170.

21. Worster, *Nature's Economy,* 340. For ecology as the subversive science, see Paul Shepard and Daniel McKinley (eds.), *The Subversive Science: Essays Toward an Ecology of Man* (Boston: Houghton Mifflin, 1969); Theodore Roszak, *Where the Wasteland Ends: Politics and Transcendence in Postindustrial Society* (Garden City, NY: Doubleday, 1972), 400; and Worster, *Nature's Economy,* 22–23.

22. Carson, *Silent Spring,* 297.

23. Carson, cited in Gottlieb, *Forcing the Spring,* 86.

24. Frank Graham, *Since Silent Spring* (Boston: Houghton Mifflin, 1970), 49. Also cited in Gottlieb, *Forcing the Spring,* 85.

25. Carson, *Silent Spring,* 24. The seminal work on Rachel Carson is Linda Lear, *Rachel Carson: Witness for Nature* (New York: Henry Holt, 1997). A more recent study is Maril Hazlett, "The Story of *Silent Spring* and the Ecological Turn," Ph.D. dissertation, University of Kansas, 2003.

26. Commoner, interview with author, 17 July 2003.

27. Barry Commoner, *Science and Survival* (New York: Viking Press, 1966), 108.

28. Rachel Carson's National Book Award acceptance speech is reprinted in Paul Brooks, *The House of Life: Rachel Carson at Work* (Boston: Houghton Mifflin, 1972), 127–129.

29. Carson, *Silent Spring,* 6. For the connection between nuclear fallout and pesticides, see Ralph H. Lutts, "Chemical Fallout: Rachel Carson's *Silent Spring,* Radioactive Fallout and the Environmental Movement," *Environmental Review* 9 (Fall 1985), 214–225.

30. Carson, *Silent Spring,* 37.

31. Carson to Walter C. Bauer, 12 November 1963 (Committee for Nuclear Information records, Western Historical Manuscript Collection, University of Missouri-St. Louis, Scrapbook no. 4). I am grateful to Linda Lear for her assistance in obtaining a copy of this letter. Carson's letter to the Committee for Nuclear Information was in response to an invitation to speak in St. Louis. By that time, however, she was quite ill and was forced to decline.

32. See the masthead of *Nuclear Information* 6 (May 1964).

33. See the masthead of *Scientist and Citizen* 6 (August 1964).

34. James R. Whitley, "Water Pollution in Missouri," *Scientist and Citizen* 6 (August 1964), 1–4.

35. Quoted in Frank Graham, *Disaster by Default: Politics and Water Pollution* (New York: M. Evans, 1966), 110.

36. U.S. Department of Health, Education and Welfare, *Report on Investigation of Fish Kills in Lower Mississippi River, Atchafalaya River, and Gulf of Mexico* (Washington, DC: Public Health Service, 1964). See also Graham, *Disaster by Default,* 106–130, and *Since Silent Spring,* 93–108; and Lear, *Rachel Carson,* 470–471.

37. Stuart H. Loory, "Science Tracks Down a Fish Killer," *New York Herald Tribune,* 23 March 1964, Rachel Carson Papers, Beinecke Rare Book and Manuscript Library, Yale University. Cited in Lear, *Rachel Carson,* 470–471.

38. The 1965 Clean Water Act was a substantial revision of the original 1960 Act. It was strengthened in 1972 and again in 1977.

39. Barry Commoner, "Fallout and Water Pollution—Parallel Cases," *Scientist and Citizen* 6 (December 1964), 2–7. Quotation is from page 2.

40. Dominick V. Rosato, William K. Fallon, and Donald V. Rosato, *Markets for Plastics* (New York: Van Nostrand Reinhold, 1969), 2.

41. Commoner, *The Closing Circle* (New York: Knopf, 1971), 127. On plastics, see Jeffrey L. Meikle, *American Plastic: A Cultural History* (New Brunswick, NJ: Rutgers University Press, 1995), and "Material Doubts: The Consequences of Plastic," *Environmental History* 2 (July 1997), 278–300; and Stephen Fenichell, *Plastic: The Making of a Synthetic Century* (New York: HarperBusiness, 1996). For the petrochemical industry, see Joe Thornton, *Pandora's Poison: Chlorine, Health, and a New Environmental Strategy* (Cambridge, MA: MIT Press, 2000);

and Gerald Markowitz and David Rosner, *Deceit and Denial: The Deadly Politics of Industrial Pollution* (Berkeley: University of California Press, 2002).

42. Commoner, "Fallout and Water Pollution," 6.

43. Commoner, *Science and Survival,* 124.

44. The best source for information on the history of synthetic detergents is William McGucken, *Biodegradable: Detergents and the Environment* (College Station: Texas A&M University Press, 1991). For the rise of synthetic detergents in the marketplace, see pages 11–19. Quotation is from page 16.

45. Commoner, *Science and Survival,* 20–21.

46. Commoner, "A Scientist Views Pollution," 3.

47. Commoner, *Science and Survival,* 21.

48. McGucken, *Biodegradable,* 7.

49. Commoner, "A Scientist Views Pollution," 7.

50. Ibid.

51. Commoner, *Science and Survival,* 25.

52. Barry Commoner, "The Integrity of Science," *American Scientist* 53 (June 1965), 174–198.

53. Commoner, *Science and Survival,* 25.

54. Paul W. Hirt, *A Conspiracy of Optimism: Management of the National Forests Since World War II* (Lincoln: University of Nebraska Press, 1994), 3.

55. Commoner, "A Scientist Views Pollution," 14.

56. Commoner, *Science and Survival,* 46.

57. Between 1950 and 1963, lithium enrichment for thermonuclear weapons released many tons of mercury to air and surface waters from the Oak Ridge National Laboratory in Tennessee. For more information, see Dennis J. Paustenbach (ed.), *Human and Ecological Risk Assessment: Theory and Practice* (New York: Wiley, 2002), 769–793. In 1993, studies suggested that mercury releases from operations were responsible for the highest potential noncancer health risks of any material used in historical activities in the nuclear lab complex. See ChemRisk, *Oak Ridge Health Studies Dose Reconstruction Feasibility Study Report,* vol. 1: *Phase I Overview.* Prepared for the Tennessee Department of Health and the Oak Ridge Health Agreement Steering Panel, September 1993.

58. On pink disease, see Ann Dally, "The Rise and Fall of Pink Disease," *Social History of Medicine* 10 (1997), 291–304.

59. See John R. McNeill, *Something New Under the Sun: An Environmental History of the Twentieth-Century World* (New York: Norton, 2000), 138–139. See also Thornton, *Pandora's Poison,* 240.

60. Office of Air Quality Planning and Standards, *Mercury Study Report to Congress,* vol. 1: *Executive Summary* (Washington, D.C.: U.S. Environmental Protection Agency, 1997).

61. Barry Commoner, *Making Peace With the Planet* (New York: Pantheon Books, 1990), 119.

62. U.S. Environmental Protection Agency, *Mercury Study Report to Congress.* See also R. Stanfield and C. Lopez, "Lethal Legacy: The Dirty Truth About the Nation's Most Polluting Power Plants" (Washington, D.C.: U.S. Public Interest Research Group, 2000).

63. Electric Power Research Institute, "Mercury in the Environment," *EPRI Journal* (April 1990), 5. See also J. G. Weiner et al., "Partitioning and Bioavailability of Mercury in an Experimentally Acidified Wisconsin Lake," *Environmental Toxicology and Chemistry* 9 (1990), 909–918.

64. Commoner, *The Closing Circle,* 185.

65. For a more complete list of mercury poisoning symptoms, see Colleen F. Moore, *Silent Scourge: Children, Pollution, and Why Scientists Disagree* (New York: Oxford University Press, 2003), 49–77.

66. Martha Moore Trescott, *The Rise of the Electrochemicals Industry, 1880–1910* (Westport, CT: Greenwood Press, 1981), 106. It warrants noting that establishing a public need for a new product is not an uncommon phenomenon. See, for example, Gary Cross, *An All-Consuming Century: Why Commercialism Won in Modern America* (New York: Columbia University Press, 2000); and Lizabeth Cohen, *A Consumers' Republic: The Politics of Mass Consumption in Postwar America* (New York: Knopf, 2003). This theme is also raised in relation to polluting technologies in Markowitz and Rosner, *Deceit and Denial.*

67. Thornton notes that "by the end of the war, more than a quarter of all munitions contained chemical agents, and all of these were chlorine based." Thornton, *Pandora's Poison,* 236.

68. The Du Pont chemist Thomas Midgley invented tetraethyl lead, the gasoline additive that would spread toxic lead particles throughout the environment, in addition to CFCs, which would come to deplete the ozone layer. This dubious distinction prompted the historian J. R. McNeill to comment that Midgley "had more impact on the atmosphere than any other single organism in earth history." McNeill, *Something New Under the Sun,* 111. For more on Midgley's contributions to speeding the state of environmental decline, see Theodore Steinberg, *Down to Earth: Nature's Role in American History* (New York: Oxford University Press, 2002), 206–210.

69. Commoner, *The Closing Circle,* 166.

70. Thornton, *Pandora's Poison,* 239.

71. Commoner, *The Closing Circle,* 145–146.

72. Ibid., 143.

73. For more on the physiological effects of mercury, see Neville Grant, "Legacy of the Mad Hatter," *Environment* 11 (May 1969), 18–23, 43–44.

74. For the Moundsville case study, see Markowitz, *Deceit and Denial,* 165–167.

75. Lutts, "Chemical Fallout," 216.

76. Sheldon Novick, "A New Pollution Problem," *Environment* 11 (May 1969), 2–9. Quotation is from page 3.

77. Göran Löfroth and Margaret E. Duffy, "Birds Give Warning," *Environment* 11 (May 1969), 10–17. See also Grant, "Legacy of the Mad Hatter."

78. Commoner, *The Closing Circle,* 146.

79. Commoner, "A Scientist Views Pollution," 15.

80. For in-depth discussion of risk analysis and the precautionary principle, see Ulrich Beck, *Risk Society: Towards a New Modernity,* translated by Mark Ritter (London: Sage, 1992); Paustenbach, *Human and Ecological Risk Assessment;* and Carolyn Raffensperger and Joel Tickner (eds.), *Protecting Public Health and the Environment: Implementing the Precautionary Principle* (Washington, DC: Island Press, 1999).

81. Commoner, *Science and Survival,* 97.

82. The seminal study of American jeremiads is Sacvan Bercovitch, *The American Jeremiad* (Madison: University of Wisconsin Press, 1978). Bercovitch argues that the jeremiad has played a major role in creating the American ethos. For an equally important though differing perspective, see Perry Miller, *Errand into the Wilderness* (Cambridge, MA: Belknap Press of Harvard University Press, 1956). While Bercovitch interpreted hope in the jeremiad's strategy, Miller emphasized the rhetorical potency of the declensionist narrative. For a discussion of the environmental jeremiad, see Theodore Roszak, *The Voice of the Earth: An Exploration of Ecopsychology* (New York: Simon & Schuster, 1993). Quotation is from Bercovitch, *The American Jeremiad,* 133.

83. Commoner, *Science and Survival,* 27.

84. Ibid., 126.

85. Edwin Diamond, "The Myth of the Pesticide Menace," *Saturday Evening Post* (28 September 1963), 16–18. Also cited in Gottlieb, *Forcing the Spring,* 85.

86. William Vogt, *Road to Survival* (New York: W. Sloane Associates, 1948), 133.

87. Fairfield Osborn, *Our Plundered Planet* (Boston: Little, Brown, 1948), 194, 200–201.

88. For literary and cinematic representations of environmental apocalypse, see Frederick Buell, *From Apocalypse to Way of Life: Environmental Crisis in the American Century* (New York: Routledge, 2003), 247–322.

89. Linus Pauling, "An Appeal by American Scientists to the Governments and People of the World," *Bulletin of the Atomic Scientists* 13 (September 1957), 264–266. Quotation is from page 264.

90. Paul Sears, "A Statement of Conviction About Overpopulation," November 1960 (Committee on Science in the Promotion of Human Welfare Papers, AAAS Archives, box 2).

91. Paul Sears, *Deserts on the March* (Norman: University of Oklahoma Press, 1935).

92. Donella H. Meadows et al., *The Limits to Growth* (New York: Universe Books, 1972), 143.

93. Worster has referred to these politico-scientists as the "new delphic voices" of the Age of Ecology. See Worster, *Nature's Economy,* ix.

94. Paul Ehrlich, *Look* (21 April 1970).

95. Stephen Fox, *The American Conservation Movement: John Muir and His Legacy* (Madison: University of Wisconsin Press, 1985), 311.

96. Paul R. Ehrlich, *The Population Bomb* (New York: Ballantine Books, 1968), xi.

97. Ibid.

98. Kirkpatrick Sale, *The Green Revolution: The American Environmental Movement, 1962–1992* (New York: Hill and Wang, 1993), 22.

99. Subtle examples of Commoner's and Ehrlich's differing opinions on the authority of scientists are sprinkled throughout their works. Notably, Ehrlich's academic title—Doctor—is conspicuously attached to his name on the cover and back of *The Population Bomb*. In comparison, Commoner's academic title is conspicuous in its absence in the various editions of *The Closing Circle*.

100. Peter J. Bowler, *The Earth Encompassed: A History of the Environmental Sciences* (New York: Norton, 1992), 504.

101. Brad Benz, "Let It Green: The Ecoization of the Lexicon," *American Speech* 75, 2 (2000), 215–221.

102. Stephen Bocking, *Nature's Experts: Science, Politics, and the Environment* (New Brunswick, NJ: Rutgers University Press, 2004), 56.

103. Ibid., 69.

104. This argument draws on Thomas Kuhn's suggestion that scientific revolutions are frequently begun by outsiders, because their perspective is different from the orthodox practitioners, who engage in what Kuhn called "normal science." See Thomas S. Kuhn, *The Structure of Scientific Revolutions* (Chicago: University of Chicago Press, 1962).

105. For tensions between ecology and environmentalism, see Bocking, *Nature's Experts* and *Ecologists and Environmental Politics: A History of Contemporary Ecology* (New Haven, CT: Yale University Press, 1997). For the history of ecology, see Bowler, *The Earth Encompassed;* Joel B. Hagen, *An Entangled Bank: The Origins of Ecosystem Ecology* (New Brunswick, NJ: Rutgers University Press, 1992); Frank Benjamin Golley, *A History of the Ecosystem Concept in Ecology: More Than the Sum of Its Parts* (New Haven, CT: Yale University Press, 1993); and Sharon E. Kingsland, *The Evolution of American Ecology, 1890–2000* (Baltimore: Johns Hopkins University Press, 2005).

106. Deborah Lynn Guber, *The Grassroots of a Green Revolution: Polling America on the Environment* (Cambridge, MA: MIT Press, 2003), 4.

107. Walter A. Rosenbaum, *The Politics of Environmental Concern,* 2nd ed. (New York: Praeger, 1977), 27.

108. Charles T. Rubin, *The Green Crusade: Rethinking the Roots of Environmentalism* (Lanham, MD: Rowman & Littlefield, 1998), 73–74. For other critiques of environmental rhetoric, see Ronald Bailey, *Ecoscam: The False Prophets of Ecological Apocalypse* (New York: St. Martin's Press, 1993); Martin Lewis, *Green Delusions: An Environmentalist Critique of Radical Environmentalism* (Durham, NC: Duke University Press, 1992); and Ron Arnold and Alan Gottlieb,

Trashing the Economy: How Runaway Environmentalism Is Wrecking America (Bellevue, WA: Free Enterprise Press, 1993).

109. The tendency to dismiss environmentalists as alarmists became a trend in the 1980s, and was indicative of the new, alarmist antienvironmentalism that emerged during the Reagan administration. For a strong critique of the antienvironmentalist rhetoric, see Buell, *From Apocalypse to Way of Life,* 3–66.

110. Commoner, "A Scientist Views Pollution," 11.

111. Commoner, interview with author, 22 November 2002.

Chapter 4: When Scientists Disagree

1. Harold Sprout, "The Environmental Crisis in the Context of American Politics," in *The Politics of Ecosuicide,* edited by Leslie L. Roos, Jr. (New York: Holt, Rinehart and Winston, 1971), 49.

2. From the organizers' manifesto, as quoted in the Associated Press, "Earth Day Organizers Hope to Halt Pollution," *The Oregonian,* 22 April 1970, 8.

3. Joseph Lelyveld, "Mood Is Joyful as City Gives Its Support," *New York Times,* 23 April 1970, 1, 30. Quotation is from page 30. See also "Angry Coordinator of Earth Day," *New York Times,* 23 April 1970, 30.

4. Robb Baker, "Earth Day: A Commie Plot?" *Chicago Tribune,* 22 April 1970, sec. 2, 4.

5. Barry Commoner, untitled talk, Brown University, 22 April 1970 (Barry Commoner Papers, LoC, box 131), 17.

6. "Angry Coordinator of Earth Day," 30.

7. Hayes's press statement is reprinted in *The Living Wilderness* 34 (Spring 1970), 12–13.

8. Nelson is quoted in Kirkpatrick Sale, *The Green Revolution: The American Environmental Movement, 1962–1992* (New York: Hill and Wang, 1993), 24.

9. Gladwin Hill, "Activity Ranges From Oratory to Legislation," *New York Times,* 23 April 1970, 1, 30. Quotation is from page 1.

10. Lelyveld, "Mood Is Joyful as City Gives Its Support," 1.

11. Ed Meagher, "No Smog on L.A. Earth Day," *Los Angeles Times,* 23 April 1970, sec. 2, 1–2.

12. Sam Hopkins and Terry Adamson, "Earth Day Marks Assault on Pollution," *Atlanta Constitution,* 23 April 1970, 1, 19. Quotation is from page 1.

13. Herbert L. Denton and Claudia Levy, "March on Interior to Highlight Earth Day Activities in D.C.," *Washington Post,* 22 April 1970, A6.

14. Maurine McLaughlin, "Housewives Hold Picnic on a Dump," *Washington Post,* 23 April 1970, A18.

15. Gladwin Hill, "Oratory and Legislation Mark Drive on Pollution," *New York Times,* 23 April 1970, 30.

16. For St. Louis, see "Earth Has Its Day," *San Francisco Chronicle,* 23 April 1970, 2. For Tacoma, see Hill, "Oratory and Legislation Mark Drive on Pollution," 30.

17. Arthur Everett, "U.S. Ignores Generation Gap, Focuses on Earth Day Drive," *The Oregonian,* 23 April 1970, 1.

18. Ibid.

19. Samuel P. Hays, *Beauty, Health, and Permanence: Environmental Politics in the United States, 1955–1985* (Cambridge: Cambridge University Press, 1987), 52. Robert Gottlieb suggests that Earth Day was "a transitional event," tied in part to the earlier efforts to spark environmental concern within the American public, but also a template for how to proceed. See Robert Gottlieb, *Forcing the Spring: The Transformation of the American Environmental Movement* (Washington, DC: Island Press, 1993), 114.

20. Walter A. Rosenbaum, *The Politics of Environmental Concern,* 2nd ed. (New York: Prager, 1977), 6.

21. Bentley's use of public funds ignited a minor controversy. On Earth Day, he stated publicly that he would pay for the telegrams himself, amid criticisms from taxpayers. Sam Hopkins, "Earth Is Getting Its Day, Finally," *Atlanta Constitution,* 22 April 1970, 1. See also "Anti-Earth Day Wires Cost Official $1,600," *New York Times,* 23 April 1970, 30.

22. Quoted in Mark Dowie, *Losing Ground: American Environmentalism at the Close of the Twentieth Century* (Cambridge, MA: MIT Press, 1995), 25.

23. "Editorial," *Ramparts* (May 1970), 2–4. Quotation is from page 2.

24. *TIME* (2 February 1970). For Nixon's State of the Union address, see "Summons to a New Cause," *TIME* (2 February 1970), 7–8.

25. "Americans Rally to Make It Again Beautiful Land," *Chicago Tribune,* 23 April 1970, 3. In *Nixon and the Environment,* J. Brooks Flippen notes the dilemma Nixon faced. On the one hand, Earth Day constituted a remarkable political opportunity to co-opt a traditionally Democratic issue, but Flippen points out that Nixon also risked "alienating traditional conservative allies." J. Brooks Flippen, *Nixon and the Environment* (Albuquerque: University of New Mexico Press, 2000), 10. In addition, Nixon aides were tentative about the partisan nature of the event; Earth Day was, after all, conceived by a Democratic senator.

26. Hill, "Activity Ranges From Oratory to Legislation," 30.

27. See Gottlieb, *Forcing the Spring,* 111.

28. For the "Herblock" cartoon, see *Washington Post,* 23 April 1970, 22.

29. For Nixon's comparisons with Roosevelt, see Gottlieb, *Forcing the Spring,* 109. See also Flippen, *Nixon and the Environment,* 74.

30. Richard Harwood, "Earth Day Stirs Nation," *Washington Post,* 23 April 1970, A1, A20.

31. See Gottlieb, *Forcing the Spring,* 110.

32. Everett, "U.S. Ignores Generation Gap, Focuses on Earth Day Drive," 1.

33. For Florida, see Gottlieb, *Forcing the Spring,* 111. See also "An Oil Spill on Market Street," *San Francisco Chronicle,* 23 April 1970, 2.

34. K. William Kapp, *The Social Costs of Private Enterprise* (New York: Schocken Books, 1971).

35. Carl Bernstein, "Area Industries Jump on Earth Day Bandwagon," *Washington Post,* 23 April 1970, A21.

36. Gottlieb, *Forcing the Spring,* 108.

37. Associated Press, "Earth Day Organizers Hope to Halt Pollution," 8.

38. "After the Talkfest on Earth Day," *Chicago Tribune,* 22 April 1970, 20.

39. James T. Patterson, *Grand Expectations: The United States, 1945–1974* (New York: Oxford University Press, 1996), 750–755.

40. Barry Commoner, *The Closing Circle* (New York: Knopf, 1971), 10.

41. Beverly Beyette, "Environmentalists: Three Who Believe," *Los Angeles Times,* 6 June 1985.

42. Commoner, *The Closing Circle,* 10.

43. Barry Commoner, untitled talk, Harvard University, 21 April 1970 (Barry Commoner Papers, LoC, box 36), 1.

44. Barry Commoner, untitled talk, Brown University, 22 April 1970, 2.

45. Ibid., 1.

46. Ibid., 20–21.

47. Ibid., 3.

48. "Ecology: Interview with Barry Commoner," NBC Interview, 17 April 1970 (Barry Commoner Papers, LoC, box 35), 22.

49. Commoner, untitled talk, Brown University, 20.

50. Commoner, untitled talk, Harvard University, 1.

51. Ibid., 2.

52. Ruth Troetschler to Commoner, 28 June 1970 (Barry Commoner Papers, LoC, box 240).

53. Mrs. Lynne H. Perry to Commoner, 24 June 1970 (Barry Commoner Papers, LoC, box 240).

54. Dr. L. E. Marshall to Commoner, 11 June 1970 (Barry Commoner Papers, LoC, box 240).

55. Sister Veronita Ruddy to Commoner, 1 January 1971 (Barry Commoner Papers, LoC, box 240).

56. Commoner, untitled talk, Harvard University, 2.

57. For a good overview of studies in human population growth, see William H. McNeill, *Population and Politics Since 1750* (Charlottesville: University Press of Virginia, 1990). Population continues to be a rich field in environmental history. For further reading, see Björn-Ola Linnér, *The Return of Malthus: Environmentalism and Post-War Population-Resource Crises* (Isle of Harris, UK: White Horse

Press, 2003); Joel E. Cohen, *How Many People Can the Earth Support?* (New York: Norton, 1995); Massimo Livi-Bacci, *A Concise History of World Population,* 3rd ed., translated by Carl Ipsen (Oxford: Blackwell, 2001); John Bellamy Foster, "Malthus' *Essay on Population* at 200: A Marxian View," *Monthly Review* 50 (December 1998), 1–18; and Jeffrey K. McKee, *Sparing Nature: The Conflict Between Human Population Growth and Earth's Biodiversity* (New Brunswick, NJ: Rutgers University Press, 2003).

58. Stephen Fox, *The American Conservation Movement* (Boston: Little, Brown, 1981), 311.

59. Paul R. Ehrlich, *The Population Bomb* (New York: Ballantine Books, 1968), 16.

60. Ibid., 15.

61. Ibid., 66–67.

62. Ibid., xi.

63. Ibid., 34.

64. Ibid., 39.

65. Lelyveld, "Mood Is Joyful as City Gives Its Support," 30.

66. Barry Commoner, "The Population Problem" (Barry Commoner Papers, LoC, box 26), 2.

67. Commoner, untitled talk, Brown University, 9–10. For Nathan Keyfitz, see Keyfitz, "National Populations and the Technological Watershed," *Journal of Social Issues* 23 (1967), 62–78. See also Clifford Geertz, *Agricultural Involution* (Berkeley: University of California Press, 1963).

68. Barry Commoner, "The World Population Crisis: Is a Humane Solution Possible?" (Barry Commoner Papers, LoC, box 49), 6.

69. Ibid.

70. Commoner, untitled talk, Brown University, 10. Commoner expanded on this argument in *The Closing Circle,* 245. See also Barry Commoner, "How Poverty Breeds Overpopulation (and Not the Other Way Around)," *Ramparts* (August–September 1975), 21–25, 58–59.

71. Barry Commoner, "Survival in the Environment: Population Crisis," presented at AAAS annual meeting, Boston, 29 December 1969 (Barry Commoner Papers, LoC, box 29), 17.

72. Commoner, *The Closing Circle,* 297.

73. Commoner, "The World Population Crisis," 8.

74. Ibid., 9.

75. "A Clash of Gloomy Prophets," *TIME* (11 January 1971), 56–57.

76. Commoner, *The Closing Circle,* 247–248.

77. Ibid., 283.

78. "Paul Revere of Ecology," *TIME* (2 February 1970), 58.

79. Commoner, interview with author, 15 November 2001.

80. Commoner, *The Closing Circle,* 114.

81. Ibid., 125.

82. Ibid., 133.

83. Ibid., 255.

84. Ibid., 282.

85. Ulrich Beck, *Risk Society: Towards a New Modernity,* translated by Mark Ritter (London: Sage, 1992), 74.

86. For more on Commoner's Four Laws of Ecology, see Michael Egan, "The Social Significance of the Environmental Crisis: Barry Commoner's *The Closing Circle,*" *Organization and Environment* 15 (December 2002), 443–457, and "Die technologische Wende und Barry Commoners Gesetze der Ökologie: *The Closing Circle* neu gelesen," *Natur und Kultur* 4 (Fall 2003), 30–47.

87. For an overview of the myriad interpretations of the causes of the environmental crisis, see Commoner, *The Closing Circle,* 5–13.

88. For the new face of environmentalism and environmental leadership, see Fox, *The American Conservation Movement;* and Gottlieb, *Forcing the Spring.*

89. Good biographical information on Ehrlich is scarce. The most comprehensive work is in David DeLeon (ed.), *Leaders From the 1960s: A Biographical Sourcebook of American Activism* (Westport, CT: Greenwood Press, 1994). See also Anne Becher, Kyle McClure, Rachel White Scheuering, and Julia Willis, *American Environmental Leaders: From Colonial Times to the Present,* 2 vols. (Santa Barbara, CA: ABC-CLIO, 2000).

90. William Vogt, *Road to Survival* (New York: W. Sloane Associates, 1948); and Fairfield Osborn, *Our Plundered Planet* (Boston: Little, Brown, 1948).

91. Indeed, their subsequent centers' locations and missions underlined the distinctions between their humanist and naturalist leanings. In 1979, Commoner moved his Center for the Biology of Natural Systems from Washington University in St. Louis to Queens College in Flushing, New York. In contrast, Ehrlich had located his Rocky Mountain Biological Laboratory in remote Crested Butte, Colorado. Commoner's urban center would focus on such concerns as urban waste disposal, while Ehrlich's center remained very active in many prominent studies of conservation biology.

92. Commoner, untitled talk, Harvard University, 3.

93. Commoner, untitled talk, Brown University, 20.

94. While Commoner's rhetoric was unmistakably socialist, Ehrlich's ambiguity not only got him in trouble with minority groups, it also associated his arguments with less popular positions, which ultimately tarnished his reputation. One notable example was the punned Miss Ann Thropy's short essay on the beneficial environmental effects of AIDS in *The Earth First! Journal,* which coincided with virulent anti-immigration polemics from the radical environmentalists Ed Abbey and Dave Foreman. The anonymous author wrote: "If radical environmentalists were to invent a disease to bring human population back to ecological sanity, it would probably be something like AIDS. . . . As radical environmentalists, we can

see AIDS not as a problem, but a necessary solution. . . . To paraphrase Voltaire: if the AIDS epidemic didn't exist, radical environmentalists would have to invent one." Miss Ann Thropy, "Population and AIDS," *The Earth First! Journal* (1 May 1987), 32. Of course, Ehrlich's position on population was far removed from Miss Ann Thropy's extreme take—and it would be wrong to associate such diatribes with his own advocacy—but Miss Ann Thropy's short article illustrated the breadth of the division between the humanist and naturalist positions and, perhaps, the humanist mistrust of the naturalist position. For more on the population and immigration positions in *Earth First!*, see Martha F. Lee, *Earth First!: Environmental Apocalypse* (Syracuse, NY: Syracuse University Press, 1995), 96–114. See also Susan Zakin, *Coyotes and Town Dogs: Earth First! and the Environmental Movement* (New York: Viking Press, 1993); and Steve Chase (ed.), *Defending the Earth: A Dialogue Between Murray Bookchin and Dave Foreman* (Boston: South End Press, 1991).

95. Commoner, *The Closing Circle*, 297.

96. Ehrlich, quoted in Anne Chisholm, *Philosophers of the Earth: Conversations with Ecologists* (New York: Dutton, 1972), 148.

97. Paul R. Ehrlich and John P. Holdren, "Dispute," *Environment* 14 (April 1972), 23–52. Quotation is from page 24.

98. The history of this formula is far more complicated and extensive than this analysis allows. See John P. Holdren, "A Brief History of 'IPAT' (Impact = Population × Affluence × Technology)," unpublished manuscript provided courtesy of Holdren, 7 September 1993. For further discussion of the formula, see H. Patricia Hynes, "Taking Population Out of the Equation: Reformulating I = PAT," in *Dangerous Intersections: Feminist Perspectives on Population, Environment, and Development*, edited by Jael Silliman and Ynestra King (Cambridge, MA: South End Press, 1999), 39–73. For the environmental movement's reaction to the IPAT formula, see Roy Beck and Leon Kolankiewicz, "The Environmental Movement's Retreat From Advocating U.S. Population Stabilization (1970–1998): A First Draft of History," *Journal of Policy History* 12 (2000), 123–156.

99. Ehrlich and Holdren, "Dispute," 31.

100. Ibid.

101. Ibid., 38.

102. Sheldon Novick, correspondence with author, 27 April 2004. A letter from *Environment* editor Sheldon Novick to Ehrlich noted the extent to which the review had been circulated in advance, "judging by the amount of discussion it produced all over the country, and the syndicated newspaper columns based on it." Sheldon Novick to Paul Ehrlich, 5 May 1972 (Paul and Anne Ehrlich Papers, Special Collections and University Archives, Stanford University Libraries, series 1, box 23). In a memorandum to *Environment*'s Science Advisory Board a couple of weeks later, Novick added: "The review was published by the authors, in mimeographed form, and widely circulated throughout the country and abroad in a manner which precluded rebuttal. It quickly became a subject of widespread discussion: I know of at least two instances in which it was used in undergraduate courses, and of two syndicated newspaper columns which were based on the mimeographed version." Shel-

don Novick to Science Advisory Board, 17 May 1972 (Paul and Anne Ehrlich Papers, Special Collections and University Archives, Stanford University Libraries, series 1, box 23). For newspaper references to Ehrlich and Holdren's draft, see Anthony Tucker, "The Prophets, and Doom," *Guardian Extra,* 28 January 1972, 12; and Harold Gilliam, "The 'Pollutionists' and the 'Depletionists' Disagree," *San Francisco Sunday Examiner & Chronicle,* 7 March 1972, 28.

103. "Communications," *Bulletin of the Atomic Scientists* 28 (June 1972), 6. Two copies of the Ehrlich and Holdren review and Commoner's response were published. See Ehrlich and Holdren, "Dispute"; and "A *Bulletin* Dialogue on *The Closing Circle,*" *Bulletin of the Atomic Scientists* 28 (May 1972), 8–27, 42–56.

104. Commoner, interview with author, 15 November 2001.

105. Novick also rejected the notion that *Environment* had deliberately scooped the *Bulletin.* "It may bear repeating that my decision to publish, and the timing of publication, were decided by me, and without reference to [the *Bulletin of the Atomic Scientists*]. The speculations of Ehrlich and Holdren about a calculated delaying tactic by Commoner are without basis in fact. Commoner's delay in providing a rebuttal, a problem we are accustomed to with most authors, forced me to delay the April issue of *Environment* by almost a month. There is nothing sinister about the fact that [the *Bulletin*] was subjected to the same delay." Sheldon Novick to Science Advisory Board, 17 May 1972 (Paul and Anne Ehrlich Papers, Special Collections and University Archives, Stanford University Libraries, series 1, box 23).

106. For Commoner and Ehrlich at the United Nations Conference on the Human Environment (5–16 June 1972), see Wade Rowland, *The Plot to Save the World* (Vancouver, BC: Clarke, Irwin, 1973), 129–131.

107. Barry Commoner, "Dispute," *Environment* 14 (April 1972), 28–52.

108. Ibid., 44.

109. Ibid., 25, 40.

110. Donald Worster, *Under Western Skies: Nature and History in the American West* (New York: Oxford University Press, 1992), 16.

111. "Communications," *Bulletin of the Atomic Scientists* 28 (September 1972), 2.

112. Pete Seeger, "*The Closing Circle:* Readers Comment," *Environment* 14 (June 1972), 40.

113. Rachel Carson, *Silent Spring* (Boston: Houghton Mifflin, 1962). See also Yaakov Garb, "Change and Continuity in Environmental World-View: The Politics of Nature in Rachel Carson's *Silent Spring,*" in *Minding Nature: The Philosophers of Ecology,* edited by David Macauley (New York: Guilford Press, 1996), 229–256.

114. Andrew Feenberg, "The Commoner-Ehrlich Debate: Environmentalism and the Politics of Survival," in *Minding Nature,* 257–282. Quotation is from page 257.

115. "When Scientists Disagree," *Nuclear Information* (May 1962), 1.

116. Virginia Brodine, "On Scientific and Political Disagreement," *Nuclear Information* (July 1962), 19.

Chapter 5: Biological Capital

1. G. B. Trudeau, *The People's Doonesbury: Notes From Underfoot, 1978–1980* (New York: Holt, Rinehart and Winston, 1981).

2. Tom Wolfe, *The Purple Decades* (New York: Berkley Books, 1983), 265–296; and Christopher Lasch, *The Culture of Narcissism: American Life in an Age of Diminishing Expectations* (New York: Norton, 1979). Wolfe's famous essay is "The 'Me' Decade and the Third Great Awakening," *New York* (23 August 1976), 26–40. For overviews of the 1970s, see Bruce J. Schulman, *The Seventies: The Great Shift in American Culture, Society, and Politics* (New York: Free Press, 2001); Peter N. Carroll, *It Seemed Like Nothing Happened: The Tragedy and Promise of America in the 1970s* (New York: Holt, Rinehart and Winston, 1982); Arlene S. Skolnick, *Embattled Paradise: The American Family in an Age of Uncertainty* (New York: Basic Books, 1991); Jim Hougan, *Decadence: Radical Nostalgia, Narcissism, and Decline in the Seventies* (New York: Morrow, 1975); and James T. Patterson, *Grand Expectations: The United States, 1945–1974* (New York: Oxford University Press, 1996).

3. Lasch, *The Culture of Narcissism,* 4.

4. Among the more prominent pieces of legislation were the National Environmental Protection Act (1970), the Clean Air Act (1970), the Clean Water Act (1970), the Federal Insecticide, Fungicide, and Rodenticide Act (1972), and the Endangered Species Act (1973).

5. Barry Commoner, untitled talk, Harvard University, 21 April 1970 (Barry Commoner Papers, LoC, box 36), 5. In 1973, E. F. Schumacher reiterated this general premise in his surprisingly successful book *Small Is Beautiful,* an economic tract that defied the maxims of growth and bigness, both perceived as integral to the free market. E. F. Schumacher, *Small Is Beautiful: Economics as if People Mattered* (New York: Harper & Row, 1973).

6. Barry Commoner, "The Social Significance of Environmental Pollution," presented at eleventh annual meeting of the National Association of Business Economists, Chicago, 26 September 1969 (Barry Commoner Papers, LoC, box 130), 4.

7. Barry Commoner, *The Closing Circle* (New York: Knopf, 1971), 250.

8. For a good introduction to ecological economics, see Juan Martinez-Alier and Klaus Shlüpmann, *Ecological Economics: Energy, Environment, and Society* (Oxford: Blackwell, 1987); Herman E. Daly, *Ecological Economics and the Ecology of Economics: Essays in Criticism* (Northampton, MA: Edward Elgar, 1999); Malte Faber, Reiner Manstetten, and John Proops, *Ecological Economics: Concepts and Methods* (Brookfield, VT: Edward Elgar, 1996); Charles Perrings, *Economics of Ecological Resources: Selected Essays* (Lyme, NH: Edward Elgar, 1997); Robert Costanza, *Frontiers in Ecological Economics: Transdisciplinary Essays by Robert Costanza* (Lyme, NH: Edward Elgar, 1997); Robert Costanza, Olman Segura, and

Juan Martinez-Alier (eds.), *Getting Down to Earth: Practical Applications of Ecological Economics* (Washington, DC: Island Press, 1996); Robert Costanza et al., *An Introduction to Ecological Economics* (Boca Raton, FL: St. Lucie Press, 1997); and Herman Daly and John B. Cobb, Jr., *For the Common Good: Redirecting the Economy Toward Community, the Environment, and a Sustainable Future* (Boston: Beacon Press, 1989).

9. Barry Commoner, "The Energy Crisis: All of a Piece," *The Center Magazine* (March/April 1975), 26–31. The quotation is from page 28.

10. The classic work on the relationship between air pollution and public health is Lester B. Lave and Eugene P. Seskin, *Air Pollution and Human Health* (Baltimore: Johns Hopkins University Press, 1977). For more recent discussions of the connection between pollution and cancer, see Devra Davis, *When Smoke Ran Like Water: Tales of Environmental Deception and the Battle Against Pollution* (New York: Basic Books, 2002); and Sandra Steingraber, *Living Downstream: An Ecologist Looks at Cancer and the Environment* (Reading, MA: Addison-Wesley, 1997).

11. Commoner, *The Closing Circle,* 253.

12. Ibid.

13. Commoner, "A Scientist Views Pollution," address before the National Industrial Conference Board, New York City, 15 December 1966 (Barry Commoner Papers, LoC, box 493), 13.

14. Walter A. Rosenbaum, *The Politics of Environmental Concern,* 2nd ed. (New York: Praeger, 1977), 31.

15. U.S. Environmental Protection Agency, *The Economics of Clean Air: Annual Report of the Administrator of the Environmental Protection Agency* (Washington, DC: Government Printing Office, 1972), 1–11.

16. Commoner, *The Closing Circle,* 273.

17. Commoner, untitled talk, Harvard University, 5–6.

18. Commoner, *The Closing Circle,* 268.

19. Ibid.

20. There is a sizable literature on the history of occupational safety and health hazards. See, by way of introduction, David Rosner and Gerald Markowitz (eds.), *Dying for Work: Workers' Safety and Health in Twentieth-Century America* (Bloomington: Indiana University Press, 1987); Christopher C. Sellers, *Hazards of the Job: From Industrial Disease to Environmental Health Science* (Chapel Hill: University of North Carolina Press, 1997); Claudia Clark, *Radium Girls: Women and Industrial Health Reform, 1910–1935* (Chapel Hill: University of North Carolina Press, 1997); and Barbara Ellen Smith, *Digging Our Own Graves: Coal Miners and the Struggle Over Black Lung Disease* (Philadelphia: Temple University Press, 1987).

21. See Gerald Markowitz and David Rosner, *Deceit and Denial: The Deadly Politics of Industrial Pollution* (Berkeley: University of California Press, 2002), 191–192. For more on industrial disease and workers' health as environmental issues, see Sellers, *Hazards of the Job;* and Davis, *When Smoke Ran Like Water.*

22. See Joe Thornton, *Pandora's Poison: Chlorine, Health, and a New Environmental Strategy* (Cambridge, MA: MIT Press, 2000), 251–257.

23. For tensions between labor and environmentalism, see Brian K. Obach, *Labor and the Environmental Movement: The Quest for Common Ground* (Cambridge, MA: MIT Press, 2004).

24. Robert Gottlieb, *Forcing the Spring: The Transformation of the American Environmental Movement* (Washington, DC: Island Press, 1993), 289.

25. Commoner, *The Closing Circle,* 271.

26. For more background on the protest over the supersonic transport project, see Mel Horwitch, *Clipped Wings: The American SST Conflict* (Cambridge, MA: MIT Press, 1982).

27. See Thomas Donaldson and Patricia H. Werhane (eds.), *Ethical Issues in Business: A Philosophical Approach,* 5th ed. (Upper Saddle River, NJ: Prentice Hall, 1996), 1–12.

28. A more recent development in this division occurred during the spotted owl controversy in the Pacific Northwest. See Richard White, "'Are You an Environmentalist, or Do You Work for a Living?': Work and Nature," in *Uncommon Ground: Rethinking the Human Place in Nature,* edited by William Cronon (New York: Norton, 1996), 171–185. See also William Dietrich, *The Final Forest: The Battle for the Last Great Trees of the Pacific Northwest* (New York: Simon & Schuster, 1992).

29. Barry Commoner, "Labor's Stake in the Environment/The Environment's Stake in Labor," keynote address at the conference "Jobs and the Environment—Whose Jobs? Whose Environment?" San Francisco, 28 November 1972 (Barry Commoner Papers, LoC, box 493), 3. See also Barry Commoner, "Workplace Burden," *Environment* 15 (July/August 1973), 15–20. Quotation is from page 15–16.

30. Commoner, "Workplace Burden," 16.

31. Commoner, "Labor's Stake in the Environment/The Environment's Stake in Labor," 9. More recent studies have made connections between PCBs and cancer. See, for example, Thornton, *Pandora's Poison,* 173–177. See also Colleen F. Moore, *Silent Scourge: Children, Pollution, and Why Scientists Disagree* (New York: Oxford University Press, 2003), 78–116.

32. Commoner, "Labor's Stake in the Environment/The Environment's Stake in Labor," 11. For the relationship between labor and the environment, see Scott Hamilton Dewey, "Working for the Environment: Organized Labor and the Origins of Environmentalism in the United States, 1948–1970," *Environmental History* 3 (January 1998), 45–63; Robert Gordon, "'Shell No!': OCAW and the Labor-Environmental Alliance," *Environmental History* 3 (October 1998), 460–487; and Chad Montrie, "Expedient Environmentalism: Opposition to Coal Surface Mining in Appalachia and the United Mine Workers of America, 1945–1975," *Environmental History* 5 (January 2000), 75–98.

33. For the "gospel of efficiency," see Samuel P. Hays, *Conservation and the Gospel of Efficiency: The Progressive Conservation Movement, 1890–1920* (Cambridge, MA: Harvard University Press, 1959).

34. Barry Commoner, "Planning to Survive," keynote address, American Institute of Planners, Boston, 8 October 1972 (Barry Commoner Papers, LoC, box 493), 13.

35. Barry Commoner, *The Poverty of Power* (New York: Knopf, 1976), 1.

36. Ibid., 2.

37. Commoner, *The Closing Circle,* 116.

38. Robert Hargreaves notes: "Even at its worst, [the war in Vietnam] never directly accounted for more than 3.5% of the gross national product. But by dissembling about the true costs of the military involvement and attempting to pay for it out of deficit spending, Johnson and [Robert] McNamara had unleashed forces that would sooner or later—but inevitably—bring America to the reckoning." Robert Hargreaves, *Superpower: A Portrait of America in the 1970's* (New York: St. Martin's Press, 1973), 111.

39. Rosenbaum, *The Politics of Environmental Concern,* 38.

40. Richard Nixon's speech was published in the *New York Times,* 8 November 1973, 32. It is also cited Carroll, *It Seemed Like Nothing Happened,* 118. For a good overview of the American energy crisis in relation to the embargo, see Martin V. Melosi, *Coping With Abundance: Energy and Environment in Industrial America* (Philadelphia: Temple University Press, 1985), 277–293.

41. For the oil crisis of 1967, see Daniel Yergin, *The Prize* (New York: Simon & Schuster, 1991), 554–558.

42. Cited in Kenneth S. Deffeyes, *Hubbert's Peak: The Impending World Oil Shortage* (Princeton, NJ: Princeton University Press, 2001), 4.

43. Carroll, *It Seemed Like Nothing Happened,* 119.

44. Hargreaves, *Superpower,* 176. Also cited in *Yergin, The Prize,* 567.

45. Carroll, *It Seemed Like Nothing Happened,* 121. Also cited in Hargreaves, *Superpower,* 176.

46. Patterson, *Grand Expectations,* 785; and Carroll, *It Seemed Like Nothing Happened,* 119. The energy crunch also extended beyond oil to natural gas. Indeed, to make matters worse, Martin Melosi notes that "in 1968, for the first time in U.S. history, more natural gas was sold than was discovered." Melosi, *Coping With Abundance,* 282.

47. Hargreaves, *Superpower,* 176. For oil importation numbers, see Yergin, *The Prize,* 567. In addition to the limitations of domestic oil, Yergin also stresses the importance of OPEC's growing strength and its ability to dictate oil prices on the global market as contributing to the severity of the 1973 oil embargo. See Yergin, *The Prize,* 554–612.

48. See Carroll, *It Seemed Like Nothing Happened,* 117–118.

49. Schulman, *The Seventies,* 125.

50. United States Department of Commerce, *Survey of Current Business* 55 (February 1975), 2.

51. Between January 1973 and January 1974, the average monthly residential bill for #2 fuel oil, for example, increased between 59 percent and 90 percent. Gas

heating prices rose by as much as 25 percent, and electricity prices by as much as 63 percent, over the same period. See Foster Associates, *Energy Prices, 1960–73* (Cambridge, MA: Ballinger, 1974), 5–7.

52. Commoner, *The Poverty of Power,* 34.

53. Cited in ibid., 265.

54. "Thinking the Unthinkable," *Newsweek* (7 October 1974), 50–51. Quotation is from page 51. In addition to such dire language, the article was accompanied by sketches of an airborne attack on oil fields.

55. Barry Commoner, "The Energy Crisis: Implications for Foundations," address at the Council on Foundations, Inc., twenty-fifth annual conference, San Antonio, TX, 10 May 1974 (Barry Commoner Papers, LoC, box 51), 1.

56. Barry Commoner, "The Energy Crisis: All of a Piece," address at "The Energy Outlook and Global Interdependence," public convocation sponsored by the Fund for Peace in cooperation with the Scientists' Institute for Public Information, New York City, 20 November 1974. The paper was published in *The Center Magazine* (March/April 1975), 26–31. The quotation is from page 26.

57. Commoner, "The Energy Crisis: Implications for Foundations," 1.

58. Yergin, *The Prize,* 588. Commoner agreed, claiming: "Oil epitomizes the energy crisis. It is the dominant source of energy for most of the world." Commoner, *The Poverty of Power,* 11.

59. Commoner, *The Poverty of Power,* 4.

60. Tom Ruppel, "Industries Grab Profits, Waste Energy—Commoner," *The Daily Collegian* (Fresno State College, 27 April 1976).

61. Commoner presented this argument in a three-part series that appeared in *The New Yorker* in February and March 1976, before it found its way into *The Poverty of Power* later that same year. During the postwar oil boom, there were seven major oil companies: Texaco, Exxon (formerly Standard Oil of New Jersey), Gulf, Mobil, Chevron, British Petroleum, and Royal Dutch/Shell. Collectively, the companies were known derisively as "the Seven Sisters." Five of the seven were American corporations. For a history of the oil companies, see Anthony Sampson, *The Seven Sisters: The Great Oil Companies and the World They Created* (London: Coronet, 1988). See also Yergin, *The Prize.*

62. Yergin, *The Prize,* 613–652.

63. Carroll, *It Seemed Like Nothing Happened,* 118.

64. *TIME* (24 September 1975), 8.

65. *Business Week* (16 November 1974), 59.

66. *Business Week* (9 November 1974), 26–27.

67. See Alvin Richman, "The Polls: Public Attitudes Toward the Energy Crisis," *Public Opinion Quarterly* 43 (Winter 1979), 576–585.

68. Patterson, *Grand Expectations,* 784. See also David Calleo, *The Imperious Economy* (Cambridge, MA: Harvard University Press, 1982), 112–113.

69. Commoner, "The Energy Crisis: All of a Piece," 26.

70. Schulman, *The Seventies,* 126.

71. David E. Nye, "The Energy Crisis of the 1970s as a Cultural Crisis," *European Contributions to American Studies* 38 (1997), 82–102. For opinion polls, see Richman, "The Polls," 583–585. For the Alaska Pipeline and Santa Barbara proposals, see J. Brooks Flippen, *Nixon and the Environment* (Albuquerque: University of New Mexico Press, 2000), 208–210.

72. Donald Worster, "The Dirty Thirties: A Study in Agricultural Capitalism," *Great Plains Quarterly* 6 (1986), 107–116. Quotation is from page 113.

73. Commoner, *The Poverty of Power,* 34.

74. "Transcript of President's Address on the Energy Situation," *New York Times,* 8 November 1973, 32.

75. Flippen, *Nixon and the Environment,* 207.

76. For the impact of coal mining, see Melosi, *Coping With Abundance.* See also John Opie, *Nature's Nation: An Environmental History of the United States* (New York: Harcourt Brace, 1998), 349–353. For a global perspective on the impact of coal mining, see John R. McNeill, *Something New Under the Sun: An Environmental History of the Twentieth-Century World* (New York: Norton, 2000), 31–32.

77. Commoner, *The Poverty of Power,* 77–78.

78. Larry Dubois, "Playboy Interview: Barry Commoner," *Playboy* (July 1974), 55–74. Quotation is from page 58.

79. Ibid., 72.

80. Dixy Lee Ray, *The Nation's Energy Future: A Report to Richard M. Nixon, President of the United States* (Washington, DC: Atomic Energy Commission, 1973), 47.

81. Ibid., 49.

82. Dubois, "Playboy Interview," 69.

83. Commoner, *The Poverty of Power,* 99.

84. Jean-Claude Debeir, Jean-Paul Deléage, and Daniel Hémery, *In the Servitude of Power: Energy and Civilisation Through the Ages,* translated by John Barzman (Atlantic Highlands, NJ: Zed Books, 1991), 170.

85. Robert W. Righter, *Wind Energy in America: A History* (Norman: University of Oklahoma Press, 1996), 150.

86. Debeir et al., *In the Servitude of Power,* 171.

87. Commoner, *The Poverty of Power,* 90.

88. Ibid., 93.

89. John L. Campbell, *Collapse of an Industry: Nuclear Power and the Contradictions of U.S. Policy* (Ithaca, NY: Cornell University Press, 1988), 4.

90. Melosi, *Coping With Abundance,* 308.

91. Thomas Raymond Wellock, *Critical Masses: Opposition to Nuclear Power in California, 1958–1978* (Madison: University of Wisconsin Press, 1998), 4.

92. Commoner, *The Poverty of Power,* 110.

93. *Wall Street Journal,* 2 May 1983, 30.

94. Robert J. Duffy, *Nuclear Politics in America: A History and Theory of Government Regulation* (Lawrence: University Press of Kansas, 1997), 54–55.

95. Ibid., 70.

96. Commoner, *The Closing Circle,* 269.

97. Dubois, "Playboy Interview," 72.

98. Ray, *The Nation's Energy Future,* 117. Ray's language in describing the solar energy option lacked optimism. She concluded: "Problems associated with public and institutional acceptability will require resolution in the near-term." Ibid. In contrast, Ray awarded $1,450,000,000 to the development of nuclear power, claiming, "Although controlled thermonuclear fusion has yet to be technically demonstrated, recent program successes indicate high probabilities of success in being able to initiate and sustain fusion reactions. This factor warrants emphasis in fusion research and development." Ibid., 115.

99. The story of the missing document is recounted in Commoner, *The Poverty of Power,* 142–144.

100. For the chronic underfunding of research and development for alternative energy sources, see Righter, *Wind Energy in America.*

101. Commoner, *The Poverty of Power,* 121.

102. Ibid., 125.

103. Commoner, *The Politics of Energy* (New York: Knopf, 1979), 33.

104. Commoner, *The Poverty of Power,* 5–6.

105. Commoner, *The Politics of Energy,* 32. A variety of prominent environmental advocates came out vociferously in favor of solar energy. Among the more popular works on the topic, see Amory Lovins, *Soft Energy Paths: Toward a Durable Peace* (San Francisco: Friends of the Earth International, 1977); and Denis Hayes, *Energy: The Solar Prospect* (Washington, DC: Worldwatch Institute, 1977).

106. Frank N. Laird, *Solar Energy, Technology Policy, and Institutional Values* (New York: Cambridge University Press, 2001), 119.

107. Allen L. Hammond, William D. Metz, and Thomas H. Maugh II, *Energy and the Future* (Washington, DC: AAAS, 1973), 61.

108. Laird, *Solar Energy, Technology Policy, and Institutional Values,* 119.

109. Richman, "The Polls," 583–585.

110. Commoner, *The Poverty of Power,* 122. In his discussion of solar energy, Commoner included hydropower and wind power, both of which were produced by the sun. Because the sun warmed the atmosphere unevenly, warm and cool air cycled around, making wind, which could be harnessed to produce energy. Similarly, some water molecules from surface waters evaporated in the sun's heat and were carried by winds to higher altitudes; they would then fall as rain or snow—creating streams and rivers whose downward rush to the sea could be used to produce energy.

111. Dubois, "Playboy Interview," 72.

112. David Bouchier, *Radical Citizenship: The New American Activism* (New York: Schocken Books, 1987), 114.

113. Commoner, *The Poverty of Power,* 262.

114. Commoner, *The Closing Circle,* 280.

115. Joel N. Shurkin, "By Another Name, Socialism Could Smell Sweeter," *Philadelphia Inquirer* book review of *The Poverty of Power* (Barry Commoner Papers, LoC, box 552).

116. John Kenneth Galbraith, *Economics and the Public Purpose* (New York: New American Library, 1975), 274.

117. Barry Commoner, "Pollution and Profit Motive," transcript of talk and Q&A on CBS, 14 December 1971 (Barry Commoner Papers, LoC, box 39).

118. Paul R. Ehrlich and Richard L. Harriman, *How to Be a Survivor: A Plan to Save Planet Earth* (New York: Ballantine Books, 1971), 136.

119. Commoner, *The Poverty of Power,* 120.

120. Commoner, "The Energy Crisis: All of a Piece," 26.

121. Commoner, *The Closing Circle,* 283–284.

122. William Cronon, *Nature's Metropolis: Chicago and the Great West* (New York: Norton, 1991).

Chapter 6: The "Other" Environmentalism

1. Frank Smallwood, *The Other Candidates: Third Parties in Presidential Elections* (Hanover, NH: University Press of New England, 1983), 210.

2. "Dr. Ecology for President," *Newsweek* (21 April 1980), 48.

3. Ibid.

4. Smallwood, *The Other Candidates,* 211.

5. Barry Commoner, *The Politics of Energy* (New York: Knopf, 1979).

6. Smallwood, *The Other Candidates,* 217.

7. Sheila D. Collins, *The Rainbow Challenge: The Jackson Campaign and the Future of U.S. Politics* (New York: Monthly Review Press, 1986), 102. For Jesse Jackson and the Rainbow Coalition, see Lorenzo Morris (ed.), *The Social and Political Implications of the 1984 Jesse Jackson Presidential Campaign* (New York: Praeger, 1984); Ollie A. Johnson III and Karin L. Stanford (eds.), *Black Political Organizations in the Post-Civil Rights Era* (New Brunswick, NJ: Rutgers University Press, 2002); Lucius J. Barker and Ronald W. Walters (eds.), *Jesse Jackson's 1984 Presidential Campaign: Challenge and Change in American Politics* (Urbana: University of Illinois Press, 1989); Thomas H. Landess and Richard M. Quinn, *Jesse Jackson and the Politics of Race* (Ottawa, IL: Jameson Books, 1985); and Lucius J. Barker, *Our Time Has Come: A Delegate's Diary of Jesse Jackson's 1984 Presidential Campaign* (Urbana: University of Illinois Press, 1988). An accessible

biography of Jesse Jackson is Marshall Frady, *Jesse: The Life and Pilgrimage of Jesse Jackson* (New York: Random House, 1996).

8. Barry Commoner, *The Closing Circle* (New York: Knopf, 1971), 268. Ulrich Beck, "Risk Society and the Provident State," in *Risk, Environment and Modernity: Towards a New Ecology,* edited by Scott Lash, Bronislaw Szerszynski, and Brian Wynne (London: Sage, 1996), 27–43. See page 28.

9. Jack M. Hollander, *The Real Environmental Crisis: Why Poverty, Not Affluence, Is the Environment's Number One Enemy* (Berkeley: University of California Press, 2003). This position is supported in John Bodley, *The Power of Scale: A Global History Approach* (London: M. E. Sharpe, 2003); Ramachandra Guha and Juan Martinez-Alier, *Varieties of Environmentalism: Essays North and South* (London: Earthscan, 1997); and Juan Martinez-Alier, *The Environmentalism of the Poor: A Study of Ecological Conflicts and Valuation* (Northampton, MA: Edward Elgar, 2002).

10. Commoner, *The Closing Circle,* 79.

11. Commoner is quoted in Dick Russell, "Environmental Racism," *Amicus Journal* (Spring 1989), 22–32. Quotation is from page 25. For a recent discussion of institutional racism, see Manning Marable, *The Great Wells of Democracy: The Meaning of Race in American Life* (New York: Basic Books, 2002).

12. For environmental justice activism in Cancer Alley, see Beverly Wright, "Race, Politics, and Pollution: Environmental Justice in the Mississippi River Chemical Corridor," in *Just Sustainabilities: Development in an Unequal World,* edited by Julian Agyeman, Robert D. Bullard, and Bob Evans (Cambridge, MA: MIT Press, 2003), 125–145; and J. Timmons Roberts and Melissa M. Toffolon-Weiss, *Chronicles from the Environmental Justice Frontline* (New York: Cambridge University Press, 2001).

13. Barry Commoner, "A Reporter at Large: The Environment," *The New Yorker* 63 (15 June 1987), 46–71. Quotation is from page 64.

14. An extensive debate has grown over the question of whether polluting industries are sited in poorer communities, or whether poorer communities are built up on lands with depressed value because of the prior existence of a polluting industry. While the first argument—which seems to carry more weight—suggests environmental racism, the latter argument rejects that race or class played a role in the disproportional siting of polluting technologies in depressed neighborhoods. For an overview of this literature, see Michael Egan, "Subaltern Environmentalism in the United States: A Historiographic Review," *Environment and History* 8 (February 2002), 21–41. See especially pages 25–29.

15. Matthew Gandy, *Concrete and Clay: Reworking Nature in New York City* (Cambridge, MA: MIT Press, 2002), 200. For asthma studies, see Willine Carr, Lisa Zeitel, and Kevin Weiss, "Variations in Asthma Hospitalizations and Deaths in New York City," *American Journal of Public Health* 82 (1992), 59–65; Douglas W. Dockery, "An Association Between Air Pollution and Mortality in Six U.S. Cities," *New England Journal of Medicine* 329 (1993), 1753–1759; R. Evans, "Asthma Among Minority Children: A Growing Problem," *Chest* 101 (1992), 368–371; and D. J. Gottlieb, A. S. Beiser, and G. T. O'Connor, "Poverty, Race and

Medication Use Are Correlates of Asthma Hospitalization Rates: A Small Area Analysis in Boston," *Chest* 108 (1995), 28–35. See also Adam Nossiter, "Asthma Common and on the Rise in the Crowded South Bronx," *New York Times,* 5 September 1995, A1. Nossiter reported on doctors' responses to an emerging asthma epidemic in the South Bronx, where hospitalization and death rates were eight times the national average. A good resource on the rising rates of asthma is the American Lung Association Web site, http://www.lungusa.org/.

16. West Harlem Environmental Action cofounder Vernice Miller, quoted in Gandy, *Concrete and Clay,* 217.

17. Samuel P. Hays, *Beauty, Health, and Permanence: Environmental Politics in the United States, 1955–1985* (Cambridge: Cambridge University Press, 1987).

18. In many respects, the articulation of an ecological language is the pivotal thrust of Donald Worster's account of the development of the ecological imagination. See Donald Worster, *Nature's Economy: A History of Ecological Ideas,* 2nd ed. (New York: Cambridge University Press, 1994). See also Roderick Nash, *The Rights of Nature: A History of Environmental Ethics* (Madison: University of Wisconsin Press, 1989), 161–198.

19. Gandy, *Concrete and Clay,* 215.

20. Literature on the human body as a site for environmental history is growing rapidly. See, by way of introduction, Christopher Sellers, "Thoreau's Body: Towards an Embodied Environmental History," *Environmental History* 4 (1999), 486–514. Quotations are from page 487. See also Christopher Sellers, "Body, Place and the State: The Making of an 'Environmentalist' Imaginary in the Post-World War II U.S.," *Radical History Review* 74 (1999), 31–64; and Maril Hazlett, "The Story of *Silent Spring* and the Ecological Turn," Ph.D. dissertation, University of Kansas, 2003. For health, body, and environment, see Gregg Mitman, *Breathing Space: An Ecological History of Allergy in America* (New Haven, CT: Yale University Press, 2007).

21. Louis Menand, *The Metaphysical Club: A Story of Ideas in America* (New York: Farrar, Straus, and Giroux, 2001), 377.

22. Gandy has described the metaphysical origins of twentieth-century American environmentalism as a "regional organicism [which] has evolved into an uneasy relation to 'nativist' doctrines that can all too easily be translated into a fear of strangers, whether plants or people." Gandy, *Concrete and Clay,* 215. This rather simplistic critique of the mainstream movement deserves complication with a deeper investigation of pluralism as a prominent feature of American environmental activism. See, for example, David Schlosberg, *Environmental Justice and the New Pluralism: The Challenge of Difference for Environmentalism* (New York: Oxford University Press, 1999).

23. Nathan Hare, "Black Ecology," *The Black Scholar* (April 1970), 2–8. Quotation is from page 2.

24. Robert Rienow and Leona Train Rienow, *Moment in the Sun: A Report on the Deteriorating Quality of the American Environment* (New York: Dial Press, 1967).

25. Hare, "Black Ecology."

26. This kind of argument poses a poignant historiographic question to existing literature on the history of the American environmental movement. Some prominent studies have tended to maintain a rather narrow focus that fails to recognize the race- and class-oriented aspects of environmental protest that Hare raised. In effect, this literature does not recognize the significance of the political economy and its relationship with environmental problems. See, for example, Adam Rome, "'Give Earth a Chance': The Environmental Movement and the Sixties," *Journal of American History* 90 (September 2003), 525–554, and *The Bulldozer in the Countryside: Suburban Sprawl and the Rise of American Environmentalism* (Cambridge: Cambridge University Press, 2001); Roderick Nash, *Wilderness and the American Mind,* 4th ed. (New Haven, CT: Yale University Press, 2001); and *The Rights of Nature;* Stephen Fox, *The American Conservation Movement: John Muir and His Legacy* (Boston: Little, Brown, 1981); Andrew Glenn Kirk, *Collecting Nature: The American Environmental Movement and the Conservation Library* (Lawrence: University Press of Kansas, 2001); and Richard W. Judd and Christopher S. Beach, *Natural States: The Environmental Imagination in Maine, Oregon, and the Nation* (Washington, DC: Resources for the Future, 2003). A few studies have sought to address this disparity. See Martin V. Melosi, "Environmental Justice, Political Agenda Setting, and the Myths of History," *Journal of Policy History* 12 (2000), 43–71; Sellers, "Body, Place and the State"; Marcy Damovsky, "Stories Less Told: Histories of U.S. Environmentalism," *Socialist Review* 22 (October–December 1992), 11–54; Scott Hamilton Dewey, *Don't Breathe the Air: Air Pollution and U.S. Environmental Politics, 1945–1970* (College Station: Texas A&M University Press, 2000); Robert Gottlieb, *Forcing the Spring: The Transformation of the American Environmental Movement* (Washington, DC: Island Press, 1993); Mark Dowie, *Losing Ground: American Environmentalism at the Close of the Twentieth Century* (Cambridge, MA: MIT Press, 1995); Andrew Szasz, *EcoPopulism: Toxic Waste and the Movement for Environmental Justice* (Minneapolis: University of Minnesota Press, 1994); and Schlosberg, *Environmental Justice and the New Pluralism.*

27. Howe is quoted in his obituary in the *New York Times,* 14 April 1996, 39.

28. Hayes is quoted in Dowie, *Losing Ground,* 25.

29. Nelson is quoted in Gottlieb, *Forcing the Spring,* 106.

30. The literature on this theme is growing rapidly. See Sylvia H. Washington, *Packing Them In: An Archaeology of Environmental Racism in Chicago* (Lanham, MD: Lexington Books, 2005); Robert D. Bullard, *Dumping in Dixie: Race, Class, and Environmental Quality,* 3rd ed. (Boulder, CO: Westview Press, 2000); Robert D. Bullard (ed.), *Confronting Environmental Racism: Voices from the Grassroots* (Boston: South End Press, 1993), and *Unequal Protection: Environmental Justice and Communities of Color* (San Francisco: Sierra Club Books, 1994); Edwardo Lao Rhodes, *Environmental Justice in America: A New Paradigm* (Bloomington: Indiana University Press, 2003); James P. Lester, David W. Allen, and Kelly M. Hill, *Environmental Injustice in the United States: Myths and Realities* (Boulder, CO: Westview Press, 2001); David Naguib Pellow, *Garbage Wars: The Struggle for En-*

vironmental Justice in Chicago (Cambridge, MA: MIT Press, 2002); and Eddie J. Girdner and Jack Smith, *Killing Me Softly: Toxic Waste, Corporate Profit, and the Struggle for Environmental Justice* (New York: Monthly Review Press, 2002).

31. See Denis Hayes, "Reclaiming the Vision of the First Earth Day," *Seattle Times,* 22 April 2004. See also Julian Bond, "Redefining the Environmental Movement," *Washington Post,* 22 April 2004. I am grateful to Denis Hayes for bringing the Julian Bond article to my attention.

32. Quoted in Dowie, *Losing Ground,* 25.

33. Gottlieb, *Forcing the Spring,* 235–269.

34. For the division between civil rights activism and environmentalism, see *TIME* (3 August 1970), 42. The article made passing reference to the environmental movement as an almost exclusively white organization. See also Eileen Maura McGurty, "From NIMBY to Civil Rights: The Origins of the Environmental Justice Movement," *Environmental History* 2 (July 1997), 301–323. See especially pages 301–305.

35. Washington, *Packing Them In.*

36. Gandy, *Concrete and Clay,* 154.

37. Commoner, *The Closing Circle,* 296.

38. Barry Commoner, "The Meaning of the Environmental Crisis," presented at United Nations Conference on the Human Environment, Stockholm, 16 June 1972 (Barry Commoner Papers, LoC, box 138), 14.

39. Commoner, *The Closing Circle,* 207.

40. Ibid., 79.

41. Barry Commoner, untitled talk, Brown University, 22 April 1970 (Barry Commoner Papers, LoC, box 131), 18.

42. Ibid. Commoner repeated the story in *The Closing Circle,* 207.

43. Commoner, untitled talk, Brown University, 19. See also Commoner, *The Closing Circle,* 208.

44. Commoner, untitled talk, Brown University, 18. See also Commoner, *The Closing Circle,* 208.

45. Commoner, untitled talk, Brown University, 18–19. See also Commoner, *The Closing Circle,* 208.

46. Commoner, untitled talk, Brown University, 19.

47. Commoner correspondence with author, 19 May 2004.

48. Commoner, interview with author, 20 November 2003.

49. Douglas H. Strong, *Dreamers and Defenders: American Conservationists* (Lincoln: University of Nebraska Press, 1988), 243.

50. For histories of trash in America, see Susan Strasser, *Waste and Want: A Social History of Trash* (New York: Metropolitan Books, 1999); Martin V. Melosi, "Down in the Dumps: Is There a Garbage Crisis in America?" *Journal of Policy History* 5 (1993), 100–127; and Pellow, *Garbage Wars.*

51. Barry Commoner, *Making Peace With the Planet* (New York: Pantheon Books, 1992), 107.

52. Gandy, *Concrete and Clay,* 309, fn 14.

53. Commoner, *Making Peace With the Planet,* 107.

54. Ibid., 109. See also Peter Montague, "Incineration vs. Recycling," *Rachel's Environment & Health News* 121 (20 March 1989), 1–2.

55. Commoner, *Making Peace With the Planet,* 119.

56. Commoner, cited in Melosi, "Down in the Dumps," 112.

57. U.S. Environmental Protection Agency, *Health Assessment Document for Polychlorinated Dibenzo-p-Dioxins* (Washington, DC: Office of Health and Environmental Assessment, 1985).

58. Commoner, quoted in Peter Montague, "Turning Point for the Chemical Industry," *Rachel's Environment & Health News* 405 (31 August 1994), 1–2. Quotation is from page 1. For Commoner's work on dioxin, see Barry Commoner et al., *Dioxin Fallout in the Great Lakes: Where It Comes From, How to Prevent It, at What Cost* (Flushing, NY: Center for the Biology of Natural Systems, 1996); and Commoner et al., *Zeroing Out Dioxin in the Great Lakes: Within Our Reach* (Flushing, NY: Center for the Biology of Natural Systems, 1996).

59. See Montague, "Turning Point for the Chemical Industry," and "How to Eliminate Dioxin," *Rachel's Environment & Health News* 508 (21 August 1996), 1–2.

60. Mark Cohen, Barry Commoner, et al., *Quantitative Estimation of the Entry of Dioxins, Furans and Hexachlorobenzene Into the Great Lakes From Airborne and Waterborne Sources* (Flushing, NY: Center for the Biology of Natural Systems, 1995).

61. For the dioxin tragedy in Seveso, see Devra Davis, *When Smoke Ran Like Water: Tales of Environmental Deception and the Battle Against Pollution* (New York: Basic Books, 2002), 200–203; Joe Thornton, *Pandora's Poison* (Cambridge, MA: MIT Press, 2000), 183–184; and Colleen F. Moore, *Silent Scourge: Children, Pollution, and Why Scientists Disagree* (New York: Oxford University Press, 2003), 240.

62. For the dioxin scare and evacuation at Times Beach, see C. D. Carter et al., "Tetrachlorodibenzodioxin: An Accidental Poisoning in Horse Arenas," *Science* 188 (16 May 1975), 738–740; Montague, "Turning Point for the Chemical Industry"; and U.S. Environmental Protection Agency, *Superfund Permanent Relocations* (October 1999), online at www.epa.gov. See also Commoner, *Making Peace With the Planet,* 72–74; and Moore, *Silent Scourge,* 240–241.

63. Barry Commoner, "Keynote Address at the Second Citizens' Conference on Dioxin," St. Louis, MO, 30 July 1994 (Center for the Biology of Natural Systems), 4. The preeminent book on dioxins is Lois Marie Gibbs, *Dying From Dioxin* (Boston: South End Press, 1995). For scientific treatments of dioxin, see Thornton, *Pandora's Poison;* and Michael McCally (ed.), *Life Support: The Environment and Human Health* (Cambridge, MA: MIT Press, 2002).

64. Environment Canada, *The National Incinerator Testing and Evaluation Program: Air Pollution Control Technology* (Ottawa: Environment Canada, September 1986).

65. Commoner, *Making Peace With the Planet,* 120.

66. Lois Gibbs, cited in Peter Montague, "Scientists Suspect Poisoning of Fish by Mercury Emissions From Incinerators," *Rachel's Environment & Health News* 198 (11 September 1990), 1.

67. Gandy, *Concrete and Clay,* 204–205.

68. For an overview of the Center for the Biology of Natural Systems' activities past and present, see the Center's website: http://www.cbns.qc.edu/.

69. Barry Commoner, "The Politics of Regional Environment: Pollution-Control and Pollution-Prevention Strategies," in *Contested Terrain: Power, Politics, and Participation in Suburbia,* edited by Marc L. Silver and Martin Melkonian (Westport, CT: Greenwood Press, 1995), 9–18. Quotation is from page 12.

70. Gandy, *Concrete and Clay,* 190. The construction of the Williamsburg plant was ultimately blocked. For that environmental justice protest, see ibid., 187–227.

71. For an extended discussion of this issue, see Girdner and Smith, *Killing Me Softly.*

72. Commoner, *Making Peace With the Planet,* 73. For another recent case, see the dispute over the risk of ammonium perchlorate, used by NASA and the Pentagon for rocket fuel and munitions since the 1950s. Recent Environmental Protection Agency reports suggest that perchlorate has resulted in the widespread contamination of groundwater throughout the United States, while NASA and Pentagon scientists have disputed the environmental agency's findings. The debate over how many parts per billion constitute a health threat—perchlorate suppresses hormonal development, and could be especially harmful to small children and fetuses—will ultimately determine the cost of the cleanup. The Pentagon and industry are currently arguing for a threshold of 200 parts per billion in drinking water, which would exempt the vast majority of the contamination from cleanup, while the Environmental Protection Agency is advocating a limit of no more than one part per billion. The potential cost of the cleanup at the Environmental Protection Agency-slated standard could amount to $40 billion over ten years. See Jennifer Lee, "Second Thoughts on a Chemical: In Water, How Much Is Too Much?" *New York Times,* 2 March 2004, D1, D4.

73. For the East Hampton pilot recycling study, see Barry Commoner et al., *Development and Pilot Test of an Intensive Municipal Solid Waste Recycling System for the Town of East Hampton* (Flushing, NY: Center for the Biology of Natural Systems, 1988).

74. Commoner, quoted in Montague, "Incineration vs. Recycling," 1.

75. For the Buffalo pilot recycling study, see D. Stern et al., *Buffalo Curbside Recycling Pilot Program* (Flushing, NY: Center for the Biology of Natural Systems, 1989).

76. Barry Commoner, untitled paper, presented at New Jersey Environmental Federation Conference, New Brunswick, NJ, 4 March 1989 (Flushing, NY: Center for the Biology of Natural Systems), 11.

77. Commoner, *Making Peace With the Planet,* 138.

78. Commoner, untitled paper, presented at New Jersey Environmental Federation conference, 11.

79. Commoner, *Making Peace With the Planet,* 138.

80. Ibid., 138–139.

81. Ibid., 29.

82. Barry Commoner, "Why We Have Failed," *Greenpeace* 14 (September/October 1989), 12–13. Quotation is from page 12. Also published in Bill Willers (ed.), *Learning to Listen to the Land* (Washington, DC: Island Press, 1991), 163–168.

83. Commoner, *Making Peace With the Planet,* 169.

84. Commoner, "Why We Have Failed," 12. My emphasis.

85. Commoner, "A Reporter at Large," 56.

86. See ibid., 47–48.

87. Ibid., 56.

88. Commoner, quoted in Montague, "Turning Point for the Chemical Industry," p. 1. See also Commoner, "Keynote Address at the Second Citizens' Conference on Dioxin," 2.

89. Commoner, "A Reporter at Large," 68.

90. Commoner, untitled paper, New Jersey Environmental Federation Conference, 13. See also Montague, "Incineration vs. Recycling," 1.

91. Commoner, "A Reporter at Large," 70.

92. Commoner, *Making Peace With the Planet,* 20.

93. Dowie, *Losing Ground.*

94. Thornton, *Pandora's Poison,* 23.

95. Schlosberg, *Environmental Justice and the New Pluralism,* 3.

96. Commoner, "Why We Have Failed," 13.

Conclusion: If We Would Know Life

1. Barry Commoner, "Is Biology a Molecular Science?," fourth Mellon Lecture at the School of Medicine, University of Pittsburgh, 17 February 1965 (Barry Commoner Papers, LoC, box 16), 40.

2. Barry Commoner, "Unraveling the DNA Myth: The Spurious Foundation of Genetic Engineering," *Harper's* magazine (February 2002), 39–47. Quotation is from page 39.

3. Stephen Fox, *The American Conservation Movement: John Muir and His Legacy* (Madison: University of Wisconsin Press, 1985), 313.

4. Barry Commoner, *Science and Survival* (New York: Viking Press, 1966), 39.

5. Ibid., 46.

6. Barry Commoner, "The Implications of Molecular Biology for Man," presented at the New School for Social Research, New York City, 21 April 1967 (Barry Commoner Papers, LoC, box 20), 21.

7. Commoner, interview with author, 17 July 2003.

8. Commoner, "Unraveling the DNA Myth," 39. The seminal work on the history of molecular biology is Horace Freeland Judson, *The Eighth Day of Creation: Makers of the Revolution in Biology* (New York: Simon & Schuster, 1979).

9. Paul Boyer reflects on the cultural transition from nuclear euphoria to Cold War terror after the Soviets detonated an atomic bomb in 1949. See Paul Boyer, *By the Bomb's Early Light: American Thought and Culture at the Dawn of the Atomic Age* (Chapel Hill: University of North Carolina Press, 1994).

10. Pnina G. Abir-Am, "The Molecular Transformation of Twentieth-Century Biology," in *Science in the Twentieth Century,* edited by John Krige and Dominique Pestre (Amsterdam: Harwood Academic Publishers, 1997), 495–524. Quotation is from page 495.

11. Peter Montague, "Barry Commoner: The Father of Grassroots Environmentalism," in *Barry Commoner's Contribution to the Environmental Movement: Science and Social Action,* edited by David Kriebel (Amityville, NY: Baywood, 2002), 5–14. Quotation is from page 5. This book consists of the presentations given in celebration of Commoner's eightieth birthday.

12. Virginia Warner Brodine, "The Day Before Yesterday: The Committees for Nuclear and Environmental Information," in *Barry Commoner's Contribution to the Environmental Movement,* 15–23. Quotation is from page 17–18.

13. Ralph Nader, "Real Junk Science: The Corruption of Science by Corporate Money," in *Barry Commoner's Contribution to the Environmental Movement,* 31–43. Quotation is from pages 31–32.

14. Barry Commoner, "What Is Yet to Be Done," in *Barry Commoner's Contribution to the Environmental Movement,* 73–85. Quotation is from page 73.

15. Ibid., 74.

16. Ibid., 85.

17. Michael A. Bryson, *Visions of the Land: Science, Literature, and the American Environment From the Era of Exploration to the Age of Ecology* (Charlottesville: University Press of Virginia, 2002), xii.

18. Stuart W. Leslie, *The Cold War and American Science: The Military-Industrial-Academic Complex at MIT and Stanford* (New York: Columbia University Press, 1993).

Bibliography

Oral Interviews and Unpublished Archival Collections

Interviews

Note: The author's taped interviews with Commoner have been donated to the Center for the Biology of Natural Systems.

Barry Commoner, interview with author, 15 November 2001.

Barry Commoner, interview with author, 22 November 2002.

Barry Commoner, interview with author, 17 July 2003.

Barry Commoner, interview with author, 20 November 2003.

Barry Commoner, correspondence with author, 19 May 2004.

Barry Commoner, conversation with author, 25 August 2005.

Barry Commoner, conversation with author, 28 December 2005.

"Ecology: Interview with Barry Commoner." NBC interview, 17 April 1970. Barry Commoner Papers, LoC, box 35.

Archives

Barry Commoner Papers. Library of Congress (LoC), Washington, D.C.

Catherine Borras. Committee files. AAAS Archives, Washington, D.C.

Committee on Science in the Promotion of Human Welfare Papers. AAAS Archives, Washington, D.C.

Committee for Nuclear Information records. Western Historical Manuscript Collection, University of Missouri-St. Louis.

Paul and Anne Ehrlich Papers. Special Collections and University Archives, Stanford University Libraries.

Government Documents and Web Sites

Government Documents

Atomic Energy Commission. *The Thirteenth Semiannual Report of the Atomic Energy Commission.* Washington, DC: Government Printing Office, 1 January 1953.

Environment Canada. *The National Incinerator Testing and Evaluation Program: Air Pollution Control Technology.* Ottawa: Environment Canada, September 1986.

Fallout, Radiation Standards, and Countermeasures. Hearings before the Joint Subcommittee on Research, Development, and Radiation of the Joint Committee on Atomic Energy, 21 August 1963.

The Nature of Radioactive Fallout and Its Effects on Man. Hearings before the Special Subcommittee on Radiation of the Joint Committee on Atomic Energy, 5 June 1957.

President's Scientific Research Board. *Science and Public Policy.* Washington, DC: Government Printing Office, 1947.

Report to the Full Committee of the Special Subcommittee on National Security of the Committee on Un-American Activities. Washington, DC: House Committee on Un-American Activities, Special Subcommittee on National Security, 1 March 1948.

U.S. Bureau of the Census. *Statistical Abstract of the United States, 1940* (Washington, D.C.: Bureau of the Census, 1941).

U.S. Department of Health, Education and Welfare. *Report on Investigation of Fish Kills in Lower Mississippi River, Atchafalaya River, and Gulf of Mexico,* 6 April 1964.

U.S. Environmental Protection Agency. *The Economics of Clean Air: Annual Report of the Administrator of the Environmental Protection Agency.* Washington, DC: Government Printing Office, 1972.

———. *Health Assessment Document for Polychlorinated Dibenzo-p-Dioxins.* Washington, DC: Office of Health and Environmental Assessment, 1985.

———. *Mercury Study Report to Congress.* Vol. 1: *Executive Summary.* Washington, DC: Office of Air Quality Planning and Standards, 1997.

———. *Superfund Permanent Relocations.* October 1999. Accessed online at www.epa.gov, 1 March 2004.

Web Sites

American Lung Association. http://www.lungusa.org/. Accessed 5 June 2004.

The Breakthrough Institute. http://www.thebreakthrough.org/. Accessed 24 May 2004.

Centers for Disease Control and Prevention. http://www.cdc.gov/nceh/radiation/fallout/default.htm. Accessed 28 April 2004.

Department of Energy. http://tis.eh.doe.gov/ohre/new/findingaids/radioactive/index.html. Accessed 28 April 2004.

———. http://www.eia.doe.gov/emeu/aer/txt/ptb0209.html/. Accessed 10 June 2004.

National Cancer Institute. http://seer.cancer.gov/csr/1975_2001/sections.html. Accessed 5 June 2004.

Books, Conference Proceedings, Theses, and Dissertations

Adamson, Joni, Mei Mei Evans, and Rachel Stein (eds.). *The Environmental Justice Reader: Politics, Poetics, and Pedagogy.* Tucson: University of Arizona Press, 2002.

Ageyman, Julian, Robert D. Bullard, and Bob Evans (eds.). *Just Sustainabilities: Development in an Unequal World.* Cambridge, MA: MIT Press, 2003.

Arnold, Ron, and Alan Gottlieb. *Trashing the Economy: How Runaway Environmentalism Is Wrecking America.* Bellevue, WA: Free Enterprise Press, 1993.

Aronowitz, Stanley. *The Death and Rebirth of American Radicalism.* New York: Routledge, 1996.

Bailey, Ronald. *Ecoscam: The False Prophets of Ecological Apocalypse.* New York: St. Martin's Press, 1994.

Balogh, Brian. *Chain Reaction: Expert Debate and Public Participation in American Commercial Nuclear Power, 1945–1975.* New York: Cambridge University Press, 1991.

Barker, Lucius J. *Our Time Has Come: A Delegate's Diary of Jesse Jackson's 1984 Presidential Campaign.* Urbana: University of Illinois Press, 1988.

Barker, Lucius J., and Ronald W. Walters (eds.). *Jesse Jackson's 1984 Presidential Campaign: Challenge and Change in American Politics.* Urbana: University of Illinois Press, 1989.

Baxandall, Rosalyn, and Elizabeth Ewen. *Picture Windows: How the Suburbs Happened.* New York: Basic Books, 2000.

Beard, Charles A. (ed.). *A Century of Progress.* New York: Harper & Bros., 1933.

Beard, Charles A., and Mary R. Beard. *The Rise of American Civilization.* New ed., rev. and enl. New York: Macmillan, 1930.

Becher, Anne, Kyle McClure, Rachel White Scheuering, and Julia Willis. *American Environmental Leaders: From Colonial Times to the Present.* 2 vols. Santa Barbara, CA: ABC-CLIO, 2000.

Beck, Ulrich. *Risk Society: Towards a New Modernity.* Translated by Mark Ritter. London: Sage, 1992.

———. *World Risk Society.* Cambridge: Polity Press, 1999.

Bell, Daniel. *The Cultural Contradictions of Capitalism.* New York: Basic Books, 1976.

Bercovitch, Sacvan. *The American Jeremiad.* Madison: University of Wisconsin Press, 1978.

Blumberg, Stanley A., and Gwinn Owens. *Energy and Conflict: The Life and Times of Edward Teller.* New York: Putnam, 1976.

Blumin, Stuart M. *The Emergence of the Middle Class: Social Experience in the American City, 1760–1900.* Cambridge: Cambridge University Press, 1989.

Bocking, Stephen. *Ecologists and Environmental Politics: A History of Contemporary Ecology.* New Haven, CT: Yale University Press, 1997.

———. *Nature's Experts: Science, Politics, and the Environment.* New Brunswick, NJ: Rutgers University Press, 2004.

Bodley, John. *The Power of Scale: A Global History Approach.* London: M. E. Sharpe, 2003.

Bookchin, Murray. *The Limits of the City.* New York: Harper & Row, 1974.

———. *Remaking Society.* Montreal: Black Rose Books, 1989.

Bouchier, David. *Radical Citizenship: The New American Activism.* New York: Schocken Books, 1987.

Bowler, Peter J. *The Earth Encompassed: A History of the Environmental Sciences.* New York: Norton, 1992.

Boyer, Paul. *By the Bomb's Early Light: American Thought and Culture at the Dawn of the Atomic Age.* Chapel Hill: University of North Carolina Press, 1994.

Bradsher, Keith. *High and Mighty: The Dangerous Rise of the SUV.* New York: Public Affairs, 2003.

Bridges, Amy. *A City in the Republic: Antebellum New York and the Origins of Machine Politics.* Cambridge: Cambridge University Press, 1984.

Brooks, Paul. *The House of Life: Rachel Carson at Work.* Boston: Houghton Mifflin, 1972.

Brown, Martin (ed.). *The Social Responsibility of the Scientist.* New York: Free Press, 1971.

Bruce, Robert V. *The Launching of Modern American Science, 1846–1876.* Ithaca, NY: Cornell University Press, 1987.

Brulle, Robert J. *Agency, Democracy, and Nature: The U.S. Environmental Movement From a Critical Theory Perspective.* Cambridge, MA: MIT Press, 2000.

Brynner, Rock, and Trent Stephens. *Dark Remedy: The Impact of Thalidomide and Its Revival as a Vital Medicine.* Cambridge, MA: Perseus, 2001.

Bryson, Michael A. *Visions of the Land: Science, Literature, and the American Environment From the Era of Exploration to the Age of Ecology.* Charlottesville: University Press of Virginia, 2002.

Buell, Frederick. *From Apocalypse to Way of Life: Environmental Crisis in the American Century.* New York: Routledge, 2003.

Bullard, Robert D. *Dumping in Dixie: Race, Class, and Environmental Quality.* 3rd ed. Boulder, CO: Westview Press, 2000.

——— (ed.). *Confronting Environmental Racism: Voices From the Grassroots.* Boston: South End Press, 1993.

———. *Unequal Protection: Environmental Justice and Communities of Color.* San Francisco: Sierra Club Books, 1994.

Burrows, Edwin G., and Mike Wallace. *Gotham: A History of New York City to 1898.* Oxford: Oxford University Press, 2000.

Bury, J. B. *The Idea of Progress.* New York: Macmillan, 1932.

Bush, Vannevar. *Science, the Endless Frontier.* Washington, DC: U.S. Government Printing Office, 1945.

Calleo, David. *The Imperious Economy.* Cambridge, MA: Harvard University Press, 1982.

Campbell, John L. *Collapse of an Industry: Nuclear Power and the Contradictions of U.S. Policy.* Ithaca, NY: Cornell University Press, 1988.

Cantelon, Philip L., Richard G. Hewlett, and Robert C. Williams (eds.). *The American Atom: A Documentary History of Nuclear Policies From the Discovery of Fission to the Present.* 2nd ed. Philadelphia: University of Pennsylvania Press, 1991.

Carroll, Peter N. *It Seemed Like Nothing Happened: The Tragedy and Promise of America in the 1970s.* New York: Holt, Rinehart and Winston, 1982.

Carson, Rachel. *Silent Spring.* Boston: Houghton Mifflin, 1962.

Chase, Steve (ed.). *Defending the Earth: A Dialogue Between Murray Bookchin and Dave Foreman.* Boston: South End Press, 1991.

Chisholm, Anne. *Philosophers of the Earth: Conversations with Ecologists.* New York: Dutton, 1972.

Clark, Claudia. *Radium Girls: Women and Industrial Health Reform, 1910–1935.* Chapel Hill: University of North Carolina Press, 1997.

Cohen, Joel E. *How Many People Can the Earth Support?* New York: Norton, 1995.

Cohen, Lizabeth. *A Consumers' Republic: The Politics of Mass Consumption in Postwar America.* New York: Knopf, 2003.

Cohen, Mark, Barry Commoner, et al. *Quantitative Estimation of the Entry of Dioxins, Furans and Hexachlorobenzene Into the Great Lakes From Airborne and Waterborne Sources.* Flushing, NY: Center for the Biology of Natural Systems, 1995.

Cohen, Michael P. *The Pathless Way: John Muir and the American Wilderness.* Madison: University of Wisconsin Press, 1984.

Cole, Luke W., and Sheila R. Foster. *From the Ground Up: Environmental Racism and the Rise of the Environmental Justice Movement.* New York: New York University Press, 2001.

Collins, Sheila D. *The Rainbow Challenge: The Jackson Campaign and the Future of U.S. Politics.* New York: Monthly Review Press, 1986.

Commission for Racial Justice, United Church of Christ. *Toxic Wastes and Race in the United States: A National Report on the Racial and Socio-Economic Char-*

acteristics of Communities With Hazardous Waste Sites. New York: United Church of Christ, 1987.

Commoner, Barry. *Science and Survival.* New York: Viking Press, 1966.

———. *The Closing Circle: Nature, Man, and Technology.* New York: Knopf, 1971.

———. *The Poverty of Power.* New York: Knopf, 1976.

———. *The Politics of Energy.* New York: Knopf, 1979.

———. *Making Peace With the Planet.* New York: Pantheon Books, 1990.

Commoner, Barry, et al. *Development and Pilot Test of an Intensive Municipal Solid Waste Recycling System for the Town of East Hampton.* Flushing, NY: Center for the Biology of Natural Systems, 1988.

———. *Dioxin Fallout in the Great Lakes: Where It Comes From, How to Prevent It, at What Cost.* Flushing, NY: Center for the Biology of Natural Systems, 1996.

———. *Zeroing Out Dioxin in the Great Lakes: Within Our Reach.* Flushing, NY: Center for the Biology of Natural Systems, 1996.

Costanza, Robert. *Frontiers in Ecological Economics: Transdisciplinary Essays by Robert Costanza.* Lyme, NH: Edward Elgar, 1997.

Costanza, Robert, Olman Segura, and Juan Martinez-Alier (eds.). *Getting Down to Earth: Practical Applications of Ecological Economics.* Washington, DC: Island Press, 1996.

Costanza, Robert, et al. *An Introduction to Ecological Economics.* Boca Raton, FL: St. Lucie Press, 1997.

Cowan, Ruth Schwartz. *A Social History of American Technology.* New York: Oxford University Press, 1997.

Cox, Donald W. *America's New Policy Makers: The Scientists' Rise to Power.* Philadelphia: Chilton Books, 1964.

Creager, Angela N. H. *The Life of a Virus: Tobacco Mosaic Virus as an Experimental Model, 1930–1965.* Chicago: University of Chicago Press, 2002.

Cronon, William. *Nature's Metropolis: Chicago and the Great West.* New York: Norton, 1991.

——— (ed.). *Uncommon Ground: Rethinking the Human Place in Nature.* New York: Norton, 1996.

Cross, Gary. *An All-Consuming Century: Why Commercialism Won in Modern America.* New York: Columbia University Press, 2000.

Daly, Herman E. *Ecological Economics and the Ecology of Economics: Essays in Criticism.* Northampton, MA: Edward Elgar, 1999.

Daly, Herman E., and John B. Cobb, Jr. *For the Common Good: Redirecting the Economy Toward Community, the Environment, and a Sustainable Future.* Boston: Beacon Press, 1989.

Davis, Devra. *When Smoke Ran Like Water: Tales of Environmental Deception and the Battle Against Pollution.* New York: Basic Books, 2002.

Debeir, Jean-Claude, Jean-Paul Deléage, and Daniel Hémery. *In the Servitude of Power: Energy and Civilisation Through the Ages*. Translated by John Barzman. Atlantic Highlands, NJ: Zed Books, 1991.

Deffeyes, Kenneth S. *Hubbert's Peak: The Impending World Oil Shortage*. Princeton, NJ: Princeton University Press, 2001.

DeLeon, David (ed.). *Leaders From the 1960s: A Biographical Sourcebook of American Activism*. Westport, CT: Greenwood Press, 1994.

Dennis, Michael A. "A Change of State: The Political Cultures of Technical Practice at the MIT Instrumentation Laboratory and the Johns Hopkins University Applied Physics Laboratory, 1930–1945." Ph.D. dissertation, Johns Hopkins University, 1991.

Dewey, Scott Hamilton. *Don't Breathe the Air: Air Pollution and U.S. Environmental Politics, 1945–1970*. College Station: Texas A&M University Press, 2000.

Diamond, Jared. *Guns, Germs, and Steel: The Fates of Human Societies*. New York: Norton, 1997.

Dietrich, William. *The Final Forest: The Battle for the Last Great Trees of the Pacific Northwest*. New York: Simon & Schuster, 1992.

Diner, Hasia R. *In the Almost Promised Land: American Jews and Blacks, 1915–1935*. Westport, CT: Greenwood Press, 1977.

———. *A New Promised Land: A History of Jews in America*. New York: Oxford University Press, 2003.

Divine, Robert A. *Blowing on the Wind: The Nuclear Test Ban Debate, 1954–1960*. New York: Oxford University Press, 1978.

Donaldson, Thomas, and Patricia H. Werhane (eds.). *Ethical Issues in Business: A Philosophical Approach*. 5th ed. Upper Saddle River, NJ: Prentice Hall, 1996.

Douglas, Mary, and Aaron Wildavsky. *Risk and Culture: An Essay on the Selection of Technical and Environmental Dangers*. Berkeley: University of California Press, 1982.

Douglas, William O. *Freedom of the Mind*. Chicago: American Library Association, 1962.

Dowie, Mark. *Losing Ground: American Environmentalism at the Close of the Twentieth Century*. Cambridge, MA: MIT Press, 1995.

Duffy, John. *A History of Public Health in New York City, 1625–1866*. Vol. 1. New York: Russell Sage Foundation, 1968.

Duffy, Robert J. *Nuclear Politics in America: A History and Theory of Government Regulation*. Lawrence: University Press of Kansas, 1997.

Dunning, Gordon M., and John A. Hilcken (eds.). *Symposium [on] the Shorter-Term Biological Hazards of a Fallout Field, Washington, D.C., December 12–14, 1956*. Washington, DC: U.S. Government Printing Office, 1958.

Dupré, J. Stefan, and Sanford A. Lakoff. *Science and the Nation: Policy and Politics*. Englewood Cliffs, NJ: Prentice-Hall, 1962.

Dupree, A. Hunter. *Science in the Federal Government: A History of Policies and Activities to 1940*. Cambridge, MA: Belknap Press of Harvard University Press, 1957.

Ehrlich, Paul R. *The Population Bomb.* New York: Ballantine Books, 1968.

Ehrlich, Paul R., and Richard L. Harriman. *How to Be a Survivor: A Plan to Save Planet Earth.* New York: Ballantine Books, 1971.

Ekirch, Arthur, Jr. *Man and Nature in America.* New York: Columbia University Press, 1963.

Ezrahi, Yaron. *The Descent of Icarus: Science and the Transformation of Contemporary Democracy.* Cambridge, MA: Harvard University Press, 1990.

Faber, Malte, Reiner Manstetten, and John Proops. *Ecological Economics: Concepts and Methods.* Brookfield, VT: Edward Elgar, 1996.

Fenichell, Stephen. *Plastic: The Making of a Synthetic Century.* New York: Harper-Business, 1996.

Fleming, Donald, and Bernard Bailyn (eds.). *The Intellectual Migration: Europe and America, 1930–1960.* Cambridge, MA: Belknap Press of Harvard University Press, 1969.

Flippen, J. Brooks. *Nixon and the Environment.* Albuquerque: University of New Mexico Press, 2000.

Ford, Daniel. *Meltdown: The Secret Papers of the Atomic Energy Commission.* New York: Simon & Schuster, 1986.

Foster Associates. *Energy Prices, 1960–73.* Cambridge, MA: Ballinger, 1974.

Fox, Stephen. *The American Conservation Movement: John Muir and His Legacy.* Boston: Little, Brown, 1981.

Frady, Marshall. *Jesse: The Life and Pilgrimage of Jesse Jackson.* New York: Random House, 1996.

Galbraith, John Kenneth. *The Affluent Society.* Boston: Houghton Mifflin, 1958.

———. *Economics and the Public Purpose.* New York: New American Library, 1975.

Gandy, Matthew. *Concrete and Clay: Reworking Nature in New York City.* Cambridge, MA: MIT Press, 2002.

Geertz, Clifford. *Agricultural Involution.* Berkeley: University of California Press, 1963.

Gibbs, Lois Marie. *Dying From Dioxin.* Boston: South End Press, 1995.

Girdner, Eddie J., and Jack Smith. *Killing Me Softly: Toxic Waste, Corporate Profit, and the Struggle for Environmental Justice.* New York: Monthly Review Press, 2002.

Goldman, Eric. *The Crucial Decade and After: America, 1945–1960.* New York: Vintage Books, 1960.

Golley, Frank Benjamin. *A History of the Ecosystem Concept in Ecology: More Than the Sum of Its Parts.* New Haven, CT: Yale University Press, 1993.

Goodell, Rae. *The Visible Scientists.* Boston: Little, Brown, 1977.

Gottlieb, Robert. *Forcing the Spring: The Transformation of the American Environmental Movement.* Washington, DC: Island Press, 1993.

Graham, Frank. *Disaster by Default: Politics and Water Pollution*. New York: M. Evans, 1966.

———. *Since Silent Spring*. Boston: Houghton Mifflin, 1970.

Guber, Deborah Lynn. *The Grassroots of a Green Revolution: Polling America on the Environment*. Cambridge, MA: MIT Press, 2003.

Guha, Ramachandra, and Juan Martinez-Alier. *Varieties of Environmentalism: Essays North and South*. London: Earthscan, 1997.

Hacker, Barton C. *Elements of Controversy: The Atomic Energy Commission and Radiation Safety in Nuclear Weapons Testing, 1947–1974*. Berkeley: University of California Press, 1994.

Hagen, Joel B. *An Entangled Bank: The Origins of Ecosystem Ecology*. New Brunswick, NJ: Rutgers University Press, 1992.

Hammond, Allen L., William D. Metz, and Thomas H. Maugh II. *Energy and the Future*. Washington, DC: AAAS, 1973.

Harding, Walter. *The Days of Henry David Thoreau*. New York: Knopf, 1965.

Hargreaves, Robert. *Superpower: A Portrait of America in the 1970's*. New York: St. Martin's Press, 1973.

Hart, David M. *Forged Consensus: Science, Technology, and Economic Policy in the United States, 1921–1953*. Princeton, NJ: Princeton University Press, 1998.

Hayden, Dolores. *Redesigning the American Dream: The Future of Housing, Work, and Family Life*. Rev. and exp. ed. New York: Norton, 2002.

Hayes, Denis. *Energy: The Case for Conservation*. Washington, DC: Worldwatch Institute, 1976.

———. *Energy: The Solar Prospect*. Washington, DC: Worldwatch Institute, 1977.

Hays, Samuel P. *Conservation and the Gospel of Efficiency: The Progressive Conservation Movement, 1890–1920*. Cambridge, MA: Harvard University Press, 1959.

———. *Beauty, Health, and Permanence: Environmental Politics in the United States, 1955–1985*. Cambridge: Cambridge University Press, 1987.

Hazlett, Maril. "The Story of *Silent Spring* and the Ecological Turn." Ph.D. dissertation, University of Kansas, 2003.

Herber, Lewis. *Our Synthetic Environment*. New York: Knopf, 1962.

———. *Crisis in Our Cities*. Englewood Cliffs, NJ: Prentice-Hall, 1965.

Herken, Gregg. *Brotherhood of the Bomb: The Tangled Lives and Loyalties of Robert Oppenheimer, Ernest Lawrence, and Edward Teller*. New York: Henry Holt, 2002.

Hewlett, Richard G., and Oscar E. Anderson. *A History of the United States Atomic Energy Commission: The New World, 1939–1946*. University Park: Pennsylvania State University Press, 1962.

Heywood, Charles William. "Scientists and Society in the United States, 1900–1940: Changing Concepts of Social Responsibility." Ph.D. dissertation, University of Pennsylvania, 1954.

Hindle, Brooke, and Steven Lubar. *Engines of Change: The American Industrial Revolution, 1790–1860*. Washington, DC: Smithsonian Institution Press, 1986.

Hirt, Paul W. *A Conspiracy of Optimism: Management of the National Forests Since World War II*. Lincoln: University of Nebraska Press, 1994.

Hodes, Elizabeth. "Precedents for Social Responsibility Among Scientists: The American Association of Scientific Workers and the Federation of American Scientists, 1938–1948." Ph.D. dissertation, University of California at Santa Barbara, 1982.

Hollander, Jack M. *The Real Environmental Crisis: Why Poverty, Not Affluence, Is the Environment's Number One Enemy*. Berkeley: University of California Press, 2003.

Horwitch, Mel. *Clipped Wings: The American SST Conflict*. Cambridge, MA: MIT Press, 1982.

Hougan, Jim. *Decadence: Radical Nostalgia, Narcissism, and Decline in the Seventies*. New York: Morrow, 1975.

Hounshell, David, and John Kenly Smith. *Science and Corporate Strategy: DuPont R&D, 1902–1980*. New York: Cambridge University Press, 1988.

Hughes, Thomas P. *American Genesis: A Century of Invention and Technological Enthusiasm, 1870–1970*. New York: Viking Press, 1989.

Hurley, Andrew. *Environmental Inequalities: Class, Race, and Industrial Pollution in Gary, Indiana, 1945–1980*. Chapel Hill: University of North Carolina Press, 1995.

Jacobs, Jane. *The Death and Life of Great American Cities*. New York: Random House, 1961.

Johnson, Ollie A. III, and Karin L. Stanford (eds.). *Black Political Organizations in the Post-Civil Rights Era*. New Brunswick, NJ: Rutgers University Press, 2002.

Johnson, Walter (ed.). *The Papers of Adlai E. Stevenson*. Vol. 6: *Toward a New America, 1955–1957*. Boston: Little, Brown, 1976.

Jolly, Christopher J. "Thresholds of Uncertainty: Radiation and Responsibility in the Fallout Controversy." Ph.D. dissertation, Oregon State University, 2004.

Judd, Richard W., and Christopher S. Beach. *Natural States: The Environmental Imagination in Maine, Oregon, and the Nation*. Washington, DC: Resources for the Future, 2003.

Judson, Horace Freeland. *The Eighth Day of Creation: Makers of the Revolution in Biology*. New York: Simon & Schuster, 1979.

Jungk, Robert. *Brighter Than a Thousand Suns: A Personal History of the Atomic Scientists*. Translated by James Cleugh. New York: Harcourt Brace, 1986.

Kapp, K. William. *The Social Costs of Private Enterprise*. New York: Schocken Books, 1971.

Kasson, John F. *Civilizing the Machine: Technology and Republican Values in America, 1776–1900*. New York: Grossman, 1976.

Kazin, Michael. *The Populist Persuasion: An American History*. Ithaca, NY: Cornell University Press, 1998.

Kevles, Daniel J. *The Physicists: The History of a Scientific Community in Modern America.* Cambridge, MA: Harvard University Press, 1995.

Kingsland, Sharon E. *The Evolution of American Ecology, 1890–2000.* Baltimore: Johns Hopkins University Press, 2005.

Kirk, Andrew Glenn. *Collecting Nature: The American Environmental Movement and the Conservation Library.* Lawrence: University Press of Kansas, 2001.

Kirsch, Scott. *Proving Grounds: Project Plowshare and the Unrealized Dream of Nuclear Earthmoving.* New Brunswick, NJ: Rutgers University Press, 2005.

Kitcher, Philip. *Science, Truth, and Democracy.* Oxford: Oxford University Press, 2001.

Kohler, Robert E. *Partners in Science: Foundations and Natural Scientists, 1900–1945.* Chicago: University of Chicago Press, 1991.

Kohlstedt, Sally Gregory, Michael M. Sokal, and Bruce V. Lewenstein. *The Establishment of Science in America: 150 Years of the American Association for the Advancement of Science.* New Brunswick, NJ: Rutgers University Press, 1999.

Kriebel, David (ed.). *Barry Commoner's Contribution to the Environmental Movement: Science and Social Action.* Amityville, NY: Baywood, 2002.

Krige, John, and Dominique Pestre (eds.). *Science in the Twentieth Century.* Amsterdam: Harwood Academic Publishers, 1997.

Kulp, J. Laurence, and Arthur R. Schulert (eds.). *Strontium-90 in Man and His Environment.* Palisades, NY: Geochemical Laboratory, Lamont Geological Observatory, Columbia University, 1961.

Kuznick, Peter J. *Beyond the Laboratory: Scientists as Political Activists in 1930s America.* Chicago: University of Chicago Press, 1987.

Laird, Frank N. *Solar Energy, Technology Policy, and Institutional Values.* New York: Cambridge University Press, 2001.

Landess, Thomas H., and Richard M. Quinn. *Jesse Jackson and the Politics of Race.* Ottawa, IL: Jameson Books, 1985.

Lapp, Ralph E. *The New Priesthood: The Scientific Elite and the Uses of Power.* New York: Harper & Row, 1965.

Lasch, Christopher. *The Culture of Narcissism: American Life in an Age of Diminishing Expectations.* New York: Norton, 1979.

Lash, Scott, Bronislaw Szerszynski, and Brian Wynne (eds.). *Risk, Environment and Modernity: Towards a New Ecology.* London: Sage, 1996.

Latour, Bruno. *Science in Action.* Cambridge, MA: Harvard University Press, 1987.

———. *Pandora's Hope: Essays on the Reality of Science Studies.* Cambridge, MA: Harvard University Press, 1999.

Lave, Lester B., and Eugene P. Seskin. *Air Pollution and Human Health.* Baltimore: Johns Hopkins University Press, 1977.

Lear, Linda. *Rachel Carson: Witness for Nature.* New York: Henry Holt, 1997.

Lee, Jennifer. *Civility in the City: Blacks, Jews, and Koreans in Urban America.* Cambridge, MA: Harvard University Press, 2002.

Lee, Martha F. *Earth First!: Environmental Apocalypse*. Syracuse, NY: Syracuse University Press, 1995.

Leopold, Aldo. *A Sand County Almanac and Sketches Here and There*. New York: Oxford University Press, 1949.

Leslie, Stuart W. *The Cold War and American Science: The Military-Industrial-Academic Complex at MIT and Stanford*. New York: Columbia University Press, 1993.

Lester, James P., David W. Allen, and Kelly M. Hill. *Environmental Injustice in the United States: Myths and Realities*. Boulder, CO: Westview Press, 2001.

Lewis, Christopher. "Progress and Apocalypse: Science and the End of the Modern World." Ph.D. dissertation, University of Minnesota, 1991.

Lewis, Martin. *Green Delusions: An Environmentalist Critique of Radical Environmentalism*. Durham, NC: Duke University Press, 1992.

Lewontin, Richard C. *Biology as Ideology: The Doctrine of DNA*. Toronto: Anansi Press, 1991.

Light, Andrew (ed.). *Social Ecology After Bookchin*. New York: Guilford Press, 1998.

Linnér, Björn-Ola. *The Return of Malthus: Environmentalism and Post-War Population-Resource Crises*. Isle of Harris, UK: White Horse Press, 2003.

Lippmann, Walter. *Drift and Mastery*. Englewood Cliffs, NJ: Prentice-Hall [1914], 1961.

Livi-Bacci, Massimo. *A Concise History of World Population*. 3rd ed. Translated by Carl Ipsen. Oxford: Blackwell, 2001.

Lovins, Amory. *Soft Energy Paths: Toward a Durable Peace*. San Francisco: Friends of the Earth International, 1977.

Macauley, David (ed.). *Minding Nature: The Philosophers of Ecology*. New York: Guilford Press, 1996.

Marable, Manning. *The Great Wells of Democracy: The Meaning of Race in American Life*. New York: Basic Books, 2002.

Marcuse, Herbert. *One-Dimensional Man: Studies in the Ideology of Advanced Industrial Society*. Boston: Beacon Press, 1964.

———. *Counterrevolution and Revolt*. Boston: Beacon Press, 1972.

Markowitz, Gerald, and David Rosner. *Deceit and Denial: The Deadly Politics of Industrial Pollution*. Berkeley: University of California Press, 2002.

Martinez-Alier, Juan. *The Environmentalism of the Poor: A Study of Ecological Conflicts and Valuation*. Northampton, MA: Edward Elgar, 2002.

Martinez-Alier, Juan, and Klaus Shlüpmann. *Ecological Economics: Energy, Environment, and Society*. Oxford: Blackwell, 1987.

Marx, Leo. *The Machine in the Garden: Technology and the Pastoral Ideal in America*. New York: Oxford University Press, 1964.

Matusow, Allen. *The Unraveling of America: A History of Liberalism in the 1960s*. New York: Harper & Row, 1984.

May, Elaine Tyler. *Homeward Bound: American Families in the Cold War Era*. Rev. and updated ed. New York: Basic Books, 1999.

Mazuzan, George T., and J. Samuel Walker. *Controlling the Atom: The Beginnings of Nuclear Regulation, 1946–1962*. Berkeley: University of California Press, 1985.

McCally, Michael (ed.). *Life Support: The Environment and Human Health*. Cambridge, MA: MIT Press, 2002.

McGrath, Patrick J. *Scientists, Business, and the State, 1890–1960*. Chapel Hill: University of North Carolina Press, 2002.

McGucken, William. *Biodegradable: Detergents and the Environment*. College Station: Texas A&M University Press, 1991.

McKee, Jeffrey K. *Sparing Nature: The Conflict Between Human Population Growth and Earth's Biodiversity*. New Brunswick, NJ: Rutgers University Press, 2003.

McNeill, John R. *Something New Under the Sun: An Environmental History of the Twentieth-Century World*. New York: Norton, 2000.

McNeill, William H. *Population and Politics Since 1750*. Charlottesville: University Press of Virginia, 1990.

McWilliams, Carey. *A Mask for Privilege: Anti-Semitism in America*. Boston: Little, Brown, 1948.

Meadows, Donella H., et al. *The Limits to Growth*. New York: Universe Books, 1972.

Meikle, Jeffrey L. *American Plastic: A Cultural History*. New Brunswick, NJ: Rutgers University Press, 1995.

Melosi, Martin V. *Coping With Abundance: Energy and Environment in Industrial America*. Philadelphia: Temple University Press, 1985.

———. *The Sanitary City: Urban Infrastructure in America From Colonial Times to the Present*. Baltimore: Johns Hopkins University Press, 2000.

Menand, Louis. *The Metaphysical Club: A Story of Ideas in America*. New York: Farrar, Straus, and Giroux, 2001.

Merton, Robert K. *Social Theory and Social Structure*. Rev. and enl. ed. Glencoe, IL: Free Press, 1957.

Miller, Perry. *Errand Into the Wilderness*. Cambridge, MA: Belknap Press of Harvard University Press, 1956.

Mills, C. Wright. *White Collar: The American Middle Classes*. New York: Oxford University Press, 1951.

Mitman, Gregg. *Breathing Space: An Ecological History of Allergy in America*. New Haven, CT: Yale University Press, 2007.

Moore, Colleen F. *Silent Scourge: Children, Pollution, and Why Scientists Disagree*. New York: Oxford University Press, 2003.

Morris, Lorenzo (ed.). *The Social and Political Implications of the 1984 Jesse Jackson Presidential Campaign*. New York: Praeger, 1950.

Muir, John. *The Yosemite*. New York: Century, 1912.

Mumford, Lewis. *The City in History: Its Origins, Its Transformations, and Its Prospects*. New York: Harcourt, Brace & World, 1961.

Nash, Roderick. *The Rights of Nature: A History of Environmental Ethics*. Madison: University of Wisconsin Press, 1989.

———. *Wilderness and the American Mind*. 4th ed. New Haven, CT: Yale University Press, 2001.

Noble, David F. *America by Design: Science, Technology, and the Rise of Corporate Capitalism*. New York: Knopf, 1977.

O'Connor, James. *Natural Causes: Essays in Ecological Marxism*. New York: Guilford Press, 1998.

O'Neill, Dan. *The Firecracker Boys*. New York: St. Martin's Press, 1994.

Opie, John. *Nature's Nation: An Environmental History of the United States*. New York: Harcourt Brace, 1998.

Oppenheimer, J. Robert. *Physics in the Contemporary World*. Portland, ME: Anthoensen Press, 1947.

Osborn, Fairfield. *Our Plundered Planet*. Boston: Little, Brown, 1948.

Patterson, James T. *Grand Expectations: The United States, 1945–1974*. New York: Oxford University Press, 1996.

Paustenbach, Dennis J. (ed.). *Human and Ecological Risk Assessment: Theory and Practice*. New York: Wiley, 2002.

Pellow, David Naguib. *Garbage Wars: The Struggle for Environmental Justice in Chicago*. Cambridge, MA: MIT Press, 2002.

Perrings, Charles. *Economics of Ecological Resources: Selected Essays*. Lyme, NH: Edward Elgar, 1997.

Petulla, Joseph M. *American Environmental History*. 2nd ed. Toronto: Merrill, 1988.

Porter, Theodore M. *Trust in Numbers: The Pursuit of Objectivity in Science and Public Life*. Princeton, NJ: Princeton University Press, 1995.

Potter, David M. *People of Plenty: Economic Abundance and the American Character*. Chicago: University of Chicago Press, 1954.

Primack, Joel R., and Frank von Hippell. *Advice and Dissent: Scientists in the Political Arena*. New York: Basic Books, 1974.

Pulido, Laura. *Environmentalism and Economic Justice: Two Chicano Struggles in the Southwest*. Tucson: University of Arizona Press, 1996.

Raffensperger, Carolyn, and Joel Tickner (eds.). *Protecting Public Health and the Environment: Implementing the Precautionary Principle*. Washington, DC: Island Press, 1999.

Ray, Dixy Lee. *The Nation's Energy Future: A Report to Richard M. Nixon, President of the United States*. Washington, DC: Atomic Energy Commission, 1973.

Reich, Leonard S. *The Making of American Industrial Research: Science and Business at GE and Bell, 1876–1926*. New York: Cambridge University Press, 1985.

Rhodes, Edwardo Lao. *Environmental Justice in America: A New Paradigm*. Bloomington: Indiana University Press, 2003.

Rhodes, Richard. *Dark Sun: The Making of the Hydrogen Bomb.* New York: Simon & Schuster, 1995.

Richardson, Elmo. *Dams, Parks, and Politics.* Lexington: University Press of Kentucky, 1973.

Rienow, Robert, and Leona Train Rienow. *Moment in the Sun: A Report on the Deteriorating Quality of the American Environment.* New York: Dial Press, 1967.

Righter, Robert. *Wind Energy in America: A History.* Norman: University of Oklahoma Press, 1996.

Roberts, J. Timmons, and Melissa M. Toffolon-Weiss. *Chronicles From the Environmental Justice Frontline.* New York: Cambridge University Press, 2001.

Rodgers, Daniel T. *The Work Ethic in Industrial America.* Chicago: University of Chicago Press, 1978.

Rome, Adam. *The Bulldozer in the Countryside: Suburban Sprawl and the Rise of American Environmentalism.* Cambridge: Cambridge University Press, 2001.

Roos, Leslie L., Jr. (ed.). *The Politics of Ecosuicide.* New York: Holt, Rinehart and Winston, 1971.

Rosato, Dominick V., William K. Fallon, and Donald V. Rosato. *Markets for Plastics.* New York: Van Nostrand Reinhold, 1969.

Rosenbaum, Walter A. *The Politics of Environmental Concern.* 2nd ed. New York: Praeger, 1977.

Rosner, David, and Gerald Markowitz (eds.). *Dying for Work: Workers' Safety and Health in Twentieth-Century America.* Bloomington: Indiana University Press, 1987.

Roszak, Theodore. *Where the Wasteland Ends: Politics and Transcendence in Postindustrial Society.* Garden City, NY: Doubleday, 1972.

———. *The Voice of the Earth: An Exploration of Ecopsychology.* New York: Simon & Schuster, 1993.

Rothman, Hal K. *The Greening of a Nation? Environmentalism in the United States Since 1945.* Orlando, FL: Harcourt Brace College, 1998.

Rowland, Wade. *The Plot to Save the World.* Vancouver, BC: Clarke, Irwin, 1973.

Rubin, Charles T. *The Green Crusade: Rethinking the Roots of Environmentalism.* Lanham, MD: Rowman & Littlefield, 1998.

Russell, Edmund. *War and Nature: Fighting Humans and Insects With Chemicals From World War I to Silent Spring.* New York: Cambridge University Press, 2001.

Sale, Kirkpatrick. *The Green Revolution: The American Environmental Movement, 1962–1992.* New York: Hill and Wang, 1993.

Schlosberg, David. *Environmental Justice and the New Pluralism: The Challenge of Difference for Environmentalism.* New York: Oxford University Press, 1999.

Schrecker, Ellen. *No Ivory Tower: McCarthyism and the Universities.* New York: Oxford University Press, 1986.

Schulman, Bruce J. *The Seventies: The Great Shift in American Culture, Society, and Politics.* New York: Free Press, 2001.

Schumacher, E. F. *Small Is Beautiful: Economics as if People Mattered.* New York: Harper & Row, 1973.

Sears, Paul. *Deserts on the March.* Norman: University of Oklahoma Press, 1935.

Segal, Howard P. *Technological Utopianism in American Culture.* Chicago: University of Chicago Press, 1985.

Sellers, Charles. *The Market Revolution: Jacksonian America, 1815–1846.* New York: Oxford University Press, 1991.

Sellers, Christopher C. *Hazards of the Job: From Industrial Disease to Environmental Health Science.* Chapel Hill: University of North Carolina Press, 1997.

Shabecoff, Philip. *A Fierce Green Fire: The American Environmental Movement.* New York: Hill and Wang, 1993.

Shapin, Steven. *The Scientific Revolution.* Chicago: University of Chicago Press, 1996.

Shapiro, Judith. *Mao's War Against Nature: Politics and the Environment in Revolutionary China.* New York: Cambridge University Press, 2001.

Silliman, Jael, and Ynestra King (eds.). *Dangerous Intersections: Feminist Perspectives on Population, Environment, and Development.* Cambridge, MA: South End Press, 1999.

Silver, Marc L., and Martin Melkonian (eds.). *Contested Terrain: Power, Politics, and Participation in Suburbia.* Westport, CT: Greenwood Press, 1995.

Simon, Julian L. *The Ultimate Resource.* Princeton, NJ: Princeton University Press, 1981.

Skolnick, Arlene S. *Embattled Paradise: The American Family in an Age of Uncertainty.* New York: Basic Books, 1991.

Smallwood, Frank. *The Other Candidates: Third Parties in Presidential Elections.* Hanover, NH: University Press of New England, 1983.

Smith, Alice Kimball. *A Peril and a Hope: The Scientists' Movement in America, 1945–47.* Chicago: University of Chicago Press, 1965.

Smith, Allen. "Converting America: Three Community Efforts to End the Cold War, 1956–1973." Ph.D. dissertation, American University, 1995.

Smith, Barbara Ellen. *Digging Our Own Graves: Coal Miners and the Struggle Over Black Lung Disease.* Philadelphia: Temple University Press, 1987.

Smith, Bruce L. R. *American Science Policy Since World War II.* Washington, DC: Brookings Institution, 1990.

Smith-Rosenberg, Carroll. *Religion and the Rise of the American City: The New York City Mission Movement, 1812–1870.* Ithaca, NY: Cornell University Press, 1971.

Steinberg, Theodore. *Down to Earth: Nature's Role in American History.* New York: Oxford University Press, 2002.

Steingraber, Sandra. *Living Downstream: An Ecologist Looks at Cancer and the Environment.* Reading, MA: Addison-Wesley, 1997.

Stern, D., et al. *Buffalo Curbside Recycling Pilot Program.* Flushing, NY: Center for the Biology of Natural Systems, 1989.

Strasser, Susan. *Waste and Want: A Social History of Trash.* New York: Metropolitan Books, 1999.

Strong, Douglas H. *Dreamers and Defenders: American Conservationists.* Lincoln: University of Nebraska Press, 1988.

Sullivan, William Cuyler, Jr. *Nuclear Democracy: A History of the Greater St. Louis Citizens' Committee for Nuclear Information, 1957–1967.* College Occasional Papers no. 1. St. Louis, MO: Washington University, 1982.

Sunstein, Cass R. *Why Societies Need Dissent.* Cambridge, MA: Harvard University Press, 2003.

Swerdlow, Amy. *Women Strike for Peace: Traditional Motherhood and Radical Politics in the 1960s.* Chicago: University of Chicago Press, 1993.

Szasz, Andrew. *EcoPopulism: Toxic Waste and the Movement for Environmental Justice.* Minneapolis: University of Minnesota Press, 1994.

Teller, Edward. *The Legacy of Hiroshima.* Garden City, NY: Doubleday, 1962.

———. *Memoirs: A Twentieth-Century Journey in Science and Politics.* Cambridge, MA: Perseus, 2001.

Teller, Edward, Wendy Teller, and Wilson Talley. *Conversations on the Dark Secrets of Physics.* Cambridge, MA: Perseus, 2002.

Tenner, Edward. *Why Things Bite Back: Technology and the Revenge of Unintended Consequences.* New York: Knopf, 1996.

Tesh, Sylvia Noble. *Uncertain Hazards: Environmental Activists and Scientific Proof.* Ithaca, NY: Cornell University Press, 2000.

Thoreau, Henry David. *Collected Essays and Poems.* New York: Library of America, 2001.

Thornton, Joe. *Pandora's Poison: Chlorine, Health, and a New Environmental Strategy.* Cambridge, MA: MIT Press, 2000.

Trescott, Martha Moore. *The Rise of the Electrochemicals Industry, 1880–1910.* Westport, CT: Greenwood Press, 1981.

Trudeau, G. B. *The People's Doonesbury: Notes From Underfoot, 1978–1980.* New York: Holt, Rinehart and Winston, 1981.

Valencius, Conevery Bolton. *The Health of the Country: How American Settlers Understood Themselves and Their Land.* New York: Basic Books, 2002.

Veblen, Thorstein. *The Higher Learning in America: A Memorandum on the Conduct of Universities by Business Men.* New York: B. W. Huebsch, 1918.

Vogt, William. *Road to Survival.* New York: W. Sloane Associates, 1948.

Wang, Jessica. *American Science in an Age of Anxiety: Scientists, Anticommunism, and the Cold War.* Chapel Hill: University of North Carolina Press, 1999.

Warner, Sam Bass, Jr. *The Urban Wilderness: A History of the American City.* New York: Harper & Row, 1972.

Washington, Sylvia H. *Packing Them In: An Archaeology of Environmental Racism in Chicago.* Lanham, MD: Lexington Books, 2005.

Weart, Spencer R. *Nuclear Fear: A History of Images*. Cambridge, MA: Harvard University Press, 1988.

———. *The Discovery of Global Warming*. Cambridge, MA: Harvard University Press, 2003.

Weaver, Warren. *Scene of Change: A Lifetime in American Science*. New York: Scribner's, 1970.

Wellock, Thomas Raymond. *Critical Masses: Opposition to Nuclear Power in California, 1958–1978*. Madison: University of Wisconsin Press, 1998.

Westwick, Peter J. *The National Labs: Science in an American System, 1947–1974*. Cambridge, MA: Harvard University Press, 2003.

Wiebe, Robert H. *The Search for Order, 1877–1920*. New York: Hill and Wang, 1967.

Wiener, Philip P. (ed.). *Values in a Universe of Chance: Selected Writings of Charles S. Peirce*. Garden City, NY: Doubleday, 1958.

Wilentz, Sean. *Chants Democratic: New York City and the Rise of the American Working Class, 1788–1850*. New York: Oxford University Press, 1984.

Willers, Bill (ed.). *Learning to Listen to the Land*. Washington, DC: Island Press, 1991.

Williams, Dennis C. *God's Wilds: John Muir's Vision of Nature*. College Station: Texas A&M University Press, 2002.

Winkler, Allan M. *Life Under a Cloud: American Anxiety About the Atom*. Oxford: Oxford University Press, 1993.

Wise, George. *Willis R. Whitney, General Electric, and the Origins of U.S. Industrial Research*. New York: Columbia University Press, 1985.

Wolfe, Tom. *The Purple Decades*. New York: Berkly Books, 1983.

Wolfle, Dael. *Renewing a Scientific Society: The American Association for the Advancement of Science From World War II to 1970*. Washington, DC: AAAS, 1989.

Worster, Donald. *Rivers of Empire: Water, Aridity, and the Growth of the American West*. New York: Oxford University Press, 1992.

———. *Under Western Skies: Nature and History in the American West*. New York: Oxford University Press, 1992.

———. *The Wealth of Nature: Environmental History and the Ecological Imagination*. New York: Oxford University Press, 1993.

———. *Nature's Economy: A History of Ecological Ideas*. 2nd ed. New York: Cambridge University Press, 1994.

Yergin, Daniel. *The Prize: The Epic Quest for Oil, Money, and Power*. New York: Simon & Schuster, 1991.

York, Herbert F. *The Advisors: Oppenheimer, Teller, and the Superbomb*. Stanford, CA: Stanford University Press, 1989.

Zachary, G. Pascal. *Endless Frontier: Vannevar Bush, Engineer of the American Century*. New York: Free Press, 1997.

Zakin, Susan. *Coyotes and Town Dogs: Earth First! and the Environmental Movement.* New York: Viking Press, 1993.

Articles, Newspapers, Essays, Reports, and Speeches

"After the Talkfest on Earth Day." *Chicago Tribune,* 22 April 1970, 20.

"Americans Rally to Make It Again Beautiful Land." *Chicago Tribune,* 23 April 1970, 3.

"Angry Coordinator of Earth Day." *New York Times,* 23 April 1970, 30.

"Anti-Earth Day Wires Cost Official $1,600." *New York Times,* 23 April 1970, 30.

Associated Press. "Earth Day Organizers Hope to Halt Pollution." *The Oregonian,* 22 April 1970, 8.

"Baby Tooth Survey Forms Going Out." *St. Louis Post-Dispatch,* 23 October 1960, 3.

"Baby Tooth Survey Opens." *The Observer,* 9 November 1960, 7B.

Badash, Lawrence. "Science and McCarthyism." *Minerva* 38 (2000), 53–80.

Baker, Robb. "Earth Day: A Commie Plot?" *Chicago Tribune,* 22 April 1970, sec. 2, 4.

Beck, Roy, and Leon Kolankiewicz. "The Environmental Movement's Retreat From Advocating U.S. Population Stabilization (1970–1998): A First Draft of History." *Journal of Policy History* 12 (2000), 123–156.

Bernstein, Carl. "Area Industries Jump on EarthDay Bandwagon." *Washington Post,* 23 April 1970, A21.

Beyette, Beverly. "Environmentalists: Three Who Believe." *Los Angeles Times,* 6 June 1985.

Bond, Julian. "Redefining the Environmental Movement." *Washington Post,* 22 April 2004.

Bookchin, Murray. "Crisis in the Ecology Movement." *Z Magazine* (July–August 1988), 121–123.

Brodine, Virginia. "On Scientific and Political Disagreement." *Nuclear Information* (July 1962), 19.

Brown, Harrison. "What Is a 'Small' Risk?" *The Saturday Review* (25 May 1957), 9–10.

"A *Bulletin* Dialogue on *The Closing Circle.*" *Bulletin of the Atomic Scientists* 28 (May 1972), 8–27, 42–56.

Carr, Willine, Lisa Zeitel, and Kevin Weiss. "Variations in Asthma Hospitalizations and Deaths in New York City." *American Journal of Public Health* 82 (1992), 59–65.

Carter, C. D., et al. "Tetrachlorodibenzodioxin: An Accidental Poisoning in Horse Arenas." *Science* 188 (16 May 1975), 738–740.

Clark, Herbert M. "The Occurrence of an Unusually High-Level Radioactive Rainout in the Area of Troy, N.Y." *Science* 119 (7 May 1954), 619–622.

"A Clash of Gloomy Prophets." *TIME* (11 January 1971), 56–57.

Cloud, John, and Amanda Bower. "Why SUV Is All the Rage." *TIME* (24 February 2003), 35–42.

Committee for Nuclear Information, Technical Division. "Closing the Information Gap." *Nuclear Information* (March–April 1963), 12.

———. "Hazard from Nevada Tests: A Reply to the Atomic Energy Commission." *Nuclear Information* (November 1963), 1.

———. "Local Fallout: Hazard from Nevada Tests." *Nuclear Information* (August 1963), 1–13.

Commoner, Barry. "Social Aspects of Science." *Science* 125 (25 January 1957), 143–147.

———. "The Fallout Problem." *Science* 127 (2 May 1958), 1023–1026.

———. "The Hazard of Fallout." *Student Life* [Washington University] (19 December 1958).

———. "The Scientist and Political Power." Unpublished manuscript, August 1962 (Barry Commoner Papers, LoC, box 14).

———. "Fallout and Water Pollution—Parallel Cases." *Scientist and Citizen* 6 (December 1964), 2–7.

———. "The Integrity of Science." *American Scientist* 53 (June 1965), 174–198.

———. "Is Biology a Molecular Science?" Fourth Mellon Lecture, School of Medicine, University of Pittsburgh, 17 February 1965 (Barry Commoner Papers, LoC, box 16).

———. "The Integrity of Science." *Science Journal* (April 1966), 75–79.

———. "A Scientist Views Pollution." Address before the National Industrial Conference Board, New York City, 15 December 1966 (Barry Commoner Papers, LoC, box 493).

———. "The Implications of Molecular Biology for Man." Address at New School for Social Research, New York City, 21 April 1967 (Barry Commoner Papers, LoC, box 20).

———. "The Scholar's Obligation to Dissent." Commencement address, University of California at San Francisco Medical Center, 10 June 1967 (Barry Commoner Papers, LoC, box 493).

———. "The Social Significance of Environmental Pollution." Presented at eleventh annual meeting of the National Association of Business Economists, Chicago, 26 September 1969 (Barry Commoner Papers, LoC, box 130).

———. "Survival in the Environment: Population Crisis." Presented at eleventh AAAS annual meeting, Boston, 29 December 1969 (Barry Commoner Papers, LoC, box 29).

———. Untitled talk. Harvard University, 21 April 1970 (Barry Commoner Papers, LoC, box 36).

———. Untitled talk. Brown University, 22 April 1970 (Barry Commoner Papers, LoC, box 131).

———. "Pollution and Profit Motive." Transcript of talk and Q&A on CBS, 14 December 1971 (Barry Commoner Papers, LoC, box 39).

———. "Labor's Stake in the Environment/The Environment's Stake in Labor." Keynote address at the conference "Jobs and the Environment—Whose Jobs? Whose Environment?" San Francisco, 28 November 1972 (Barry Commoner Papers, LoC, box 493).

———. "The Meaning of the Environmental Crisis." Presented at United Nations Conference on the Human Environment, Stockholm, 16 June 1972 (Barry Commoner Papers, LoC, box 138).

———. "Planning to Survive." Keynote address, American Institute of Planners, Boston, 8 October 1972 (Barry Commoner Papers, LoC, box 493).

———. "Workplace Burden." *Environment* 15 (July/August 1973), 15–20.

———. "The Energy Crisis: All of a Piece." Address at "The Energy Outlook and Global Interdependence," public convocation sponsored by the Fund for Peace in cooperation with the Scientists' Institute for Public Information, New York City, 20 November 1974. Published in *The Center Magazine* (March/April 1975), 26–31.

———. "The Energy Crisis: Implications for Foundations." Address at Council on Foundations, Inc., twenty-fifth annual conference, San Antonio, TX, 10 May 1974 (Barry Commoner Papers, LoC, box 51).

———. "How Poverty Breeds Overpopulation (and Not the Other Way Around)." *Ramparts* (August–September 1975), 21–25, 58–59.

———. "A Reporter at Large: The Environment." *The New Yorker* (15 June 1987), 46–71.

———. Untitled paper. Presented at New Jersey Environmental Federation conference, New Brunswick, NJ, 4 March 1989 (Center for the Biology of Natural Systems, Queens College).

———. "Why We Have Failed." *Greenpeace* 14 (September/October 1989), 12–13.

———. Keynote Address at the Second Citizens' Conference on Dioxin, St. Louis, MO, 30 July 1994 (Center for the Biology of Natural Systems, Queens College).

———. "Unraveling the DNA Myth: The Spurious Foundation of Genetic Engineering." *Harper's* magazine (February 2002), 39–47.

Condon, E. U. "Science and Our Future." *Science* 103 (5 April 1946), 415–417.

Cousins, Norman. "The Schweitzer Declaration." *The Saturday Review* (18 May 1957), 13–16.

Dally, Ann. "The Rise and Fall of Pink Disease." *Social History of Medicine* 10 (1997), 291–304.

Darnovsky, Marcy. "Stories Less Told: Histories of U.S. Environmentalism." *Socialist Review* 22 (October–December 1992), 11–54.

Deakin, Doris. "Mothers Ask—What Should We Feed Our Kids?" *Nuclear Information* (October 1959), 1–4.

Denton, Herbert L., and Claudia Levy. "March on Interior to Highlight Earth Day Activities in D.C." *Washington Post,* 22 April 1970, A6.

Dewey, Scott Hamilton. "Working for the Environment: Organized Labor and the Origins of Environmentalism in the United States, 1948–1970." *Environmental History* 3 (January 1998), 45–63.

Diamond, Edwin. "The Myth of the Pesticide Menace." *Saturday Evening Post* (28 September 1963), 16–18.

Dockery, Douglas W. "An Association Between Air Pollution and Mortality in Six U.S. Cities." *New England Journal of Medicine* 329 (1993), 1753–1759.

"Dr. Commoner Cites Scientists' Dilemma." *St. Louis Globe-Democrat,* 13 October 1960, 4.

DuBois, Larry. "Playboy Interview: Barry Commoner." *Playboy* (July 1974), 55–74.

Dudman, Richard. "Washington University Teacher Attacks Teller's Atomic Fallout Views; Accused of 'Fighting Windmills.'" *St. Louis Post-Dispatch,* undated (March 1958).

"Earth Has Its Day." *San Francisco Chronicle,* 23 April 1970, 2.

"Editorial." *Ramparts* (May 1970), 2–4.

Egan, Michael. "The Social Significance of the Environmental Crisis: Barry Commoner's *The Closing Circle.*" *Organization and Environment* 15 (December 2002), 443–457.

———. "Subaltern Environmentalism in the United States: A Historiographic Review." *Environment and History* 8 (February 2002), 21–41.

———. "Die technologische Wende und Barry Commoners Gesetze der Ökologie: *The Closing Circle* neu gelesen." *Natur und Kultur* 4 (Fall 2003), 30–47.

Ehrlich, Paul R., and John P. Holdren. "Dispute." *Environment* 14 (April 1972), 23–52.

Electric Power Research Institute. "Mercury in the Environment." *EPRI Journal* (April 1990), 5.

Evans, R. "Asthma Among Minority Children: A Growing Problem." *Chest* 101 (1992), 368–371.

Everett, Arthur. "U.S. Ignores Generation Gap, Focuses on Earth Day Drive." *The Oregonian,* 23 April 1970, 1.

"Excerpts From Message by Schweitzer." *New York Times,* 24 April 1957, 2.

"Fallout: Moment of Tooth." *Newsweek* (25 April 1960), 70.

Fleming, Donald. "Roots of the New Conservation Movement." *Perspectives in American History* 6 (1972), 7–91.

Forman, Paul. "Behind Quantum Electronics: National Security as a Basis for Physical Research in the United States, 1940–1960." *Historical Studies in the Physical and Biological Sciences* 18 (1987), 149–229.

Foster, John Bellamy. "Malthus' *Essay on Population* at 200: A Marxian View." *Monthly Review* 50 (December 1998), 1–18.

Gilliam, Harold. "The 'Pollutionists' and the 'Depletionists' Disagree." *San Francisco Sunday Examiner & Chronicle,* 7 March 1972, 28.

Gordon, Robert. "'Shell No!': OCAW and the Labor-Environmental Alliance." *Environmental History* 3 (October 1998), 460–487.

Gottlieb, D. J., A. S. Beiser, and G. T. O'Connor. "Poverty, Race and Medication Use Are Correlates of Asthma Hospitalization Rates: A Small Area Analysis in Boston." *Chest* 108 (1995), 28–35.

Grant, Neville. "Legacy of the Mad Hatter." *Environment* 11 (May 1969), 18–23, 43–44.

Green, Harold P. "The Oppenheimer Case: A Study in the Abuse of Law." *Bulletin of the Atomic Scientists* 33 (July 1977), 12–16, 56–61.

Hare, Nathan. "Black Ecology." *The Black Scholar* (April 1970), 2–8.

Harwood, Richard. "Earth Day Stirs Nation." *Washington Post,* 23 April 1970, A1, A20.

Hayes, Denis. "Reclaiming the Vision of the First Earth Day." *Seattle Times,* 22 April 2004.

Hazlett, Maril, and Michael Egan. "Technological and Ecological Turns: Science and American Environmentalism." Paper presented at the History of Science Society annual conference, Cambridge, MA, 22 November 2003.

Herber, Lewis. "The Problems of Chemicals in Foods." *Contemporary Issues* 3 (1952), 206–241.

Hill, Gladwin. "Activity Ranges From Oratory to Legislation." *New York Times,* 23 April 1970, 1, 30.

———. "Oratory and Legislation Mark Drive on Pollution." *New York Times,* 23 April 1970, 30.

Holdren, John P. "A Brief History of 'IPAT' (Impact = Population × Affluence × Technology)." Unpublished manuscript, 7 September 1993.

Hopkins, Sam. "Earth Is Getting Its Day, Finally." *Atlanta Constitution,* 22 April 1970, 1.

Hopkins, Sam, and Terry Adamson. "Earth Day Marks Assault on Pollution." *Atlanta Constitution,* 23 April 1970, 1, 19.

Kalckar, Herman M. "An International Milk Teeth Radiation Census." *Nature* 182 (2 August 1958), 283–284.

Kevles, Daniel J. "The National Science Foundation and the Debate Over Postwar Research Policy, 1942–1945." *Isis* 68 (March 1977), 5–26.

———. "Cold War and Hot Physics: Science, Security, and the American State, 1945–56." *Historical Studies in the Physical and Biological Sciences* 20 (March 1990), 239–264.

Keyfitz, Nathan. "National Populations and the Technological Watershed." *Journal of Social Issues* 23 (1967), 62–78.

Kirsch, Scott. "Harold Knapp and the Geography of Normal Controversy: Radioiodine in the Historical Environment." *Osiris* 19 (2004), 167–181.

Kulp, J. Laurence, et al. "Strontium-90 in Man." *Science* 125 (8 February 1957), 219–225.

Langone, John. "Edward Teller: Of Bombs and Brickbats." *Discover* 5 (July 1984), 62–65.

Lee, Jennifer. "Second Thoughts on a Chemical: In Water, How Much Is Too Much?" *New York Times,* 2 March 2004, D1, D4.

Lelyveld, Joseph. "Mood Is Joyful as City Gives Its Support." *New York Times,* 23 April 1970, 1, 30.

Libby, Willard F. "An Open Letter to Dr. Schweitzer." *The Saturday Review* (25 May 1957), 8–9, 36–37.

Löfroth, Göran, and Margaret E. Duffy. "Birds Give Warning." *Environment* 11 (May 1969), 10–17.

Logan, Yvonne. "The Story of the Baby Tooth Survey." *Scientist and Citizen* (September–October 1964), 38–39.

Loory, Stuart H. "Science Tracks Down a Fish Killer." *New York Herald Tribune,* 23 March 1964.

Lutts, Ralph H. "Chemical Fallout: Rachel Carson's *Silent Spring,* Radioactive Fallout and the Environmental Movement." *Environmental Review* 9 (Fall 1985), 214–225.

Martin, George. "Grounding Social Ecology: Landscape, Settlement, and Right of Way." *Capitalism Nature Socialism* 13 (March 2002), 3–30.

Marx, Leo. "Does Improved Technology Mean Progress?" *Technology Review* 90 (January 1987), 32–41, 71.

Maxwell, Michael Scott. "Poisoning the World." *The Daily Telegraph,* 10 November 1966, 21.

McFayden, Richard E. "Thalidomide in America." *Clio Medica* 11 (1976), 79–83.

McGurty, Eileen Maura. "From NIMBY to Civil Rights: The Origins of the Environmental Justice Movement." *Environmental History* 2 (July 1997), 301–323.

McLaughlin, Maurine. "Housewives Hold Picnic on a Dump." *Washington Post,* 23 April 1970, A18.

Meagher, Ed. "No Smog on L.A. Earth Day." *Los Angeles Times,* 23 April 1970, sec. 2, 1–2.

Meikle, Jeffrey L. "Material Doubts: The Consequences of Plastic." *Environmental History* 2 (July 1997), 278–300.

Melosi, Martin V. "Down in the Dumps: Is There a Garbage Crisis in America?" *Journal of Policy History* 5 (1993), 100–127.

———. "Environmental Justice, Political Agenda Setting, and the Myths of History." *Journal of Policy History* 12 (2000), 43–71.

Meyerhoff, Howard A. "Boston, 1953." *Science* 117 (20 February 1953), 3.

"Milk and the Strontium-90 Problem." *Information* (February 1959), 1–2, 4.

Miller, Perry. "The Responsibility of Mind in a Civilization of Machines." *The American Scholar* 31 (Winter 1961–1962), 51–69.

Miss Ann Thropy. "Population and AIDS." *The Earth First! Journal* (1 May 1987), 32.

Montague, Peter. "Incineration vs. Recycling." *Rachel's Environment & Health News* 121 (20 March 1989), 1–2.

———. "Scientists Suspect Poisoning of Fish by Mercury Emissions From Incinerators." *Rachel's Environment & Health News* 198 (11 September 1990), 1.

———. "Turning Point for the Chemical Industry." *Rachel's Environment & Health News* 405 (31 August 1994), 1–2.

———. "How to Eliminate Dioxin." *Rachel's Environment & Health News* 508 (21 August 1996), 1–2.

Montrie, Chad. "Expedient Environmentalism: Opposition to Coal Surface Mining in Appalachia and the United Mine Workers of America, 1945–1975." *Environmental History* 5 (January 2000), 75–98.

Moog, Florence. "Nuclear War in St. Louis: One Year Later." *Nuclear Information* (September 1959), 1–4.

Needell, Allan. "Preparing for the Space Age: University-Based Research, 1946–1957." *Historical Studies in the Physical and Biological Sciences* 18 (1987), 89–110.

Nossiter, Adam. "Asthma Common and on the Rise in the Crowded South Bronx." *New York Times*, 5 September 1995, A1.

Novick, Sheldon. "A New Pollution Problem." *Environment* 11 (May 1969), 2–9.

Nye, David E. "The Energy Crisis of the 1970s as a Cultural Crisis." *European Contributions to American Studies* 38 (1997), 82–102.

"An Oil Spill on Market Street." *San Francisco Chronicle*, 23 April 1970, 2.

"Paul Revere of Ecology." *TIME* (2 February 1970), 58.

Pauling, Linus. "My Efforts to Obtain a Passport." *Bulletin of the Atomic Scientists* 8 (July 1952), 253–255.

———. "An Appeal by American Scientists to the Governments and People of the World." *Bulletin of the Atomic Scientists* 13 (September 1957), 264–266.

Pruitt, William O., Jr. "Comments From Other Scientists." *Nuclear Information* (November 1963), 11.

Rees, Mina. "Warren Weaver." *Biographical Memoirs* 57 (1987), 493–530.

Reiss, Louise Z. "Baby Tooth Survey—First Results." *Nuclear Information* (November 1961), 1–6.

———. "Strontium-90 Absorption by Deciduous Teeth." *Science* 134 (24 November 1961), 1669–1673.

Reynolds, J. B., and Barry Commoner. "Hearings Reveal New Facts." *Nuclear Information* (May–June 1959), 6.

Richman, Alvin. "The Polls: Public Attitudes Toward the Energy Crisis." *Public Opinion Quarterly* 43 (Winter 1979), 576–585.

Rome, Adam. "'Give Earth a Chance': The Environmental Movement and the Sixties." *Journal of American History* 90 (September 2003), 525–554.

Ruppel, Tom. "Industries Grab Profits, Waste Energy—Commoner." *The Daily Collegian* [Fresno State College] (27 April 1976).

Russell, Dick. "Environmental Racism." *Amicus Journal* (Spring 1989), 22–32.

Saad, Lydia, and Riley Dunlap. "Americans Are Environmentally Friendly, but Issue Not Seen as Urgent Problem." *Gallup Poll Monthly* 415 (April 2000), 12–18.

Schweitzer, Albert. "Appeal to End Nuclear Tests." *Bulletin of the Atomic Scientists* (June 1957), 205.

"Schweitzer Urges World Opinion to Demand End of Nuclear Tests." *New York Times,* 24 April 1957, 1.

Sears, Paul. "A Statement of Conviction About Overpopulation," November 1960 (Committee on Science in the Promotion of Human Welfare Papers, AAAS Archives, box 2).

Sellers, Christopher. "Body, Place and the State: The Makings of an 'Environmentalist' Imaginary in the Post-World War II U.S." *Radical History Review* 74 (1999), 31–64.

———. "Thoreau's Body: Towards an Embodied Environmental History." *Environmental History* 4 (1999), 486–514.

Servos, John. "The Industrial Relations of Science: Chemical Engineering at MIT, 1900–1939." *Isis* 71 (December 1980), 531–549.

Shellenberger, Michael, and Ted Norhaus. "The Death of Environmentalism: Global Warming Politics in a Post-Environmental World." Published online at http://www.thebreakthrough.org/images/Death_of_Environmentalism.pdf. Accessed 21 December 2005.

Shurkin, Joel N. "By Another Name, Socialism Could Smell Sweeter." *Philadelphia Inquirer* book review of *The Poverty of Power* (Barry Commoner Papers, LoC, box 552).

Smith, Allen. "Democracy and the Politics of Information: The St. Louis Committee for Nuclear Information." *Gateway Heritage* (Summer 1996), 2–13.

Smith, Merritt Roe. "Technology, Industrialization, and the Idea of Progress in America." In *Responsible Science: The Impact of Technology on Society.* Edited by Kevin B. Byme. San Francisco: Harper & Row, 1986.

Stanfield, R., and C. Lopez. "Lethal Legacy: The Dirty Truth About the Nation's Most Polluting Power Plants." Washington, D.C.: U.S. Public Interest Research Group, 2000.

Stoll, Mark. "Green Versus Green: Religions, Ethics, and the Bookchin-Foreman Dispute." *Environmental History* 6 (July 2001), 412–427.

"Summons to a New Cause." *TIME* (2 February 1970), 7–8.

Taussig, Helen Brooke. "Dangerous Tranquility." *Science* 136 (25 May 1962), 683.

———. "The Thalidomide Syndrome." *Scientific American* 207 (August 1962), 29–35.

Taylor, Dorceta E. "American Environmentalism: The Role of Race, Class, and Gender in Shaping Activism, 1820–1995." *Race, Gender & Class* 5 (1997), 16–62.

"Thinking the Unthinkable." *Newsweek* (7 October 1974), 50–51.

Thomas, Wilbur L., Jr. "The Real Issue of Black Survival in Our Polluted Cities." East St. Louis, IL, 20 February 1970 (Barry Commoner Papers, LoC, box 307).

"Transcript of President's Address on the Energy Situation." *New York Times,* 8 November 1973, 32.

Tucker, Anthony. "The Prophets, and Doom." *Guardian Extra,* 28 January 1972, 12.

Ubell, Earl. "Scientists Out to Give Ideas Popular Appeal: American Association to Reorganize in Face of 'Intellectual Bankruptcy.'" *New York Herald Tribune,* 29 December 1952, 15.

Visscher, Maurice B. "Scientists in a Mad World." *The Nation* (24 January 1953), 69–71.

Wang, Jessica. "Science, Security, and the Cold War: The Case of E. U. Condon." *Isis* 83 (1992), 238–269.

Weaver, Warren. "AAAS Policy." *Science* 114 (2 November 1951), 471–472.

———. "Fundamental Questions in Science." *Scientific American* 189 (September 1953), 47–51.

———. "Confessions of a Scientist-Humanist." In *What I Have Learned: A Collection of Twenty Autobiographical Essays by Great Contemporaries From the Saturday Review.* New York: Simon and Schuster, 1968.

Weiner, J. G., et al. "Partitioning and Bioavailability of Mercury in an Experimentally Acidified Wisconsin Lake." *Environmental Toxicology and Chemistry* 9 (1990), 909–918.

"When Scientists Disagree." *Nuclear Information* (May 1962), 1.

Whitley, James R. "Water Pollution in Missouri." *Scientist and Citizen* 6 (August 1964), 1–4.

Wolfe, Tom. "The 'Me' Decade and the Third Great Awakening." *New York* (23 August 1976), 26–40.

Wolfenstein, Lincoln. "The Tragedy of J. Robert Oppenheimer." *Dissent* 15 (1968), 81–85.

Worster, Donald. "The Dirty Thirties: A Study in Agricultural Capitalism." *Great Plains Quarterly* 6 (1986), 107–116.

Wyant, W. K., Jr. "50,000 Baby Teeth." *The Nation* (13 June 1959), 535–537.

Index

Urban and Industrial Environments

Series editor: Robert Gottlieb, Henry R. Luce Professor of Urban and Environmental Policy, Occidental College

Maureen Smith, *The U.S. Paper Industry and Sustainable Production: An Argument for Restructuring*

Keith Pezzoli, *Human Settlements and Planning for Ecological Sustainability: The Case of Mexico City*

Sarah Hammond Creighton, *Greening the Ivory Tower: Improving the Environmental Track Record of Universities, Colleges, and Other Institutions*

Jan Mazurek, *Making Microchips: Policy, Globalization, and Economic Restructuring in the Semiconductor Industry*

William A. Shutkin, *The Land That Could Be: Environmentalism and Democracy in the Twenty-First Century*

Richard Hofrichter, ed., *Reclaiming the Environmental Debate: The Politics of Health in a Toxic Culture*

Robert Gottlieb, *Environmentalism Unbound: Exploring New Pathways for Change*

Kenneth Geiser, *Materials Matter: Toward a Sustainable Materials Policy*

Thomas D. Beamish, *Silent Spill: The Organization of an Industrial Crisis*

Matthew Gandy, *Concrete and Clay: Reworking Nature in New York City*

David Naguib Pellow, *Garbage Wars: The Struggle for Environmental Justice in Chicago*

Julian Agyeman, Robert D. Bullard, and Bob Evans, eds., *Just Sustainabilities: Development in an Unequal World*

Barbara L. Allen, *Uneasy Alchemy: Citizens and Experts in Louisiana's Chemical Corridor Disputes*

Dara O'Rourke, *Community-Driven Regulation: Balancing Development and the Environment in Vietnam*

Brian K. Obach, *Labor and the Environmental Movement: The Quest for Common Ground*

Peggy F. Barlett and Geoffrey W. Chase, eds., *Sustainability on Campus: Stories and Strategies for Change*

Steve Lerner, *Diamond: A Struggle for Environmental Justice in Louisiana's Chemical Corridor*

Jason Corburn, *Street Science: Community Knowledge and Environmental Health Justice*

Peggy F. Barlett, ed., *Urban Place: Reconnecting with the Natural World*

David Naguib Pellow and Robert J. Brulle, eds., *Power, Justice, and the Environment: A Critical Appraisal of the Environmental Justice Movement*

Eran Ben-Joseph, *The Code of the City: Standards and the Hidden Language of Place Making*

Nancy J. Myers and Carolyn Raffensperger, eds., *Precautionary Tools for Reshaping Environmental Policy*

Kelly Sims Gallagher, *China Shifts Gears: Automakers, Oil, Pollution, and Development*

Kerry H. Whiteside, *Precautionary Politics: Principle and Practice in Confronting Environmental Risk*

Ronald Sandler and Phaedra C. Pezzullo, eds., *Environmental Justice and Environmentalism: The Social Justice Challenge to the Environmental Movement*

Julie Sze, *Noxious New York: The Racial Politics of Urban Health and Environmental Justice*

Robert D. Bullard, ed., *Growing Smarter: Achieving Livable Communities, Environmental Justice, and Regional Equity*

Ann Rappaport and Sarah Hammond Creighton, *Cooling the Ivory Tower: University Leadership to Slow Global Warming*

Michael Egan, *Barry Commoner and the Science of Survival: The Remaking of American Environmentalism*